D0820578

Greek Tragedy

by the same author

IN THE MOUNTAINS OF GREECE
FORM AND MEANING IN DRAMA

H. D. F. KITTO

Greek Tragedy

A LITERARY STUDY

METHUEN & CO LTD
11 NEW FETTER LANE LONDON EC4

First published October 26th, 1939
Second edition July 1950
Reprinted 1954
Third edition, 1961
Reprinted 1966
Printed and bound in Great Britain by
Cox & Wyman Ltd,
Fakenham, Norfolk
3.2
Catalogue no. 02/3325/31

880.9
K62g³

164983

Preface

A book on Greek Tragedy may be a work of historical scholarship
or of literary criticism; this book professes to be a work of criticism.
Criticism is of two kinds: the critic may tell the reader what he so
beautifully thinks about it all, or he may try to explain the form in
which the literature is written. This book attempts the latter task.
It is neither a history nor a handbook; it has, I think, a continuous
argument, and anything, however important, that does not bear
on that argument is left out.

Longinus says, in his fine way, ἡ τῶν λόγων κρίσις πολλῆς
ἐστι πείρας τελευταῖον ἐπιγέννημα: literary criticism is the last
fruit of long experience. My criticism is the fruit, if it is fruit, of an
experience different from that which Longinus had in mind, the
experience of putting awkward questions to a class and having to
find answers to them – why did Aeschylus characterize differently
from Sophocles? why did Sophocles introduce the Third Actor?
why did Euripides not make better plots? This book is nothing
but the answers to a series of such questions; the answers may be
wrong, but the questions are right.

I make one basic assumption of which nothing that I have read
in or about Greek Tragedy has caused me to doubt the soundness.
It is that the Greek dramatist was first and last an artist, and must be
criticized as such. Many Greeks, like many moderns, thought he
was a moral teacher. No doubt he was, incidentally. Many English
schoolmasters assert that cricket inculcates all sorts of moral virtues.
No doubt it does, incidentally; but the writer on cricket does
well to leave this aspect of his subject to the historian of the British
Empire.

Not that any dramatist, especially the Greek, who was so consciously a citizen, can be indifferent to morality. His material, the
thoughts and actions of men, is essentially moral and intellectual,
more obviously moral than the musician's, more obviously intellectual than the painter's, and he must be honest with his material.

MILLS COLLEGE LIBRARY
Mills College Library
Withdrawn

But the material will not explain the form of the work. There is something deeper that does this, something apprehensive, not dogmatic, something as intuitive as that, whatever it is, which moves a composer or painter to activity. Aeschylus, Sophocles and Euripides each have a different fashion of tragic thought; this it is that explains the drama.

When therefore we say that the Greek dramatist was an artist, we are not using a tired platitude meaning that he preferred pretty verses and plots to ill-made ones; we mean that he felt, thought, and worked like a painter or a musician, not like a philosopher or a teacher. Being a dramatist he must deal with moral and intellectual questions, and what he says about them is a natural subject of study; but if we are to treat the plays as plays and not as documents we must, as in criticizing painting, free ourselves from 'the tyranny of the subject'. If we can grope our way to the fundamental tragic conception of each play or group of plays, we can hope to explain their form and style. If not, we expose ourselves to the temptation of thinking that changes of form and style were sought for their own sake (which may be true of us but is not true of the Greeks), or to the temptation of treating form and content separately, or of falling back on that unreal figment 'the form of Greek Tragedy', something which evolves historically and takes the individual plays with it. For us, there is no such thing as 'the form of Greek Tragedy'. The historian, looking at Greek Tragedy from the outside, can use this conception, but our business is with individual plays, each a work of art and therefore unique, each obeying only the laws of its own being. There were limits fixed by the conditions of performance (practically the same for Euripides as for Aeschylus); within these wide limits the form of a play is determined only by its own vital idea – that is, if it is a living work of art, a $\zeta\hat{\omega}o\nu$, and not an animal 'after Landseer'.

We shall therefore always begin by trying to understand the nature of the dramatic conception that underlies a play or group of plays. We shall ask what it is that the dramatist is striving to say, not what in fact he does say about this or that. The 'meaning' contained in many a dramatic speech or chorus may be as direct as the 'meaning' of a passage in Aristotle's *Ethics*, but that 'meaning' which alone will explain the form of the play is something more akin to the 'meaning' of a Rembrandt or of a Beethoven sonata.

Mills College Library
Withdrawn

It is, of course, much more intellectual, for the dramatist's apprehensions go at once into imagery closer to our intellectual life than the imagery of the painter or composer. The difference of medium, and consequently of method, is so great that direct comparison between drama and these other arts is rarely of much use except to the one who makes it. Nevertheless, we must remember where we are, and hold fast to the difference between the 'meaning' of a philosopher and the 'meaning' of an artist.

Can we go further? Can we explain, by reference to the communal life of which the poets were a part, how it came about that they 'meant' these particular things? We can certainly guess, and some of our guesses will no doubt be right; perhaps we can do more, but I have not regarded this as any business of mine, as our present concern is criticism and not biography. Criticism, it seems to me, can without discredit begin with what is in the poet's head, without inquiring how it got there.

The literary importance of Greek Tragedy has not yet been forgotten by Professors of English, who sometimes expect their pupils to have some acquaintance with it. It is because I hope that this survey may be of interest to students of literature who have no Greek that I have given translations where possible. But we Hellenists have our feelings, like other men, and I have left in Greek two recurring words: ἁμαρτία (hamartia) is the tragic flaw of Aristotle's theory, and ὕβρις is hybris.

My obligations are many and difficult to count; I hope I have been honest in acknowledging debts. I realize uncomfortably that often I quote others only to disagree with them. I am grateful to the Editor of *The Times*, who very willingly gave me permission to use copyright material valuable to me. My warmest thanks are due to my colleague Mr A. W. Gomme, for reading my scripts and making many salutary remarks about them. For the same friendly and critical services, most generously given, I owe a debt which now I cannot pay to my late colleague W. E. Muir, whose early death has taken away a good scholar, a firm and sensitive judge of literature, and one ποθεινὸς τοῖς φίλοις.

H. D. F. K.

THE UNIVERSITY
GLASGOW
March 1939

NOTE TO THE THIRD EDITION

As the chorus remarks in the *Agamemnon*, even an old man can learn. I was unwilling to emit, in this edition, statements which I no longer believe to be true; therefore I have entirely rewritten chapters III and IV, on the *Oresteia* and the Dramatic Art of Aeschylus, the sections on the *Ajax*, *Trachiniae*, and *Philoctetes*, with certain minor reconstructions and many consequential changes. The discovery of about two square inches of papyrus compelled me also to remodel, though not very seriously, the first part of chapter I.

H. D. F. K.

THE UNIVERSITY
BRISTOL

Contents

I LYRICAL TRAGEDY *page* 1

    1. THE 'SUPPLICES' 1

    2. THE 'SUPPLICES' AND PRE-AESCHYLEAN TRAGEDY 22

II OLD TRAGEDY 31

    1. INTRODUCTION 31

    2. THE 'PERSAE' 33

    3. THE 'SEPTEM' 45

    4. THE 'PROMETHEUS VINCTUS' 55

III THE 'ORESTEIA' 64

    1. THE 'AGAMEMNON' 64

    2. THE 'CHOEPHORI' 78

    3. THE 'EUMENIDES' 87

IV THE DRAMATIC ART OF AESCHYLUS 96

V MIDDLE TRAGEDY: SOPHOCLES 117

    1. INTRODUCTION 117

    2. THE 'AJAX' 120

    3. THE 'ANTIGONE' 125

    4. THE 'ELECTRA' 131

    5. THE 'OEDIPUS TYRANNUS' 138

VI THE PHILOSOPHY OF SOPHOCLES 145

VII THE DRAMATIC ART OF SOPHOCLES 151

    1. THE THIRD ACTOR 151

    2. THE CHORUS 158

    3. STRUCTURAL PRINCIPLES 171

VIII   THE EURIPIDEAN TRAGEDY   *page* 187

    1. INTRODUCTION   187

    2. THE 'MEDEA'   190

    3. THE 'HIPPOLYTUS'   203

    4. THE 'TROADES'   210

    5. THE 'HECUBA'   216

    6. THE 'SUPPLIANT WOMEN'   223

    7. THE 'ANDROMACHE'   230

    8. THE 'HERACLES'   237

IX   THE TECHNIQUE OF THE EURIPIDEAN TRAGEDY   250

    1. INTRODUCTION   250

    2. CHARACTERIZATION   252

    3. THE CHORUS   259

    4. RHETORIC AND DIALECTIC   265

    5. DRAMATIC SURPRISE AND ORNAMENT   272

    6. PROLOGUES AND EPILOGUES   278

X   THE 'TRACHINIAE' AND 'PHILOCTETES'   288

    1. THE 'TRACHINIAE'   288

    2. THE 'PHILOCTETES'   298

XI   NEW TRAGEDY: EURIPIDES' TRAGI-COMEDIES   311

XII   NEW TRAGEDY: EURIPIDES' MELODRAMAS   330

    1. THE 'ELECTRA'   330

    2. THE CHORUS IN NEW TRAGEDY   341

    3. THE 'ORESTES'   346

    4. THE 'PHOENISSAE'   351

    5. THE 'IPHIGENEIA IN AULIS'   362

XIII   TWO LAST PLAYS   370

    1. THE 'BACCHAE'   370

    2. THE 'OEDIPUS COLONEUS'   381

    INDEX   399

CHAPTER I

Lyrical Tragedy

1. The 'Supplices'

The first two editions of this book opened with the assertion that the *Supplices* is the earliest work of European drama. It now seems possible – some would say certain – that this is not true; that the trilogy was first produced not in or near 492 B.C. but much later, probably in 464, after the *Persae* and the *Septem*. The belief in the earlier dating never rested, of course, on any documentary evidence but chiefly on considerations of style, some of which (as I record with some complacency) I had rejected as evidence of date: namely, that in this play the real protagonist is not an actor but the chorus, and that the second actor is handled rather clumsily. Nevertheless, the general impression of archaism, combined with what Bowra well called 'the loaded magnificence of the style',[1] seemed reason enough, in the absence of direct evidence, to think it an early play.

This view was indeed challenged, notably by E. C. Yorke.[2] Yorke analysed a certain metrical phenomenon in the seven plays – resolution of a long syllable in the iambic trimeter – and showed that if the frequency of such resolution increased with the poet's increasing years then the *Persae* (472 B.C.) is the earliest play, and that the *Supplices* would fall between it and the *Septem* (467). But the assumption is hazardous; closer inspection suggests that the dramatic quality of a scene had something to do with the incidence of these resolutions – as is certainly the case in Sophocles.

But in 1952 there was published a fragment of papyrus from Oxyrhynchus,[3] which to all appearance derives ultimately from the didascalia, the official record of the dramatic contests in Athens.

[1] C. M. Bowra, *Ancient Greek Literature*, p. 81.

[2] *Classical Quarterly*, 1938, p. 117.

[3] P. Oxy., 2256, frag. 3.1b – perhaps most readily available in Murray's revised Oxford text of Aeschylus.

The fragment says that in the archonship of somebody whose name begins Ar . . . (unless these two letters were the beginning of the word *archon*, which is not very likely) Aeschylus won the first prize with this trilogy, Sophocles the second prize, and Mesatos the third. If the reference is to the first production of the trilogy, which is the natural interpretation, but not indubitably the correct one, then the production certainly did not take place near 490, when Sophocles was a boy five or seven years old. He won his first victory, at what may have been his first attempt, in 468. The only year in the neighbourhood that provides a suitable archon is 464: Archedemides. The obscure Mesatos remains a difficulty. In Epistle V of Euripides he is mentioned alongside Euripides' younger contemporary Agathon, which would put him firmly in the later part of the century. The epistle is indeed what we harshly call a 'forgery', written possibly as late as the fifth century A.D. Yet a forger has every reason to be careful over detail: this one may have known what he was talking about. There is indeed an inscription[1] which records names of dramatists apparently in the chronological order of their first successes, and places a certain . . . . tos next to Sophocles. If this name was Mesatos, and not for example an unrecorded Stratos or the like, it would agree with the papyrus very well.

The fragment is so carelessly written that the Oxyrhynchus editor said of it 'There are things about this text which make one sceptical of its authority'; and there is another fact which should be taken into account. F. R. Earp, in his *Style of Aeschylus* (1948), submitted the plays to an exhaustive stylistic analysis. In every one of his statistical tables the *Supplices* comes out on top, indicating – if such evidence has value – that it is the earliest of the seven. Nothing led Earp to suspect that it could be later than the *Persae*, and his results, in other respects, are self-consistent. It has been suggested, as a compromise, that the trilogy was kept in cold-storage for some twenty-five years, for political reasons.[2] Not perhaps impossible, but unlikely, and the reasons adduced seem to me entirely to misjudge the 'political' significance of the play; as will be argued below, it is hard to see what more Aeschylus could have done to make it clear that his 'Argos' was not contemporary Argos.

---

[1] I. G. II, 2325.

[2] A. Diamantopoulos, *Journal of Hellenic Studies*, LXXVII, Part 2, 200 ff.

The nature of the theme (if I have correctly interpreted it) and the power with which it is handled certainly do not suggest the immaturity of youth. Therefore, though without any burning conviction, I accept the evidence of the papyrus at its face value, and turn to more interesting matters.

Some of the older judgements of the play were based in part on the belief that it is a primitive work, partly on a sheer inability to understand a form of drama which is unfamiliar to us. It is natural, but wrong, to approach a work of art with a preconceived idea of what it ought to do, and how; such criticism may go very far astray. The critic tries to read into the play what he expects to find, and when he does not find it he is disappointed. Thus, Tucker found that the *Supplices* 'fails in dramatic effect. . . . There is no thrilling action in the piece, and despite its admirable poetry it would have fallen flat' but for the spectacular effect of the chorus. Bowra, many years ago now, wrote: 'Such action as there is consists of their [the suppliants'] efforts to secure protection, and the arrival of a herald from Egypt announcing the presence of the rejected suitors'[1] – a summary which leaves out the situation which makes the play a tragedy. Or, starting with the doctrine that Aeschylus was a religious teacher and the educator of his people, Erzieher seines Volkes, we may say, with Pohlenz, that the play concerns the protectors more than the protected, which is true, and holds up to the Athenian democracy the inspiring picture of a whole people, the Argives, taking upon itself the greatest dangers because it puts religious duty before everything – which is not true, since Aeschylus takes some trouble to point out that the King and his people are in a cleft stick: if they will not protect the suppliants, they will have to brave the anger of the offended gods.

By all means let us think some passages in the play clumsy; nevertheless the greater part of it handles a profoundly tragic situation – and a familiar one – with immense power. Our first duty is to discover where Asechylus laid the emphasis; we may assume that he built the play as he felt it. Certainly, those who find it undramatic cannot tell us, except by accident, what it is about, for they will not have seen the drama.

It begins dramatically enough. The chorus enters, dressed in Egyptian fashion, and chanting to the processional anapaestic

[1] *Ancient Greek Literature*, p. 81.

rhythm a great invocation of Zeus, the Zeus who protects the Suppliant and has brought these victims of violence safely across the sea from the Nile to Argos; and with Zeus are presently linked the other gods, those of the sky and those of the underworld. The particular situation is being placed in the widest possible context. The *parodos* gives us the necessary facts easily: Danus, the flight from the suitors, the suppliants' own Argive descent. Why they are fleeing from the suitors is not yet made clear; the chorus mentions hybris, and θέμις εἴργει, Right forbids. We are given a clear impression of these young women – full of energy, passionate in their resistance, firm of faith in the gods.

The parodos is followed by a long ode. A slow and steady rhythm is started, and the chorus proceeds to dance and sing some 140 verses. There is no suggestion of immediate action, debate or intrigue; the ode, one-sixth of the whole play, would take something like fifteen minutes in performance, the time of an ordinary symphony-movement. This shows what wind is blowing in the theatre: the audience, clearly, is in no hurry to see the actors and action.

Since the rhythms of the poetry give us a slight and distant impression of the nature of the dances and their visual effect, we will give them a little attention. The ode opens, with Zeus and Epaphus, in the stately 'Dorian' rhythm. With the more personal tone of the second pair of stanzas the chorus turns to the impulsive choriambic: $|{-}\cup : \cup{-}|{-}\cup : \cup{-}|$ (duple, not triple, time), but still closes quietly with a smooth iambic (or trochaic) verse. The third pair are well balanced: they open with a steady hexameter, work up to choriambic, and again end smoothly. In the fourth pair we return to Zeus and to a steadier rhythm; and this leads to the unmistakable outburst of

> ἰάπτει δ' ἐλπίδων
> ἀφ' ὑψιπύργων πανώλεις
> βροτούς, βίαν δ' οὔτιν' ἐξοπλίζει

where the weight of the rhythm marks the climax of this part of the ode.[1] The next pair introduce something new: harsh, clumsy spondees and tribrachs, which seem appropriate to the passionate

---

[1]
$$\cup - (\cup) - (\cup) - \cup -$$
$$\cup - \cup - (\cup) - \cup - (\cup) -$$
$$\cup - \cup - (\cup) - \cup - \cup - (\cup) -$$

lamentation and foreign-sounding invocations in the two stanzas and their refrains. It would be a reasonable inference, perhaps even a necessary one, that the accompanying dance was of the same character. The audience was not simply listening to poetry; it was experiencing a combination of the three arts, poetry, dance, and music, all surely saying the same thing, each reinforcing the others.

In view of what was to happen to the tragic Chorus before the century was out, it is not superfluous to notice how closely the poet sticks to his dramatic theme. We are always told, with good reason, that Aeschylus was a great religious poet; what impresses one in this ode is that he is a great dramatic lyrist, never making philosophic or mythological or decorative diversions. So dynamic a combination of rhythms is essentially of the dramatic poet, composer, choreographer. To the chorus, Zeus is to be their protector; Io is their claim on Argos; they think naturally of Philomela; they do not stay to narrate her story, as a late Euripidean chorus might. Then comes the appeal to the Justice, the Dike, of the gods, followed by those two splendid stanzas in which, for their own assurance, they sing of the power of Zeus. Here we reach an almost Hebraic intensity, but it is the intensity of the dramatic poet, not of the philosopher or theologian. After this, the change described above: Greek by descent, they are Egyptian by upbringing. They began in Dorian rhythm and spoke in true Greek strain; they end with the rhythms of despair, with wild, uncouth language, and with threats of hanging themselves at the altars of the gods – threats which they are presently to apply to the King of Argos.

'So, through the mouth of the chorus, does Aeschylus declare his faith in a Zeus who is the refuge of the oppressed.' This kind of thing is easily said, and has been said. Unfortunately, either this is nonsense or the play itself is. It is a hypothesis which scholars have sometimes found convenient, that the dramatists would use the chorus as their 'mouthpiece'; sometimes even that anything said in a play represents what the dramatist would have us believe. As this directly concerns our understanding of Greek drama, we may take the present opportunity of considering it.

An example of the extreme view comes to hand in Professor Hugh Lloyd-Jones's article *Zeus in Aeschylus*,[1] in which it is said, about the *Septem*: 'We are repeatedly told that Zeus and Dike

---

[1] *Journal of Hellenic Studies*, LXXVI (1956). The passage quoted is on p. 59.

are on the side of Eteocles and the defenders; this is implied at
443–6, 565–7, and 630, and is clearly stated at 662–71, where
Eteocles calls Dike the maiden daughter of Zeus and affirms that
Polyneices, from his earliest years, has had no part in her.' It will
be enough to consider the last of the four passages. If Aeschylus
intended us to believe this about Zeus, Dike and Eteocles, he was
a very inept dramatist and his audience were remarkable people.
For what happens? With this declaration on his lips Eteocles goes
out to meet his brother in single combat, and each of them is killed.
Is not this sufficient comment on what Eteocles has said? Or did
Aeschylus imagine that in a play words have meaning, but events
none?

But there is also the audience to consider. Returning to the
Supplices, we might picture two of Aeschylus' fellow-citizens
trudging home to their village after the trilogy, ruminating on
what they had seen. They would recall (we will suppose) that in
the *parodos* and again later (vv. 529 f.) the ill-used Suppliants
appealed to Zeus to protect them and drown their oppressors at
sea. How was Aeschylus to prevent them from remembering, too,
that in fact the wicked Egyptians turned up in Argos, undrowned,
perfectly dry? and from concluding either that there is no point in
praying to Zeus, or that Zeus is something other than the Suppliants imagined?

In short, unless the mental processes both of Aeschylus and of his
audiences were something beyond our comprehension, the poet
had one mouthpiece and one only: the play in its entirety, not in
bits and pieces. This chorus, certainly, is not Aeschylus' 'mouthpiece' but his creation – and a very dramatic one.[1]

During the ode, one figure has remained stationary, Danaus.
Now he comes forward to speak, and what he has to say hardly
makes our blood run faster. He tells his daughters that he is as
prudent by land as he has been at sea; with unnecessary amplitude
he tells them that a company of men is approaching. He is dull.
Having said that, we should ask ourselves what is the substance of
the short scene. To us it may be a bore, but the question is – if we
can answer it – what response to it did Aeschylus expect from his
audience? Two things happen: first, Danaus counsels his daughters

---

[1] The urn-speech in Sophocles' *Electra* further illustrates this very elementary
argument. – Below, p. 177.

to place themselves as suppliants at the altar of Zeus, and to be submissive, as becomes the suppliant; second, prayers are offered to Zeus, Apollo, Hermes. There is no difficulty in the prayers; we are once more to understand that the gods are going to preside over the action of the trilogy, that it will have no merely personal or local orbit. As for the other point, it seems reasonable to suggest that it is a preparation for what is to come and has been fore-shadowed already: these Danaids can hardly be called submissive, 'like doves' (v. 223), towards the King; and this may prove to be not merely an interesting bit of decorative character-drawing, but something central to the whole trilogy. Do the Danaids fully under-stand and accept the laws of the god to whom they are appealing?

Pelasgus enters – it is convenient to use the name, though Aeschy-lus does not – and is invited to say who he is. In reply, he traces his lineage from 'earth-born Palaechthon', describes at length his kingdom, which embraces all Greece and Macedonia too, and then goes on to explain why this particular region is called Apia. (Aeschylus, like Euripides, and unlike Sophocles, did not always eschew matters of extraneous interest.)

Why all this? It is often assumed that for reasons of current politics Aeschylus wished to gratify Argos, or to commend friendship with Argos, rather than with Sparta, to his fellow-citizens. The assump-tion would be better founded if we were firmly assured of two things: that Aeschylus was rather stupid, and that in his Athens any approach to poetic imagination was punishable by death. Pelopon-nesian Argos, smarting under her supplanter Sparta, was one thing; this misty Pelasgian Argos, comprising regions that Agamemnon never knew, is utterly different; it would have been poor propa-ganda to retire so far from any historical reality. Contemporary Argos might have been gratified if an Athenian poet had asserted, or implied, her title to pre-eminence in the Peloponnese, but Argive Dodona and Macedonia are not politics. And if we are to think of current politics (and forget Zeus for the moment), would the Athenian voters in the audience be favourably disposed towards Argos by the thought that their own city, at this remote time, was an unmentioned detail in this vast Pelasgian kingdom? In fact, when Pelasgus does refer to the plain in which historical Argos stands, he calls it not Argos but Apia; and when he ends his long speech, perhaps not very happily, by saying 'Be brief; this city does not

love long speeches', everyone in the audience would instantly think
not of Argos but of Sparta.

Surely what Aeschylus is doing is plain enough. As he universal-
izes the particular action by interweaving with it the agency of
gods, so he escapes from local boundaries by imagining a vast
kingdom. His mythical Argos, with its anachronistic democracy,
stands for Greece in general, *any* Greek city. His Argos that stretches
beyond the Pindus has something in common with Shakespeare's
Bohemia which has a sea-coast.

The stichomythia that follows has been called 'a long-winded
genealogical orgy'.[1] This is to misunderstand it. What we have is
the proof of their Argive descent which the Suppliants give to
Pelasgus. Certainly it does not need much acumen to see that the
proof is very thin; all they prove is that they know the story. But
in a play pitched on this lyrical plane it would be a mistake to
demand a rigid proof. If one lay ready to hand, well and good; if
not, then it is almost enough that the forms of proof are duly gone
through. Our real interest is to know if Pelasgus will accept the
claim; only in a later and sophisticated form of Greek drama
will such a proof itself become a source of dramatic interest and
delight.

Though the first part of this act is not very exciting, what remains
makes ample amends. From v. 324 until the end of the scene, and
beyond it, we have a presentation of a tragic situation that will hold
its own with any. The power and certainty of it are astonishing.
Twenty-four verses are enough to explain the coming of the chorus
and to show the King that a chasm is opening beneath his feet.
Πέφρικα λεύσσων he cried: 'I see, and shudder.' He is in a cleft
stick: either he must undertake a dangerous and unwanted war,
or he must risk the anger of the gods. This having been made clear
to the unhappy King, the Danaids take advantage of their lyrical
position to push home their appeal by a liberal use of the urgent
dochmiac metre, accompanied no doubt by some passionate dance-
figure.

In the whole of this scene, with Danaus not indeed off the stage,
but quite otiose in the background, we can see what kind of
dramatic effect late sixth-century tragedy might have produced in
the hands of a master, the tragedy that used only a single actor with

[1] H. W. Smith, *The Drama of Aeschylus*, p. 40.

the chorus.[1] All is formal, as formal and vivid as a Miltonic sonnet. The doubts, fears, considerations of prudence that pass through the King's mind are distilled into five-verse stanzas, as formal as are the lyric stanzas of the chorus. The character, speech, arguments of Pelasgus are formalized in the same degree, necessarily; there is no pretence that we are following, with Sophoclean subtlety, the successive thoughts or emotions that pass through his mind. 'Let no quarrel, unexpected and unforeseen, come upon the city. The city has no need of these.' 'Assist you I cannot, without hurt; yet to reject your prayers, that too is hard.' Translated, the words are unimpressive, but no one familiar with the early Greek manner will miss the power either of the formal speech or of the formal scene, submitted to so severe a discipline. Our standard must be Simonides' epitaph, not a speech from Oedipus. Equally formal is the short speech 406–17, with its last line echoing the first. To call it stiff and undramatic is easy and wrong. The whole play is cast in a lyrical, unnaturalistic mould; we must not at one moment praise the odes for being Pindaric and at the next censure the dialogue for not being Sophoclean.

While the King stands motionless, contemplating the terrible alternatives, the chorus dances before him in the heavily swinging cretic rhythm (five-time). It seems to have something of a hypnotic force; it presents the appeal of the suppliants carried beyond the reach of language. We are told that Pelasgus is no character, only an abstraction. This is not quite true; he has all the character that the situation requires, and if Aeschylus had given him more, it would have been only an irrelevance. Character-drawing for its own sake is not necessarily a dramatic virtue. Pelasgus has mind and strength, for he can remain steady even under this assault. He emerges clear-eyed: 'There is no issue free from disaster.' With no rhetoric, but with an eloquent restraint, he leads up to his anguishing point: ὅπως δ' ὅμαιμον αἷμα μὴ γενήσεται, 'But that our kinsmen's blood be not shed . . .' – the overmastering thought to which he returns a moment later: ἄνδρας γυναικῶν οὕνεχ' αἱμάξαι πέδον, 'That in a women's quarrel men's blood should stain the ground . . .!' (449, 477). His uninvited guests have brought him to a pass where he has to choose between a war whose horrors he does not gloze over, and the unnamed terrors of the gods' wrath. Until this day he was the

[1] See below, pp. 22 ff.

contented ruler of a prosperous state; now he is in torture. Unless
Aeschylus was not a builder but only a decorator, this must be the
centre of his thinking in this play, as it certainly is the centre of its
tragic feeling. Because certain women away in Egypt have suffered
violence, and because they have an ancestral claim upon Argos,
this has come upon him; and this, perhaps, does something to explain
the slightly too bland tone of his opening speech: it was to prepare
for the contrast. Pelasgus has tried reason. He has argued that
marriage between cousins is no bad thing: it keeps the family
together. He has asked 'what if your laws sanction this marriage?'
All is swept aside; the Danaids detest the marriage, and appeal to
Dike. Through no Aristotelian ἁμαρτία, through no deficiency of
character or sense, the King, and his people, have suddenly fallen
into this awful dilemma.

It is perhaps the most purely tragic of tragic situations: a total
divorce of suffering from guilt or responsibility, a situation that
Aristotle would not accept, because he found it shocking, μιαρόν.
Perhaps it is too soon to ask what Aeschylus thought about it; we
may, however, spare a moment for the observation that it is fairly
constant in the tragic poets, though Aristotle rejected it and other
philosophers have been uneasy about it.[1] It is the situation that
engulfs Antigone; as she says, 'What law of the gods have I trans-
gressed? Why should I look to Heaven any more?' Some have
duly found the required ἁμαρτία in her, being in this respect more
loyal to Aristotle than to Sophocles. There is Orestes; there is
Hamlet, and many others in Shakespeare: the good Duke of York
in *King Richard II*, torn between his sworn loyalty to an unjust
king and his loyalty to a kinsman whom that king has wronged.
There is Blanche in *King John*, fated to see her wedding stained
with bloodshed, unable to wish success to either side in the impending battle between her kinsmen. Perhaps most tragic of all are the
Father who has killed his Son and the Son who has killed his Father
in *King Henry VI Part III*. In their several degrees all suffer, and
none is in any way responsible. Macneile Dixon's answer is that
the tragic poets, wiser than the philosophers, recognize that there
is a tragic flaw, but one that sometimes is not in the character of the
sufferer, but in the universe itself. I doubt if the tragic poets would
agree. The miseries that fill *King Henry VI* are explicitly ascribed by

[1] See W. Macneile Dixon, *Tragedy*, pp. 128 ff.

Shakespeare to moral violence: see the prophecy made by Warwick (Part I, II, 124 ff.), so like the opening verses of the *Iliad*. Falconbridge says (*King John*, II, i, 574 f.) what Shakespeare so often implies:

> *The world itself is peisèd well,*
> *Made to run even upon even ground.*

When it does not run even, when disaster befalls the innocent, the reason is, in Shakespeare, as in the *Antigone*, that human folly has made the ground uneven. What Aeschylus thinks about the tragedy of Pelasgus and his citizens remains to be seen. He created it, he presents it powerfully; it will be strange indeed if he has not thought about it.

Pelasgus is overwhelmed by the situation; his mind is numb. But the poet has not yet done with him. The Danaids have already applied the screw to him; they proceed to turn it with a deliberation that seems almost devilish:

> – *We have one more word of supplication.*
> – *I am listening.*
> – *We have strings and cords for our robes.*
> – *That is very proper in women.*

A commonplace verse? As commonplace as Duncan's 'This castle hath a pleasant seat'.

> – *New ornaments for the altars.*
> – *You are giving me riddles. Speak clearly.*

They do. They explain that they will insult and defile the altars of the Argive deities by hanging themselves there.

> – *It is a thing that scourges my heart.*
> – *Now are your eyes open.*

So too are ours. If the King will not protect the Suppliants at the price of his citizens' blood staining the ground, the whole land will have to endure the anger of Heaven. The people itself must choose.

The ode that now begins opens with an impressive invocation of Zeus, the Supreme Power. The prayer is repeated, that Zeus may destroy the Egyptian pursuers at sea. Then the Danaids dwell on the strange story of their ancestress Io, loved by Zeus, persecuted over sea and land by Hera, half-transformed into the shape of a cow, guided to Egypt, and there delivered by Zeus of a glorious son, whom all proclaimed the son of Zeus, for none but Zeus could have overcome the wrath of Hera. The story, as handled here, seems to have an affinity with the Prometheus trilogy and with the *Oresteia*: out of violence and cruelty and confusion come at last order and harmony. In the *Oresteia* we can follow the presentation of the dramatist's thought to the end; in the Danaid trilogy and in the *Prometheia* we are unluckily in the position of one who has to leave the theatre at the end of the first of the three plays: we can only surmise where it will end, what the poet has in mind. However, this ode, centrally placed, makes it once more plain that the supreme power of Zeus will dominate the whole. As to this, it is customary among scholars to say that Aeschylus exalted the religion of Zeus; we might consider a different way of putting it. Aeschylus asserts, here as elsewhere, that there *is* a supreme power; that is to say, there is a unity in things, some direction in events, which imply a supreme power; and this he identifies with Zeus. In him the Suppliants have put their trust – but it by no means follows that Zeus is exactly what they suppose. Some disillusionment awaits them.

Zeus is made prominent also in the short *epeisodion* that follows, the shortest in extant Greek drama. Danaus brings the good news that the Argive assembly, with impressive unanimity, has resolved to protect the Suppliants, at any cost. It has been said that here Aeschylus was concerned to give to Athens a picture of the ideal democracy, to show how Leaders and Led should work together. If this is all we can see in the passage, this, no doubt, is what we shall see. But half of the speech is devoted to the tragic dilemma, which is now put before the people as the Danaids have already put it before Pelasgus; and Danaus' last words are 'Zeus brought it to fulfilment.' We spoke, a moment ago, of Orestes; let us mention him again, for is not this desperate choice that is forced upon the Argives very like the choice that confronts Orestes? If Zeus is supreme, and is not malignant or incompetent, how do these things come about?

The short episode is followed by a long hymn of gratitude. This too is severely formal in style. The chorus invokes blessings on

Argos; not vague ones, like Prosperity, Peace, Honour. It happens that Peace with Honour do figure among the desirable things, but they appear in explicit form: 'May they offer to foreigners, before girding themselves for war, satisfaction by fair agreement.' Nothing Utopian; they pray for what is possible. Prosperity also is concrete: 'May the lambs in their fields be fertile; may the land be rich in crops in each season.' They bless thoughtfully, and in the accusative and infinitive construction, like a law or proclamation.

Once more the rhythmical figures are worth attention. After the brief anapaestic prelude there are four pairs of stanzas; the rhythms fall into three groups. Group A, which begins each or the first six stanzas (followed in each case by Group B), consists mainly of two metrical phrases, — ∪ ∪ — ∪ —, and its variant ∪ ∪ ∪ — ∪ —, the dochmiac: short, energetic phrases, marked by Mazon[1] *assez agité*. Group B is mainly — ∪ — ∪ ∪ — ∪ —, the glyconic, or its equivalent — ∪ — ∪ ∪ — —, the pherecratean. These are calmer rhythms. The alternation of the two groups evidently gives variety within a firm framework, but it also reinforces the sense, as we should expect: in the first pair of stanzas, the *assez agité* rhythm conveys the prayer, and Group B conveys the reason why the prayer is being made. In the second and third pairs, the suffering which is being deprecated is, usually, given to Group A, and the opposite state of happiness to Group B. Group C appears in the last two stanzas, which sum up the whole in a prayer for peace with gods and men; it is a bigger, more swinging rhythm, well characterized by Mazon as *large et décidé*:[2]

$$\cup - (\cup) - (\cup) - \cup - \cup - (\cup) -$$
$$\cup - \cup - (\cup) - \cup - \cup - (\cup) -$$
$$\cup - \cup - (\cup) - \cup -$$
$$\cup - \cup - (\cup) - \cup -$$
$$\cup - \cup - (\cup) - \cup - \cup - (\cup) -$$

We can see therefore, however dimly, something of the firm and intelligent lines of the whole composition. It is followed by a dramatic turn of events. Danaus, who (we must suppose) has been looking out to sea, has descried a ship that bears the hated Egyptians.

---

[1] In his *Budé* edition of Aeschylus.

[2] This rhythm made a brief appearance in the first ode (above, p. 4), and is used extensively in the *Agamemnon* (below, pp. 114 ff.).

No miracle has occurred to stop them; Greek gods, in serious tragedy, do not work miracles, except within a perfectly intelligible and intelligent dramatic convention.[1] Therefore the next few dance-movements are very different in character; the Danaids are terrified. Danaus assures them that the altars will protect them until he returns with help, that the Argives will fight in their defence, that the Egyptians will not find an easy landing, in the dusk; but the terror of the chorus gives a vivid impression of the ruthlessness of the Egyptians.

Danaus goes off to summon help. Aeschylus is using only two actors; therefore the one playing Danaus must be given an exit in order to reappear as the Herald. We may guess too that Aeschylus was not reluctant to have the suppliants entirely unprotected, except for the altars; the violence of the Egyptians becomes the more apparent. Of the ensuing ode there is no need to say more than that it leaves us in no doubt that the Danaids will do anything rather than yield. Then comes a wild scene badly battered in our MS. tradition: we must imagine the orchestra filled with wild movement, violence made manifest. For the moment, the dance and music are more important than the words.

No one will complain that the passage between Pelasgus and the Herald is undramatic, or lacking in character-drawing. Pelasgus' proud refusal to give his name, the dignity with which he rejects the Herald's demand, his readiness to throw the taunt of beer-drinking at the Egyptians, make him much more than a lay-figure. But when the Herald makes his exit, with the threat of war, all the stuffing seems to go out of the play. The King's short speech about the entertainment of the Danaids in Argos is well enough, but why must these vivid young women ask that Danaus be sent back to determine the matter for them? Would it not have been a natural and satisfying conclusion to the play if the Danaids had now made their way into the city under the impressive escort of the King himself?

When he comes, Danaus does little to increase his dramatic stature. He tells his daughters that the citizens have been very considerate to him, but this information hardly justifies his reappearance. For the rest, he talks to his daughters like a father, and an anxious one: they are beautiful, very desirable; life in a foreign city

---

See below, pp. 147 and 314.

is difficult and can be perilous; let them guard against the snares set by Aphrodite.

As for the persistent flabbiness of Danaus, it is often said that it is a sign of immaturity in the dramatic art of Aeschylus; he has not yet mastered the art of using the two actors with the chorus. It is indeed not easy to think of this play as coming half-way in time between the *Septem* and the *Oresteia*, yet we must be careful. Aeschylus was never a conventional or a cautious dramatist; once he saw a tragic theme, he was not easily deterred from dramatizing it. In the *Persae* he wrote a play that lacks a central character and is nearly all narrative; in the *Prometheus* he has a central character who cannot move, and delivers a long series of long speeches. These are signs of courage rather than of immature technique. Danaus, beyond a doubt, had an independent role in the second and third plays of the trilogy; in the first he is a mere shadow of his daughters. Aeschylus did not mind.

We may be tempted to think that Aeschylus brought back Danaus merely because he is the father of the Danaids, and then could find nothing for him to do except talk like a father. But is this enough?

There are those to whom the final scene of the *Agamemnon* is a sad anticlimax. It is – if we allow ourselves to think in terms of modern drama, with its emphasis on the interesting individual; but we have the *Oresteia* complete, and we can see, if we will, how the dramatic themes used in the Aegisthus-scene not only develop themes used already in the *Agamemnon* but also are a necessary and powerful preparation for much that follows. It is very far from being an anticlimax. Therefore, though of course nothing can be proved, we should consider the possibility that the same may be true here, and not be too quick in accusing Aeschylus of ineptitude. What is said here about the difficult position of foreign guests in a strange city, especially when they are beautiful young women, may have been a much more organic part of the whole than is visible to us.

But there is something else. When a dramatist does not do the obvious thing, as when Aeschylus does not make Pelasgus escort the Danaids into the city, his critics should take the elementary precaution of asking if, by not doing it, the dramatist has achieved some other effect which the obvious would have precluded. The play does, in fact, end with a stroke which is quite unexpected and

typically Aeschylean, and could not conveniently have been contrived if Pelasgus were waiting to take the Danaids into Argos.
They raise a hymn in honour of the city; they invoke the virgin-
goddess Artemis, and pray that they shall not come under the law
(ἀνάγκη) of Aphrodite. Then Aeschylus suddenly liberates the
tongues of a group of serving-women whom hitherto we have
taken to be supernumerary silent actors.[1] It is very like what he does
in the *Choephori*, when at a crisis he suddenly gives a voice to the
silent actor Pylades.[2] This too is a crisis. The serving-women sing:
'My prudent hymn does not disregard Aphrodite. She, with Hera,
comes nearest in power to Zeus . . . For the fugitives I foresee cruel
grief and bloody wars. Why has the pursuit been so swift and sure?
What is fixed, that will surely come to pass. The will of Zeus cannot
be opposed.' That is, marriage is the natural law; to oppose it is
idle. The further exchanges between the two choruses cannot be
sorted out with complete certainty, but the serving-women seem
to warn the Danaids that they are praying for too much; the
purposes of Zeus are not to be discerned by men, and one cannot
appease the unappeasable. Such is the thought on which Aeschylus
brings to a close the first of the three plays.

How did the trilogy continue? and what is it all about? Unfortunately, we can be only tentative. The keystone of the myth was
that the Danaids were compelled to marry their cousins, that on
the wedding-night each of them, by arrangement with Danaus,
murdered her husband, except one, Hypermestra, who spared hers
through her desire for children, and that she became the ancestress
of a royal house in Argos, including Heracles. Aeschylus had indeed
a masterful way with legends, but naturally he did not make them
unrecognizable; he certainly incorporated in his trilogy these
features of the story, but about important details we remain in the
dark.

The *Supplices* is the first play in the trilogy; the fact has been
denied, but that shows only that in criticism there is no position so
untenable that some intrepid spirit will not be found occupying it.
It is known that Aeschylus wrote a play called *The Egyptians*; it is
likely that this was the second part of the trilogy, and that the

---

[1] There is no indication of this in our MSS., but the passage is not otherwise
intelligible.

[2] See below, p. 86.

Egyptians formed the chorus. If so, the Danaids did not appear –
to the relief, perhaps, of the actor playing Danaus. From this play
only one word remains: Zagreus. It is not illuminating. The third
play was *The Danaids*, and here we are much more fortunate with
our fragments. Atheneus records that Aphrodite appeared as a
character in the play and delivered a speech of which he quotes
seven verses:

> The holy Sky loves to pierce the Earth, and love for the union
> seizes the Earth. Rain from the moist Sky falls upon her and makes
> her swell. She brings forth for man flocks of sheep and Demeter's
> grain; from this liquid marriage trees grow to their perfection;
> and it is I who am the cause.

The fragment does not greatly help us to reconstruct the plot:
obviously, Aphrodite is defending the action of Hypermestra, and,
at least by implication, condemning her sisters; but in what circumstances we cannot be sure. It does however emphatically restate
and amplify the theme announced in the *finale* of the *Supplices*, and
thereby gives a clear indication of the general scope of the trilogy.

It is not quite a hymn to the glory of Zeus. We may indeed say
with truth: 'It is from Zeus that the whole trilogy derives its
significance, and around his name that the composition [the *parodos*]
is designed.'[1] But what is Zeus? Aeschylus tells us more than once
that he does not know. Thomson continues: 'A question of religion
is thus raised which is going to dominate the whole play, or rather
the whole trilogy. Is Zeus indifferent to justice? Will he allow
brutality to triumph?' But this is so evidently a question expecting
the answer No that none but a simple-minded dramatist would
ask it. Aeschylus' questions were not so easy. Pohlenz makes two
interesting remarks on the Zeus of the play:[2] 'His mind is an abyss
which no mind can fathom: Seine Sinn ist ein Abgrund den kein
Blick ermisst,' and 'Zeus does not abandon his own: Zeus verlässt
die Seinen nicht'. The first is true, tragic, and Aeschylean; the
second, if true, is not tragic, but belongs to a German chorale as
much in feeling as it does in rhythm. Who protects the Danaids?
Not Zeus. Zeus does not answer their prayer and drown the Egyptians; they escape the hated marriage only by the murder for which,

[1] G. Thomson, *Greek Lyric Metres*, p. 82.

[2] *Griechische Tragödie*, pp. 35 and 38.

probably, they must atone. Are they 'die Seine'? We must not hastily
assume this because they appeal to Zeus and win our sympathy.
Zeus has two daughters, Artemis and Aphrodite: the Danaids, like
Hippolytus in Euripides' play, give all their devotion to Artemis
and none to Aphrodite – as, presumably, the Egyptians give all
theirs to Aphrodite and none to Artemis. Both goddesses are parts
of a whole, and the Whole is Zeus. The trilogy is not a pious
demonstration; it is a tragedy.

How far can we go in reconstructing it? Did the threatened war
take place, or was it somehow averted? Argos of the Pelasgi became
Argos of the Danai; therefore Danaus succeeded to Pelasgus. But
how? Ancient authorities knew two variants. Apollodorus records
that Pelasgus ceded the throne voluntarily to Danaus; Pausanias,
that the change was made by a decision of the people. If Aeschylus
used either of these versions, the former, though improbable, seems
the more likely. Pelasgus did indeed say 'The people is quick to
blame', but his own behaviour was so irreproachable that one does
not easily foresee deposition. Hermann argued that there was a war,
and that Pelasgus was killed; Wilamowitz, that there was no war,
but a compromise.[1] Surely Hermann's view is the more probable;
the prophecy of the serving-women supports it. Wilamowitz found
unnecessary difficulty in explaining how, if there was a war, the
chorus of the second play could be the Egyptians. But we need not
assume that Aeschylus condemned himself to dramatize every bit
of the story. If in the second play the Egyptians are already victorious, or Pelasgus slain, then the arranging of terms between them
and the Argives and Danaus would give enough material for a play.
The objection to Wilamowitz' view is the compromise: why
should the Danaids give way, except under dire compulsion?
'Honourable marriage, not a violent one,' says Wilamowitz. But
the Danaids have made it quite clear that they will have no marriage
of any kind. One point to bear in mind is the description we have
been given of the great extent of Pelasgus' kingdom; one does not
easily imagine that it was defeated in war with Egypt. Yet the
Pelasgi did become Danai. Perhaps therefore we may surmise that
honours were even in the battle, but that Pelasgus was killed. Thus
Argos, now leaderless, might without dishonour offer the throne to

---

[1] G. Hermann, *de Aeschyli Danaidibus* (Opusc. II, 319 ff.) Wilamowitz, *Interpre-
ationen*, p. 20.

Danaus if he could make terms with the Egyptians, and he, with some justification, could concert his plot with his distracted daughters. Certainly the death of Pelasgus would be no unlikely consummation of the tragic dilemma in which we have already found him placed; and if we feel inclined to ask if the Zeus of Aeschylus would permit the destruction of a king who had come to the defence of suppliants, we should reflect that this Zeus is no comforting embodiment of a pleasing 'natural justice': he did not prevent the wicked Egyptians from reaching Argos, and in the *Agamemnon* he has a King destroyed because the king has done precisely what he, Zeus, intended. These Greek gods usually prefigure the sort of thing that does happen rather than what we may think ought to happen.

Now we may consider the Danaids: their trial, their punishment. Were those who killed their husbands arraigned for murder, and before the people of Argos, on the grounds that they had brought blood-pollution on the land? Or was it Hypermestra who was accused?[1] We could approach this question with a little more confidence if we knew what happened to the forty-nine; but we do not. The myth which condemned them to draw water for ever in leaky vessels is certainly not Aeschylean. Another story had it that Lynceus, Hypermestra's husband, avenged his brothers by killing all his sisters-in-law and Danaus too: we will not easily believe that Aeschylus used so violent a denouement.

The appearance of Aphrodite in the third play stands in a very natural relation with the close of the *Supplices*. Now, Pindar uses a myth in which the Danaids are put up for marriage, not very gloriously, as prizes for all-comers to contend for in a foot-race: they were stationed at the end of the course, and each successive suitor, as he reached it, took his choice.[2] It seems likely that Aeschylus used the same myth; Mazon indeed conjectured that Pindar may have taken it from Aeschylus. So the forty-nine Danaids would be compelled to accept the $K\upsilon\pi\rho\acute{\iota}\delta o\varsigma\ \mathring{a}\nu\acute{a}\gamma\kappa\eta$, the universal law of nature, against which they protested in the first play. We might further conjecture that if the suitors were not Argives the city would at once be relieved of any pollution which their

[1] Mazon says: 'Hypermestra est d'abord l'objet de la colère de Danaos, car elle a trahi les siens, en laissant vivre un vengeur des Egyptiades.' (Edn. Budé, *Notice*, p. 8)

[2] Pythians IX, iii ff. This ode was composed in 474 or near it.

continued presence might entail. Hypermestra on the other hand remains in Argos and becomes the ancestress of the new royal line and of Heracles. So at last does a descendant of the Princess Io return to the land from which Io had been driven by the jealousy of Hera. This would imply that it was the forty-nine who were put on trial, not Hypermnestra. The punishment, if indeed this is what Aeschylus contrived, is obviously not a punishment for homicide, but for disregard of Aphrodite. So far as the Egyptians are concerned, perhaps the decision was that they deserved what they got. And since we are guessing, let a final guess be ventured. Bearing in mind the bold dramaturgy of the *Eumenides*, where Apollo defends Orestes, the Erinyes accuse him, and Athena sits in judgement with human colleagues, may we not think it conceivable that in the *finale* of the Danaid trilogy there appeared not one goddess but two, Artemis alongside Aphrodite? Her function would be to denounce the lustfulness of the Egyptians, and thereby to secure the acquittal of the Danaids from the charge of murder.

All this is very uncertain. We shall be on rather firmer ground if we return to the play that has survived and ask ourselves what it is about.

Drama, we are told, always involves conflict. In the *Supplices* it abounds: the Danaids conflict with the Egyptians; Pelasgus and his citizens have to choose between conflicting policies either of which will bring them death and possibly destruction; finally, so far only adumbrated, there is in the Danaids themselves the latent conflict between Artemis and Aphrodite – a conflict that should not exist. Yet over all there stands the ultimate power of Zeus.

> *The world itself is peisèd well,*
> *Made to run even upon even ground.*

We have asked if Aeschylus too built on this foundation. Some part of the *Supplices* may be thought consistent with it. Pelasgus' dilemma need not imply an irrational universe, a Zeus whose mind, in so far as it is not quite obscure, is self-contradictory. It is a perfectly normal tragic sequence, familiar to us also from the classical English tragic poet:[1] moral violence, an offence against Dike, breaks out in Egypt when the Egyptians resolve to marry

---

[1] I have briefly discussed this in an essay on the *Histories* of Shakespeare: *More Talking of Shakespeare*, pp. 33–54 (Longmans, 1959).

their cousins against their will. Resisting this, the Danaids flee, and show no little violence themselves when they threaten to defile the altars. Pelasgus is faced with a conflict of duties, in which we, like Pelasgus, may seek a just resolution, but the search is vain; not because the universe is irrational, ἄνευ δίκης, but because the course of dike has been violently disturbed by the Egyptians. It is for this reason that Pelasgus finds 'no way out except through disaster' (v. 442). In such a case we can pray the gods to come to our rescue, but (as Antigone found) the gods will not. Neither in mature tragedy nor in life itself do we find that the gods who made the laws will intervene in a particular case to prevent the laws from operating. Zeus does not prevent the Egyptians from reaching Argos safely, nor from so far prevailing that the Danaids have to marry them. Yet neither does Zeus prevent the Danaids from murdering them, nor – if our reconstruction is near the truth – do they have to pay in blood for their bloodshed. They must indeed make atonement to Aphrodite, but when this is done, dike is re-established.

This, perhaps, is acceptable so far as it goes, but there is another theme in the play: Io. Her story, we can be quite certain, had for Aeschylus some deep significance: in a later trilogy too he used it, interwoven with the story of Prometheus. Each trilogy is now a fragment, so that we can be only tentative. In *Prometheus Vinctus* the cruelty and indeed tyranny of Zeus towards Prometheus is in juxtaposition with his cruelty towards Io. Prometheus can prophesy that out of Io's suffering blessing will come,[1] and that from her descendant Hypermestra will spring the royal line of Argos, and Heracles who will release Prometheus; but at the beginning the love of Zeus for the young princess is presented as no more than a passion which Zeus is determined to satisfy,[2] and if her father will not compel Io to yield to him, Zeus will destroy his whole family with a thunderbolt. It is a blind passion not essentially different from his blind rage against Prometheus. Yet in each case the violence passes. In these two broken trilogies much, necessarily, remains obscure; yet the idea emerges fairly clearly from the Io story that sheer violence and chaos in the universe give place in time to peace and order. Fortunately one trilogy remains intact; that one certainly

[1] *P.V.* 846–76.
[2] *P.V.* 640–86, especially 649 f. and 654.

enforces the same idea. How prominent it may have been in the
Danaid trilogy one cannot tell.

2. The 'Supplices' and Pre-Aeschylean Tragedy

Greek tragedy passed through distinct forms, and unless we wish
to stultify our criticism by complaining that the *Troades* is not so
'well-constructed' as the *I.T.*, or by finding the *Septem* stiff in
comparison with the *Tyrannus,* it is well to make clear the main
features and peculiar virtues of each. The significant forms seem to
be four, of which the first three are clearly marked. Aristotle
remarks briefly, and without a word of explanation, that Aeschylus
introduced the second actor, and Sophocles the third, with scene-
painting. The meaning of these innovations will be the theme of
much that follows; for the moment it is enough to observe that
they give us important landmarks. Tragedy was profoundly
modified by each. We have the Thespian lyrical tragedy with one
actor, the early Aeschylean with two, the Sophoclean with three.
It will be convenient to call the early Aeschylean Old Tragedy, the
Sophoclean Middle, and the late-Euripidean drama New. The
differences we have in mind are other than those personal to the three
poets. The *Medea* has more in common with the *Antigone* than with
the *I.T.*; and New Tragedy was written by both Euripides and
(apparently) Agathon. From Old Tragedy our surviving plays are
the *Septem, Persae* and *Prometheus* – the last in spite of its three
actors, and even if Professor G. Thomson is right in putting it later
than the *Oresteia.* The *Supplices* is a link between Old Tragedy and
the still older Lyrical Tragedy which is the subject of our present
inquiry.

   Neither about the form nor about the essential spirit of pre-
Aeschylean drama have we any direct evidence.[1] We know that
it was enacted by one actor and chorus,[2] but this does not take us

---

[1] Kranz, *Stasimon,* is full of interesting speculation on the development of choric
forms, but here we are concerned with the dramatic form of the plays as a whole.

[2] What the size of the chorus was I resolutely refuse to discuss; but one question
interests me. It is generally accepted that it was a chorus of fifty, and Wilamowitz,
in his robust way, said that it was ridiculous to suppose that the later chorus of twelve
could possibly have impersonated the fifty daughters of Danaus. This has some force;
but in the last play, when Hypermnestra had presumably severed herself from her
sisters, did Aeschylus use a chorus of forty-nine? The effect of a dance with one dancer
missing would be striking, and perhaps not too bold for Aeschylus.

far. Aristotle speaks of tragedy casting off the satyric element and discarding the trochaic metre, but there is little help here. In the first place, Pickard-Cambridge[1] gives serious grounds for supposing that Aristotle was only theorizing, and in the second, even if Aristotle's account is true, we cannot imagine that tragedy was satyric in style and irresponsible in spirit so late as 535 B.C., when Peisistratus made it part of his enlarged and glorified Dionysiac Festival. We know from Aristotle that it took a long time for Comedy to be thought worthy of a place in the festival: the tragedy of Thespis must surely have been a serious form of art.

However, if we limit ourselves to the period immediately preceding Aeschylus we may form a general impression by arguing backwards from the *Supplices,* an apparently hazardous enterprise which is made possible by the dramatic idleness of Danaus. The play is in all essentials single-actor drama up to the point where Danaus is able to do something useful by going into Argos.

The first and most obvious merit of the *Supplices* is the power of the lyrical passages. Aeschylus deals with the chorus as surely and confidently as Sophocles with dialogue. There is no sign of hesitancy. If we had no external evidence, we should still be certain that the lyrical was the oldest part of tragedy, for it is sufficiently obvious that Aeschylus had behind him a long tradition. But not only is the composition of the odes firm and varied; the characterization too is mature. These people are no band of singers and dancers, but the Danaids, and they could never for a moment be confused with the Chorus of another play. Sophocles' choruses, praised though they are by Aristotle, never reach this degree of characterization.[2] We realize clearly enough in the *Ajax* that they are Salaminian sailors, in the *Antigone* Theban senators; these all sing in character, but their character is not stamped on their songs or speech as the character of the Danaids is. They will sing πολλὰ τὰ δεινά and we think of them as pure Chorus; a moment later they will say something to Creon, and we realize that they are Theban senators; the Suppliants never for a moment allow us to forget that they are the Suppliants.

We can go further. Aeschylus makes this character dynamic as well as vivid. Greek tragedy never interested itself, except perhaps

---

[1] *Dithyramb, Tragedy, and Comedy,* pp. 128 ff.

[2] Not a complaint but a compliment, see p. 158 f.

in some lost trilogies of which the *Prometheia* is a possible example,
in the development of character,[1] but it did gradually reveal an
already developed character. Aeschylus does this simply but very
powerfully with his chorus here. The Danaids are partly Greek,
partly barbarian; their reliance on Zeus emphasizes the one strain,
their violence the other. The first long choric movement closes
very dramatically with the emergence of the barbarian strain, and
sets up a contrast which Aeschylus uses repeatedly, like some powerful and unifying basic rhythm. Sophocles never did this either;
Aeschylus scarcely again. We shall see later why not.

For pre-Aeschylean tragedy then we can postulate a high level
of competence in the management of the chorus and in its dramatization. 'The Chorus was the Protagonist.' This is the conclusion
drawn from its position in the *Supplices,* and it is a doubtful one.[2]
We must not think of the *Supplices* as Greek Tragedy, example
no. 1 or no. 2. It is the *Supplices,* a unique and individual play; and
Aeschylus never quite learned the art of turning out plays to a
pattern.[3] The myth which he uses in this trilogy is obviously
unusual in this respect, that the chief agent was not an individual
but a crowd. If the fifty daughters of Danaus were to appear on the
stage at all, it could only be as chorus. The same problem cropped
up in a later trilogy, and was solved in the same way. In the
Eumenides one of the actors was a multiple personality, and these
Furies inevitably and effectively become the chorus and virtually
co-protagonist with Orestes. We do not say of this that Aeschylus
is becoming primitive again, returning to the dramatic traditions
of his youth; neither should we make too certain that the dramatic
position of the chorus in the *Supplices* is a sign of date only. This
special degree of dramatization is not necessarily in the tradition
at all, but was probably a direct consequence of the layout of this
particular myth. The lyric element was predominant, but we have
no reason to suppose that it was in this specific sense dramatic; it

---

[1] Professor Webster has argued (*Introduction to Sophocles,* pp. 94 ff.) that it did,
but only by assuming that an important change of mind (e.g. Ajax resolving not to
kill himself after all) is development of character. What is the Greek for 'character'
in this sense? It cannot be φύσις, and it obviously is not ἕξις; and τὴν γνώμην
μετατίθεσθαι does not mean 'develop your character'.

[2] Aristotle, it should be noticed, does not say that the chorus was the protagonist
but τὰ τον χοροῦ, the lyric element, which is a different thing.

[3] See below, p. 96.

probably stood to the chorus of the *Supplices* as the chorus of the *Agamemnon* does to that of the *Eumenides*.

We may now look again at the futility of Danaus. The difficulty that Aeschylus has in using him is not simply a sign of primitive technique and inexperience, but a special consequence of this legend. To the end of his life no amount of dramatic difficulty stopped Aeschylus from making a play once he had seen in its story a tragic idea; we need only look at the *Prometheus* to see that. Sheppard's comment therefore, that Aeschylus has invented the tool but cannot yet use it properly, must not pass unchallenged. The second actor is used well enough when he is the Herald, and we need not doubt that Danaus was effective enough in the later plays, when he had an independent part. The character of the daughters is one of the two important dramatic forces that make the *Supplices,* and this may not be overshadowed by any strong characteristic in the father. For Danaus, if he is to do anything dramatic here, can do it only by becoming a third dramatic force, additional to the chorus and the King. He must be the driving-force behind his daughters, or oppose them, or present their situation from another point of view; and none of these things belonged at all to Aeschylus' tragic conception of the story. He is therefore only 'an eponymous ancestor dressed up for the stage', but because the situation allowed nothing else, not because Aeschylus knew no better.

This unusual position of the chorus in this play explains too why it is specifically dramatic in a way in which later choruses (except the Furies) are not. Had Aeschylus in the *Agamemnon* or Sophocles in the *Antigone* attempted to dramatize his chorus as fully as Aeschylus does here, he would have detracted from the dramatization of the stage-characters and done something which might have been interesting but would have obscured the tragic idea. If there is one thing which may be said without reserve of all Greek Tragedy (so long as it remained tragic), it is that it never admits anything which does not directly contribute to the tragic idea. It has to the full the austerity and logic of every other classical Greek art, and it will use neither characterization nor anything else needlessly.

We may now for the moment leave the Chorus. We have seen that Aeschylus is already as much at home with it as he is in the *Septem* or the *Oresteia*. His personality grew, but in this respect his art was already mature, and we may infer that those who had immediately preceded him were also, in their own degree, masters of this part of drama. What of the other parts?

'The *Supplices* is deficient in characterization.' This is a misconception. Certainly Danaus' few incursions into character are tedious, but Danaus is already explained. There remain the Herald and the King. For Heralds the good and sufficient rule is, as H. W. Smyth says, 'like master like man', and no quarrel will be picked with Aeschylus on this score. But Pelasgus is said to be no character; he is no Eteocles, no Oedipus. And why should he be? His tragedy turns on no ἁμαρτία; it is not even remotely based on his character. Be he what he will, he is lost, and Aeschylus is too good an artist to invest him with irrelevant character. All we need is that he should be morally and intellectually big enough to realize to the full what has come upon him and to see the dilemma in which he and his people are placed; and this we have. Sophocles drew character so brilliantly not because he was good at it but because his tragedy turned on it; Aeschylus drew Pelasgus as he did, not because he was a primitive and could do no better but because his tragic conception demanded this and nothing more.

Aeschylus' power of presenting character was fully equal to his need, and we may find that in other respects he was not following a tradition of puerility. The passage of the turning of the screw is masterly: Aeschylus never did anything better. Was this something new to the Greek stage, or was it in the tradition? The power of it is surely pure Aeschylus, but in a sense – in its clarity and its directness – it is pure Greek. All we can say is that the possibility of such dramatic effects lay to hand if there was a poet capable of using it. It is clear too that iambic speech of a dramatic kind was no novelty. That there were earlier masters of this art we may perhaps infer from such passages as 468–89, which do not read like the poetry of a pioneer. Croiset remarks, 'The poetic style, though it has admirable qualities of strength, grandeur and brilliance, is defective in its excessive tendency to remove itself from the level of normal speech. To avoid resemblance with prose it loads itself with an excess of images sometimes bizarre, of artificial periphrases, of turns of speech almost enigmatic.'[1] This is just, if we remember that iambic speech brought into so close a connection with lyric speech must avoid the prosaic at all costs. We think of the artificial antithesis between sea

[1] *Eschyle*, p. 67.

and land (77), 'Dust, the dumb messenger of an army' (180), ἀβουκόλητον τοῦτ' ἐμῷ φρονήματι (929). These things are significant perhaps not of an early stage in the writing of iambics but of Aeschylus himself. In another early play we find one more bad shot, worse than any of these: 'the voiceless children of the undefiled,' meaning fish (*Persae* 577). These strained phrases of the *Supplices* are genuine Aeschylus, like the homely vividness of δεδορκὸς ὄμμα, μηδ' ἄγαν ὠνωμένον ('an eye clear, not too wined-up'), which reappears in the ox on the Watchman's tongue in the *Agamemnon*. We have here the real Aeschylus in his strength and weakness, and one can but feel that the weakness would have been more pronounced had he not had some earlier masters on whom to model his style.

We know then that in the dramatic lyric, and, we may feel fairly certain too, in the dramatic iambic, Aeschylus had some considerable predecessors. Can we venture to form a more definite idea what this earlier tragedy was like?

We infer a chorus which, though not an actor like the chorus of the *Supplices,* is yet essentially dramatic, expressing in its long movements the urgency of some tragic situation, and bringing to bear on the actor some moral or spiritual force. The normal chorus then, as later, was surely a group of citizens, senators, captives or the like representing in its passionate formalism a big collective idea or emotion – the city, the vanquished, the wronged; a body surpassing the individual stature, but not a mere abstraction deprived of all personality. Even if less fully characterized than the Suppliants, it was probably more fully characterized than later choruses; for of the two forces which clashed in the drama, one necessarily proceeded from them. There was no room for the 'idealized spectator'.

Against this chorus stands the single actor. He, too, must have been drawn in outline only, like Pelasgus, for a detailed character-drawing would be wrong against this background, and the exiguous dramatic personnel would not have allowed it, nor the type of tragic idea called for it. The actor must represent the complementary idea to the chorus – the King, the victor, the wrongdoer. Pelasgus is the perfect type, neither an abstraction nor very individual. His diction, like his characterization, must harmonize with that of the chorus, for any approach to naturalism would be out of drawing. In conformity with the strictly-regulated lyrical measures which form the bulk of the play he must speak regularly. A passage like

Suppl. 347–406 obviously belongs by nature to this kind of drama, and so does stichomythia, provided that it is formal enough. Intellectual subtlety and eristic could play no part here.

It is the usual assumption that the pre-Aeschylean tragedy was only a sort of Oratorio: 'Aeschylus found Cantata and turned it into Tragedy.' If the word Cantata can be stretched to cover such essentially dramatic and tragic things as the major part of the *Supplices* (still discounting Danaus), then there is nothing to be said; but if the word means a series of exchanges between a chorus and an actor, both playing a part but neither being specifically dramatic, then the assumption seems to be unjustified. Phrynichus was evidently more lyrical than dramatic, but we need not assume that everyone else was a Phrynichus too. The early plays about which we are best informed are his *Capture of Miletus* and *Phoenissae,* and these seem to have been pathetic narrative-drama rather than tragedy; real cantata in fact. But it may be noticed that such chronicle-subjects were not the normal ones, and were particularly difficult to put into dramatic form. Aeschylus, most would admit, was not altogether successful with his historical play the *Persae.* If no other work of his had survived, we might now be saying that tragedy remained lyrical or narrative in form conception until Sophocles rescued it. But we know that the *Persae*, in style and structure, is not typical of Aeschylus; the middle part of the *Supplices* and the whole of the *Septem* are much more specifically dramatic in form. By analogy it seems likely that normal pre-Aeschylean drama was more specifically dramatic than the *Phoenissae* and the *Capture of Miletus*. Again, we are perhaps inclined to overestimate the importance of the second actor and to underestimate the possibilities of the single actor with chorus. From the *Supplices* we may gain some idea of the kind of plot and the kind of tragic situation that early drama could have dealt with; and if it is shown that the possibility of real drama is there, no one who knows his Greeks will care to deny that the possibility was realized.

The plot, like the diction and the characterization, must have been highly conventionalized, not in the least naturalistic. This was inevitable, for unless the actor was to spend most of his time in the changing-room, free movement of plot was impossible. The chorus enters and expounds the situation; the actor enters and gives us an impression of his general position. Now all the dramatic forces are present; something may be kept back, as in the *Supplices* the threat of suicide is kept back,[1] but nothing new can enter. It is more important, however, to notice that nothing new is wanted. The limitation, like most limitations to the great artist, does not mean poverty, but intensity. It means here the opportunity to display one form of Tragedy, and that perhaps the profoundest, in its purest form, free from distracting irrelevancies; and that is the form of Tragedy which we have in the *Supplices,* the spectacle of the hero isolated before some awful rift in the universe, looking, like Pelasgus, into the chasm that must engulf him. The simple form of Thespian tragedy was marvellously fitted to such a tragic idea, ἄνευ λύπης οὐδαμοῦ καταστροφή, No issue free from disaster; and it is hard to suppose that nobody saw the fact before Aeschylus altered the form with his second actor. The cantata theory does not explain the *Supplices*.

It has been assumed that the crisis is that of the actor, not of the chorus, and that in this sense the actor really was, or became, the protagonist. The assumption is necessary. It may not have been true when Thepis won his famous victory in 534, but it obviously was when tragedy got within hail of Aeschylus. The single actor necessarily attracts the eye; he must be the centre of our most poignant interest, as he is the focus of the moral forces working in the play. The chorus is the voice of Humanity, its sufferings the common sufferings of Humanity; only those of the actor can be made tragically significant. He is bound to stand out above the crowd; his must be the choice at the crisis; he, the individual, must be seen at grips with his destiny. Drama in which the chorus takes first place can only be pathetic; it is not in the strictest sense tragic to be the population of a captured city or the victim of cruel oppression; and though the chorus in the Danaid-trilogy as a whole is the protagonist, really a tragic hero that acts tragically and suffers tragically, it is because it is not a normal chorus, simply a representative group, but an individual character multiplied fifty times. They are tragically one-sided like Hippolytus, not a community like the chorus of the *Persae* or *Agamemnon*.

We may therefore tentatively, but not without some evidence,

---

[1] Kept back, that is, from the King. Aeschylus might have given us a cheap dramatic surprise by keeping it back from us too, but he was an artist, and a Greek artist. (See below, p. 282.)

suggest the following as a type, not the only one but the best, of early tragedy.

First ode.

Entrance of the Actor and disclosure of the general situation.

Second ode, in which pressure is brought to bear on him.

The crisis grows. Kommos?

Third ode.

Actor faces the crisis and takes his decision.

Fourth ode.

The result. Messenger?

Fifth ode.

It is a simple form, but not infantile. It is a form which permits the most exquisite and most powerfully dramatic lyricism, and can express the profoundest and most moving of tragic situations. Its 'stiffness' is no defect. 'Is it not possible,' said the Dramatic Critic of *The Times,* commenting on the Delphi production of the *Supplices* in 1930, 'that the pre-Aeschylean drama already held a key that gave it freedom from the bonds of naturalism – a key for which modern dramatists from Strindberg to Lenormand have been desperately striving?' It is, I think, not possible only, but certain.

CHAPTER II

Old Tragedy

1. Introduction

We come to that form of Greek drama whose outward mark is the use of two actors and the chorus.[1] Our task must be to try to gain some idea why this form was brought into existence, why Aeschylus wanted the second actor, why he did not want a third; in other words, what the special virtue of this type of tragedy was. We have been maintaining that it is not necessary to regard Lyrical Tragedy as something immature and incomplete which was waiting anxiously for Aeschylus to give it form and significance; so too we must be careful not to think of Old Tragedy merely as Greek drama without the third actor, another, though less, incomplete form. Regarded historically or biologically it may be a primitive form; regarded aesthetically it is not. It is perfectly adapted to the purpose for which it was designed, and is therefore complete. Aeschylus added one actor and not two, not, fundamentally, because he was conservative and cautious (no dramatist has been bolder), nor because his technique was not yet equal to managing three actors, but because his tragic conceptions demanded this form and not the other.

Why Aeschylus introduced the second actor and invented his characteristic use of the statutory trilogy will be discussed later,[2] but it seems well to anticipate one or two points here. It is quite certain that he had no idea of using the second actor as an antagonist to the first, turning tragedy into an ἀγών, a contest, between the two. This comes only upon the third actor's appearance and is quite foreign to Aeschylus' tragic thinking. The essence of Old Tragedy

---

[1] The *Prometheus* is included in this group, in spite of its three actors, because the use of the third is quite incidental.

[2] See below, pp. 44, 106 f., 152.

was not one character joined in conflict with another, but the
solitary hero facing his own destiny or playing out an inner drama
of his own soul – like Pelasgus.[1] Pelasgus is not more solitary
than Eteocles and Prometheus; Eteocles does not grapple with
Polyneices but with himself – not because Aeschylus was hampered
by his small cast, but because he did not want Polyneices.

But if the second actor did not revolutionize drama in this respect
he did in another; he enabled plot to move, to move longitudinally,
in action, as well as vertically, in tension. The plot of Lyrical
Tragedy was, in a certain sense, static; when chorus and actor met,
the ring was closed. Now it is not; there is a second actor who can
come in with fresh news – as Darius does, or the Spy in the *Septem* –
or can present different facets of the situation to the hero – as do
Oceanus and Io in the *Prometheus*.

This movement of plot seems not to have been contrived merely
for dramatic reasons, for the sake of making drama more lifelike.
It is natural for us to think like this, but the innovating artist thinks
differently; at least we may be fairly confident that Aeschylus' firs
reason for innovating was that the older form did not enable him
to say what he wanted to say. We have a fine example of his use of
static plot in the middle part of the *Supplices,* but already this is
part of a much wider dramatic theme. The second actor makes it
possible, dramatically, to set the hero in a position which not only
seems, but also is, innocent. Now the situation can change; messengers bring news or heralds make proclamations, and what was
safe becomes perilous. Of this dramatic method the *Septem* is the
perfect example; there we see no sudden pit opening beneath the
hero, but a horror growing before our eyes. Technically this is
no doubt a vast improvement, but it was not first thought of in this
way. The tragic implications of the second actor are even more
important than the dramatic ones. Since the situation moves, the
hero must be of a certain kind; he must – if we are to have tragedy
– be of such a moral constitution as to oppose himself to this
movement, not to conform to it. The hero of the pure tragedy
of situation was Man, almost undifferentiated; the hero of the
Septem must be like Eteocles, one who will not, like the normal
man, say at v. 653, 'Circumstances alter cases; of course I cannot

---

[1] For convenience, I speak here confidently; really Aeschylus is the critic's despair,
because he would never write two plays alike, not even in the *Oresteia*.

fight my own brother.' In other words, the moving plot was designed to display and test moral character, to give room for moral choice and for its results.

Such seems to have been the genesis of the second actor. Once there he could naturally be put to other uses; Darius for example gives us our first dramatic surprise; and we shall see one or two approaches to realism – of which indeed we had one example already in the *Supplices*: the King could hardly have mentioned beer to the chorus, but he can to the Herald.

When we examine the three plays that survive from this stage of drama we at once meet an illuminating difficulty; in two of the plays Aeschylus is wrestling with material which will hardly go into drama at all. In the *Persae* he is sailing closely into the wind of Epic; in the *Prometheus* his imagination is seized with a subject which any other dramatist would have rejected, in this form, as impossible. The technical interest of the *Persae* is to follow the steps whereby an essentially epic story is made ready for the stage; of the *Prometheus* to see how Aeschylus extracts the inner dramatic movement of a situation essentially immobile; of the *Septem* to see Old Tragedy at its best.

2. The 'Persae'

The *Persae* is possibly unique among historical tragedies. The play was produced in 472 B.C. The battle of Salamis, the central incident in the play, had been fought only eight years earlier, and only a few miles from the theatre. A large part of the audience must have taken some part in the battle; all who were Athenians had been refugees from the city; the temples on the Acropolis, destroyed by the Persians, were still in ruins. But the second great Hellenic victory at Plataea, in 479, had broken the invaders, and in the intervening years the maritime Confederacy of Delos, with Athens as its chosen leader, had liberated Ionia from Persian rule and had removed the Persian menace. The completeness of the victory must have seemed a miracle.

Therefore, as the dramatization of recent events was no new thing – for Phrynichus at about 493 had staged his unfortunate *Capture of Miletus* and in 476 his version of the Persian War – it was natural for Aeschylus to be attracted to the subject. As it happens,

we are fairly well supplied with facts about the war, and we know
a little about Phrynichus' play, so that we are in a position to see
what was Aeschylus' idea in such a dramatization – not only to see
what he did but also what he refused to do – and we can to some
extent compare his dramatic outlook with Phrynichus'.

About Phrynichus' play we know this: the scene was laid in
Susa, the chorus consisted of Phoenician women, and a eunuch,
placing seats for the Persian nobles, speaks a prologue in which the
defeat at Salamis is mentioned. The prologue begins

$$Τάδ' ἐστι Περσῶν τῶν πάλαι βεβηκότων$$

a verse which, by what Mazon finely calls 'a courtesy-salute',
Aeschylus uses for his opening, but substituting the ominous
οἰχομένων.[1]

From these few facts Croiset has drawn some interesting conclusions. As the chorus is composed of women, these nobles must
have been given some other part in the play, and one actor must
have been their spokesman, leaving for the other the part of messenger. There could not therefore have been much dramatic complication, especially as the defeat was already known in the palace.
The staple of the play must have been lyrical lamentation – at
which we known Phrynichus excelled. Surprise there could not
have been; as Mazon says, it seems to have been less a tragedy than
a cantata. Phrynichus used Aeschylus' second actor but remained
faithful to his own conception of tragedy; we shall presently find
Aeschylus in his turn doing a similar thing.

By taking the same theme only four years later Aeschylus shows
that he had something new to contribute. He, too, lays the scene
in Susa. That was necessary. Only from the Persian point of view
was the event tragic, and truly tragic not in the Persian camp but in
the centre of the threatened empire. Again, there is the point
roughly expressed by saying that remoteness of place compensates
for nearness in time. The great danger was that the poet should be
betrayed into naturalism, into situations where realistic treatment
was the only possible one. The events were still fresh in men's
memories, and details would be inimical to the development of a
broad moral theme, such as alone would justify the dramatization
of a recent event. The danger could be avoided only by going to

[1] See J. T. Sheppard, *Greek Tragedy*, pp. 45–46.

Susa. There only could the story be sufficiently simplified. Moreover Susa gave opportunities, such as Aeschylus never despised, of striking scenic effects. In this respect, therefore, Aeschylus had to follow Phrynichus.

The choice of Persian nobles and not women as the chorus is significant. Technically it was an improvement in that it set free an actor to play other roles and so to develop the dramatic force – in which Phrynichus had little interest. Morally it is even more important. In a play whose chorus was Phoenician women the prevailing tone must obviously have been pathetic, 'Alas for the dead!' With a chorus of Counsellors the tone becomes deeper. 'Alas for our fallen nation!' The chorus of the *Persae* can take the historical view, and can develop the tragic theme which Aeschylus sees in the story – they, and they alone, can show us that Xerxes' policy of boundless aggression is responsible for the disaster.

Nor does Aeschylus follow Phrynichus in allowing the news of the disaster to be already known when the play opens. He was composing a drama, not a threnody, and needed therefore all the dramatic movement he could get. But this raises an interesting question: if Aeschylus was concerned – as he must have been – to create dramatic situations out of this epical material, why did he not anticipate Herodotus, and begin his play with a triumphant message from Xerxes announcing the capture and sack of Athens? What could be more obvious, or more effective? Let the play begin with scenes of rejoicing: they will be the perfect foil for the catastrophe to come. Incidentally, this stroke would have circumvented one awkward moment, the transition from the first ode to the first episode (vv. 140 ff.). 'Come,' says the Leader of the Chorus, 'let us deliberate. How is Xerxes faring?' Since they have no idea how he is faring, there is no material for deliberation; but we have to be informed who they are, and why they are there. The chorus is, in fact, in an unprofitable situation, and we are glad when the Queen arrives, to rescue them from it.

Since the *Persae* is not a play in which mundane realism is of importance we need not exaggerate this blemish; but it is one, and one that would have been unnecessary if a first message of triumph had been contrived, for then the chorus would have had matter for debate. So that we ask, once more, why Aeschylus did not begin with a message announcing victory.

MILLS COLLEGE
LIBRARY

It is, of course, possible to say – though hard to believe – that at this date Aeschylus was incapable of so dramatic a stroke. It is perhaps safer to assume that a dramatic idea obvious to us was accessible to Aeschylus also, and to inquire if the true explanation does not lie deeper. Before, doing that, we may raise other questions of the same kind, and in trying to answer them we may become a little clearer on two matters, about the relation between Old Tragedy and Epic, and about the meaning and purpose of the *Persae* itself. For it has been said, wrongly, as I think, that the play represents a stage in the development of drama at which drama had not yet emancipated itself from the epic tradition and technique; while as for the other point, are we to call it a religious or a patriotic play? Politics and religion were certainly not so clearly separated in the fifth century as they are today; nevertheless, if one critic says 'This is a religious play about the punishment of ὕβρις' and another, 'This is a patriotic piece celebrating the victory,' they are not saying the same thing, and it is perhaps possible to prove that the one is substantially right and the other substantially wrong. For if Aeschylus was a competent dramatist, not struggling with a form that he had imperfectly mastered, proper appreciation of his form should lead us directly to a proper appreciation of the content. If we ask ourselves the right questions about the form of the play we shall be led, I think, straight to the conclusion that he did not set out to compose, for the stage, a piece in celebration of Salamis and Plataea – a theme which might have made good epic – but to create drama, and nothing but drama, on the theme of ὕβρις and its inevitable punishment. What patriotic celebration there is – and there is obviously some – is incidental.

For his material, Aeschylus had the Persian invasion; but we find that he used it with the same freedom that the dramatists were accustomed to use in handling myth – and for the same purpose, namely, to remove everything irrelevant to the dramatic idea and to emphasize what is significant, in order that every detail of the plot may be dramatically efficient. In Aristotelian language, οἷα ἐγένετο, what happened, is modified until it becomes οἷα ἂν γένοιτο what *would* happen; drama becomes 'more philosophic than history'.

Believing that the form embodies the thought, and that Aeschylus was able to manage his form as he wished, let us look at it, asking ourselves certain questions about the plot and the manipulation of the material. One such question we have asked already: why does Aeschylus not begin with the news of a considerable success? Other questions are: why does he represent Darius as the prudent King who never set foot out of Asia, although Darius had invaded Scythia, and had had something to do with Marathon? Why does he so exaggerate the importance of the small action on Psyttalia? Why does he represent Xerxes' retreat from Salamis as an incontinent flight, such that he arrives at Susa as a broken fugitive? Why does he invent that quite impossible disaster on the Strymon? Why, in describing the battle of Salamis, does he so notably avoid mentioning individual names and personal exploits? Why does he represent as impious the building of the bridge across the Hellespont, when the ordinary Greek attitude to these contrivances seems to have been (as we should expect) one of interested admiration?

Needless to say, answers have been given to most of these questions, and not all of them are bad answers. The difficulty is that they are all different, while the questions are the same – namely, why did Aeschylus shape his play like this? As for the character of Darius, we are told that the Athenians, not having the *Cambridge Ancient History,* did not know very much about him; further, that the prudent Darius makes a strong contrast with the furious Xerxes, and that dramatists like contrasts of character. They do – but was Aeschylus altering history only for a dramatic 'effect'? As for the autumnal freezing of the Strymon, the Strymon was a long way off, and probably the Athenians did not know much about its habits; in any case, Aeschylus loved marvels. (This answer is a bad one – for this reason if for no other, that instead of trusting to Athenian ignorance, Aeschylus goes out of his way to call the frost ἄωρος, unseasonable.) As for the action on Psyttalia, it has been suggested that here Aeschylus had in mind the need for promoting social unity in Attica: he is showing the Athenians that every class of citizen had his share in the glory of Salamis, the poorer classes afloat, the hoplites on the island. But exaggeration is poor propaganda. Then, Xerxes' disorderly flight is honest misconception; alternatively, Aeschylus is ridiculing the Persians – again, a poor way of celebrating a victory. That no Greek names are used is a master-stroke of artistic simplification, which at the same time avoids the invidious – though we may perhaps feel some doubt here; for suppose that

Aeschylus had chosen to treat his theme in epic style, with a Catalogue of Ships, in a speech bristling with Greek names – should we
not have found this 'artistic' too, and filled our commentaries with
parallels from Milton? The 'artistic', after all, is only what is necessary and right. Let us then show that the theme demanded precisely
this treatment; then we shall know why it is artistic.

Of the answers given here, some are plausible, some may be even
partially true. But they are extremely various, invoking as they do
politics, ignorance, and the pursuit of certain isolated dramatic
effects. If we found one single answer to all the questions – including
the first one, not yet answered at all – we should feel some assurance
that we were on the right track. And we do find such a single answer
in the assumption that Aeschylus was not writing a play – epic,
patriotic, or anything else – about the victory, but was constructing
a religious drama out of the Persian War, in just the same spirit
that he constructed another out of the Trojan War. Xerxes' ὕβρις
led him to break a divine law. He sinned as Paris sinned, and
Agamemnon; and like those sinners he was punished by Zeus
through instruments chosen by Zeus, Paris through the two sons
of Atreus, Agamemnon through Clytemnestra, Xerxes through the
Greeks and Greece. The difference – a profound one indeed – is
that in the *Agamemnon* the 'justice' inflicted is in each case a crime,
itself calling for justice, while in the *Persae* the punishment is simple
and final. With this important reservation the parallel holds, and it
explains the play.

First, the 'mythical' treatment of recent history. Mr D. S.
MacColl relates how a sitter complained to a Scottish sculptor that
the bust he had made of him was not like him. 'It's no every mon,'
said the sculptor, 'can be like his bust.' That was Darius' trouble.
Xerxes was to be smitten by Heaven because he had committed
ὕβρις. The poet, wanting a clear symbol of that ὕβρις, uses the
sharp distinction between Europe and Asia; here are bounds laid
down by Heaven. Obviously, history or no history, Darius cannot
be allowed to have passed these bounds, or the judgement of
Heaven would have fallen on him. Darius must therefore be wise
and prudent; he must scrupulously have respected this law. The
contrast of character is indeed effective, but it is a by-product.

What of the description of the battle, Psyttalia, the precipitous
flight of Xerxes? To Aeschylus, the Greek forces are an Avenger,

an instrument in the hands of Heaven. Individual names must therefore be suppressed at all costs. This is the reason why the treatment of the battle is 'artistic'. One individual exploit is, in fact, referred to plainly enough, the stratagem of Themistocles. And what does Aeschylus say about it? That there came to Xerxes some Alastor, or some evil spirit.

As for Psyttalia, that becomes a second blow from the god, one that destroys not Persian allies, like Salamis, but the Persian nobility itself. And then Xerxes flees in terror. In fact, he did not; in the play, he does – because his real adversary is more than human. And as for the Strymon, let us not talk of Athenian ignorance, or Aeschylus' love of marvels. In the first place, the preliminary sufferings of the Persians on the retreat are all attributed to 'natural', not human, causes; not harassing attacks by patriots in the mountains, but hunger and thirst. It is the very soil of Greece opposing the invader. In the second place, it is 'the god' who freezes the river, 'out of season'; and when the Persians were on the ice, thanking the gods for their deliverance, 'the god scattered his rays', and the Persians were drowned. There is a direct parallel to this in the *Agamemnon*. 'Let them remember,' said Clytemnestra, 'to spare the temples, for they still need a safe return.' They did not spare the temples, and they found no safe return, for 'those bitterest enemies, fire and water, conspired together' to destroy the fleet. This conspiracy of enemies is no idle decoration, but a sign that the god was at work, here as in the *Persae*.

Now the reason becomes clear why Aeschylus will have no preliminary message of victory. The God of Aeschylus does not move in the mysterious way of the God of Sophocles; he is direct, and when he hits, he hits straight and hard. He does not mock first. The news that Athens was already destroyed would suggest that he did; it would be a 'dramatic' effect ruinous to the idea. And finally, the reason why Aeschylus makes such an ominous point of the bridge is not to be found in plain fact; it is not that he thought differently about it from Herodotus, or supposed that the Persians might; it is simply that he needed his symbol of Xerxes' ὕβρις. The bridge can be made an explicit case of Xerxes' transgression of limits fixed by Heaven; and Aeschylus' audience, not unaccustomed to poetry, can accept it as such, whatever they may have thought privately about this civil engineering.

c

We find, then, the same answer to every question; the form shows the content. The *Persae* is as purely dramatic, in conception, as any other play by Aeschylus. It has no real connexion with epic, and should not be used to buttress a theory that Tragedy is in some sense descended from the epic. The 'epic colouring' comes from an accident, not from essentials – the accident that much of the action must be presented through narrative; and after all, in this respect, the *Persae* is very like the *Prometheus*. In the *Prometheus* the action is partly past action, partly inner action in the mind of the hero; in either case, necessarily conveyed in a series of speeches. Neither play has any real link with epic; indeed, one of the notable points in the account of Salamis is precisely the way in which Aeschylus has avoided epic expansiveness and detail. What we have here is pure drama; not indeed the form we are accustomed to, but one which we can readily understand once we lay aside prepossessions derived from later forms. 'Slices from Homer' was a brilliant phrase, but one that hardly does justice to the real independence and integrity of Old Tragedy.

We may now examine in detail how Aeschylus put this dramatic conception into dramatic shape. Since the days of Sophocles, especially as interpreted by Aristotle, tragic form has implied clash of character, converging lines of intrigue, surprise, and 'happiness' passing into 'unhappiness'. Aeschylus could not work like this; his religious philosophy could not be expressed through this form. That God will punish the sinner is certain; the only surprise possible is the swiftness and completeness of the punishment; the only movement possible is from foreboding to fulfilment.

It is easy for us to say 'God punishes the sinner', and to think that we know what it means; but what it means to us, if anything, may not be what it meant to Aeschylus: Platonism, our Judaeo–Christian inheritance, and a few other influences have made a difference. It is well therefore to watch with some care what Aeschylus does.

First he makes the chorus give an impressive roll-call of the principalities and powers that compose the 'irresistible flood of men' who have rolled westward against Greece. The gods, we learn, have given to Persia domination by land; the Persians have learned also to look unafraid upon the sea. (Darius's Ghost has something to say about this later.) But the mood of confidence gives place to a mood of anxiety, and the change is brought about not by anything so specific as the arrival of untoward news, but by the reflection – one of which Plato would have strongly disapproved – the god, the *theos*, is deceptive, δολόμητις, 'guileful', and that Atê will smile and lure a man to his ruin.

The Queen-mother arrives and tells of her ominous dream; it quickens vague apprehension into real fear. The chorus advises her: let her offer sacrifice to those *theoi* whom, as we learn later, from the *Agamemnon* (vv. 69 ff.), nothing will appease; no gods will save you from the consequences of what you have done. But before she goes to make ready her sacrifice, Aeschylus defies naturalism by making her ask certain questions about Athens. Obviously, the questions, awkwardly placed, were devised for the sake of the answers. In the line-by-line dialogue that follows we are often bidden to see the mood of patriotic satisfaction: the Athenian poet is inviting the Athenian audience to rejoice in the victory to which Athens contributed so much. Does the passage not twice refer to the Athenian victory of Marathon? – Yes; but the style is very severe, not exactly rabble-rousing; as a patriotic poet Aeschylus might have done something much more effective than this. The passage does mention Marathon twice – but also the discovery of a rich vein of silver at Laureion, and the facts that the Athenians did not rely on the bow (cf. vv. 85 ff.) but on the spear and shield – as of course did all the other Greeks – and were not subjects of a despot but free citizens. Since also the style here is so entirely un-emotional, it would be more prudent to suppose that Aeschylus was mentioning facts which tend to strengthen the fear of the stage-audience. That is at least the way in which the Queen takes it: her final comment is 'Not much comfort here for the parents of our soldiers!'

The immediate arrival of the Messenger converts the fear into frightful reality. In the four speeches that Aeschylus wrote for him there are several points to notice, chiefly that Salamis is not their climax. In the lyrical dialogue that begins the scene the name of Athens is twice mentioned with horror – and it is the last time but one that the city is mentioned at all, a strange fact, if the poet thought he was glorifying the city. The first of the four speeches is another roll-call, this time of Persian notables whose bodies are now swilling around in the waters of Salamis. Then comes the vivid story of the battle. Though Athens provided nearly two-thirds of the Greek fleet, Aeschylus never alludes to the fact, but steadily refers to 'the Hellenes'. What secured the victory – in the play? Two things: first, the valour and discipline of the Greeks, aided by the deceptive stratagem of 'a Greek from the Athenian camp' and by the over-confidence that led Xerxes straight into the trap; second, the *theoi*: it was the *theoi* that 'gave the glory of the seafight to the Greeks' (vv. 454 f.), and it was 'a hostile *daimôn* or Alastor' that deceived Xerxes. The *daimôn* may be no more than a sign of dutiful piety (or of superstition, as some scholars prefer), or it may make good sense. We must wait and see. At least, signs of thoughtful construction are appearing. The *daimôn* recalls the 'guileful' *theos*; the self-discipline of the free Greeks is contrasted with the situation of the Persian captains, who went into battle under the despot's threat that any who flinched would have his head cut off; and all knew that it was with the silver from Laureion that the Athenians had built their large navy.

Now the Messenger dismays the stage-audience, and surprises us, by saying that the half has not yet been told. What follows is not historically accurate, and if we are among those unfortunates who think that historical tragedy must at least be good history, that is the end of the matter: it is a poor play, and we can only wonder why Aeschylus wrote it. According to Herodotus, some Athenian hoplites under Aristeides landed on Psyttaleia and destroyed the Persian troops who had been posted there: the Athenian poet suppresses Aristeides, does not mention that the hoplites were Athenians but calls them 'Greeks', and transforms the Persian 'troops' into the very flower of the Persian army, 'those who were best and noblest, those whom Xerxes trusted most'. If we keep our eyes not on Greek history but on the play, we have no difficulty in understanding why Aeschylus did it: he is not grossly exaggerating the military importance of the action on Psyttaleia, but making the Queen and chorus feel even more shame and humiliation.

Finally, as we saw above, the stage-audience is overwhelmed with two more disasters, and in neither of them do Athenians or Greeks play any part at all: as Darius later says (v. 792), the very soil of Greece turns on the invaders; and then, when Greek valour and the soil of Greece have virtually finished the job, the *theos* himself, appearing at last almost in person, clinches everything. The *theos*, working in or through various natural agencies, has been with us from the beginning; the chorus obviously says the right thing when, at the beginning of its next ode, it declares that it is Zeus the King that has filled the cities of Persia with mourning. What we have to do is to make sense of this, for presumably it made sense to the audience for which Aeschylus was writing.

So far we have heard little about Xerxes' own character and motives. If we must have a tragic hero, we are being disappointed. We have been told that he is a θούριος ἄρχων, 'vehement commander', an ἰσόθεος ξώς, 'man equal to the gods' (vv. 73, 80); the Queen tells us that he intended to avenge Marathon, but instead has lost everything (475 ff.): that is about all. Now, when the Ghost rises, we learn more. Darius is appalled when he learns that his son had dared to bridge the sea, 'thinking to control the *theoi*, even Poseidon'. We recall that the *theoi* had given it to Persia to be dominant by land; they seem not to have approved of the attempt to go further: it is to be the theme of the next ode that ships have been their ruin. The Queen and Darius agree that some *daimôn* had come upon Xerxes, to take away his judgement. For some modern scholars, this *daimôn* is something 'supernatural'; Aeschylus does not seem to agree, for later (753 ff.) he makes the Queen give an entirely natural explanation: Xerxes, being in any case 'vehement', was beset by evil advisers who so taunted him that he neglected the counsels of prudence that his father had given him. In this respect Xerxes resembles Paris in the *Agamemnon*: he too was assailed by the *daimôn* Temptation, daughter of Ruin; being like 'bad bronze' he was unable to resist, and paid the usual penalty. It is nothing supernatural; it is disastrously natural. Temptation, Folly, are ever-present realities.

Presently Darius is prophesying the crowning disaster of Plataea. Some have found a grave inconsistency here: if only a very few Persians survived the Strymon, whence comes the powerful army that is to be destroyed, apparently for the second time? In these matters it is a real affliction to be clever without being intelligent: Aeschylus, like Sophocles (see below, p. 298), knew when to make mistakes. Again we should think of the stage-audience, and of the real audience too. Because Aeschylus has carefully *not* said that Xerxes left in Greece a large army under Mardonius, the prophecy of yet more ruin is the more appalling.

Again Aeschylus is not very careful to be historical. In sober fact, the Athenian army, at Plataea, contributed notably to the Greek victory; our Athenian poet does not even mention that they were present at the battle, but gives all the credit to 'the Dorian spear' – and to Zeus; for we are now told that the Persian host had burned temples and defiled holy places, and that Zeus, 'a chastiser of pride', 'a stern accountant', will punish them for their impiety.

There is another point to notice here. It is easy to say (as I said myself in earlier editions of this book), that the play suffers from the fact that it has no strong central character. Aeschylus himself was evidently unaware of this important requirement: he could so easily have represented this army as another victim of Xerxes' ambition and folly, but instead he makes it the victim of its own reckless impiety. It is true that we can help the poet out of this little scrape by saying that Xerxes was responsible, since he was in command when the Persians burned the temples on the Acropolis; but Aeschylus did not think of saying this, and it is bad criticism to put into a play what its author did not. It obviously is the case that for the time being Aeschylus was content to forget Xerxes, who will not serve as a tragic hero; what he has not forgotten in the *theos* and the fact – or the belief – that he punishes hybris. The hybris of Xerxes was one kind of presumption, the kind that *we* should call folly rather than sin; the army shows hybris of another kind, which we *would* call sin. What they have in common is the presumptuousness of thinking that you can do *anything*, that there are no limits. The same *theos* or *theoi* punish both.

This enables us to make more sense of the concluding scene, and of the end of the present one too – for Darius and the Queen make a strange fuss about receiving Xerxes when he arrives, and arraying him once more in robes that befit his royal station. In the event, he appears before us as he is, in rags, or the Aeschylean equivalent of rags. From this final scene we have irretrievably lost what presumably mattered most – the dance-movements, the music, and the visual contrast between the nobles of the chorus and the battered King; but we can still appreciate the accusing, even menacing, tones in which they speak to one whom they can no longer regard as 'equal to the gods'; also his own miserable confession that it is all his own fault. Early in the play (vv. 212 ff.), the

Queen had said 'If he succeeds, all will admire him; if he fails –
at least the nation cannot call him to account'. The corresponding
word was used by Darius too: 'Zeus is a stern accountant'. We
do not see Xerxes in royal robes; he has been called to account
by Zeus.

We rightly call it a 'religious' play; after that, we have to elicit
the meaning of the word 'religious', for it is not quite what we
might expect. Aeschylus dramatizes for his fellow-citizens a myth
that bears a startling resemblance to the events in which they had
just played a leading part. The play is clearly not a celebration of the
city's greatness, nor is it the tragedy of a not very heroic tragic hero.
It is not simply an edifying Morality on the theme that the gods
punish human presumption: the 'religion' is exploratory rather
than declaratory, for it explores *how* the *theos* operated in the present
case. Silver-mines had something to do with it, and superior
weapons, and a superior political system and a superior spirit, and
overconfidence. Xerxes was tempted and gave way; commanding
so much power, he, a man 'equal to the gods', thought he could
command anything, without limit. But the *theos* is guileful; things
did not go according to plan; not because Zeus aided his Greeks,
but because there was so much that Xerxes had not taken into
account. Atê smiled upon him: the great host advanced triumphantly
and burned Athens. Then Atê smiled again – to herself. It has been
said that history teaches one lesson, namely that men do not learn
from history. Perhaps the same is true of drama. At all events, sixty
years later another great and irresistible force assembled, this one
not in Sardis but in the Piraeus, and it too sailed to utter destruction.
Anyone who cares to read Thucydides VI and VII with attention
and awareness will find it an interesting companion-piece to the
Persae.

3. The 'Septem'

One-third of the fifth century had passed when Sophocles won his
first victory, and in the following year, 467, Aeschylus showed what
Old Tragedy could do by producing the *Septem*. When two-thirds
of the century had passed and new things were again in the air,
Sophocles turned to this Theban legend and crowned Middle

Tragedy by producing the *Tyrannus*. Each play marks an epoch, and marks it emphatically and worthily. The *Tyrannus* displays the virtues peculiar to Middle Tragedy with a completeness and a finality that show that something new must soon be attempted or tragedy decay; and the *Septem* is as perfect an example of Old Tragedy. It has that complete balance of form and content which is the chief glory of the *Tyrannus*, and in our lamentably small inheritance from Old Tragedy it is the only play which places first actor, second actor and chorus in that relation which seems to have been predestined. The *Prometheus,* though it is vaster in conception and has been much more important in the world's education, lacks the beauty and the poise of the *Septem*, and the *Oresteia* is, in our definition, not Old Tragedy. It is a tribute to the Theban story, and one which the formal sense of the Greeks would have approved, that not only these two climacteric plays, the *Septem* and the *Tyrannus,* but also that last and most strangely beautiful of Greek dramas the *Coloneus* turned to it for inspiration.

We saw, or inferred, that the lyrical tragedy of the single actor was peculiarly fitted to convey one kind of tragic situation, that in which the hero, irrespective of his character, irrespective of what he may do, is engulfed as Pelasgus was engulfed. Such a drama cannot and need not move, but nothing is more foolish than to assume that on this account it is undramatic. The drama lies in the lyrical plane, and consists of an increasing tension. The second actor enables the plot to move, and now the true dramatic thrill will arise out of this movement. Instead of watching a Pelasgus caught inextricably, we shall watch the reaction between the moving situation and the hero; and, since the tragic issue depends on this, that the hero shall not be such as to accommodate himself harmlessly to this movement, the hero will have to be characterized. Pelasgus is lost whatever kind of man he is; Eteocles, though in peril, is not lost if he is sensible enough to listen to the chorus. The greatness of the *Septem* lies in this, that it so perfectly realizes the peculiar virtue of Old Tragedy, to be the tragedy of character, and of a single character; that it relates this character closely and significantly to every movement in the situation; and that it achieves the perfect balance between the actors and the chorus. This last we could not say of the *Persae,* nor shall we be able to say it of the *Prometheus*; we shall, however, say something very similar of the *Tyrannus*.

Of the first two plays of the trilogy we know practically nothing, but at least the outline of the story is well established. As subject for this third play Aeschylus had the accomplishment of the curse laid upon his sons by Oedipus; as material, the Argive expedition to Thebes and the death of the brothers in single combat. With these, the only necessary, data it is clear that Aeschylus had a free hand in arranging his plot, and no formidable task in finding enough action to fill a play. It is interesting to see what he chose, and more interesting to see what he rejected; for the plot which he made is not inferior in tragic effect to the renowned plot of the *Tyrannus*, and is as perfectly suited to the genius of Old Tragedy as that to Middle. The difference is characteristic; Sophocles' plot is wonderful through what is can bring in, Aeschylus' through what it can leave out.

The remarkable omission is Polyneices. The play is all Eteocles. It is perhaps not surprising that Polyneices does not appear in person – this might have been difficult to arrange plausibly; what is surprising is that nothing is made of the quarrel and its effect on Eteocles' mind, that there is no parleying between the two, no defiance, no mention even of Polyneices before the fatal moment. One cannot imagine any later dramatist taking this theme and leaving out the central situation; it is *Hamlet* without the Prince.

The reason for this is not that Aeschylus had some idea of keeping back Polyneices' name for the sake of dramatic effect. He has, in fact, based his plot on such a silence, but the complete concentration on the one brother is anterior to this. Aeschylus was not interested in both brothers, only in one. His mind and dramatic imagination were absorbed in the questions of Man's relation to God, fate, the Universe, not in his relation to Man. Sophocles, it is safe to assert, would have made of this situation a study in the fatal play of the one brother's character on the other's; Aeschylus sees in it the question of one man and his destiny. The second brother is the dramatic but not the moral point of the play. A scene between Eteocles and Polyneices therefore was exactly what Aeschylus did not want; it would have implied an interaction of characters which was not his dramatic preoccupation – if it had been, he and not Sophocles would have introduced the third actor; and the day when scenes like this were engineered for the sake of their own excitement was still far distant. In the *Septem* we have again the hero alone with his fate.

His isolation is magnificently complete. The second actor is
a colourless person, or persons, since it is a matter of perfect indifference whether the Spy and the Messenger are the same man or not.
They are mere instruments in the plot. The chorus too is reduced
in stature; no longer the centre of the action, for Eteocles is that;
less sharply characterized than the Suppliants. To this chorus a
single broad characteristic, Fear, is attributed – an emotion natural
to a group – and this is put to important use in the plot; but for the
greater part of the play the chorus is pure Chorus, not a personal
agent like the Suppliants. But although Eteocles, the actor, opens
this play and leaves us in no doubt who the Protagonist is this time,
the chorus is still so integral a part of the structure that artistically it
shapes the whole drama.

Aeschylus then chooses one brother, and invents a situation –
a particularly fine one – in which all the interest is concentrated
upon him. But this is only the beginning. The plot has to be made
to move, and the poet has to decide how destiny is to overtake its
victim. If by pure fluke – then the ancient nonsense[1] about Fate in
Greek Tragedy would all be true and there would be no tragedy;
if by his deliberately seeking out Polyneices in the open field, we
might have an edifying display of wickedness, but again no tragedy,
only melodrama. Dramatically it will be best if we can be shown the
destined fratricide passing from an apparent improbability to a
dreadful probability; morally, if we can see that, Eteocles being
what he is, no other outcome was possible; that the inherited doom
is but the projection of inherited situation and inherited character.
If the plot of the *Septem* merits comparison with that of the *Tyrannus,*
it will be because Aeschylus has succeeded in giving it this shape by
simple and natural means, and by the use of the conventions proper
to Old Tragedy. He has done this, with the minimum of means
and the maximum of effect.

The opening scene is splendid in setting, poetry, and characterization. Eteocles' strength is measured against the sombre background, the imminent peril in which the city stands, and we are
made to feel at once that he is assuredly a man worthy to meet the
crisis. Calmly and prudently he makes his dispositions; he is completely in command. But suddenly (v. 70), when we hear his

---

[1] And not all of it ancient. Willems (*Melpomène,* pp. 43, 91, 93) can speak of Aeschylus' characters as 'jouets', 'assujettis aux caprices des dieux'.

invocation of 'a father's avenging curse', we realize that the threatened city is no more than a background for the working-out of Eteocles' own doom. Certainly the public danger shows us what desperate men the brothers are, or Polyneices at least, but unless we are to see them only in the light of public dangers suppressed, the working-out of the doom must rise in the dramatic scale above even the threat to Thebes. Aeschylus is a confident dramatist.

In this scene there is no suggestion that the brothers are to meet that day in personal combat.[1] Eteocles is King, and as King he makes his dispositions for the city's defence, which, as the Messenger tells him, involves posting at the seven gates 'the chosen champions, the bravest of the city'. Polyneices too is the leader of an army. His name is carefully kept back, and we are not encouraged to think that the two leaders will engage. We do know what the outcome must be; but to Eteocles, and to us if we analyse the actual situation, the possibility seems remote that this day will see the fulfilment of the curse.

But the chorus alters things. In striking contrast to the manly dignity of the opening scene there comes pouring in pell-mell[2] a chorus of young women, frightened to death by the enemy without, appealing wildly to the Gods within. Against this turbulent background Eteocles stands firm. Again we are given the measure of the man – but there is more than this in the incident. So dangerous an element are the women in the besieged city that to reassure them Eteocles says that he will himself stand at one of the gates. The alteration in the natural and foreshadowed plan is made almost casually, a mere by-product, apparently, of the turbulence of the women. The chorus, we think, has already justified its existence by providing so admirable a background; now we see something more than simple decoration in it. The improbability that the brothers will meet has become sensibly less, and that through no fault in Eteocles.[3] He has no reason to suppose that Polyneices too

[1] My debt to Verrall here will be obvious. I have never seen an answer to Bayfield's question (*C.R.*, 1904, pp. 160 f.), what can be the point of vv. 653 ff. if Eteocles has suspected that Polyneices would himself be one of the Argive Seven?

[2] And with the excited dochmiac rhythm, not the marching-anapaest which was usual. Aeschylus forgot for the moment how statuesque Greek Tragedy is.

[3] Kranz (*Stasimon*, p. 172) points out that this Chorus gradually loses character, becoming plain representatives of the city and calling Eteocles τέκνον (686). This is what we should expect: the Chorus is vividly characterized *only while it is to affect the action*: date is irrelevant.

will fight in person; he acts out of sheer prudence – but we know, and his unconsciousness is terrible.

Having at last coerced the chorus into decent order, Eteocles goes about his business, leaving the chorus to sing its vivid ode on the terrors that fall upon a city captured – terrors which Polyneices is prepared to inflict on his own city.

Now comes the long and crucial scene. The Spy tells the King what he has discovered. Seven champions have been chosen from the Argive host to assail the gates. Each, at each gate, is described – his character, his appearance, and the device and motto on his shield. Against each Eteocles appoints the appropriate defence, and the chorus each time sings a short stanza. If we are content to accept anything from Aeschylus provided that it is good poetry and good morality, waiting for our dramatic thrills until tragedy shall have grown up, we may find the scene long, formal and dull. Formal it is, as Pelasgus' colloquy with the chorus was formal, and for the same reason, that the chorus is still a controlling element in the play, not a background for the actors; for the reason too that this formality is the perfect accompaniment to the volcanic fire that smoulders underneath the surface. This elaborate parade of heraldry, this antiphony of vices and virtues, are an ironical and ceremonial procession, leading Eteocles to his death.

There are seven gates, and we can guess, though Eteocles has no suspicion, that Polyneices is to take the seventh. Eteocles therefore has six chances of safety – but the whole point of the scene is that Aeschylus does not leave it to chance. He makes Eteocles not merely a prudent commander but also a man of acute moral perceptions, and ruins him this way. Against each attacker, who is prefigured equally in his physique, his device, his motto, his language, he appoints not merely an adequate fighter, but the man best fitted by his moral character to meet that particular assailant. Each time it is impossible for Eteocles to say, 'I am the man to withstand this form of wickedness.' He does not meet his natural opponent until he comes to the seventh gate.

At the first Tydeus blasphemously rages. 'Whom,' asks the Spy, 'do you oppose to him?' It is not, I think, without design that Aeschylus makes the answer begin Κόσμον μὲν ἀνδρὸς οὔτινος τρέσαιμ' ἐγώ: 'No man's array could daunt me.' It sounds as if Eteocles is going to take the first gate. For ten verses we are kept in suspense; then we hear the pronoun again: 'I, against Tydeus, will set the good son of Astacus' – and we see that it was impossible. Five chances remain, and Eteocles does not know that Polyneices is fighting.

Capaneus is worse than Tydeus. 'Who will await without flinching this man and his boasts?' Eteocles continues his unconscious minuet with Death; again it is inevitable that he should think of another than himself. Four chances.

The third gate; Eteoclus. Surely the King will accept an omen? Eteocles against Eteoclus? No; Megareus, 'by a happy chance,' has been sent already – a fine stroke. At the fourth gate stands Hippomedon, another Capaneus; and the opponent marked by nature for him is Hyperbius. This time the King does accept an omen; Zeus on the one shield will overcome once more Typhoeus on the other. Next, the romantic figure of Parthenopaeus, whose match in character and therefore in battle too must be an ἀνὴρ ἄκομπος, a man who boasts not. The choice, to Eteocles, is once more obvious; Actor is sent, and one chance of safety is left.

But alas! At the sixth gate stands the nobly tragic figure of Amphiaraus, 'the seer, most virtuous of men and bravest in the fight,' doomed himself not to return home and, by standing at this gate, doomed to cause the fulfilment of another's curse, the curse of Oedipus upon his sons; for now more than ever it is impossible for Eteocles to think of himself. We all knew, of course, that Amphiaraus belonged to the story. He was bound to come in, and as a tragic figure, but we did not know it would be like this. It is a searing flash of tragic irony, hardly to be paralleled in Aeschylus, not approached elsewhere. This last chance, seeing that the opponent was Amphiaraus, never existed; it remains only for Eteocles to hear who is his own opponent, to hear of the insensate rage which animates Polyneices and challenges his own.

Of the power with which this scene is brought to a close there is no need to speak. We are given, in a sudden revelation, the other side of Eteocles, his hatred of his brother, his inability and his unwillingness to control his mad and fatalistic leap upon his doom.[1]

[1] I can see no sign here, or anywhere else in the play, that Eteocles is devoting himself to death in order to save Thebes and Pohlenz' theory of Greek Tragedy. It is a dramatic idea that he should do this, but not, I think, Aeschylus'. This aspect of the curse, that any offspring of Laius would destroy Thebes, is kept very much in the background; obviously Aeschylus cannot allow us to feel that if Eteocles is
(continued)

This is the consummation of the rigid control which has been exercised so long.

Throughout this scene the chorus is active, singing and dancing a stanza after each pair of speeches, and keeping to the one theme, the danger that hangs over Thebes. It is because the chorus is interwoven with the dialogue in this way that the speeches have so antiphonic a ring; brisk dialogue between these formal lyric utterances would be impossible. The whole is architectural in conception, a perfect balance: the plastic chorus trembling for the city, the hero, who can see so clearly and be so blind, advancing slowly upon his fate, the almost automatic Spy supplying the facts. The second actor, being only an instrument, cannot diminish the stature of the hero; the only personal force allowed to enter, beside the hero's, is that of the chorus, and this, being the communal emotion of fear, does not compete with the hero's personality, but sets it in a frame which isolates it and makes it the more impressive.

In the ode that follows the interest widens somewhat; we are approaching the end of the trilogy. Forgetting for the moment their own peril the chorus thinks only of the ruin of the royal house. The image of the Chalybian Stranger appears, a characteristic piece of Aeschylean imagery, this time entirely at the service of its inventor; a strained note wonderfully expressive of strained minds. The ode rolls on in sombre magnificence, touching only for a moment the common peril, and comes to rest on the Curse, as the Messenger comes in with his news of victory sounding strangely remote.

The actors have now had their say; we are in a region where only the chorus can live. Middle Tragedy would have ended this story with a soberly eloquent messenger-speech describing the end of the two brothers, and a brief lament from the chorus. Rightly so, for such descriptions of the actual event are the logical conclusion of its more realistic treatment. Old Tragedy omits the details, for these do not belong to its more lyrical tone. Passing judgement is a foolish pastime; it is enough to say that this end also is logical and beautiful.[1] This last scene, too, is a warning that we should not be

---

sensible enough to listen to the chorus Thebes is lost. Accordingly it is not mentioned until *after* the fatal choice is made (vv. 745 ff.). Méautis also (*Eschyle*, 105 ff.) makes an interesting Eteocles, but one who depends too much on the γε of v. 71 and on inferences which are possible but not necessary.

[1] The scene between the Herald and Antigone which appears in our text is spurious.

too ready to explain the last scene of the *Persae* by citing the absence
of the music and dance. They are missing here too, but the nobility
of the funeral hymn is none the less apparent. It is a long hymn, for
it has to bear the weight of the whole trilogy, and it is carefully
worked, illuminated by an imaginative symbolism which sounds
nearly non-Greek – the Pontic Stranger. We met him in the previous ode (v. 727). The Messenger corroborates, as it were, with his
Σκύθη σιδήρῳ (817); and through the simple σὺν σιδάρῳ of v. 883
and the double σιδαρόπλακτοι of vv. 912–13, we come to the full
personification, in vv. 941 ff.

πικρὸς λυτὴρ νεικέων
ὁ Πόντιος ξεῖνος ἐκ πυρὸς συθεὶς
θηκτὸς σίδαρος.[1]

The imagery is felt so vividly that the Stranger becomes almost a
supernatural actor whom only the chorus can see. This ode is no
stop-gap, no mere libretto, but a dramatic lyric composition
thought out and felt as intensely as anything in the play, bringing
the trilogy to a close on the verge of a new dimension.

We can now see the answer to some of the questions that the
second actor raised. He does not in any way encroach upon the
loneliness of the hero; Eteocles is as solitary as Pelasgus. The second
actor was not intended to be a foil or complement to the first;
simply to supply him with the facts to which he has somehow to
accommodate himself. There is no interplay between the two. The
Spy brings certain forces to bear upon Eteocles and Eteocles absorbs
them all; we do not look back to see what effect he in his turn has
on the Spy, as we look back when any two Sophoclean characters
come into contact. Nor is the function of the chorus very different.
The chorus has indeed personality, but this is used only as one single
'moment' in the situation. Once its panic has caused Eteocles to
take his first fatal step, its personal influence is exhausted and it
becomes pure Chorus. There is no real interplay of personality, and
we are as far as ever from the Sophoclean cross-scene.

What the second actor does is to make the situation grow.
Instead of the static situation of the *Supplices* which grows only
in intensity, we have one that moves, thanks to the fresh information

---

[1] 'Cruel resolver of strife, the Pontic stranger that leaps out of fire, the whetted
sword.'

that the Spy can bring in.[1] This has the important consequence
that the hero has to be characterized. It did not matter much what
sort of man Pelasgus was; it matters vitally what Eteocles is. If
he is not the man that he is – the bold but prudent commander, a
man of profound moral insight but combining this with the fatal
recklessness that carries him over the brink – then nothing happens.
The *Septem* is our earliest tragedy of character, Eetocles the first
Man of the European stage.

We see Eteocles in the round, not as an outline like Pelasgus nor
as a flat character like Xerxes; but we must beware of treating
Aeschylus' characterization as a matter of chronology. Aeschylus
does not, in these essentials, 'improve,' nor is Sophocles' characterization an 'improvement' on his. It is different because the tragic
idea is different. Agamemnon is conspicuously less in the round than
Eteocles because his tragedy is differently conceived; and why are
we told that Oedipus grows angry with his subordinates, Creon a
bully to his, while Eteocles has simply no attitude at all to his
Spy? Not because Aeschylus is still learning the art of dramatic
characterization and is as yet unconscious that these are good
dramatic effects. He refrains from dramatizing Eteocles' bearing
towards the Spy just as he refuses to tell us how he behaves to his
wife, or whether he has one: because it has no significance to
Eteocles' tragedy. The impatience of Oedipus, the harshness of
Creon, are significant; that is why the traits are there. The Greeks
left it to the modern masters of characterization to exhaust the
possibilities of the insignificant.

That is to say, the characterization is as highly conventionalized
as the style, the diction, and the plot – for it is highly conventional
that the attack and defence of Thebes should be morally idealized
like this. The use of convention must be thorough, or disharmony
will follow. The stiff structure of the play, the disregard of naturalism, the restricted use of characterization, are not the quaint
archaisms of a drama which has not yet grown up, but conventions
deliberately sought to keep at bay the intrusion of a naturalism that
would destroy the illusion.

---

[1] It is one mark of the superiority of the *Septem* over the *Persae* that in so far as
Eteocles is affected by anything personal, it is by the chorus. The chorus affects him
by being something, the other actor only by saying something. The personality of
the chorus, being communal and kept in the orchestra, will obscure that of the hero
less than a personality beside him on the stage.

The severe lines of the play are, however, relieved in one notable respect. The plot offers no turns, twists and palpitations, but is simply one terrific crescendo; yet a striking relief is obtained by the manipulation of the chorus. To this are allotted two main themes, the danger to the city and the danger to Eteocles. At first the former predominates; when Eteocles has quelled the chorus into submission and begins to reject his chances one by one, it is still – naturally – the common danger that fills the mind of the chorus. Eteocles draws visibly nearer to disaster, but still Aeschylus keeps back with his chorus, 'timing' his stroke, until at the last moment, when Eteocles rushes out, the danger to the city is forgotten and the chorus throws all its weight into the theme of the fall of Laius' house. Thus we watch the dramatic movement through two mediums, in the action and in the minds of the chorus; and the chorus, being woven into the very fabric of the drama in this way, plays a more important part than it does in the *Persae*, even though it has had to give up to the actor the privilege of opening the play. The technical history of Greek Tragedy is largely an account of the efforts to make the Chorus an integral part of a continually changing system. Several times the balance was lost and found. It is achieved here, and the tremendous power of the play is the result. It is perfectly shaped, the theme is exactly realized in the form, the plot is sheer genius, and the characterization and poetry are as fine as anything Aeschylus ever did. 'Nothing but well and fair.'

4. The 'Prometheus Vinctus'

The *Prometheus,* whatever its date,[1] belongs to the type of drama that we are calling Old Tragedy. Although in the prologue it uses

---

[1] As to the date, the judicious remarks in Sikes and Willson's edition (Introd., pp. 35 ff.) still seem to me to give what can profitably be said, that it lies between the *Septem* (467) and the *Oresteia* (458); though the almost apocalyptic theme might incline one to put it nearer the *Oresteia* than the *Septem*. Professor G. Thomson (in the introduction to his edition) argues for a date later than the *Oresteia,* and I would not deny the possibility, but his analysis of the doctrine of πάθος μάθος is, to me, unconvincing, and in any case too uncertain a thing to be made a basis for precise chronology; and his stylostatistics at most only prove that the play is a late one. And let us not forget that what stylostatistics prove is not date but style – until it is further proved that the poet's style did change chronologically. Euripides' did, but not Sophocles' – not at least without very large reservations – and I should hesitate to make so simple an assumption of so bold a dramatist as Aeschylus. (On Aeschylus' style Pohlenz puts a pertinent question to those unhappy men who believe that Aeschylus did not write this play: Why *should* Prometheus talk like Cassandra?)

three actors,[1] and that to some purpose, for the rest of the play the whole interest is centred on the hero and his fate, everything being subordinated to him as rigidly as in the *Septem*. We look always from the minor persons to the hero, never back again, except perhaps to a very slight degree with Oceanus; certainly we have no juxtaposition of characters in the least like that of Agamemnon with Clytemnestra.[2] Indeed, as if to assert in their extremest form the rights of the older drama, Aeschylus gives us a hero who literally cannot move, and a plot that can be regarded as a reaction from that of the *Septem*. The new and busy drama that was coming into fashion is put firmly in its place. In the prologue Prometheus is enchained by Hephaestus, under the direction of the personified abstractions Might and Force, and from this point to the arrival of Hermes the situation remains unchanged. The chorus of Oceanids comes to sympathize, and Oceanus to urge submission; Io passes by in her flight and provokes fresh indignation against the common persecutor; but, in the crude sense, nothing 'happens' until Hermes orders Prometheus to reveal his secret and Prometheus is thrust down to Tartarus for his disobedience. In the real sense we have two related dramatic movements during these scenes. The cruelty of Zeus and Prometheus' determination to resist to the end are more and more clearly revealed; and a powerful dramatic movement is drawn from the gradual disclosure of the secret which is Prometheus' weapon against Zeus.

Aeschylus was committed here to the task of turning a long series of events into drama almost without the help of action. He has to outline the relations between Zeus and Prometheus from the beginning – how Prometheus deserted the Titans and helped Zeus to victory because the Titans were too unintelligent, Zeus not, to make use of his stratagems (297 ff.); how he saved the human race from Zeus (231 ff.); how, doing this from sheer pity of man, he went further and taught man all the arts of life. The rage of Zeus, the punishment of Prometheus, his continued defiance and his long-distant hope complete this part of the story, and form the

---

[1] On the idea that in the prologue Prometheus was represented by a lay-figure and that therefore there were only two actors, Croiset is good: 'Il n'est pas donné à tout le monde de croire à ce mannequin' (*Hist. Litt. Gr.*, III, 188, note).

[2] It is this that makes me reluctant to accept Professor Thomson's date, for the *Prometheus* seems definitely to close an epoch; but I am far from supposing that such epochs do not overlap.

only part which can be represented on the stage. Aeschylus in fact dramatizes the emotions and not the events.

In this, there is not much obviously dramatic material. The enchainment, clearly, will make a scene, but a state of continued defiance is not the most apparent source of dramatic action. There were certain other difficulties. The dealings of omnipotent gods one with another are not easily made dramatic; what really happens when the irresistible meets the immovable? Homer, undoubtedly, made his gods not very godlike partly because this was the only way of using them as dramatic agents; Aeschylus takes over the primitive conceptions, some of them, that underlay his myth, in particular the shadowy conception of a Necessity stronger even than the gods. In this we need see no more than a dramatic convenience. Aeschylus is not propounding a theological idea, but making a contest between the two gods possible; for if nothing is superior to Zeus, Prometheus can have no hold on him. Other difficulties are simply ignored, as for example how it was that Prometheus was able to save the human race in defiance of Zeus. The two are treated vaguely as co-ordinate powers, Zeus certainly the stronger, but not omnipotent.[1]

The powers of Zeus being in this way limited, his adversary's continued defiance becomes dramatically significant; but it cannot be drama except in the spirit of lyrical drama, whose essence is not movement and action but dramatic emotion and intensification. The real dramatic movement here is one which takes place in the mind of the immovable Prometheus, and Aeschylus' presentation of this is one of the greatest achievements of the Greek stage.

Aeschylus begins this apotheosis of Old Tragedy by boldly grafting on to it Sophocles' invention of the Third Actor. On Aeschylus' use of this we shall have more to say when we come to the *Agamemnon*. It has been said that he used three actors together only on the condition that all three should not speak at once, but such timidity is not in the least like Aeschylus. He rarely wanted three actors to be speaking together because his tragic conceptions did not run in this direction. Here at least the case is perfectly clear. The third actor enabled Aeschylus to represent the crucifixion scene in progress without sacrificing the great dramatic effect of Prometheus' disdainful silence; his mind is fixed on Zeus, and he will not

[1] Méautis (*Eschyle*, pp. 78) discusses this point very sensibly, and Bogner (*Philologus* 1932, 470) points out that in spite of Homer the gods are not 'fixed'; Zeus could be made subject to Μοῖρα.

condescend to speak to his minions. But if Prometheus will not speak, someone else must, and a monologue from the crucifier would be less interesting and valuable than the dialogue that can now be arranged. Aeschylus might indeed have produced his chorus at once, but this would have used up too quickly the dramatic movement available, and would have sacrificed another dramatic effect, the utter solitude of the spot. The third actor solves all these difficulties. Cratos (with Bia as a supernumerary) directs Hephaestus, and Prometheus remains silent. One, two, or three persecutors – it is all the same to him. Further, now that two agents are present, it is more dramatic and interesting if they are characterized differently, and this obvious point is turned to a good use: Cratos is quite inhuman, Hephaestus reluctant, and sympathetic towards his fellow-god. Moreover the contrast, interesting in itself, gives us a powerful sense of Prometheus' stature that he so superbly ignores it, and it contains a strong criticism of Zeus. Hephaestus is a 'hostile witness' in that he belongs to the side whose privileges Prometheus has infringed; fire in particular, 'thy flower' as Cratos reminds him, he has stolen and given to man. Yet Hephaestus shows the greatest repugnance to his task. He admits that Prometheus has acted wrongly ($\pi\acute{\epsilon}\rho\alpha$ $\delta\acute{\iota}\kappa\eta s$), but the punishment is of a savagery which only the newness of Zeus' sovereignty can explain. However, neither the accusation nor the sympathy draws a single word from Prometheus.

When they are gone Prometheus, we may suppose, remains silent for some time. The prologue is over and the play begins, a play of one static situation whose whole movement is an inner one, beginning with the almost interstellar silence of this remote spot[1] and ending with the thunder of splitting mountains. It is built on a series of impacts – the chorus, Oceanus, Io, Hermes, upon Prometheus – but impacts that produce light and heat rather than movement. Prometheus is shown in a series of carefully arranged relations; first alone, then with the chorus of Oceanids, then with Oceanus, then with Io. The choice of these and the order of their appearance is not arbitrary, but it is by no means inevitable; we cannot say that they come $\kappa\alpha\tau\grave{\alpha}$ $\tau\grave{o}$ $\epsilon\mathit{i}\kappa\grave{o}s$ $\mathring{\eta}$ $\tau\grave{o}$ $\mathring{\alpha}\nu\alpha\gamma\kappa\alpha\hat{\imath}o\nu$, by Aristotle's law of inevitable or probable sequence. It would be possible and just as natural for Io to appear before Oceanus – but this does not involve Aristotle's censure of plays in which scenes could be transposed

---

[1] The loneliness and silence are both mentioned by Hephaestus in his first speech.

without making any difference. Aristotle's rule is not valid here.
There is a law, but it is one of increasing tension, not of 'natural'
or logical sequence. To transpose Oceanus and Io would outrage
no logic – except the logic which makes Prelude precede Fugue and
Scherzo follow Andante. Oceanus and Io are not there to assist in
the presentation of a logical series of events, for as we have seen
Aeschylus is dramatizing a state and not events; they come simply to
develop the inner drama, Prometheus' defiance of Zeus.

After the crucifixion Prometheus is seen alone, uttering his
indignation to earth and sky.[1] The purpose of the scene is fairly
clear. It still postpones the entrance of the chorus, which is an effect
not to be used up too soon, and it brings home to us that silence
and remoteness of which Hephaestus spoke, a powerful dramatic
effect (and an essential part of the punishment) which is not to be
frittered away. The benefactor of mankind has no one to whom he
can turn but inanimate nature. But in this short passage there is
more than dramatic economy and pathos: the solitude gives a wider
amplitude to the rhythm of the piece. As Sophocles shows us Electra
alone before he subjects her to the dramatic forces which make his
play, working as it were from the lowest possible pitch to the highest,
so Aeschylus prolongs this solitude as much as he can: it is the best
possible contrast to the terrific catastrophe in which the play is to end.

The next step is to introduce the chorus, a band of half-imagined
sea-maidens; a splendid contrast to Prometheus, the rock chained
to a rock. These gentle interlocutors allow Prometheus, in Aeschylus' good time, to relate his services both to Zeus and to mankind;
but besides this obvious purpose they have another: by their
sympathy to draw from Prometheus more and more of his indignation with Zeus, to lead up to his first allusion to the secret (189 ff.),[2]
and to reinforce the picture already suggested of the cruelty of the
new tyrant. The character of this chorus is determined largely by

[1] Schmidt-Stählin (I, 2, p. 73, note 5) state, as part of the argument that the *P.V.*
is spurious, that Aeschylus does not know the monody: 'Aischylos kennt diese Form
nicht.' What this means, I cannot imagine. If it means that we know for a fact that he
never wrote one, it is not true and is a *petitio principii*. If the implication is that in a
dramatic situation like this Aeschylus would not have had the wit or the courage
(if courage was wanted) to use a monody, it is worthless. If it means that Aeschylus
would never have allowed himself to get into such a situation, it overrates Aeschylus'
dramatic caution. The monody does not appear in Sophocles until the comparatively
late *Electra* not because Sophocles did not 'know it' until then, but because until
then he had no use for it. The reasons for the monody in the *Electra* are perfectly plain
if one looks for them, and are very similar to the reasons for the monody here.

[2] Hephaestus has given the first hint (v. 27); 'Thy deliverer is not yet born.'

the needs of the dramatic rhythm. The climax in the disclosure of
Zeus' cruel ways and in the resistance to him is being reserved for
Io; the chorus therefore must be comparatively gentle.

As for the series of speeches which Prometheus makes to the
chorus, we must observe what they are; in the actual performance
the point would be clear enough. Aeschylus is not simply explaining
the situation for us, how it has arisen. What Prometheus has done
for Zeus, what he has done for Man, are not only things which
have led to the present situation; they *are* the present situation, part
of Prometheus' present mind – for the essential drama is precisely
his present mind. Milton does the same for Samson (the *Agonistes*
is pure Old Tragedy) in those opening speeches in which Samson
compares what he is with what he was; speeches which make one
wonder how any critic has ever had the audacity to call Milton
'undramatic'.[1]

In order to bring a new force to bear on Prometheus and to
deepen our sense of his hostility to Zeus – and incidentally to break
this sequence of speeches – Aeschylus introduces Oceanus; a
friendly, politically-minded person who can give advice and offer
mediation as the chorus cannot. Prometheus' reply is to urge him
not to concern himself in what may bring him to ruin; Zeus is
implacable and invincible. The punishment of Atlas is described,
and the might and punishment of Typhoeus, with an elaboration
which might superficially seem undramatic, inasmuch as it keeps
Oceanus waiting. But in this timeless play, which is not concerned
with a series of events, waiting does not matter; the description is
dramatic, not decorative, because it springs directly (even the description of Etna) from the dramatic theme of the play, Prometheus'
thoughts about Zeus. The sole purpose of the Oceanus-scene is to
give us the measure of Zeus' power and of Prometheus' defiance of it.

When Oceanus has been firmly dismissed the chorus develops
the theme by singing explicitly of Zeus' tyranny, and, ranging
over the whole world, it represents all nations as mourning Prometheus' fate. This wide gathering of peoples goes with the geographical speeches delivered to Io; it goes, too, in feeling, with the
account that follows it of Prometheus' services to Man. Here, too,

---

[1] Whether in the *Agonistes* or in *Paradise Lost*. Where *Paradise Lost* is undramatic it
is so because Milton, unlike Aeschylus, could not set any limit to the power of his
God.

Milton is Aeschylean. When Michael and Adam 'Both ascend In the visions of God', and from the summit of Paradise survey the extent of the world and the future course of Man,[1] Milton is (at first) very close in spirit to Aeschylus as he surveys the extent of the world and the past course of Man – even if, later, we may begin to feel that in Aeschylus it was the hero, in *Paradise Lost* the poet, who was in chains.

The silence which Prometheus maintains at the end of the ode and the despair into which he falls at the end of his next speech are powerful moments in the dramatic rhythm of the whole. Here, in the middle of the play, as he contemplates what he has done for man, he is at his lowest ebb – a contrast with his determined rejection of Oceanus' offers of help, a greater contrast with what is to follow Io's appearance.[2] The scene ends with Prometheus' second allusion to the secret; Zeus, too, is subject to Necessity – but what Necessity has in store for him it needs a more powerful personality than that of the chorus to wring from Prometheus.

When the chorus has suggested to Prometheus that he has honoured Man, the helpless weakling, too much and Zeus too little, this more powerful personality appears. Io, rushing frantically to and fro pursued by her imaginary gad-fly, is the complete contrast to the chained Prometheus, but is equally a victim of Zeus and his 'private law';[3] she is almost an impersonation of the God's simple-minded cruelty. Her part is still further to stimulate our indignation with Zeus, and to provoke Prometheus to disclose the secret of Zeus' final overthrow – so bringing on the catastrophe. Io's account of her fearful persecution, though it has little to do with Prometheus, is an essential part of the rhythm of the play; and the geography, like the details of Etna, lends its weight to our sense of what the victims of Zeus have to suffer, and so carried us on towards the climax.

[1] *P.L.,* XI, 370 ff.

[2] Again a similarity can be seen between this play and the *Electra*. (See below, p. 172f.) And the two speeches here, the first dealing with the most primitive of the arts which Prometheus has taught man, the second with the higher arts of civilization, must surely have been in Sophocles' mind when he was constructing the second ode of the *Antigone*.

[3] Ἰδίᾳ γνώμᾳ (543) recalls ἰδίοις νόμοις κρατύνων (403). Both adversaries are acting 'privately'; a clear suggestion that some more universal system is to be established at the end. – Méautis (*Eschyle,* p. 82) makes the point that Io, suffering at the hands of Zeus, is a sort of parallel to Prometheus, so that her eventual release is warrant for his – as indeed it is her descendant who will release him.

That is to say, the feeling of the whole scene is essentially lyrical. In spite of the geographical details, the conception and movement of the whole is nearer the drama of music than the drama of the intellect and of prose. Indeed, in presenting it through actors and not a chorus, Aeschylus puts himself into difficulties. To avoid repeating the story of Prometheus' wrongs he has to ride off on the Aeschylean Τοσοῦτον ἀρκῶ σοι σαφηνίσας μόνον (621). The past history of Io (which cannot be spared) is brought in not unnaturally – supposing the Oceanids to be Hellenic – by the simple curiosity of the chorus, and the sequence of speeches is once more carefully broken, this time by dialogue about the secret (757 ff.); but when Prometheus restricts Io to a choice between two speeches and then delivers one to her and the other as a gift to the chorus, we cannot but feel that the material is putting the form to a severe strain (780–5), especially as a few verses later Prometheus contradicts his own unexplained reluctance to talk by giving us an 'extra' for which no one has asked (823 ff.). These rather uncomfortable artifices are not signs of primitiveness or lack of skill. Aeschylus could make plays well enough, if that was all that was wanted, but he was more than a playwright. His material here, whose dramatic quality is imaginative rather than directly intellectual, would perhaps have gone gratefully into a big ode like the opening odes of the *Supplices* or *Agamemnon,* but the dramatic situation did not allow this, Prometheus not being a chorus; so that a certain artificiality is inevitable. Aeschylus, however, like Plato, would go whithersoever the argument led, and a mere dramatic inconvenience never deterred him (or Euripides or even Sophocles, for that matter) from making tragedy where he saw a tragic idea.

A smaller problem that arose during this play was that of bringing in and sending off actors who are wanted not to do anything but to be something. Shakespeare, on one incomparable occasion (*The Winter's Tale,* III, 3), gets rid of a character by the simple stage-direction *Exit Antigonus, pursued by a bear*: Aeschylus finds a solution ready to hand and extremely dramatic in the gadfly. The second victim of Zeus resumes her dreadful flight in circumstances which bring our indignation to its highest pitch.

Is not the succeeding ode a little disappointing? It is dramatic, in the sense that it is apposite to the situation; the chorus prays that it may never inspire a god with love but find love in its own station of life – a perfectly natural reflection on the fate of Io; but it is dramatic in the later manner, accompanying the action, not controlling or transfiguring it. This chorus, as we saw, is necessarily a weaker figure than Io, and as lyrical force it has been superseded by her and cannot build a higher climax upon her exit.

The sufferings of Io, past and to come, have carried the dramatic rhythm to a height that only the catastrophe can crown. The secret, given more and more definition at each stage of the drama, is now blazed forth by Prometheus to an incredulous and terrified chorus. Now it moves even Zeus. He sends his 'lackey' Hermes to extort the secret with the direst threats. Prometheus refuses, and, still enchained, is thrust down to Tartarus amid deafening convulsions of the firmament – the fulfilment of the unearthly stillness with which the play began. Yet even this majestic climax is, like the enormous church of Beauvais, only a promise; we are only one-third of the way through the trilogy.

Such is Aeschylus' way of dealing with this part of his myth. The solitary hero is everything; and not what he does, but what he feels and is. Of action, between the prologue and the catastrophe, there is none. Prometheus' narratives, though they may give the illusion of action, were not designed for this. It is a drama of revelation, not action; of increasing tension in a situation which does not move. In spite of the second and third actor, in spite of the freedom and limpidity of style that distinguished this play from the rest of Aeschylus, the *Prometheus* is the last triumphant affirmation, in an extreme form, of the rights of the oldest tragedy.[1]

[1] I have discussed the interpretation of the trilogy in *J.H.S.*, 1934, pp. 14 ff. In brief, my suggestion was, and is, that Aeschylus presented a contest between Zeus (= Power, Order) and Prometheus (= Intelligence). Both have to concede something, and assimilate something, before they are reconciled in the later perfect cosmic order of Zeus. Such an evolutionary theme explains the prominence given to the evolution of civilization in our play, and it accords very well with the evolutionary theme which becomes prominent in the *Oresteia* (See below, pp. 70, 94).

I should like to take this opportunity of thanking Professor L. A. Post, who has, I think, strengthened my original argument by citing a passage I had overlooked, Plato, *Ep.*, II, 310e–11b (*A.J.P.*, LVII, 206–7). Plato, speaking of his relation to Dionysius, remarks that wisdom and great power naturally attract each other; and after citing stock examples from history and poetry (Solon–Croesus, Teiresias–Creon), he adds, 'In my opinion Prometheus and Zeus, too, were joined in this sort of relation by the ancients.' The passage is interesting, and it is a flattering suggestion that one may perhaps be right with Plato.

The myth in the *Protagoras* (320c ff.) is also worth considering in this connexion. Practical wisdom, τὴν περὶ τὸν βίον σοφίαν, Man had from Prometheus: τὴν δὲ πολιτικὴν οὐκ εἶχεν. ἦν γὰρ παρὰ τῷ Διί. Zeus, in Plato's version of the myth, was the source of social morality and order.

CHAPTER III

The 'Oresteia'

1. The 'Agamemnon'

To the modern reader the *Oresteia* is not easy of access. Its great
amplitude, the dramatic power of many of its scenes, the bold
character-drawing, the splendour of the poetry – these and other
such qualities declare themselves at once, but time after time
Aeschylus fails to do things that we expect, or does things that we
do not expect, so that for the moment we lose imaginative touch
with him. He will quite clearly say or imply things that are so
strange, so startling, that instinctively we resist them and try to
explain them away. The result can be that although we feel the
grandeur of the whole, it remains a remote grandeur, remote both
in style and thought; we think it archaic, and make allowances.
What we should allow for is not so much Aeschylus' archaism but
our own modernity; we so easily assume that the methods and aims
of our own epoch are immutable parts of drama itself.[1]

For example, the most recent editor of the *Agamemnon*, Professor
Page, writes like this about the Herald-scene: 'The tension is
heightened by his futile cheerfulness; we wish he would go away,
that we might know the worst at once'; and like this about the
Aegisthus-scene: 'The play is nearly over, but first we must watch,
with whatever emotions, the antics of Aegisthus.' Obviously, when
the Herald arrives we expect two things: that he should 'advance
the plot', and that he should be an interesting character. In both
respects he disappoints us. Obviously, when near the end of the
play Aegisthus is added to the superb Clytemnestra, he ought to
make a climax, but he turns out to be not much more than a vulgar
poltroon, and even so spends much of his time narrating ancient
history. Therefore we find the scene an anticlimax; we blame

[1] See below, pp. 97–103.

Aeschylus, instead of questioning our basic assumptions. More than one commentator has found it necessary to be indulgent to Aeschylus for his stiff and undramatic handling of the chorus at the moment when Agamemnon is being murdered; also for the strange way in which Cassandra is kept silent for so long, especially when Clytemnestra and the chorus-leader are trying to talk with her, and Aeschylus introduces the bizarre idea that perhaps the lady does not understand Greek. Pinero would have done none of these things, nor even Sophocles. We invent canons for Greek tragedy, or take refuge in the idea that Aeschylus had not yet mastered his job. But such criticisms prove only one thing, that those who make them have not fully understood what is going on. We expect one thing; Aeschylus gives us another. He needs no indulgence. He could write for the theatre as intelligently as any dramatist and more powerfully than most. All we have to do is to understand what *he* thought his plays were about; then everything becomes clear – including the fact which we should never forget, that in his own time he was not a highbrow dramatist but an immensely popular one.

It would be salutary if any man who undertook to comment on the *Oresteia* should first disengage from the plays the material that Aeschylus uses in them, and then, using all this material, should draft the scenario for a Shakespearian play or plays covering the same ground. In the *Agamemnon* alone the material includes the story of the House of Atreus, Iphigeneia, the Trojan War, the story of Cassandra, and the double murder. The exercise recommended above would make it clear that Aeschylus has not ordered his material in the obvious way; it might also cast doubt on Wilamowitz' notion (which seems to be in some slight danger of revival) that the Greek playwrights had no dramatic ambitions beyond the very simple one of putting Saga on the stage. Aeschylus leaves until nearly the end of his play those events which come earliest in time: Thyestes committed adultery with his brother's wife (1193 f.), Atreus avenged himself on Thyestes, and finally Thyestes' son on Atreus' son – by adultery and murder. All this is narrated by Aegisthus in the last scene of the play, in a kind of second prologue, as one might hastily call it. The trilogy is sometimes given the sub-title *The Curse in the House of Atreus*. Perhaps there is no need to quarrel with that, but we may at least observe that the first play is two-thirds finished before ever the Curse is mentioned, and that the trilogy does not end with the lifting of the Curse but with a reconciliation between the Erinyes and the Olympian deities, brought about by Athena, and not in Argos but in Athens, with the prosperity of Attica as the important issue. Perhaps, therefore, the sub-title falls short of indicating what Aeschylus thought his trilogy to be about.

He chose the later story for his beginning, the story that begins with Paris' abduction of Helen. Now, the indications are – though some scholars will disagree – that Aeschylus had what we may call a *mind*; also that he gave some thought to the composition of his trilogy. If these assumptions are acceptable we shall suspect that he saw reason in constructing the play on these lines; that although Paris and Helen had nothing to do with the Curse, nevertheless, there is a really organic link between the two stories. When we see Agamemnon lying dead and Clytemnestra standing in triumph over him, as a direct result of what he had done at Aulis, and when to this spectacle there is added Aegisthus, who claims the vengeance as his own, we shall expect that, if Aeschylus was really an artist and not a poor artisan, this debouchment of two separate stories into one common catastrophe will make immediate sense. And not only that, for we are looking not at one body but at two; we are justified in expecting that the tragedy of Cassandra has an organic and not only a history-book relation with that of Agamemnon. If all this does not combine into a unified and intelligible idea, then let us by all means praise Aeschylus for other things, but refuse to follow those who call him a great dramatist. Those who deserve that title build well, and with meaning.

'I pray the gods to rid me of this toil . . . lying on this roof, like a dog watching the nightly company of the stars, wet with dew, waiting season after season – waiting for a signal that Troy is captured. . . .'

It is a strong beginning. The man on whom is laid the solemn duty of opening the *Oresteia* is no more than a common soldier, but Aeschylus makes him live; he is no mere instrument, like the Spy in the *Septem*. He is the first of the minor characters who comes to life. Yet we must be careful, lest we think that Aeschylus created him for the fun of the thing, enriching his play with a decorative detail drawn from life. Why did he invent this man, of whom we never hear again? At once, he sounds the note of apprehension: all is not well within the palace. To his joy he sees the beacon-light. His trouble is over; the King will soon return – but all is not well. This effect Aeschylus is going to repeat in the Herald scene: the King is coming – but all is not well. But the Watchman does more than this. Aeschylus, being a poet, and a dramatist, will convey some of his thought through his imagery. This prayer for ἀπαλλαγή πόνων, release from toils, repeated by more important characters in the trilogy, becomes the prayer of suffering humanity, waiting for its own release; the light that the Watchman sees blazing out of the darkness culminates, after several other false lights, in the torch-lit procession that escorts the Eumenides to their new home in Athens, and really does put within man's grasp, if he will take it, 'release from misery'.

The increased stature, in this play, of the minor characters does not diminish that of the chorus. Half the play is in lyrics; the first ode, over two hundred verses long, takes twenty minutes in performance. It is articulated clearly in four sections, made distinct, for us, by the metres, for the original audience by the dance-figures and music as well.[1] An ode composed on this scale is no mere prelude to action, no mere decoration; in fact, it lays down, as firmly as can be, the intellectual foundations of the whole trilogy. It deserves attention.

It begins with sixty verses in anapaests, the regular march-rhythm. Nearly ten years have passed since the two sons of Atreus set out for Troy, ministers of retribution (Dike), to punish the crime of Paris. They were sent by Zeus. As some god, Apollo or Zeus, or Pan, hears the cry of a vulture robbed of its young and sends an Erinys to avenge it, so has Zeus sent the two kings to avenge the wrong Paris did to Menelaus – to avenge it in war, with strife for Greeks and Trojans alike. But the second part of the composition brings a check, the omen of the two eagles feasting on the body of a pregnant hare. The violence has aroused the indignation of Artemis; the seer is afraid that she, in her anger against her Father's winged eagles, may demand such a sacrifice as will create, at home, an abiding wrath, a μῆνις, against the commander of the army.

Here we may take stock, since this is drama on a scale not native to us. The war was conceived by Zeus; yet another deity will not

[1] See below, pp. 114 ff.

allow it to go forward except on terms that will bring retribution
on him who wages the war. Artemis is not concerned with anything
that Agamemnon has done already, but with what he is going to
do. In order to emphasize this, Aeschylus (who was no more
subservient to his sources than Shakespeare was) alters the accepted
myth. This was that Agamemnon had angered Artemis by shooting
one of her stags and boasting of it. Since this was of no use to
Aeschylus he abolishes the stag, substitutes the eagles, and makes the
cause of Artemis' anger (so far as we see at the moment) not
Agamemnon but Zeus and his feasting eagles. (Of what is going to
follow in this chapter, experts in the history of Greek religion have
told me that it is quite impossible that Aeschylus could have meant
such things; the only reply I can think of is that he certainly *said*
them.)

Artemis' terms are that Agamemnon shall do such a thing as
will involve him in wrath, $\mu\hat{\eta}\nu\iota\varsigma$, and retribution. Is she more
enlightened than Zeus? Not in the least; she is nothing like Prome-
theus. Aeschylus does not mention her again; she is nowhere brought
to heel by Zeus. On the contrary, we are told explicitly that everything here has been brought about by Zeus, the cause of all things
(1481–9), including therefore what Artemis contrived for Agamemnon. Later in the trilogy we meet something like civil war
among the gods, but not in this play, nor does it concern Artemis.
Nor in fact is she more 'enlightened' than Zeus, or than the Apollo
whom we hear of later in the play: they are all unforgiving des-
troyers.

Why does Artemis demand the sacrifice? What moves her
indignation is the wanton destruction of life committed by the
eagles; not that they eat a hare, for eagles must eat, but that they
eat the unborn young, too. The point of the comparison is the
indiscriminate destruction of life that this war must bring. It was
not only an inevitable but also a declared part of the plan of Zeus:
he will bring about, 'in the cause of an unchaste woman, many a
combat, as the knee is planted in the dust and the lance is shivered,
for Greeks and Trojans alike' (60–67). As for the Trojans, we shall
hear in the third ode that they made themselves accomplices with
Paris and suffered the inevitable penalty, but the Greeks at least were
innocent. About them, Aeschylus later (437–74) writes two of his
most moving stanzas: brave men are killed in this war 'for another

man's wife' – war which the Elders themselves had thought indefensible (799–804) – and the public anger in Argos against the King is so bitter that the chorus fears his assassination. This would be a natural result of the war, even though it was conceived by Zeus; and if rage concerning the dead is visited in this way on Agamemnon, it will be the counterpart, on the level of ordinary reality, of the indignation felt by Artemis towards the eagles. Deeds of this kind have their consequences; 'the gods are not regardless of those that shed blood' (462) – 'the gods', not Artemis alone.

Her price is Iphigeneia. Here also Aeschylus is combining legends in a most imaginative and purposeful way. Except that Agamemnon, not for the last time, is blind to realities, nothing could more effectively deter him from the war: if he must shed so much innocent blood 'for an unchaste women', let him first shed his own daughter's innocent blood – and take the consequences. In effect, Artemis is doing to him what Clytemnestra does to him later, when she tempts him to tread on the tapestries and so make his guilt manifest. Iphigeneia stands as symbol of the reckless destruction of life which later makes the chorus tremble for Agamemnon; she also brings it about that the assassin is not some enraged citizen of Argos, but Clytemnestra. In killing Agamemnon she is, consciously, avenging her private wrongs, but, since 'the gods are not regardless of those that shed blood', she is also satisfying Artemis' anger and avenging the dead slain before Troy. In fact, the sacrifice of Iphigeneia is the strongest of the links that bind the story of Troy to the story of Atreus.

At first sight it may seem incredible that Aeschylus should have presented the gods as behaving like this, but there is no escape from it. Zeus conceived the war to avenge Menelaus and sent the Atreidae to fight it; Artemis, hating the slaughter, ensures that this, too, shall be avenged: the gods do not overlook bloodshed, and to be a sacker of cities is dangerous. Agamemnon has not exceeded his commission (for the overthrow of the altars in Troy is a separate issue; this was committed by, and visited upon, the army); he is destroyed, by Zeus, or by 'the gods', or through Artemis (for this is immaterial), for doing what Zeus ordained in the way that Zeus foresaw. This is what Aeschylus says, as plainly as a dramatist can. It all makes good and important sense, if we are willing to concede that Aeschylus knew how to make and control a play.

We come to the third section. Zeus, 'whoever He is,' shall be invoked as the Ultimate. He is the triumphant god who overthrew the god who had overthrown *his* predecessor; the victor who established the law: Learn through suffering; the god whose favours come through violence. ('Lead, kindly Light,' was not a Greek idea.) We notice two things. There was a time when Zeus was not the supreme god, but made himself such by sheer force. This we shall remember with profit when we reach the end of the *Eumenides*. We notice also that Zeus is not called the god of Wisdom and Justice, rather the god of learning through experience, hard experience; at least, what Aeschylus says about him is that he brought a new law, Learn by suffering. How was this new? We cannot imagine that under his predecessors men learned without suffering; Aeschylus did not believe in a past Golden Age. The only interpretation is that under the earlier gods man suffered but did not learn; nothing came of hard experience. This is what the poet commemorates here; under the reign of Zeus, learning, progress, becomes possible.

So far the action has been presented only on the divine level. Now at last we see something of Agamemnon, and have to ask ourselves the usual question: what is the dramatist's idea of the relationship between what the gods do and what the human agents do? In this, naturally, Aeschylus does not differ fundamentally from Sophocles and Euripides: the human agents are absolutely autonomous; when the same action is attributed to both gods and men, the effect is to make us contemplate it as an individual action which has the nature of a universal. Both the inception and the conclusion of the war are ascribed to Zeus and to Agamemnon; Agamemnon, correctly, speaks of Zeus, when he offers him thanks for the victory, as $\mu\epsilon\tau\alpha\acute{\iota}\tau\iota\sigma$, quite literally, 'partner', even though divine partner.[1] Zeus 'sent' Agamemnon, 'like an Erinys,' to fight the war; when victory comes it is Zeus who cast around Troy the net from which none could escape (355–67). But elsewhere the war is treated as a purely political event; we have seen how the chorus tells Agamemnon that they regarded it as a hideous mistake (vv. 799–804). The Herald, naturally, ascribes the glory both to Zeus and to Agamemnon. Such duplication is not only standard Greek practice; it is also familiar in our own religious observances. If a clever man,

[1] On this often misunderstood passage see Fraenkel's note, *Agamemnon*, 811.

after a Harvest Festival service, should say, 'But you can't have it both ways: who *is*, in your idea, responsible for the harvest, God Almighty, or Farmer Jones?' we should feel inclined to tell him that he was out of his mental depth. Agamemnon is autonomous. When first we see him, through the eyes of the chorus, he does not seem to realize that he is being 'sent' by Zeus, but regards the war as his own idea, and certainly, when he is caught in his dilemma it does not occur to him to appeal to the god who is 'sending' him, nor does Zeus help him. Page rightly demands an explanation of the ἀνάγκη, the inevitability, to which Agamemnon has to bow (v. 218), and he complains, rightly, that commentators have not given one. His own is not persuasive; it is that all the human agents in the plays are helplessly driven by irrational, supernatural Powers – plain Demons, like Temptation, Hope, Infatuation; the human agents are not to be blamed, for they cannot help themselves. These various Demons exercise their power for no purpose; they do it because they will. That this makes nonsense of the drama, Page admits; from Aeschylus he expects nothing but confusion, great poetry and powerful drama[1] – a strange combination indeed. However, Aeschylus does appear to blame Paris for giving way to Peitho or Temptation: at least, he says that Paris had 'kicked over the altar of Dike' (v. 381–4); and he does persuade us that Clytemnestra, for one, acted from positive and definite reasons of her own – taking offence, for example, at Agamemnon's murder of her daughter, and not much relishing the idea of having in her house her husband's mistress. Perhaps therefore there may be more probability in an explanation of the ἀνάγκη which does not reduce the trilogy to intellectual confusion; the confusion is too dearly bought.

Agamemnon has taken it for granted that a war for a wanton woman is a proper thing: it is his conception of Dike. It is also Zeus' conception, and Zeus is going to follow it by destroying the destroyer. The 'necessity' is the necessity of shedding innocent blood in such a war, which Artemis anticipates by requiring him first, as a condition, to shed some innocent blood of his own family, as a foretaste, and to take the consequences. He can avoid shedding Iphigeneia's blood, and a lot more innocent blood, only by giving up the war and his revenge on Paris. This, as he explains, is impossible;

[1] *Agamemnon*, ed. Denniston and Page, *Introduction*, p. xv.

D

therefore he must, of necessity, shed the blood.[1] He must take
the consequences of his own policy. The obvious implication is that
we have here a conception of Dike that cannot work, even though
it is the present will of Zeus. If this is not already plain, the rest of
the play will make it so: the instinct for violent and bloody retribution dominates and unifies the whole play, and in the end it leads
to complete breakdown; we are to see how it is morally, philosophically, and politically bankrupt.

The Queen speaks. About her the Watchman has given us a hint;
the ode makes us see in her the destined avenger: on the one level,
the avenger of Iphigeneia, on the other, of the hare and of all those
killed before Troy. In this scene Aeschylus is concerned not so
much to draw her character as to suggest her stature: the beacon-
speech lifts what was no more than a competent piece of organiza-
tion to the level of something elemental. The first word is 'Hepha-
estos': the fire-god himself has brought her the news, and when
she has finished, the chorus marvels. Again she speaks: she gives a
vivid picture of the tumult and slaughter within the conquered city
– and we remember the omen, and the anger of Artemis. Then she
utters a warning: let them remember to spare the holy places, for
they still need a safe homecoming.

Another long ode follows. Its prelude corresponds closely to that
of the first ode; the prime mover in it is Zeus. He has cast over the
city such a net that neither young nor old could escape; it is total
destruction. The ode proper begins with Paris. He, corrupted by
wealth, was assailed by temptation, and fell; he trod underfoot
the beauty of holy things, and the gods do not overlook such. As
bad bronze, hammered, shows its impurities, so did Paris, hammered
by Temptation, show his. Helen's light-hearted sin bequeathed war
to Greece; it caused mourning in Menelaus' house; mourning, too,
in every house in Greece. It caused anger too, when the ashes began
to return home in the place of the living men who had set forth:
anger against the Kings who championed retribution, for another
man's wife; and such anger is like a public curse. The gods do not
overlook bloodshed; the Erinyes lie in wait; the chorus fears some
dark deed of vengeance. From whom? The context allows only one
answer: from some of those who have been so angrily muttering

---

[1] Page's assertion that in any case the other Greek commanders would have killed
Iphigeneia is not an assertion that Aeschylus makes.

against the Kings. 'May I never be a sacker of cities!' The ode sets us a proportion sum: The crime of Paris : the punishment of Paris :: the crime of Agamemnon : ? .

To the six weighty stanzas Aeschylus adds an Epode, performed apparently either by three sections of the chorus or (more probably) by the three section-leaders. Here again Page raises a pertinent question and, as I think, gives the wrong answer.[1] The question is: Why at this point does the Chorus unexpectedly doubt what hitherto has been taken for granted, namely that Troy has veritably fallen? Why do they now suggest that Clytemnestra is little better than a fool? Page's answer is, in effect, that Aeschylus had little idea how to construct a choral ode; he brings this one down in ruins. Not, perhaps, very likely. We shall see in a moment that Aeschylus had good dramatic reason for causing *somebody* to say this sort of thing about the Queen. It is, of course, inconsistent with what the chorus has just been singing Yet three individuals detached from the chorus are a very different dramatic *persona* from the united body; it does not, therefore, seem an inevitable conclusion that Aeschylus, here, completely baffled his audience.

The Herald is no doubt more of a character than was the Spy in the *Septem*, but Aeschylus was not greatly concerned with that. In one respect he is like the Messenger in the *Antigone*: a person who comes into the play expressing conventional ideas which to us, who have been in the play from the beginning, are fraught with irony. The Herald, like the Watchman, is profoundly glad to be rid of it all. They all suffered; many are dead. But Victory has come! – Victory being another of the false lights that illuminate the whole trilogy. 'Give glory to the conqueror! He has utterly cast down Troy with the crowbar of Zeus who brings retribution, and with it he has devastated the land. The altars and temples of the gods are no more; the seed of the whole country is destroyed.[2] remember what Clytemnestra said: 'Let them remember! They still need a safe return.'

The Queen speaks again – not replying directly to the Herald; for in this kind of drama, in which we are to see the human agents

---

[1] See his note *ad loc.* (See also p. 170, below.)

[2] The verse about the altars and temples is removed from the text by many editors, chiefly because it appears, in almost exactly the same form, in the *Persae* (811). If it is an interpolation, the interpolator was a genius. I have given my own reasons for resisting the deletion elsewhere (*Form and Meaning in Drama*, pp. 15 ff.).

in direct relationship with the gods, their personal relationship with each other is of small importance. First she triumphs contemptuously over the chorus: 'They called me a fool! They said my news was not true!' At once, we can see how the detail serves, again, to increase her stature; we see also why Aeschylus made the chorus question the truth of the news; presently we shall see something more. Then turning to the Herald, she sends a false message of welcome to her husband.

Now the Herald has another long speech, and it is a frightening one, if we know how to read the scene. Those two ancient enemies Fire and Water have conspired to blast the Greek fleet on the way home; only one ship is known to have reached land – Agamemnon's, saved by some divine hand that held the tiller. Some god has brought Agamemnon safe home – to Clytemnestra.

This is not intimate drama; it is architectural in scale. Now we can restate our sum: The sin of Paris : the destruction of Paris :: the sacrilege of the Greek host : the destruction of the Greek host :: the sin of Agamemnon :   ? .

The third ode carries a stage further this screwing-up of tension. The Trojans, by welcoming Helen, made themselves partners in Paris' crime. As a lion-cub, a delightful plaything when young, must grow up and fulfil its nature, making the farmyard run with blood, so did Helen's coming first cause happy bridal hymns, and then cries of mourning and lamentation. 'It is not prosperity that angers the gods but wickedness. Hybris provokes more Hybris, and then the day of reckoning comes at last. Dike leads everything to the end appointed.' *Enter* Agamemnon, *royally, with a young woman*. Was ever a dramatic entry more finely prepared?

It is commonly said that the chorus, in its address to the King, is trying to warn him against the Queen. I cannot see that a single word points to the Queen. They know of her adultery, of course; that she has designs on his life they cannot believe, even when Cassandra tells them (see in particular 1251 f.). On the other hand we know well enough what it is that they do fear: it is that the public indignation in Argos may vent itself in some dark deed. They speak of the difference between the sincere and the insincere friend – a warning to which the King responds with characteristic complacency – and indicate their own sincerity by telling him bluntly what they had thought about his war. It is disaffected citizens that they have in mind, not Clytemnestra.

The scene goes on, loaded with irony. Agamemnon cannot see the falsity of his wife's welcome, nor can he resist her when, in startling fashion, she brings a metaphor to life. Paris 'trod on the beauty of holy things'; Clytemnestra spreads rich tapestries at his feet and tempts him, in his turn, to tread on the beauty of holy things. He knows, in a general way, what he is being asked to do – and he does it: he risks the φθόνος, the 'indignation', of the gods.

About the woman in the chariot there is not a word – not because Aeschylus could not use the third actor, but because he could. We know Clytemnestra; we know that Agamemnon, by bringing Cassandra, has driven the last nail into his coffin. What need for talk? Only one thing is said about her – by Agamemnon, to Clytemnestra: 'Take the foreign lady in, and treat her kindly.' To realities he is blind, as he was when he began his war, and when he killed his daughter.

The chorus, in its fourth ode, is tortured by an anxiety that it can scarcely understand. 'The King is safe home, yet I cannot rejoice. I hear the chant of the Erinyes. Blood spilt on the ground calls for more blood. Except that one thing must balance another, I could be at ease.' About the woman in the chariot, sitting aloof, not a word.

Now comes a short scene which is extremely puzzling – until one sees its meaning. At last someone does take direct notice of Cassandra: Clytemnestra comes out from the palace to tell her, in grimly ironic terms, to come in and take part in the sacrifice. This time Clytemnestra does not triumph; neither she nor the chorus-leader can establish any contact with her. The dramatic technique here is superb; it has often been dismissed as mere ineptitude. Cassandra takes no notice of anything said to her; the others are baffled, and the desperate suggestion that she, not knowing Greek, may need an interpreter, is the measure of their bewilderment. Soon it will be the chorus that needs an interpreter (v. 1254). Clytemnestra is totally defeated. The fact is obvious, but why does Aeschylus contrive it? The reason begins to appear when at last Cassandra does speak, or rather scream – not against Agamemnon, or the Greeks, or even the folly of her brother Paris, but, most unexpectedly, against Apollo, 'my destroyer'. Throughout the

long scene that follows she insists that she is Apollo's victim, and
she gives the reason quite explicitly: Apollo wanted her, and bribed
her; she, having accepted the god's gift of prophecy, then recoiled,
denied the god, and is now being destroyed by his 'rage', κότος
(1211). It is Apollo who has brought her here, to this bloodstained
haunt of the Erinyes, this house of so many crimes, past and future.
Agamemnon whose folly has brought her here, the vindictive
Clytemnestra who will kill her like an animal at the butcher's block,
are nothing but the god's unconscious agents. It was to prepare us
for this that Aeschylus for so long kept her aloof, as if in a world
of her own; and when at last she does go into the palace, it is not
before she has torn off her prophet's insignia, in a kind of trance,
and made us feel that it is none other than the god himself who, in
his anger, is driving her in to die.

We hear Agamemnon's death-cries. What Aeschylus does here
with the chorus has often been pitifully misunderstood. The shock
splits the solid chorus into twelve dismayed individuals; but what
they debate is not, as is often said, whether they should break in
and try to rescue the King. Some of them think that the cries mean
nothing; others, that the King is already dead, and what they are
confronted with is what they had feared in their second ode – a
political assassination, a *coup d'état*. The man who proposes (1349)
that they should raise the citizens against the murderers is not
shuffling off responsibility; he is talking plain common sense. What
none of them expect, in spite of Cassandra's warning, is what they
immediately see: Clytemnestra standing over the two bodies,
glorying in her deed and justifying it – and, like Agamemnon at
Aulis, not suggesting in the least that she herself is not entirely
responsible for what Cassandra has described as the work of a god,
and which Clytemnestra later calls the work of the Daemon of the
family.

Only now do we hear of the Curse, the *daemon*, in the House of
Atreus – though we shall hear more about it when Aegisthus enters.
Two things become clear: the nature of the daemon, and its
connexion with what was our chief preoccupation in the first half
of the play, namely, the sin of Paris and the war of revenge. The
successive crimes within the palace, and the war, all are instances of
violent, instinctive bloody vengeance for injury received. As the
scene continues, with Clytemnestra more and more taking on the

aspect of a doomed criminal (though the agent of Apollo), the successful hunter who will herself be hunted, we are reminded more and more insistently of the laws that govern this aspect of human action. There is the law of Dike – not 'justice' but 'requital' – that wrongs done must have their revenge, 'the doer must pay.' Clytemnestra pathetically hopes, like Agamemnon before her, that the law may not operate in her case: 'May it be well' (1568 ff.; cf. 217, 846–54), but we know that the hope is vain; for there is also the law of Hybris, that one outrage begets another, until the day of reckoning comes. The power of the scene comes partly from this, that the superb and triumphant Queen, by her own act, has placed herself in the same position as the King over whose body she is exulting.

From the wrong point of view, what follows is an anticlimax. Aegisthus is mean, cowardly, unredeemed by any touch of greatness – which no one would say of Clytemnestra. His long speech could be written down as only a second exposition, a necessary but not exciting rehearsal of past history. His assumption, with Clytemnestra, of royal power, and the futile resistance of the chorus, might be thought to fall flat, coming after so splendid a scene as what has gone before.

But Aeschylus thought it was a climax, and Aeschylus was right. This is no drama to be interpreted solely in terms of individual character and action. Through the visions of Cassandra, Aeschylus has already brought into one focus Atreus' revenge on Thyestes, Clytemnestra's on Agamemnon, Apollo's, and Clytemnestra's, on Cassandra, the revenge of the 'cowardly wolf' (1224), and the crime still to come. All are committed in this palace, all the work of the Erinyes whom Cassandra sees haunting the palace – as was Agamemnon's war too, for Zeus had sent him 'as an Erinys'; and Zeus is the cause of all things (1485 ff.). Other images reinforce this chain of similar acts. The repulsive Aegisthus is made to enter greeting the 'day that brings retribution'; when last we heard the adjective, δικηφόρος (525), it was used of 'the crowbar of Zeus' whereby Agamemnon had overthrown Troy. Again, with satisfaction Aegisthus sees his enemy lying dead 'in a robe woven by the Erinys'; it is 'the net of Death', the δίκτυον Ἀιδου, (1115), which Cassandra had seen Clytemnestra throwing over Agamemnon. Another metaphor has come to life: the net which Zeus, by the hand of Agamemnon, had cast around Troy (355–61). The climax is partly this, that so repulsive a deed, performed by so repulsive a creature as Aegisthus, is nevertheless the same in kind as the other acts of vengeance, performed whether by gods or men; partly in the fact that the whole series now issues in chaos – for that is the significance of the theme of Tyranny, begun here, and continued in *The Choephori*. Aeschylus, like Shakespeare, uses the overthrow of a legitimate king by a usurper as a symbol of political, social and moral chaos. The chorus had feared that public resentment against the blood shed caused by Agamemnon might result in 'some dark deed done by night'; the bloodshed has indeed been avenged – not, however, by angry citizens, avenging the blood spilt at Troy, but by a wife avenging the blood spilt at Aulis before ever Agamemnon could sail for Troy, that which was to brand Agamemnon as a man of blood and to ensure his punishment; also by her accomplice, an adulterer and a usurper, avenging an earlier crime in the house. So is Argos delivered into the hands of a tyrant who holds his power not $\Delta\iota\acute{o}\theta\epsilon\nu$, 'by grace of God,' like Agamemnon (43) but lawlessly; and the rightful heir and successor is in exile.

2. The 'Choephori'

The *Oresteia* is a trilogy, but from no point of view is the division between the second and third plays either so wide or so deep as that between the first and second. As soon as the *Choephori* begins we are made to feel that we are in a new world, though it is still one which is far from being comfortable. The imaginary period of time that separates us from the *Agamemnon* is indeed only some ten years, but from the very first line we are aware that something new has come upon the scene, something that was conspicuously absent from the *Agamemnon*. Orestes enters, with his friend Pylades; he prays to Hermes in his capacity of intermediary between the living and the dead. The beginning of his speech, unluckily, is in fragments, but enough is left to show that Orestes is laying on his father's tomb gifts which, being an exile, he could not offer at the proper time, and that he is praying to Hermes to protect and help him.

On Orestes falls the task of avenging the outrage done to his father. Here is nothing new; it was foreseen by Cassandra. The law of Dike is eternal; the question is, how its demands are to be met. So far they have been met in the spirit of blind and guilty retribution; Orestes approaches the task very differently. For the first time we meet an avenger whose motives are pure.

Soon he sees approaching a solemn procession led by Electra. The two men make room. From the chorus of Asian captive-women we learn that after many years an unsleeping Wrath has spoken; its voice rang out in the night, and caused terror. Later in the play (527–39) we learn what Clytemnestra's dream was: she was suckling a snake which she had brought to birth, and it bit her breast. In her terror she has sent Electra to make at last offerings at the tomb, hoping so to conciliate the anger of the dead. But nothing can atone for blood spilt on the ground.

So much we learn from the chorus. It is the same dramatic imagery that was used later by Sophocles in his *Electra*: at the moment when the avenger comes back from exile, Clytemnestra has a dream that clearly foreshadows the vengeance. In each case the purpose is the same: to show that the vengeance is no mere personal exploit or crime. Of course it is the bold act of Orestes, but it is also one in which the unseen powers of the universe are involved.

'But with what form of prayer,' asks Electra, am I to make the offering? Am I to say to the dead, as the custom is, "Make fair return for what we give"? 'Pray,' says the chorus, 'that he help his friends, and that upon those who caused his death some *daemon* or some man may come.' 'As judge (δικαστής) or as avenger (δικη-φόρος)? – 'Say simply: one who shall take blood for blood.' – 'And is this a lawful prayer? – 'Lawful indeed, to requite one's foes with harm.'

To requite one's foes with harm was normal Greek ethics, and there is no reason to suppose that Aeschylus questioned it. The interesting thing in the passage is the distinction that Electra makes. The word δικηφόρος ,'retribution-bringing,' we heard twice in the *Agamemnon*, and it gives no comfort here. It is the word used by the Herald of the crowbar of Zeus that overthrew Troy, and by Aegisthus of the day which brought his revenge. But the word δικαστής, in common parlance 'juryman', shows a glimmer of something less crude, though we have to wait long before the glimmer becomes daylight.

Now Electra prays – to Hermes, the powers below, to Earth, to Agamemnon – that they will pity her, and help Orestes. She says that she is treated like a slave; the murderess has married the murderer; the wicked pair have robbed Orestes of his wealth and are wasting what Agamemnon had won. And she adds another prayer – this, too, being unlike anything that was said or thought by anyone in the first play:

αὐτῇ τέ μοι δὸς σωφρονεστέρα πολὺ
μητρὸς γενέσθαι, χεῖρά τ' εὐσεβεστέραν

'And to myself grant that I may be more chaste than my mother, and more reverent in action.'

All the essentials of the new tragic situation are now present: the first half of the play does but give them definition and emphasis. Electra, like Orestes, is bound by her duty to the dead. As things stand, it is inescapable that the dead man shall be avenged by his children, even through matricide: there is no one else to do it. But it is a vengeance which they, unlike any of the avengers in the *Agamemnon*, seek to inflict with clean hands and a pure heart; yet how can Orestes' hands not be soiled with his mother's blood? These new avengers, free of any guilty motives, must yet do what is worse than anything done in the *Agamemnon*; herein lies the tragic power of the play.

Electra's long prayer is followed by an impressive rite: she pours on the tomb the belated libation which Clytemnestra sent, and the chorus accompanies the action with a hymn invoking Agamemnon's aid against his enemies.

There follows a scene which is not easy to understand – the recognition scene, which Euripides parodied in his *Electra*. Electra sees a lock of hair placed on the tomb as an offering; she finds it so like her own that she concludes that it must be from her brother, whether put there by him, or by someone else as a memorial to him. Then she sees footprints, and finds that they exactly match her own. Now, it is easy enough to make fun of a tragic passage by repeating it in a realistic context, and that is what Euripides does, making it the more amusing by speaking not of footprints but of boot-marks. New Tragedy became very clever at such things as recognition-scenes, not having any more serious preoccupations; but there are two things to notice before we dismiss Aeschylus as a fumbler. One is that the passage is not a recognition scene: that follows immediately, when Orestes steps out of his hiding-place and declares himself. So far as the mere plot is concerned, there is no reason why Aeschylus should not have made him do this as soon as Electra and the chorus have ended their prayers. It seems to follow that he had some other purpose in interposing this passage. A second point lies in what Orestes says later (225–8): 'When you see me in person you are slow to recognize me, though when you saw the lock of my hair and the outlines of my feet your thoughts had wings, and you fancied you were seeing me.' This contrast between Electra's present sensible caution and her previous excitement should warn us that if we take the previous passage in the most pedestrian spirit of which we are capable, we may be missing the point.

Crudely speaking, the passage is unnecessary; no subsequent action is based on the assumption that the supposed resemblances are valid, and Electra herself conceives that the hair may not be Orestes' at all, but of some enemy (198). As the passage, so to speak, stands free, not helping to support the plot, it follows that Aeschylus wrote it for some other reason. We should reflect that the scene was written for the theatre, and that the actor would have received instructions or hints, where necessary, from Aeschylus. We have one hint ourselves: in her final line, Electra speaks of her 'anguish and tumult of mind' (211). There is the possibility, therefore, that Aeschylus intended it to work up to a highly emotional climax – and that would make a difference. (One has heard musicians say of a passage that it looks awkward on paper but succeeds beautifully in performance.) Our question should be, not 'Why was Aeschylus such a simpleton as to suppose that a brother's and a sister's foot-prints would match? but 'Is it likely that this scene, which looks so awkward on paper, may after all have been well calculated for performance?'

It does not help the plot; it does, however, give us what nothing else in the play does: a picture of Electra's inner emotions. The long lyrical passage that is coming, the Commos, is a Lament and an Invocation; religious in conception, not personal. Only here do we see Electra as the waiting sister, torn between hope and despair, isolated among Agamemnon's enemies and the citizens whom they

have cowed, utterly dependent on her brother's coming. That is
to say, the undertone of the scene is lyrical; Euripides would have
written it as a monody. Performed in plain argumentative style
the scene could hardly come off; how far a more intense, quasi-
lyrical performance might justify the illogicalities, each reader
must try to assess for himself. Certainly we shall not understand
either its intention or effect if we take it to be only a primitive
Recognition-scene.

Brother and sister are reunited, at last. What grief Electra has been
enduring, what joy she feels now, we infer, if we must, from the
passage that we have been considering. Orestes, to her, is father,
mother, brother, and sister – 'the sister so pitilessly sacrificed': that
is all. It is the only reference in the play to Iphigeneia; it is remarkable that it is made not by one of Agamemnon's enemies but by
Electra. It suits Aeschylus purpose in the second and third plays to
present Agamemnon in different colours: his blindness and folly, the
bloodshed, the violence of his conquest, are forgotten; he is always
the glorious king, foully slain. The reason for this may appear later.

Nor is Orestes allowed to express private joy. Instead, he prays to
Zeus, and he repeats, from the beginning of the *Agamemnon*, the
image of the eagle: he and Electra are the young of a slain eagle,
driven from their nest, robbed of their sustenance. We remember
how some god heard the cry of the birds robbed of their young
and sent an Erinys to avenge them; we remember, too, what
happened to the avenger, thanks to the wrath of Artemis. This is
not the only passage in the *Choephori* where the repetition of
imagery makes us wonder uneasily if events, too, must be repeated.
Electra (394 f.) prays that Zeus may strike down the guilty; we
recall how Zeus struck down Paris – and then Agamemnon, who
had done the striking. The chorus (386 ff.) prays that they may be
able to sing the ὀλολυγμός, the cry of triumph, over a man and a
woman slain; we remember the ὀλολυγμός sung by Clytemnestra
(*Agam.* 587 and 1236), and the ugly hymn sung by the Erinyes over
Agamemnon's body (*Agam.* 1473). There are repeated prayers for
victory (148, 487, 868); we remember certain previous acclamations
of victory (*Agam.* 854, 1673), and how transitory that victory
proved. The *Choephori* derives much of its tragic power from this,
that in it we see the new avengers, very different in spirit from the
old, but menaced by the same threats.

And yet with a difference, for Orestes is acting under the direct command, indeed the dire threats, of Apollo (269 ff.).

Hitherto, divine and human agency have been coincident but independent; this is the first time that a god issues a direct command to a man. Yet the difference is not radical; only a matter of dramatic presentation. The gods are beginning to move from the background to the forefront of the drama, but the human agent still has his own reasons for acting as he does; Orestes is no puppet. He says (297 ff.) that he must follow the god's command, but even without it he must still avenge: he is compelled by his grief for his father, by his own poverty, by the thought that his own people are in shameful subjection to cowardly tyrants. The double motivation here is important, and is what we should expect. If Orestes were acting against his own judgement, in terror, then we might begin thinking of divine compulsions that are arbitrary and beyond reason; as it is, we see clearly that Apollo's compulsion is simply another, a more universal, expression of the compulsion which the situation of itself lays upon Orestes. The decisions is not only Apollo's; it is also his own.

The Commos follows (306–478), part hymn, part invocation, performed around the tomb by the chorus, Electra and Orestes in concert. It is of the first importance to realize that there is nothing psychological here; it is not character-drawing, it is not the means by which Orestes' determination is brought to the sticking-point. Orestes is already fully resolved. It is true that he will have his moment of awful misgiving when he actually confronts his mother, but the horror of the act does not come into play until that moment. The *commos* does not advance the plot in any way; it contains nothing new except the statement that Clytemnestra had mutilated Agamemnon's body; but this is not put forward as an additional incentive for Orestes; it only intensifies what we know already, that Agamemnon's enemies have been treating him with every form of dishonour.

We see, around the tomb, the 'united company' (458) of Agamemnon's friends, paying to him at last the proper tribute of a funeral hymn. They are demonstrating their loyalty to him, seeking to make their voices heard by him, imploring his aid against his enemies and theirs, exciting his anger against his murderers and their own oppressors by telling him of their own shameful position

and of the danger that the line of Atreus may cease to exist. With
this there is a gathering-together and an emphatic restatement of the
old themes. A blow must requite a blow; the doer must suffer;
blood calls for blood. They appeal to Zeus that he will slay the
slayers. Only the kinsmen, by strife and blood, can set the family
free. 'Ares (Violence) will confront Ares; Dike will confront Dike.'
But if Dike conflicts with Dike (as presently Olympians conflict
with Erinyes), the universe is chaotic, and Dike cannot yet be
'Justice'.

It is the same dark, hopeless picture that we had in the *Agamemnon*,
full of menace, all the more tragic that Orestes, faced with the
worst of all crimes, has motives which are so pure: 'She shall pay
for dishonouring my father, and when I have slain her, let me die'
(438). The only source of light in this darkness is Apollo's promise
to protect Orestes, and our faith that somehow, some time, the
reign of Zeus must become the reign of Order.

After this long lyrical preparation the action gathers speed.
Orestes hears of Clytemnestra's dream; accepting the omen he
declares that he will turn himself into the serpent that bit its mother.
Once more, imagery reinforces thought: Orestes already has
likened Clytemnestra to a serpent who killed an eagle (248 f.); he
must repeat what she has done.

He expounds his plan: as they slew δόλῳ, by guile, so by guile
shall Aegisthus be slain – for here he says nothing about Clytemnestra. But the ensuing ode sets her and her lawless passion and her
abominable crime vividly before us. 'Yet,' they say, 'the root of
Dike is firm; Doom forges the sword; the unforgetting Erinys
brings home again at last the offspring of old crimes to requite the
polution.'

'Boy, boy!' It is the offspring of the old crime knocking at the
door of the palace. We do not know which the slave will bring, the
master or the mistress. It is Clytemnestra who comes, and hears the
guileful story of Orestes' death. She speaks of the implacable Curse
on the house; it has now lighted on Orestes, 'though, in his prudence, he had taken himself far from the quicksands. Now is the one
hope of the house destroyed.' We should remember that the actor
playing the part is wearing a mask; still, the falsity of the language
is apparent; it is the Clytemnestra of old. From the Nurse, later, we
shall hear how 'she showed a sad face to the servants, and hid the

smile within her eyes at things which have fallen out well – for her.'

As for the Nurse, in our enjoyment of this vivid sketch we must be careful not to miss the point of the whole scene by supposing that Aeschylus wrote it only for the purpose of brightening up Drama. It has been read as comedy – a sad defacement of the play. We may observe that a lifelike character here was by no means inevitable. The audience would not have felt cheated had Clytemnestra sent a quite formal messenger to tell Aegisthus to come at once, on a private matter; and had he then come alone, no questions would have been asked. But Aeschylus arranges things differently. He makes the chorus do what Greek choruses are supposed never to do: to take a part in the action. The message given to the Nurse is that Aegisthus shall come with a bodyguard; the chorus persuades her to alter it. The superiority of this over a purely formal treatment of the incident is clear enough. It does indeed result in the interesting figure of the Nurse – and that is all we shall see, so long as we suppose that the dramatist's chief preoccupation is character-drawing. But there is much more. In the first place, the theme of Guile receives extra emphasis: as they have sown, so shall they reap (556 f.). When Orestes has entered the palace, and before the Nurse comes out of it, the chorus has invoked πειθὼ δολία, 'Guileful Persuasion';[1] and when Clytemnestra, later, understands what is happening, she too says (887 ff.) 'By guile do we perish, even as we slew.' So is the working of Dike made the more manifest. A second point that emerges is the moral isolation of the criminals: the common people hate them and willingly do what they can to frustrate them – the chorus, and the Nurse; and the slave who calls to Clytemnestra says, in an aside (883 f.), 'Her head seems near the block, and rightly will it fall.'

As for the supposed touch of comedy, if we have understood what the Nurse is saying, and why she says it, we shall not be tempted to smile when she talks of a baby's napkins. The mother of the man who is reported dead is 'hiding the laughter in her eyes'; it is the old slave-woman who is broken-hearted: what happened before, she says was grief past bearing, but this is worse, that her Orestes should be dead, the baby to whom she gave her whole life (748–53).

While we await Aegisthus the chorus sings an impressive ode in

[1] A demon?

which it prays to Zeus, Apollo, Hermes, all the gods worshipped within the palace: 'May the old crime bear no more offspring within the house!' Clytemnestra, in the *Agamemnon* (1567–77), had expressed the same hope; now she is at the point of death. How can this prayer be fulfilled? More than once, in this play, we have been assured that a blow calls for a blow, that blood demands blood. There are indeed grounds for hope, but serious grounds also for grave fear.

Until Orestes is actually face to face with Clytemnestra, sword in hand, Aeschylus has not encouraged our minds to dwell on the horror of matricide; the conflict has been a cosmic, not a psychological one. Now, at the supreme crisis, the conflict within Orestes' own soul does come to the front, and is dealt with in typical Aeschylean fashion. Half a dozen lines are enough – because Aeschylus is a good enough dramatist to exploit the conventions of his theatre and make them do most of the work. Pylades is that conventional figure of the Greek stage the supernumerary actor who never speaks; we have fully accepted him as such. Therefore when he does speak, it has the effect of a thunderclap. His grim three lines, reminding Orestes, and us, of Apollo's command, brush aside even so powerful a deterrent as the one now working on Orestes' mind. Technically, the device is antistrophic to the one used in the previous play with Cassandra: here the effect is achieved by giving speech to an actor whom we expect to be silent; there it is achieved by imposing silence on an actor whom we do expect to speak.

There follows the short colloquy between mother and son. He is able to rebut her pleas of justification, not however without making us feel uneasy on his behalf, in this universe in which Ares conflicts with Ares and Dike with Dike. She pleads that Destiny, Μοῖρα, not herself, caused Agamemnon's death; he replies the same Destiny is now causing hers. May it not then also cause the death of Orestes? He says 'You killed whom you should not; now suffer what you should not.' She threatens him with the pursuit of her Erinyes if he kills her; he can reply only that if he does not kill her, his father's Erinyes will pursue him. Nothing could more forcibly express the bankruptcy of the cosmic and social system of Justice which we have been contemplating hitherto.

The last scene, evidently, was designed to recall the scene in the *Agamemnon* in which the murderess appeared standing triumphantly over the two bodies. Clytemnestra had said: 'Here they lie, side by side, the lover and his mistress.' Orestes says: 'Here they lie, joint tyrants, joint assassins, joined in death.' Orestes causes to be displayed and held up to the all-seeing Sun the vile contrivance in which she had enmeshed Agamemnon; 'such a crafty thing as a footpad might use, to murder and then to rob.' This, too, we saw in the previous scene, the 'net woven by the Erinyes' that Aegisthus joyfully acclaimed, the visible counterpart of the net which had been thrown around Troy by Zeus. It has now become distinctly less impressive. The future may be dark and menacing, but at least we can look back and see what a great moral advance has already been accomplished. But the onset of the unseen Erinyes makes it clear that the advance has been made in vain so long as Dike can require acts like this.

3. The 'Eumenides'

There are scenes in the *Agamemnon* which are a little tedious until we understand what Aeschylus was thinking about. The *Eumenides* enables us to make the opposite mistake: from the beginning to the end it is so spectacular that there is danger of supposing that Aeschylus was only letting off theatrical fireworks, with occasional reference to past or present Athenian history. This is the play about which the story became current that the horrific appearance of the Chorus made boys in the theatre faint and women to have miscarriages – a silly enough tale, but one understands why it should have been invented. About Spectacle in drama Aristotle writes rather coolly; Aeschylus on the other hand contrived it with enthusiasm, and nowhere more so than in this play.

The first scene, laid before Apollo's temple in Delphi, establishes a mood of dignity, calm and beauty. The tradition was that Apollo took possession of Delphi by force. In this play Aeschylus abolishes the force; all is order and peace. The first of many theatrical strokes is that the Priestess, having entered the holy shrine, comes out again in terror, on all fours; she has seen within such hideous monsters that she can hardly describe them. Next, we see Apollo himself, in all his majesty, the Apollo who has been aptly compared with the nearly contemporary Apollo in the pediment at Olympia. He assures Orestes of his protection, and delivers him for safe-keeping into the hands of Hermes, the god to whom Orestes was praying at the beginning of the *Choephori*. The Erinyes, overcome by sleep, lie huddled on the floor. Apollo speaks of them just as the Priestess did: they are loathsome creatures from the lowest pit.

The scene is left empty, but for the sleepers. Now the Ghost of Clytemnestra rises, and this woman is even more impressive dead than alive. Even to these awful beings she speaks with authority: she reproaches them for their sleeping, she tells them of her dishonoured place among the dead, and she spurs them on in their pursuit of her son and murderer. Grunting and groaning they gradually awaken, and at last we see them, performing some dance in the holy place, and protesting violently against the chicanery of Apollo. The god returns. After a sharp altercation, full of indignation on the one side and of hatred and disdain on the other, he drives them out, and they resume their pitiless pursuit of Orestes.

We have had four scenes of the utmost effectiveness, and yet we are only at v. 235; at v. 235 in the *Agamemnon* we were still listening to the first long ode. Here is dramatic movement indeed; and it continues, with no slackening of speed or intensity, through the tremendous conflict on the Acropolis in Athens to the solemn procession with which the trilogy ends.

But not only is the action vigorous; it is also astonishing. We are entitled to be surprised that a religious poet represents deities in bitter conflict. Apollo, and the Priestess, describe the Erinyes in terms that may well remind us of Satan and his hellish crew: Apollo tells them that if they do not leave his temple at once he will shoot at them with his arrows and make them spew up the human blood they have drunk. But *Paradise Lost* will not prepare us for what is to come here. The conflict is referred to Athena; she in turn refers it to a jury consisting of herself and eleven of the wisest Athenian citizens[1] – another not very Miltonic idea. One would expect the verdict to be overwhelming. Apollo seems to have all the cards in his hands: he is the radiant god of Delphi, a son of Zeus, and he says with emphasis that never has he given to men a response that had not been given to him by Zeus (616–18). Therefore the command that he gave to Orestes came from Zeus. As for Apollo's adversaries,

---

[1] The proof that this was the composition of the jury is given in *Form and Meaning in Drama*, pp. 65 ff. It is, briefly, that vv. 711–34 cannot be reasonably stage-managed unless Athena is one of the twelve.

Aeschylus does all he can to emphasize their primitiveness and the gulf that separates them from the Olympians: Athena, for instance, speaks to them as if she had never seen them before, and observes that they resemble neither gods nor men. Yet when the votes are counted, they are equal, even though Athena has voted for Orestes; the superb Apollo comes as near to failure as the Erinyes do to success. Further, the role of Apollo, which begins so impressively, ends so unimpressively that from the text it is impossible to tell where he makes his exit; he simply evaporates.

There are other things that should surprise us, especially if we approach drama, even Aeschylean drama, with a healthy prejudice in favour of common sense and good craftsmanship.

It is made abundantly clear that the Erinyes are quarrelling not with Apollo merely but with the Olympians as a group. They say repeatedly that they are Elder Deities, and they protest against the pretensions of the Younger Gods who, they say, have more than once contravened Apportionment, or Moira, and Dike (149, 163 f., 321-7, 723-8), and 'ride roughshod', καθιππάσασθαι, over the ancient daughters of Night (150, 731, 778 f.) – and half the jury seem to agree with them. It is in agreement with this that we receive the impression that the Olympian gods form a harmonious group under Zeus. The Priestess informs us that Apollo received his gift of prophecy from Zeus, that the sons of Hephaestus made smooth his path to Delphi, that Pallas Pronoia (Forethought) is honoured in his responses, that Dionysus, too, has a home in Delphi. Further, in his first altercation with the Erinyes, Apollo tells them that by their action they are doing outrage to the sacred institution of marriage, guaranteed by the pledges exchanged by Zeus and Hera and presided over by Aphrodite. That Apollo has never spoken without the authority of Zeus is a fact which we have already mentioned; and we may add to all this that Athena, when her turn comes, makes it equally clear that she also speaks for Zeus: from him comes her wisdom (850), and when she has succeeded in conciliating the Erinyes she ascribes the victory to Zeus – to Zeus Agoraios, a title which can be surprisingly translated 'Zeus of Public Meetings'. There is no question but that the Olympians, virtually, are one Godhead – and older deities are accusing them of injustice and aggression.

Now, in reading or watching the third play of a trilogy we are entitled to remember the first, and to expect that the dramatist himself has not forgotten it. There are indeed scholars who assume that a dramatist naturally composes a play more carelessly, or incompetently, than they would themselves compose a learned article, and therefore explain away what they find inconvenient in a play by invoking a principle of natural error, inconsistency; which, in a serious artist, would amount to sheer irresponsibility: the artist may be inspired, but it is not too much to expect him to have intelligence and technique as well.

Already in the trilogy we have heard a good deal about the mutual relations of the Olympians and the Erinyes: in the *Agamemnon* and the *Eumenides* these relations are very different. In the *Agamemnon*, Zeus, or Pan, or Apollo, sends an Erinyes to punish the wrongdoer, and of course the Erinys does the god's bidding without question. We are told that the crimes committed in the house of Atreus were the work of the Erinyes; nevertheless the chorus can say that it has all happened 'through Zeus, who is the cause of all things'. Still more arresting is it, in view of what happens in the third play, that in order to satisfy his rage against Cassandra, Apollo availed himself of the blood-drinking Erinyes who were haunting Atreus' house; yet in the *Eumenides* he speaks of them with unrestrained loathing and contempt. There is certainly an inconsistency. The question is whether the reason for it is negligence or incapacity, or whether Aeschylus – having perhaps thought about his plot for a week or two before beginning to write – positively meant something by it and expected his audience to understand.

A subsidiary question is involved: are the Erinyes of the third play intended to be the same as the Erinys or Erinyes of the first? Of course the answer is Yes; those whom we see in the *Eumenides* are, in appearance, nature and function, identical with those whom Cassandra describes in the *Agamemnon*; in each play they are the incarnation of blind, automatic vengeance – as also is the Erinys who pursued Helen across the sea (*Agamemnon* 749). The question is hardly worth asking except that it brings to light a minor 'inconsistency' which was certainly designed by Aeschylus, for a good artistic reason: in the *Eumenides* the Erinyes are sometimes the Erinyes of Clytemnestra, sometimes the Erinyes at large. They are introduced as the former; as such they are charged with the execution of Clytemnestra's vengeance, and are interested in nothing else;

as such they exalt the claims of the female over those of the male. But they are not speaking as the Erinyes of Clytemnestra when they say that their function is to punish homicide (421), the killing of a father or mother (514–16), injury done to guests (546), violence that overthrows a house (354–59); and no audience in its right mind would suppose, when the final reconciliation comes to pass, that only the Erinyes of Clytemnestra were installed in Attica, leaving an unspecified number unreconciled, somewhere in the void – including the Erinyes of Agamemnon, of whom we heard in the *Choephori* (925), who were in fact not called into existence, because, Orestes did avenge his father. This is not confusion, except to a pedant; it is simplification: the audience will think each time of direct, implacable, unreasoning vengeance. Aeschylus is following the sound dramatic canon: Never explain what will in any case be obvious.

In the *Agamemnon* the Olympians can work in concert with the Erinyes because both parties are primitive; but their joint system of Justice, which they share with all the human actors in the play, ends in chaos: the king who received his sceptre from Zeus (*Agamemnon* 45) was, by the working of Zeus' own plan, murdered by and supplanted by a lawless tyrant; and Orestes finds himself in the impossible position that he both must and must not avenge his father. The Erinyes have no objection to chaos, no interest in the fabric of human society. The impossible dilemma in which Orestes is placed does not perturb them, for if Orestes kills his mother her Erinyes will hound him to death, while if he does not, then the Erinyes of Agamemnon will. It is quite simple. But the younger gods have other ideas; it was, after all, Zeus who introduced the idea that out of suffering understanding should come. The Olympians, or some of them, were particularly concerned with the fabric of human society – as protectors of cities, or of streets, houses or families, and as law-givers. These gods were concerned with the political side of life, unlike others – Dionysus, Demeter, Eros, Aphrodite in some of her aspects, Ares – whose field was the non-political.

Here, in the trilogy, comes the split between the Olympians and the Erinyes. From the chaos in which the *Agamemnon* ends, Zeus, the Olympians, will force a way out; if need be, Zeus will impose new laws of his own devising; he will invade ancient rights, infringing Moira, because in no other way can order be imposed on chaos. The dilemma can be stated in general form thus: there can be no such thing as Justice if a king, husband, father, can be murdered with impunity, since ordered society would be at an end. On the other hand, there are instinctive, intimate loyalties and sanctities without which society cannot continue: to the body politic, matricide is no less deadly than regicide – and we have just seen that with matricide Aeschylus combines parricide and outrage to guests.

It is the purpose of the first half of the *Eumenides*, the Apolline half, to show that the Olympians are whole-heartedly, and one-sidedly, champions of the King, of Authority. It was in preparation for this that in the *Choephori* Agamemnon was presented in a different light; that his destruction of Troy, for example, became not an act of violence to arouse apprehension on his behalf but a glorious exploit. In the first part of the *Eumenides* there is indeed a radiance that plays around Apollo; there is purity, beauty, order; and this has its human counterpart in the purity of motive shown by the new avengers. We have moved out of darkness, but we are not yet on even keel; neither Apollo's extreme and designedly unconvincing arguments about the primacy of the male, nor the lofty disdain that he shows towards the older deities, crude though they are, allow us to feel that we are on firm ground. How can we be, while there is civil war in Heaven? The situation resembles that in the *Prometheus,* where Zeus has an adversary who can call him a young and tyrannical despot.

But in the second part of the play the dominant figure is Athena. She supersedes Apollo, and by implication she corrects him: her courtesy towards the Erinyes contrasts markedly with Apollo's contempt. They are, as she says, beings unlike gods or men; yet 'to speak ill of another when he has given no offence (ἄμομφον ὄντα) is wrong'. Lest we begin to guess idly at the reasons why Aeschylus invented this contrast between gods let us observe that it is a coherent part of a wider pattern. In the first place, it is because of this courtesy and tolerance of Athena that the Erinyes agree to accept her arbitrament: from Apollo's total hostility no conciliation could have come about. But more than this: Athena takes a wider view than Apollo. She agrees with, and repeats, what is the chief substance of the Erinyes' plea, that Fear must not be removed – the fear of the certain punishment which they bring upon those guilty of bloodshed. She criticizes the methods used by the Erinyes: there is a hint of disapproval when it is made clear (422–4) that there will be no end to their pursuit of Orestes, and a moment later she chides them for trying to snatch an unfair victory by the Oath. (This means that they had challenged Orestes to deny on oath that he had killed his mother – which he could not do, his defence being not denial of the charge, but justification; but to the Erinyes motive and circumstance are irrelevant; only the bare act matters.) Another grave weakness in their case appears in the pleadings. They argue (605) that matricide is worse than the killing of a husband since the son is a blood-relative of the mother but the husband is no relative to the wife. The argument does not prove, as some have thought, that Aeschylus was thinking, whether as antiquarian or as a political theorist, of ancient tribal customs; it does prove that he was thinking of his play: it is the counterpart of the one-sided argument of Apollo. He, reasonably, defended the marriage-bond as the keystone of society; the Erinyes declare no interest in this. They, reasonably, insist that the tie of blood must remain inviolable; Apollo argued that the mother is no real parent at all. The jury, reasonably, says, not quite 'A plague on both your houses', but at least that each party is half right and half wrong.

The unanswerable part of the Erinyes' case is that crimes like matricide, parricide, outrage to a guest, may not go unpunished. 'In vain,' they say, 'will men cry to Dike, to the Erinyes. Fear must not be cast out. What man will be just if he fears nothing? Avoid anarchy and avoid despotism; the middle road is best.' This argument Athena repeats as her own: 'I would have my citizens revere this court and shun anarchy and despotism. Do not cast out Fear; what man will ever be just if he fears nothing?' (690–9). Anarchy and despotism are the extremes that meet – in moral and political violence; for despotism is the violence of the one or the few, anarchy the violence of the many. During the fifth century, Athens knew both.

As for the trial, there are other points, apart from the voting and the arguments used, which we noted as worthy of surprise: that the acquittal of Orestes is not the climax of the play, that a dispute between the older and the younger gods is decided not by the Supreme God but by his daughter and eleven human jurors sitting and voting together, and that Apollo evaporates. The last fact is quite logical: Aeschylus will show no interest in Apollo as a Divine Person when such an interest would not help the drama; he does not write a farewell speech for Apollo: 'Now I return to Delphi, a wiser god.' Apollo, as a representative of Zeus, has been superseded, in the play, by another, Athena.

Human participation in the trial is a logical continuation of that correlation of the human and the divine which we have met throughout. These gods do not push men about; indeed, Clytemnestra's Ghost pushes the Erinyes about. In this conflict humanity is most deeply concerned: on its outcome depends political and social stability, or its alternatives of anarchy or despotism. Is authority, in any circumstances, to override that Dike which the Erinyes execute? On the other hand, are the very foundations of the social order to be challenged with impunity? From this point of view perhaps Apollo's open bribing of the Court is not so shameless as it might, superficially, appear: he is promising Athens political power. But he is one-sided; what of the ruination which the Erinyes threaten? True well-being, as the sequel shows, comes only from the proper conciliation and blending of these opposites. Human welfare is at stake; humanity must share the responsibility of the decision. What Athena, Santa Sophia, brings is tolerance, level judgement – inasmuch as she, an Olympian, accepts the valid half of the Erinyes' case – reason (Peitho, Persuasion), and mercy – inasmuch as equal votes acquit. These are divine attributes in man; as Haemon says to Creon (*Antigone*, 683 f.): 'It is the gods that have implanted reason in man, the greatest of all blessings.' The Court of the Areopagus, the prototype of all courts of justice, is a divine institution, a barrier against violence, anarchy, despotism; and at the first meeting of this court Athena sits with her fellow-citizens. Wrath, $\mu \hat{\eta} \nu \iota s$, as the means of Dike, gives place to Reason.

Zeus has moved forward from violence and confusion, in which the Erinyes were his unquestioning agents, to arbitrary interference, which angered the Erinyes, and from that to reason and mercy, which angers them still more. The conflict may not continue; how is it to be ended? Athena, mentioning thunderbolts (827 f.), gives a reminder of the invincible power with which Zeus overcame Cronos (*Agam.* 167–73), but this time he prevails not by thunderbolts but through Athena's gift of persuasion (*Eum.* 885 f., 970–5):

she convinces them that in the new dispensation, if they accept it, although their methods of exacting Dike will be different, their privileges will not be infringed, but extended; that there is need of them in the Polis, if it is not to be rent by discord. Though reason and mercy are to be admitted, fear is not to be cast out, and Dike in its widest sense (*Eun.* 903–15) is to be their care. They accept; and so, as Athena quaintly says, Zeus of Public Meetings, Ζεὺς Ἀγοραῖος, has prevailed. Except that Aeschylus is *not* quaint. Had it been possible to bring Atreus, or Thyestes, or Paris, or the question of the war, or Clytemnestra, or Aegisthus, before a responsible, disinterested Assembly, the demands of Dike could have been met and chaos averted. It is in this final conciliation that Zeus becomes truly Teleios (*Agam.* 973 f.). It remains for men to revere and dread his agents and allies, not now the black-robed Erinyes but the red-robed Eumenides.

Did the trilogy have any reference to contemporary politics? This is generally assumed, and the assumption seems plausible. About three years before it was produced, the powers of the Areopagus, the ancient council of ex-archons, had been curtailed in favour of the popular Assembly, Ephialtes and Pericles being the chief sponsors of the reform. Those who would like Aeschylus to be a good Conservative argue that the *Eumenides* contains a protest; those who would like him to be a Liberal argue that he was pointing to the original function of the Court: jurisdiction in cases of homicide, which the reformers had scrupulously respected. Neither argument shows a very profound understanding either of the trilogy or of Aeschylus. In Athens, political strife could now and then become violent: Ephialtes, for example, had been murdered. The trilogy certainly makes a protest – against blind rage and violence, against both despotism and anarchy. It does not end in undiluted optimism but with a conditional assurance: the Eumenides, ex-Erinyes, will give prosperity to a city that reveres Dike; a city that does not will expose itself to their wrath.

CHAPTER IV

The Dramatic Art of Aeschylus

Aeschylus will do anything. It seems impossible to reduce his dramatic procedure to any kind of system. For example: some of his plots are full of action, like the second half of the *Choephori* and the whole of the *Eumenides*, yet for most of the time the *Septem* and the *Supplices* are quite static, the *Prometheus* has a chief actor who cannot move, and consists almost entirely of speeches, and the *Persae* is nearly all narrative. In the *Eumenides* he manages what are virtually five actors with the greatest of ease; in the *Supplices* he cannot manage even two – a fact that is the more interesting now that we can no longer assume that Aeschylus wrote the play in his comparative youth, when he had not yet learned how to use the two actors.[1] It is the same with his character-drawing: on the one hand we find vivid portraits or sketches, as of Clytemnestra or the Nurse; on the other, mere outlines, as of Pelasgus or Danaus or Xerxes.

Aeschylus is, in fact, not unique among the Greek tragic poets in his refusal to behave properly. Sophocles, admired for his sense of form as much as for anything, has left us with two plays which are said to break in the middle. He is not quite so αὐθάδης, self-willed, as Aeschylus, but Euripides runs him close, for he could construct the most brilliant plots, as of the *I.T.*, which Aristotle obviously admired, but on the other hand wrote plays which have induced some of his critics to call him a 'botcher', and to make the patronizing suggestion that he invented the *deus ex machina* for the purpose of extricating him from plots from which he could find no other means of escape.

This seems a convenient moment at which to consider the whole

---

[1] This never was a very good argument: we do not say that the *P.V.* must be early because Aeschylus had not yet learned how to make a plot or manage dialogue. It is not in the least likely that Aeschylus should have introduced the second actor when he had little idea what to do with him or how to use him. This is not the way in which an artist works.

situation. What we find is this: Aristotle gives a clear recipe for the making of a good play, and it is one which he is commonly supposed to have deduced from the practice of his classical dramatists, yet they themselves appear to have treated such principles with considerable indifference. What should we do? We can, of course, run over each play with an Aristotelian tape-measure and pronounce it a fit or a misfit, as the case may be, but few would think this an enlightened kind of criticism. It is too much like the exploit of a music scholar of the early nineteenth century who declared, of Bach's 48 fugues, that not one of them was correct; or like the celebrated Rockstro who compiled what long remained the standard textbook on sixteenth-century counterpoint; for Rockstro explained that he had been compelled to invent most of the examples given in the book since Palestrina, Vittoria and the rest did not provide suitable ones. Academic criticism, at its worst, can be exceedingly funny.

We can safely start from the assumption that these three dramatists were intelligent men: their audiences were agreed that Aeschylus and Sophocles were the best tragic poets that Athens had, and in the other arts Athenian standards of craftsmanship were very high. Therefore when one modern critic tells us of two scenes in the *Agamemnon* that they are manifestly a bore, and another that the dramaturgy of the *Eumenides* is 'naïve' (and presumably not worth considering seriously, since he does not consider it at all),[1] it is perhaps worth while to entertain the hypothesis that they may have missed something somewhere, perhaps through looking for the wrong thing – especially when neither of them has taken account of such things as the elaborately constructed verbal imagery in the play, which may not have got there by accident.

The dictum that all great art is timeless must be received with caution: it certainly does not mean that any ordinarily sensitive spectator can stroll up to some ancient work of art, in whatever medium, and upon inspection understand and appreciate it; he may be disabled by certain unexamined prepossessions of his own, not shared by the artist. To take an extreme illustration: if he should take it for granted that the visual arts necessarily obey the known principles of perspective, he would not be able to say anything worth listening to about most Greek vase painting.

[1] H. Lloyd-Jones, *Journal of Hellenic Studies*, LXXVI (1956), p. 64.

Not many of us are as naïve as that, yet criticism of the Greek dramatists, and for that matter of Shakespearian tragedy too, is beset with assumptions that differ from this only in degree. Thus, we take it as an axiom that all drama is built around the character, actions, motives, and fate of one central character whom we may call the Tragic Hero; further, that the dramatist develops the action, or the plot, logically, step by step. It is all in Aristotle; in any case it is self-evident. Therefore when we find a dramatist not doing these things, or doing them only intermittently, we think it a defect, and either call him incompetent or try to explain it away. We do not at once reflect, that, so far as modern drama is concerned, the all-significant tragic hero is an idea of the Renaissance, quite foreign to medieval drama, and that insofar as Shakespeare was still in touch with the medieval tradition, it is foreign to him also; and that since in what remains of fifth-century Greek drama it fails to work, as often as not, its appearance in Aristotle might be connected with the contemporary Greek equivalent to our Renaissance.

Again, we can be misled by our historicism. We look back over three-quarters of a century of Greek tragic drama. We observe that during this period certain developments occurred in what we call the Greek tragic form. We record them – a rational thing to do, certainly, but it is not criticism, and if we are not careful it may impede criticism, that is, understanding. We record, for example, that Aeschylus did not join scene with scene with the dexterity of Sophocles, nor portray character so vividly, nor use the third actor with such freedom. In these respects, we say, Sophocles advanced the art of tragic drama; Aeschylus, to this extent, remained something of a primitive. So be it; there is nothing to complain of in this, but there is something to be careful about; for are we using the word 'primitive' in a purely historical sense, with reference only to our abstraction, 'the Greek tragic form,' or are we giving to it critical overtones, meaning that Aeschylus did not have full control of his dramatic technique? But obviously, dramatic technique, any technique, is not an absolute; it is relative to the job to be done. The danger of this historical approach is that it may tempt us to think only negatively of such features in Aeschylus' style: he did not do these things because, so to speak, he lived a bit too soon. Perhaps this could be true, but first we should try to think of them positively;

they may be features of the dramatic art which were developed by Sophocles for good reasons of his own, and for equally good reasons avoided, or not invented, by Aeschylus. In Aeschylus' drama they might have been merely silly.

As for the tragic hero, we may think it an immutable law of drama that a play should revolve around a single personage. Not all the dramatists agree. A play must have its unity; probably nothing that we are agreed to call a great work of art lacks this. But the unity of a play does not necessarily subsist in one character; it is not Agamemnon nor Clytemnestra who gives its unity to their play, nor Xerxes to the *Persae*, nor Hecuba to the *Troades*. Even when there is, beyond any question, a central and dominant character in a play, we can still, thanks to the modern interest in personality and the individual, entirely misunderstand the degree of importance which he had in the mind of the dramatist, and so more or less seriously misunderstand his play.

Let us take a Shakespearian example. There is no question who is the central character, the tragic hero, in *Coriolanus*. Now, when the play was last produced at Stratford, one of the critics observed that it loses its hold towards the end – not an unusual judgement on the play. The reason he gave was that 'when Coriolanus leads an enemy army against Rome merely to gratify a private grudge against the city, our belief in his fundamental nobility becomes difficult to sustain'. This, consciously or not, is perfectly Aristotelian: the tragic hero must be ὅμοιος, 'like us', since if he is not we do not feel pity for him; we must be able to believe in his fundamental nobility. It is also modern. Unfortunately, it is not Shakespearian. To a similar effect the Shakespearian scholar E. E. Stoll imputes it as a shortcoming to the play that the drawing of Coriolanus' character is 'external': Shakespeare does not explore the mental processes which led Coriolanus to join the Volsces – to which Granville Barker sensibly replied that in Coriolanus there *were* no such mental processes. But apart from this, both of the criticisms, and many others that might be mentioned, rest on what is to us the obvious assumption that here is a play about the tragic hero Coriolanus. On this assumption the play does not really work, and is therefore commonly regarded as a comparative failure.

But what if the assumption is not perhaps entirely wrong, but far short of the truth? Shakespeare was bred in the sixteenth century, when the medieval way of thought had not yet become incomprehensible, when ideas about God's creation, the divinely appointed order, with its earthly counterpart the ordered State, under the King, 'the deputy anointed by the Lord', still had an accepted meaning; when 'the body politic' was not a tired metaphor but a pregnant idea. But we have lost all this; if then it is all assumed in the play, to which we bring quite different assumptions, it is not surprising that *Coriolanus* is often regarded as not one of Shakespeare's best tragedies. To demonstrate that all this *is* assumed would take us too far from Aeschylus. Still, we may notice that in the first scene of the play Menenius relates, at some length, the ancient and medieval parable of the belly and the rebellious members. To us, this is quaint; we think that its purpose is only to characterize Menenius as an amusing old man; even Granville Barker, a sensitive critic, sees nothing in the parable and the whole scene, in which Menenius is chiding the violence of the plebeians, except that it delays, for dramatic reasons, the first entrance of the Hero. But what if modern sophistication has caused us to miss the point? It seems much more likely that the parable would immediately call to the minds of Shakespeare's audience a whole set of familiar ideas circling round the divinely appointed order, the ideal commonwealth, and the human body as an example of that order. From such a point of view the play gains immeasurably in solidity and strength – and Shakespeare's audience did go to church, and listen to long sermons. The plebeians, with their 'bats and clubs', the malicious tribunes, the haughty Volumnia, the splendidly arrogant Coriolanus, are all in their degree rebellious members, and between them they bring Rome into dire peril; and the last act, in which we lose interest because we can no longer believe in the fundamental nobility of the hero is, in fact, one of the most moving and tragic that Shakespeare ever wrote: action, statement, metaphor, imagery all combine to make us see in Coriolanus one who is trying to deny and oppose all the laws, ties, obligations of Nature – very like Ajax, who tries to live his life independently of the gods; and when, like Ajax, he finds too late that the laws of Nature are too strong for him, he can only go to his death. Once we have seen the scale of the play, it matters little to us if we can believe in this fundamental nobility or not, and it becomes clear that exploration of Coriolanus' motives would have been only a distracting irrelevance. In order to see the scale of it, no more is necessary than that we should be sceptical about our own assumptions, and read the play in the persuasion that Shakespeare probably meant all that he does and says, and designed it with intelligence. Its unity comes not from Shakespeare's conception of Coriolanus' character; this indeed serves to focus the idea of the play, but its real unity comes from further back, in the general rejection of Nature's laws.

Great art is *not* timeless, unless we will take the trouble to understand its idiom, which may be very different from our own. To a certain interpretation of a Greek play one scholar has objected that 'it does not accord with the experience of reading the play'. In itself the argument is valueless: the reply is '*Whose* experience?' We know how the eighteenth century read Shakespeare's tragedies. It had entirely lost Shakespeare's mental and religious background, and naturally substituted its own, and its own ideas of 'taste'. Therefore the plays were rewritten, in order that such as Juliet and Cordelia should not die: this was contrary to 'natural justice', as Johnson lucidly explains in his preface to *King Lear*, in which he warmly approves of the happy ending contrived by Nahum Tate. Now we laugh heartily; we see that Johnson's experience of reading the play (which he found intolerably distressing) tells us much more about Johnson and the eighteenth century than it can about *King Lear*. Yet Johnson had edited Shakespeare; but it had never occurred to him to disengage from the plays Shakespeare's own assumptions and habit of thought; he assumed that his own were right and eternal. Consequently the plays did not make sense to him. Therefore, when critics find rudimentary blunders in the Greek dramatists, a degree of at least temporary scepticism seems justifiable.

Unlike our own medieval ancestors, we are not accustomed, as part of our ordinary imaginative experience, to drama in which the action can be shared by men and gods alike. The fifth-century Athenians were so accustomed – and not in drama only, for there was also Homer. Our ideas of drama are very different; if not based on Aristotle's, they are at least in general conformity with them. Therefore it is interesting that Aristotle himself makes no allowance for divine action, except as a dramatic convenience: his one reference to the gods, in the *Poetics*,[1] is that 'by convention, the gods foresee everything' – they are useful, no more. That is to say, the dramatic

[1] 1454 b 5.

field has become smaller. We are now dealing only with the character, motives, actions, of an individual, and their logical results, not
with anything greater than the individual. The centre of gravity, as
we might say, is now placed within the dramatic field defined by
the human dramatic characters, and from this the Aristotelian canons
follow – as we should expect – logically: the balanced character of
the hero and the *internal* logic of the plot. Now that the hero is all
that we have to contemplate, we must be able 'to believe in his
fundamental nobility' – which we need not do with Agamemnon
or Hecuba; there may not now be incursions from the wider
universe, like the Sun-god's chariot in the *Medea*. A further natural,
if not even inevitable, consequence, now that the wide prospect of
the earlier drama has been lost, is Aristotle's insistence on τὸ
φιλάνθρωπον, which, in effect, is indistinguishable from Johnson's
'natural justice'. For instance, it is remarkable, but quite logical,
that in his treatment of πάθος, the deed of violence, Aristotle counts
as the second-worst of the four possibilities the one which is normal
in the tragic poets, and prefers the one which gives us a dramatic
frisson but avoids the tragic issue: τὸ μιαρὸν οὐ πρόσεστι, 'the shocking effect is avoided.' Aristotle would not allow a blameless character to meet with disaster; it is μιαρόν, 'shocking'; it contravenes
τὸ φιλάνθρωπον, 'natural justice.'[1] The fourth century seems close
to the eighteenth. Certainly the fifth-century dramatists often
obliged Aristotle by attributing grave ἁμαρτία (and sometimes
nothing else) to those whom they brought to ruin – but not on
principle, or not on Aristotle's principle; for there is no contributory fault in Pelasgus or Antigone or the Hecuba of the *Troades*.
Aristotle is right to this extent, that such unmerited suffering is
intolerable, because without meaning, if we have so shortened our
focus that we no longer see it against the wide background which
the poet devised, but only in the immediate situation. In that case,
if the sufferers bore no responsibility, what befalls them would
be no more significant than a railway accident. This is the reason
why Aristotle, rightly from his point of view, insisted on ἁμαρτία;
there was no wide background in the drama that he was considering.
In short, it seems that if we agree with Pope:

> *Presume not God to scan;*
> *The proper study of mankind is Man,*

[1] *Poetics*, 1453 b 27–1454 a 5, and 1452 b 34–1453 a 5.

we must also agree with Johnson, that Shakespeare made some terrible mistakes. It is a pity that we cannot know what Aristotle really made of Aeschylus; one would imagine, very little.

To this general discussion, long though it is, one final point may be added. It is not difficult for the modern reader to see that Aristotle's system makes virtually no contact with the drama of Aeschylus; it is with Sophocles that our real difficulty begins. The whole framework of the Aeschylean drama is so spacious, the independent or interdependent role of men and gods is so evident, that there is little temptation to try to interpret it in Aristotelian terms. But the texture of Sophoclean drama is much more closely woven. It looks, at first sight Aristotelian; it makes so much sense (like Shakespeare's too) if we read it with Aristotelian or modern assumptions that when from time to time it does not make sense – when a play seems to break down in the middle – it does not occur to us to question our assumptions; it seems enough to say that the dramatist, for once, was not in very good form. Yet in fact, although his idiom is different, Sophocles' drama has the same kind of wide background as that of Aeschylus, and makes complete sense only if it is read in the same way.

The upshot of this discussion is that we should not be surprised if an examination of Aeschylus' art, based on modern assumptions, produces only a string of negatives. As we have seen already, he seems to have had in mind no ideal pattern to which a play should conform. Again, his interest in character was limited; not one of his dramatic persons comes within miles of being the rounded character postulated by Aristotle, with the possible exception of Eteocles. Pelasgus is not much more than an outline, Danaus hardly even that. We might prefer a Xerxes who was more sharply drawn – one for example who took his overthrow with resignation and dignity, and made wise dispositions for the future; Aeschylus gives us nothing of the kind. To him, Xerxes is a man who has offended Heaven and has been crushed; what does his personal character matter? The word *drama* can be paraphrased *what is going on*; elaboration of character would only distract attention from what is really going on; therefore it is kept to the minimum, whatever in each case the minimum may be. Our own lively interest in individuals can mislead us. For example, perhaps we hail the Nurse in the *Choephori* with delight: here, at last, is a really lifelike character;

E

Greek tragedy is at last becoming positively dramatic. Lifelike, of course; as lifelike in her broken-hearted sorrow as Clytemnestra in her wicked hatred – and set in the same deep perspective; and this perspective is what we shall not see, if we lean back in our seats enjoying an unexpected bit of naturalism. Aeschylus devised it in strict relation to 'what is going on'. The chorus, hoping desperately that retribution shall fall on the murderers, has been praying to Hermes and to $\Pi\epsilon\iota\theta\grave{\omega}$ $\delta o\lambda\acute{\iota}a$, Guileful Persuasion. The Nurse, in her sorrow for Orestes and her hatred for the murderers, is very willing to help deceive Aegisthus; as in Sophocles' play also, the guile which they used against Agamemnon is being turned against themselves. She is indeed a real person; they are all real persons, or the drama would have no effect. But she is made into this particular real person not for the sake of 'realism' but of something further: she does not know it, but she is working alongside gods: Hermes and Peitho.

Orestes, too, needs care. His character is indeed not elaborately drawn, but we must not ascribe what character he has merely to the fact that Aeschylus' ability to draw character is increasing. When Orestes declares that he would have avenged his father in any case, we must not think that we have exhausted the point when we say that it shows his heroic stature; as we have seen,[1] there is more in it than that. It is not the characters that shape the plot either in Aeschylus or in Sophocles.

Nor is it the story. Wilamowitz had the idea that the essence of Greek tragedy was that it represented saga. No doubt in the hands of inferior tragic poets it did just this, and no more, just as, according to Aristotle,[2] the second-rate epic poets simply narrated what happened to Theseus or Heracles; they were merely guided by the story; Homer shaped his material according to some idea of his own. But although Athens no doubt had tragic poets who could not walk without crutches, they have not survived to trouble us. We need only look at the plays we have to see that the poets made of the myth precisely what they wanted.

For a trilogy about Prometheus, myth – that is to say, Hesiod – offered ample material, and Aeschylus used much of it, just as much as he needed, and no more; and where it was of no use to him, he

[1] Above, p. 83.
[2] *Poetics*, VIII.

altered it. Myth, or Hesiod, offered him, for a Prometheus, a minor god of no great importance who cunningly stole fire and gave it to mortals; Aeschylus turned him into a god who had given man, one might say, everything that distinguished him from brute creation, and could measure himself even against Zeus. It was not myth, but Aeschylus, that created the not negligible idea of a Zeus who, like a Polyneices or Eteocles, has upon him a father's curse (*P.V.* 910–12); it was not myth, but Aeschylus, who brought the Oceanids to come and sympathize with Prometheus, and who represented the whole world and its inhabitants as mourning for him. Aeschylus did find in myth most of the material for his story of Io, but it was Aeschylus, not myth, who interwove her story with the story of Prometheus – and nothing could more vividly illustrate his total indifference to Aristotle's law of internal logic than the sudden arrival of Io into the middle of the *Prometheus Vinctus*. She has, of course, her part in the story, otherwise her arrival would have been too violent, probably, even for Aeschylus, but what matters in the play is that she, like Prometheus, is a victim of the arbitrary cruelty of Zeus.

So one could continue. It was not myth, but Aeschylus, who decided that the cause of Artemis' anger at Aulis should be, not something that Agamemnon had done already, but something that he was going to do; or, alternatively, something that the eagles of Zeus were doing.[1] To all appearance it was not myth, but Aeschylus, who brought Orestes to trial before not the Twelve Gods but a human jury. If for 'myth' we read 'history' the same is true. It was not history, but Aeschylus, who caused Xerxes to be deceived not by Themistocles but by 'some Spirit or Alastor', the Persians to be stricken by panic after Salamis, and to be destroyed in their thousands on their retreat by hunger, thirst, and a deceptively frozen river.

That is to say, Aeschylus, like all great tragic poets, was not the obedient servant but the imperious master of his sources: the *Persae*

---

[1] Aeschylus made a bad mistake here, as D. L. Page has explained (*Agamemnon*, ed. Denniston and Page, xxiii). 'Here [viz. in the traditional story of the stag] was a suitable background for Aeschylus' narrative: the mortal offends the goddess, and her anger involves him in further wrongdoing; the original wrong was his fault, and all that follows can be traced back to it. Alternatively (and better) the wrath of Artemis might have been more clearly linked to the chain of destiny which binds the house of Atreus.' It is indeed well that we know, by revelation, apparently, what Aeschylus really meant; otherwise we should not know what a poor dramatist he was.

is much less unhistorical that the 'history' of Duncan and Macbeth constructed for them by Shakespeare. Tragic poets use, and manhandle, myth or history, rather than invent their own plots, for the sake of the solid advantages to be gained from it, advantages which are indicated, though not exhausted, by Aristotle's remark: 'Of events which have not happened, we are not immediately persuaded that they are possible, but what has happened obviously is possible'; and later, 'Therefore, even if a poet should chance γενόμενα ποιεῖν, to take his plot from real events, he has none the less "made" (ποιεῖν) his plot, for there is no reason why some historical events should not be οἷα ἂν γένοιτο, significant of a universal truth, and what *can* happen; and it is in this respect that the poet is their creator (ποιητής).'[1] The use of myth saves the dramatist from the tedious necessity of giving solidity and importance to his story. *Hamlet* in modern dress may be all very well, but a Hamlet who lived in Balham and was called Smith would need a powerful lot of buildingup. But for all practical purposes, Aeschylus invented (ποιεῖν) his myths; he made them entirely his own, and used them as he wished. They hampered him to this extent, that if his trend of thought required, for example, that a vengeful spouse bent on murder was frustrated by a loyal son, then he could not use the Orestes myth. No doubt the relation between thought and myth was not quite so free as this; no doubt the trend of thought was often suggested by contemplation of a myth; nevertheless, all the evidence is that Aeschylus made the myth convey what *he* meant, not that his plays dutifully followed existing stories.

Let us now consider the word 'myth' in its Aristotelian sense of 'plot'. It is perhaps one of our instinctive assumptions that one thing a play must do is to tell a story. Perhaps it must, even though, as in a medieval cycle, it may be so familiar a one as the story of the Creation, the Fall, the Redemption, and the Last Judgement. But the relation between story and drama varies considerably: in the merely narrative element of drama Aeschylus had relatively little interest.

For example, he invented the trilogy-form, and we naturally think like this: 'In the trilogy, with its wide range of time and subject, Aeschylus was able to trace the course of this hereditary evil, and to follow the crime from its original commission down to

[1] *Poetics*, IX, 1451 b 17 and 29.

the period of its final expiation.'[1] Quite so; first, Atreus and Thyestes, then Agamemnon, Clytemnestra, and Aegisthus, then Orestes and the final expiation. Paris and Helen would be something of an excrescence – part of the original 'history' that could not well be left out? Iphigeneia, as Professor Page has observed, would need a much more cogent link with the Curse than Aeschylus has supplied (unless we can understand him), and although Cassandra as the victim of Agamemnon and Clytemnestra would be a logical part of the story, Cassandra as the victim of Apollo (which is what she says she is) would make no sense; and Aeschylus did not think that 'the final expiation of Orestes' was the point at which he should stop. It is clearly not the shape of the story that dictated the shape of the trilogy; 'what is going on' is rather different.

Aeschylus' relative indifference to mere narrative is forcibly illustrated by one thing that happens in the *Agamemnon* – or rather, by one thing that does *not* happen. The Herald has come, bringing to the Elders of Argos the long-awaited news of the victory. Then, with reluctance, but in powerful style, he tells them of a great disaster: the whole fleet, so far as he knows, has been destroyed, the army drowned. Having finished his tale of overwhelming catastrophe, he disappears. What will the chorus say now? Argos has suffered a crippling blow, and sons of their own will have been in the ships. What this incredible chorus does is to begin a chant about Helen, the ruin that she brought to Troy, Hybris, and Justice. We hear no more of the lost fleet; never again is the storm mentioned, not even by Agamemnon, one of the few survivors. Homerists ought to give their attention to this: what is clearer than that there must have been at least two Aeschyli? The earlier one will have composed the second part of the play, which shows no knowledge of the storm. The first part must have been written, or rewritten, by a later poet – and not the storm-speech only, because the coming storm is clearly implied in the close of Clytemnestra's second speech: 'Let them remember, when they are in the captured city . . .'

Oddly enough, readers of the play are not in the least perturbed by the failure of the chorus to be sensible at this point. Naturally; the reason is plain enough: all our attention is absorbed by the theme of crime and its punishment; to it, the storm makes its own immediate contribution, and that is enough; it has done its work. What the

[1] A. E. Haigh, *The Attic Theatre* (3rd. edn.), p. 14.

chorus deals with next, namely Helen and the Trojans, is a perfectly logical continuation, though the logic of it is that of Aeschylus' own dramatic conception, not of the story or situation. Had Aeschylus made the chorus mourn the loss of their own sons at sea, we should feel it to be an irrelevance. His loyalty, which in turn successfully claims ours, is not to the events but to the idea.

It is this fact that explains the notably spacious texture of his drama; it is not closely-knit and carefully articulated, like the drama of Sophocles. These, as was suggested above, are positive, not negative facts: since it is, explicitly, a drama of gods and men, not one of individuals and their complex relations, Aeschylus, so to speak, keeps us at the proper distance, that we may see the whole in due perspective. Again, since it is not an intellectually lazy drama, but one that made considerable demands on the imaginative energy of the audience, he took care not to make the task harder by introducing decorative diversions; interesting personal relationships therefore are kept to a minimum. In the last scene of the *Persae*, why did Aeschylus not bring back Atossa to receive and say something suitable to Xerxes? He had the second actor at his disposal, doing nothing in the changing-room. But his interest was in the relations between Xerxes and the god; those between Xerxes and his mother would only distract attention.

In this matter our natural assumptions can easily mislead us, as is shown by Headlam's treatment of the passage between Clytemnestra and the Herald. Headlam begins by observing that messengers in Greek drama are regularly rewarded, 'in accordance with Greek and oriental custom.' Clytemnestra, however, at the beginning of her speech, does not address the Herald at all, but the chorus. Then, turning abruptly to him, she tells him that she has no need of the details of his story, gives him a message for Agamemnon, and retires without giving him any reward, not even a word of thanks; whereupon the Herald, according to Headlam, comments unfavourably on the Queen's manners. How natural! – if only this were naturalistic drama. But the whole idea of this personal bit of byplay is foreign to the Aeschylean drama. It would not in any way help to forward or illuminate the theme of the play; it would not help the audience to see, in Clytemnestra, the avenger appointed by Artemis. But the proof that it is a modern misconception does not rest on these considerations only: we have only to look a little further into

Aeschylus to see that such aloofness between persons is standard practice. The Herald himself does not greet the chorus when he enters, nor receive a greeting from them until he has completed his first speech. Agamemnon, when he enters, behaves towards the chorus just as Clytemnestra does towards the Herald; the chorus welcomes him in some thirty verses, but he speaks twenty-nine before he acknowledges its presence, and then abruptly says: τὸ δ'ἐς τὸ σὸν φρόνημα, 'As for your advice...' Do we then conclude that no one in the play has decent manners? Aegisthus enters without a word either to the chorus or to Clytemnestra: What do we do, sitting in the audience? – do we speculate on Aegisthus' manners, and wonder why he does not speak to the Queen? or, unconcerned with this kind of thing, do we listen intently to what he is saying: 'Hail, day that brings retribution, now that I see him enmeshed in a robe woven by the Furies'? Assuredly we cannot do both: it was in order that we might do the one that Aeschylus avoided the other, and does not bring Aegisthus and Clytemnestra into any sort of contact. The only occasion in this play when an incoming character directly addresses someone on the stage is when Clytemnestra at once, and by name, addresses Cassandra. The special reason for this we have seen already.[1]

Looking further afield, we find that Pelasgus does indeed at once speak to the chorus, naturally: that is why he has come; but he takes no notice whatever of Danaus. The messenger in the *Persae*, 'in accordance with oriental custom,' ought, I imagine, to do obeisance to the queen-mother; but no, he addresses neither her nor the chorus of Elders, but 'the cities of all Asia, the land of Persia, and its store of wealth'. He speaks, presumably, straight at the audience. When the Spy of the *Septem* returns with his news (v. 375) he begins with no preamble whatever; he gives no sign that he is addressing Eteocles in particular until he says (v. 395): 'Whom will you oppose to this man?'

That is to say, when the occasion demands it, as when Pelasgus meets the Danaids, or the Egyptian herald, Aeschylus will bring the characters into their natural relationship; if it does not, he shows no embarrassment in completely neglecting it, just as he neglects entirely, and without embarrassment, the time that would have been spent by Agamemnon in sailing from the Troad to Nauplia through

[1] Above, p. 76.

a storm, the pursuit of Orestes by the Erinyes from Delphi to Athens in the middle of a play, or the fact that in real life a group of Argive notables would take some little notice of the news of a national disaster. Aeschylus is not involved, and does not wish to involve his audience, in anything but the dramatic realization of his theme; he will disregard collateral facts and consequences just as he will disregard personal relationships. One often has the impression that his characters are speaking to each other over a distance of fifteen or twenty yards, not of five or ten feet, as on our stage; often, that they are not speaking to each other at all, but straight at the audience, as when Aegisthus makes his first speech in the *Agamemnon*. In such a case the other actor will be simply immobile – and the very immobility can be extremely dramatic, as in the case of Cassandra.[1] Certainly we may call it 'stiff technique', and observe that Sophocles is more supple (though Sophocles keeps Creon immobile for long stretches of the *Antigone*), but it is more profitable to consider it positively: it is the technique that Aeschylus' normal dramatic theme demands; the more supple treatment would not be so good.[2] It is a matter of scale: the scale of this drama is more like that of Stonehenge than of a conversation-piece.

Once the nature of Aeschylean drama has been established, with the dramatic conventions that it implies; once it has been seen that he is neither dramatizing a story nor making drama about individuals of a certain kind in a certain situation, but about man and the gods, and certain verities of the human universe, then the major fact stares one in the face: Aeschylus was, above all things, a superb man of the theatre. He professed to be a tragic dramatist (though in his epitaph he preferred to be remembered as a soldier), he was signally honoured by Athens as a tragic dramatist, and it is as such that he deserves to be considered.

If it is the mark of the great tragic poet that he renders visible and memorable certain basic truths or conceptions, whether they be old or new (and this is not of the first importance, except to doxographers; for we do not value Shakespeare because he represents a great advance on the thought of Abelard or Aquinas), then it is not

---

[1] On the possible long immobility of Clytemnestra, see Page's interesting note on *Agamemnon* 489 ff. (though I find it difficult to suppose that she does not leave the stage, following Agamemnon, at v. 974). For the immobility of Creon in the *Antigone*, see *Form and Meaning in Drama*, 146–7, 165, 170, 173.

[2] This is not to deny that there are some real awkwardnesses, as in the management of some of Prometheus' speeches.

easy to think of a dramatist who did this more imaginatively and powerfully, nor with a more architectonic control. In him, thought and the dramatic image of thought become the same thing. Of the *Prometheia*, fragmentary though it is, we can say, using conceptual terms, that it deals with the maturing of civilization in respect of the balance to be achieved between dynamic intelligence and such qualities as pity, mercy, on the one hand, and on the other, power and authority. Aeschylus does not speak in conceptual terms; had he done so, he would not have been a dramatist. Though he had not read Aristotle he knew all about mimesis; what he thought or felt he 'represents' through his chosen dramatic imagery; he begins his trilogy, not by a philosophic essay in verse, but visually, with the scene of Prometheus, the god of eloquent name, being crucified by Brute Force. With perhaps even greater imaginative energy he concludes the *Oresteia* by making his idea visible and incarnate in the conflict and its reconciliation between the older and the younger gods. This is not Allegory. The allegorist thinks in conceptual terms and then gives capital letters or Christian names to his concepts; the dramatist, whether he has thought in abstract terms or not, sees and expresses his thought in his dramatic structure; the two are indivisible. Did Aeschylus begin thinking out the *Oresteia* from a sense of the tragic wastefulness of this long chain of bloodshed, or from a picture of a king returning triumphantly from a stupid war, to be murdered by his wife and supplanted by her paramour, or from thoughts about Orestes, caught in an intolerable situation where he must either commit an atrocious crime or lose all honour and self-respect; or did he begin with reflections on violence, crime, vengeance, and the bearing of all this on the well-being of the city which he was proud to have served as a soldier? We cannot possibly tell where it all began;[1] all we know is where it ended – in the *Oresteia*. Thought and dramatic imagination 'all compact' made a solid and convincing work of art, every cranny of it instinct with life. It is inevitable that those who maintain that Aeschylus had no mind worth speaking of must also believe that he was not a competent dramatist either – for if the *Agamemnon*, for instance, ends with a scene which is a tedious anticlimax, how can we assert that Aeschylus knew how to make a play?

[1] Except that it did not begin with a theological doctrine about Zeus, and that a primitive one. From such a germ the *Oresteia* could not have come into existence.

The phrase 'superb man of the theatre' was used advisedly. The word *drama* means, roughly, 'something going on'; the word *theatre* means literally 'a place where one looks' – and also listens. One looks not only at actors enacting events, and occasionally at certain stage-properties in use, but also at dancers performing certain evolutions designed for them by the dramatist; one hears not only speech but also song and music. A dramatist is not simply a poet; the poet does not have to consider, and *qua* poet cannot use, music, dancing, grouping, nor such vulgar things as hammers and nails, nets, swords, boots. As a poet writing for the theatre Aeschylus did have to consider all these things, and as a good man of the theatre he was able to weld them into a unity. The competent dramatist will not only think, as it were, longitudinally, backwards and forwards, using the fact that his audience will necessarily look at one scene or one event in the light of what has gone before, or of what it knows is going to happen later;[1] he will also think in depth; at any moment he will use some of the means at his disposal, verbal, aural, or visual, some or all of them, to make clear what is really going on.

Of the longitudinal construction enough has been said in the foregoing chapters; here we will consider, as best we can, Aeschylus' ability to construct in depth – as best we can, because obviously little of the original evidence remains to us.

We have seen already, and now need only recall, how in the *Oresteia* Aeschylus allies poetic imagery with stage-properties: how the net cast around Troy by Zeus becomes first the net 'woven by the Erinyes' in which we see the body of Agamemnon, and then 'such a thing as a footpad might use'; how the light which the Watchman is imagined to see, which Clytemnestra describes as leaping from mountain to mountain, which the chorus of the *Choephori* hails prematurely when the two murderers are killed (v. 961, πάρα τὸ φῶς ἰδεῖν), becomes visible light only at the end of the trilogy; how the metaphor of trampling underfoot holy things leaps suddenly to life as Agamemnon passes to his death.

The dramatic event will often pass the decisive comment on something that has been said. The Suppliants beseech Zeus to drown the wicked Egyptians – and Zeus refuses to do it; Eteocles has no

---

[1] It is only the scholar who can isolate one dramatic moment from the continuous succession, taking it out of its context.

doubt that Dike will destroy his unjust brother – and both of them are destroyed; Agamemnon, warned by the chorus of disloyalty in Argos, replies that what is amiss he will cure by cautery or the knife – and he is run through by Clytemnestra's sword; Clytemnestra, no less blind than he, stands over his dead body and says she is willing to compromise with the Spirit of the Pleisthenids; she is content that it shall depart and plague some other house. 'Cold irony' (Sidgwick), or 'deep anxiety' (Fraenkel), or 'a cool and practical and thoroughly sensible suggestion' (Page)? No, none of these; Aeschylus, like several later dramatists, knew how eloquent it could be merely to repeat a situation: Agamemnon shed blood, and now is dead; she also has shed blood. He hoped that all might be well; now she hopes the same. It is very simple, and very effective; 'Neither by prayers nor burnt-offerings nor libations will you bend the inflexible temper of the gods.'

These are moments when spectacle is working alongside speech, not as a decoration, but as an additional means of expressing thought. Many others could be added, notably the long middle scene of the *Septem*, if we accept the idea that the six defenders of Thebes are on the stage, alongside Eteocles, himself the seventh, waiting for their orders. Richmond Lattimore has said: 'The base of it all is the brute fact that Thebes had seven gates.'[1] This is as true as it would be if one said, of a Beethoven string quartet, that the base of it all was the brute fact that the composer had only four instruments to play with; all depends on whether the artist has been able to assimilate the brute fact, to make the limitation a source of strength, even of inspiration. Aeschylus surely has here. When we see only two left, Lasthenes and the King himself, one can imagine how great the tension must have been; enormously increased, and significantly, when the sixth Argive turns out to be Amphiaraus.

There are moments when Aeschylus relies on spectacle alone. Aristophanes would have us think that it was a mannerism with Aeschylus to keep an actor portentiously silent for long spells. We will not complain of a comic poet that he makes us laugh; nevertheless, one does not need to be an expert of the theatre to know that this effect is a difficult one to bring off; difficult for the actor, who must impose himself on the audience merely by being there; embarrassing for the audience, if the silence and inaction are

[1] *The Poetry of Greek Tragedy,* p. 44.

prolonged for a moment longer than the dramatic tension can bear. In the surviving plays there are two certain, and different, instances: Cassandra and Prometheus. The first half of Cassandra's silence shows how effectively Aeschylus could make spectacle talk: the mere presence of Cassandra, when Clytemnestra also is there, is eloquent. Later, when Clytemnestra and the chorus speak to her in vain, her immobility becomes the centre of the drama; for once, it is speech that is futile, and the silence that draws all our attention.

The silence of Prometheus is different because it is unmixed; there is no accompanying speech or movement. It follows the ode in which the chorus has protested against the cruelty of Zeus. The whole earth, it says, groans in sympathy with Prometheus; all who live in Asia, and the Amazons, and the inhabitants of Scythia, Arabia, the Caucasus, lament him; the same cry is heard, too, from the waves of the sea, from dark Hades, from the springs of all the rivers. Now the silence begins. The chorus, presumably, remains motionless; Prometheus certainly does. The real dramatic movement is, for some time, continued by the mere spectacle of the chained god, and by the imagined cry of sympathy from the whole universe – except from Olympus. Then at last Prometheus speaks: 'Think not that I am silent from disdain or stubbornness . . .' An eloquent silence.

Then there is the choral dance. Though the music and the dances have perished, they have left something behind them, namely the rhythm which they shared with the verse – for the rhythms of Greek lyric poetry are not, except the simplest of them, speech-rhythms at all; they make no sense if we try to declaim them. We have noticed already[1] how dramatic are the wild and unsteady rhythms of the *parodos* of the *Septem*; the *Agamemnon* enables us to go further. When the chorus, at v. 192, begins to relate what happened at Aulis it uses a rhythm not yet heard in the play, a simple four- or six-bar iambic phrase of which the metrical scheme is given above, p. 4, since it is used also in the *Supplices*. Twice the six-foot iambic line appears pure, with no prolongations, though with a rare resolution. Anyone who cares to look at vv. 406–8 and 423–5 will see at once the dramatic reason for this very smooth variation: the music and the dance-figure are obviously made to reinforce the sense and feeling of the words, as in several other places,

[1] Above, p. 49.

for instance v. 196, where the heavy rhythm of παλιμμήκη χρόνον τιθεῖσαι is hardly accidental.

This rhythm increasingly dominates the fourth and longest section of the first ode. It recurs in the second ode; in fact, quite unusually, it prevails throughout, with the exception of the songlike refrain which ends each stanza, and of a most intelligible incursion into the more emotional anacreontic rhythm at 447–51 and 467–71. Here, as it happens, we can use the rhythm to check our understanding of 'what is going on'. It has been said, with some plausibility, that in this ode the chorus first expresses its joy at the long-awaited victory, then, as it counts the cost, changes to a mood of apprehension. But joy and apprehension demand different dance-rhythms, and music; here there is no change, therefore the mood does not change. There is no contrast, but steady continuation. Aeschylus is not, in fact, so far characterizing his chorus as to make them rejoice at the victory; indeed, if he were doing this, we should begin to wonder later on why they do not similarly mourn the loss of the fleet.

It is even more exceptional that the same rhythm reappears in the middle of the third ode: 737–41=750–54, and for most of what follows. Now, these facts do not, perhaps, seem very exciting, but their obvious corollary is. Whenever it appeared, the rhythm was obviously realized in some associated dance-figuration and music; what these were we cannot possibly tell, but we can easily divine their dramatic purpose and effect: we note that the rhythm is used first to convey to us what Agamemnon did at Aulis; then, in the second ode, with what Paris did and suffered, with the war which Helen bequeathed to Greece, with Ares, money-changer of men's bodies and with the hatred which is gathering in Argos towards Agamemnon. Then, in the third ode, the associations which it has already acquired are made explicit as the chorus sings, to this same dance and music, of hybris and its inevitable outcome. What we have been watching, in the long-sustained pattern of this dance, is the visual expression of the moral or intellectual basis of the whole play. Then, as the dance reaches its conclusion, Aeschylus causes the 'sacker of cities' to make his royal entrance into the theatre – with Cassandra. Except that this, in fact, is not the end of this dance-figure, for we see it again, at 1485–1509 and at 1530–6=1560–6. With what ideas does the dramatist associate the rhythm now? With the same: Zeus is the cause of all things; the violence presses on; the storm must break; the law abides, that the doer must pay. This is indeed to use and combine the resources of the theatre to some serious purpose and with some intelligence.

The ancient *Life of Aeschylus* assures us that 'he far surpassed his predecessors in the composition of plays, their *mise en scène,* the brilliance of his productions, the costumes of the actors, and the impressiveness of the chorus'. We can well believe it; from the text itself it is evident that he greatly relied on visual and aural effects for arresting and directing the attention of his audience. We may simply recall here what has been said already about such scenes as the entrance of the chorus in the *Septem,* the visual contrast between Prometheus and the Oceanids, the frenzied dance of Io, the wild movements, reflected in language and metre, of the Danaids upon the arrival of the Herald, the whole of Cassandra's part. In the *Choephori,* where so much of the verbal imagery recalls that of the *Agamemnon,* one can hardly miss the significance of a certain visual repetition. Orestes stands beside the two dead bodies: 'See the two tyrants of our country! How proudly they sat on the throne – and still are they joined together!' So also had Clytemnestra stood, on the same spot, over two dead bodies: 'There lies he, this woman's defiler; and she, too, his faithful partner on shipboard and in bed.'

For Aeschylus' attention to costume we may cite the oriental dress of the Danaids (*Supplices,* 234 ff.), and two dramatic changes of costume: one at the end of the *Oresteia,* when the Erinyes change into the Eumenides, putting off black and putting on purple; one in the *Persae,* when the Queen, who made her first entry with all royal pomp, returns (vv. 607–9) on foot, and in plain dress. Finally, anyone who has seen the *Agamemnon* performed will recall the sinister splendour of the rich tapestry as it is unrolled before Agamemnon, and how much the sheer colour adds to the drama of the moment.

These are meagre relics to have rescued from the vanished richness of the original productions, but at least they serve to show that the art of Aeschylus was indeed an art of the theatre and of drama, not of poetry only. Wherever we can still catch sight of his visual effects we can see that they are no mere decorative addition; Aeschylus thought of spectacle, poetry, movement, and presumably music, too, as partners, each reinforcing the others; each, on occasion, continuing the drama without the others.

CHAPTER V

Middle Tragedy: Sophocles

1. Introduction

Aeschylus is a profound religious dramatist, Euripides a brilliant, uneven representative of the new spirit which was so uncomfortable in the old forms, and Sophocles was an artist. We all know what an artist is: he is one who makes things which are beautiful or at least pretty, and if he is an artist of the right kind what he makes is good for us. Our public thinks like this, and so did the Greeks – with more excuse. Critics of the last century never ceased thanking Heaven that Sophocles believed in the Gods – their profound satisfaction lives on in the writings of examinees – and, assured that Sophocles was an artist of the right kind, they turned to the grateful and interesting task of examining and admiring his astonishing technique.

But an air of conventionality could be felt. Aeschylus has his religion, Euripides his views and his very tragic single-scenes; what was there to say about Sophocles except that his religion and politics were admirable and his art perfect? One concentrated on the art; indeed, when the *Electra* was mentioned one had to. The 'happy ending' of this play and its avoidance of moral strife were a little puzzling. The poet who also wrote the *Antigone* has been accused of a certain complacency, of a bluntness of moral perception, and the *Electra* has been explained by the assumption that Sophocles retired into the Homeric age to write it. It was said that Sophocles interested himself chiefly in the persons who did these things; he took the events for granted and studied the characters of the actors in them – as if one could study character in a moral vacuum.

This simple view of the artist brought other difficulties, and in spite of the close attention which Sophocles has received during the last twenty years some of them remain. The most troublesome, oddly enough, are structural. When Euripides fails to perform what is evidently the artist's first duty, to turn out a shapely play, we are not surprised; we may invent a series of special explanations, a different one for each offending play, or take refuge in a general theory of incompatibility or ineptitude, but we are not surprised. When Sophocles does the same thing we are perturbed; he did know better; yet the *Ajax* and the *Trachiniae* fall into two parts almost as badly as the *Andromache* and the *Hecuba*, and the end of the *Antigone* has been accused of throwing the play out of balance. Sophocles does not indeed descend to unrelated scenes, nor does he combine two distinct legends into one unsatisfactory plot, but the structure of the *Ajax* and the *Trachiniae*, since the plays were made by Sophocles, is at least as puzzling as that of the *Suppliant Women*, *Hecuba* or *Andromache*, which can plead the magic excuse 'Euripides'.

One way out of the difficulty was to say as little as possible about the *Antigone*, to think of special excuses for the *Ajax*, and to write off the *Trachininiae* as a total loss. Such criticism fails in all respects; especially does it fail to explain why the dichotomy is so unnecessarily absolute in the *Trachiniae*. A modern method is to call unsatisfactory plots diptychs or triptychs (which makes them sound better at once), and to suppose that there was a period in Sophocles' artistic career in which he thought that this was a reasonable, apparently the only reasonable, way of making drama. Therefore the *Trachiniae* is assigned by some scholars to a date near that of the *Ajax*; but in his methods of composition Sophocles was no more obedient to the calendar than Aeschylus had been.

The explanation that will be attempted here is that Sophocles, because he was a great artist, had something more important to do even than to make beautiful plays, namely to express as directly as his medium allowed certain tragic ideas which sprang out of a certain apprehension about human life. If he was only a technician with a bias towards beauty some of the 'faults' are quite inexplicable. Being a great dramatic artist he must, like Aeschylus, have had a tragic way of thinking; from this his drama sprang, to express this his plays were shaped. When a critic can improve a play of Sophocles', he may be sure that he is only giving it a turn that Sophocles had already rejected. If then we can penetrate, however dimly, to this bedrock of the dramatist's thought, we may hope to understand the plays more intimately.

We may hope for more. Τρεῖς δὲ καὶ σκηνογραφίαν Σοφοκλῆς, says Aristotle in his bald way: 'Sophocles introduced the third actor and scene-painting.' What explains the plays should explain, too, why Sophocles imposed on Greek Tragedy the form he did; questions of form and technique are fully resolved only when fully related to the mind of the artist who makes and uses them. What we should like to relate is Sophocles' introduction of the third actor, his interest in character and skill in drawing it, his marked leaning to irony in language and plot, his curtailment of the part of the Chorus, his typical tragic hero and plot – every element of his homogeneous art.

Before attempting this we may remove two obstacles. The first is to Sophoclean criticism what Aeschylus' religion is to Aeschylean; Sophocles' character-drawing is so important that it is often taken (not perhaps consciously, but in effect) to be the determinant thing. Thus one critic writes, in a blithe moment, 'He even alters and manipulates the mythic material so that he may the more readily and brilliantly practise his hobby.'[1] This does indeed fall short of blasphemy, but it overlooks the essential difference between Sophocles and Dickens. It has been argued that the three Creons are portraits of the same character – which may be true. But it is not true that 'it is hardly conceivable that so great an artist . . . primarily interested in the study and delineation of character, could have failed to see or could consciously have ignored the need for consistency in character'.[2] There is no such need: Sophocles was not creating a portrait-gallery. The only need is that each play should present as vividly as possible the tragic idea that lies behind it.

The other stumbling-block is the fact that most Greek theory of art is moral. The Greek theory of art is nothing to us, who are concerned exclusively with the Greek practice of art. There are as many possible theories of art as there are ways of regarding art; the Greeks regarded it from the moral point of view not because the Greek artist thought in a different way from any other but because their thought was predominantly political, and art, like drainage, undoubtedly performs some function in the state.[3] Sophocles was

---

[1] C. R. Post, *Harvard Studies*, 1912, p. 72.

[2] D. Peterkin, *Class. Philology*, 1929, p. 264.

[3] Mr. Belloc, in one of his prefaces, states that he wrote the book 'for gain'. This implies a financial theory of art, but it should not affect Mr. Belloc's literary critic.

no doubt aware that his plays were good for Athens (though the passage in the *Apology* suggests that he could not prove this to Socrates); he may have tried to make them such. But no amount of morals will make a good play, and no moral analysis will explain a play.

2. The 'Ajax'

It is very probable that this is the earliest of Sophocles' extant plays, produced perhaps as early as 450. Sophocles gained his first victory in 468, being then nearly thirty years old; the *Ajax* therefore is not the work of a novice. Criticism has been uneasy about it, for the reason that although the hero kills himself at v. 865 the play goes on for another 550 verses, introducing two fresh characters and a long and bitter dispute about his burial. The earliest criticism we possess is a scholium on v. 1123: Ἐκτεῖναι τὸ δρᾶμα θελήσας ἐψυχρεύσατο καὶ ἔλυσεν τὸ τραγικὸν πάθος, 'Wishing to extend the play Sophocles becomes a bore and dissipates the tragic tension.' Even if the judgement is sensible, the reason given is silly. Sophocles was not incompetent; had he wanted only to 'extend the play' he would have done it at the other end. There was no difficulty in making a reasonable play about Ajax: it could have begun with Ajax brooding over his supposed wrongs, coming to his decision to murder the judges, making his attack and failing in it (messenger speech), passing from the exultation of frenzy to the despair of sanity, and then killing himself. The question of his burial, if that were wanted, could then be raised and settled with reasonable dispatch.

It seems to be the almost universal assumption, shared by the scholiast, that the play is simply a play about Ajax. For example: 'Avec Ajax disparait l'interêt principal du drame, qui consistait surtout dans la peinture des êmotions diverses d'une âme heroique, confiante dans sa valeur jusqu'à l'excès, jusqu'à l'orgeuil impie. Dans la seconde partie de la pièce Teucre prend la place de son frère.'[1] In other words, the play is that familiar thing tragedy of character, of the Aristotelian kind. There are indications that Sophocles thought it was something bigger.

Ajax is by far the most impressive and the strongest character in the play. This is easily said, and is not true, for the strongest and most impressive character is Athena, and it against her that Ajax

[1] Dalmeyda, *Revue des Etudes grecques*, 1932, p. 8.

has pitted himself. However, it is not easy to think of a tragic hero anywhere who for sheer magnificence surpasses Ajax, whose fall gives a more poignant sense of tragic waste – unless it is Shakespeare's Coriolanus, who so much resembles him. But what led Sophocles to think, as presumably he did, that the vulgar Menelaus and the hardly less vulgar Agamemnon had some intelligible part to play in his tragedy?

It is a modern fashion to call the play a 'diptych'. This does not help us; it only says, in different words, that we do not find it a unity. We are assured that the Greeks attached great importance to burial – as we also do. But why should this persuade Sophocles to spoil a play? Because (we are told) Ajax was an Attic cult-hero; therefore he must have been buried, since hero-cults centre on the hero's tomb. But in the first place Ajax in the play is not a Hero but a man, just as he is in the *Iliad*; not a single word makes us think of him as anything else. Then, why present the future hero in such a way that his enemies have plausible reason for treating his body as offal? Again, burial is equally important in the *Antigone*, and Ajax resembles Polyneices to this extent, that he has made himself a public enemy who has imperilled the safety of all; Agamemnon thinks like Creon, and publishes the same decree: is there nothing in the parallel beyond the importance of burial? Certainly Polyneices was no cult-hero.

We are told that the final scenes are necessary because they 'rehabilitate' Ajax. But do they? And if they do, is the 'rehabilitation' demonstrably Sophocles' purpose in contriving them, or is it a by-product? Teucer does indeed tell Agamemnon what Ajax has done for him and the Greeks; Odysseus recalls, with gratitude, his services; but neither makes any attempt to palliate the crime, and, as we shall see, the arguments of Odysseus are concerned with much greater things than even the merits of Ajax. We are not fifth-century Greeks but moderns: may it not be that we are looking at the play from a point of view which is natural to us, but not necessarily that of Sophocles and his audience? We say 'The hero is guilty of presumption against the gods, and is punished for it'.[1] This is true, but it leaves us with Menelaus and Agamemnon embarrassingly on our hands. Is it the whole truth?

Xenophon, in his *Memorabilia* (IV, 4, 19–24), records some

[1] C. M. Bowra, *Ancient Greek Literature*, p. 93.

observations made by Socrates to Hippias on the 'divine' or 'unwritten' laws, and the way in which they differ from man-made laws: it is that with luck one can avoid being punished for breaking a human law, but never for breaking a divine law, such as the divine law forbidding incest, or enjoining gratitude to benefactors; and the reason is that when a divine law is infringed the punishment follows (as we should say) automatically. The incestuous union, so Socrates argues, inevitably produces weakly children, and ingratitude strips a man of true friends. Such is the way in which the gods punish offences against their laws. This is no Socratic paradox; it is exactly what we must infer from the *Antigone*. Creon is told that he has angered the gods and that they will punish him. The punishment comes precisely as Teiresias foretold; yet Sophocles makes it quite clear that Creon's ruin is the direct and natural outcome of what he, himself, has done to Antigone, Haemon, Eurydice. If we say of this and of other such instances that the gods are, in effect, the natural or inevitable course of things, we shall no doubt be omitting much, but we shall be stating an essential truth. Does this help us to make complete sense of the Ajax?

Ajax is drawn as being, with all his greatness, self-reliant to the point of arrogance. He knows his own merit; he will rely on this alone, and he will have it acknowledged. The 'gown of humility' would sit on him as ill as it does on Coriolanus. In his consideration for others he is not notable. Things must bend to his will; he must impose his own pattern on life. Of his pride, Menelaus talks angrily, and no one in the play contradicts him. As Bradley said of Coriolanus, he is an 'impossible person'. The judgement on the arms is the crisis. Was the award dishonest? Ajax, of course, says it was, and so do his men, the chorus; Sophocles does not. We may notice that Ajax dies with two prayers on his lips: that his body may first be found by Teucer, and that the gods may wreak ample vengeance for his wrongs on the Atreidae and the whole Greek army. The first prayer is answered; the second is not. The wrongs exist only in Ajax's own mind. He has received what is to him a shattering reverse and a deadly insult, and he cannot accommodate himself to it: his answer is to attempt a treacherous and frantic murder, the nemesis of his obstinate pride.

His 'impossibility' is presented also in religious terms, notably in the first scene where he is most pitiably a puppet in the hands of

Athena. This we understand more fully when the Messenger tells us how Ajax, twice, disdained the help of gods: he was strong enough to prevail alone. Twice, also, the Messenger says that Ajax is unable κατ' ἄνθρωπον φρονεῖν, 'think human thoughts', to recognize the limitations of humanity and to behave accordingly. There is much reason to suppose that this matter of κατ' ἄνθρωπον φρονεῖν was very much in Sophocles' mind when he was thinking out his play; time after time we are reminded of the conditions in which human life must be lived.

We may notice how often Sophocles refers to the instability of human things. Athena says: 'One single day can overthrow or raise up anything human' (131). Ajax himself (679–83) reflects that neither friendship nor enmity endure, and he is echoed in this by Odysseus (1359). Clearly akin to this is the great passage, in Ajax's 'ironical' speech, about the majestic rhythm of Nature: day follows night, summer follows winter, nothing remains steady for ever – and here we may remember that Athena's anger also will remain only for one day, though one day was enough for Ajax. The irony of the speech cuts deeper than some have seen. Life being like this, a matter of change, also of sudden reversals, what should our response be? Odysseus indicates one response, the wise one. Athena, pointing to Ajax in his humiliation, says: 'You see, Odysseus, the power of the gods?' Odysseus answers: 'Therefore, though he is my worst foe, I pity him, thinking as much of myself as of him; for I see that none of us who live is more than a phantom, an empty shadow'; to which Athena rejoins: 'Therefore shun pride; it is the wise that the gods cherish.' Pity, generosity, gratitude for what has been well done, forbearance towards injuries: these are what Odysseus urges in the final scene too, thinking here also, as he says, of himself, as well as of Ajax. To Agamemnon he deprecates the rigid (σκληρά) temper. Practising what he preaches, knowing that many a friend becomes an enemy, many an enemy a friend, he offers friendship to Teucer in the place of enmity; and it is a tragic moment when Teucer dares not allow Odysseus to touch the body, lest it anger the spirit of Ajax.

Ajax's response is utterly different; it is the impossible one. Hence the deep irony of the speech. He is completely sincere when he says that he is moved with pity for Tecmessa and his son; the quality of the poetry, if nothing else, can assure us of that. The grave irony is that he has put it out of his power to do anything for them; he can only hope that Teucer will be able to defend them. As winter 'makes room', ἐκχωρεῖ, for summer, as night 'gives place,' ἐξίσταται, for day, so must he now 'make room', 'get out of the way'. He would have life on his own terms; that being impossible he must now die. The gods whose help he disdained have been too strong for him.

The constant term of reference, clearly indicated by the presence of Athena in the first scene and by her intervention which saves the Atreidae and humiliates Ajax, is nothing less than the position o Man in the universe and the demands which this makes upon him, demands which he must meet, or perish. It is this that gives resonance to the grave and beautiful speech of Tecmessa (485 ff.). She speaks of the blind stroke of fate, the ἀναγκαία τύχη, which destroyed her fortunes; and she lets us see how she faced it. She, who has suffered and accepted such a reversal, is speaking to Ajax who has suffered a much less serious one. The juxtaposition is eloquent.

So, warned by Sophocles that this is the level on which we should try to respond to his play, we come to Menelaus. He is quite unnecessary to the plot; one son of Atreus would have been enough. But Sophocles apparently wanted him, and wanted him to be vulgar and mean. Why? In the *prologos* we saw the great Ajax humiliated; now we see him lying dead. There Athena spoke of pride, and Odysseus of pity; here we listen to Menelaus talking of revenge, and a revenge that is not only degrading to our common humanity, that so great a man should be so dishonoured in death, but is also empty; for as Odysseus says to Agamemnon, 'You cannot harm Ajax; you would only be infringing the gods' law' (1343–4). Sophocles makes Menelaus repeat ideas which we have met already in the play:

$$νῦν \ δ' \ ἐνήλλαξεν \ θεὸς$$
$$τὴν \ τοῦδ' \ ὕβριν$$

Now the god has brought reversal on his insolence (1058); ἕρπει παραλλὰξ ταῦτα, 'These things go by turns . . . Now *I* can show pride' (1087 f.) – which, as the chorus tells him, is more hybris. 'But for the gods,' he says, 'I should be a dead man.' Teucer's reply is swift: 'Then do not dishonour the gods who saved you.' In effect, the play has almost been asking the Socratic question: πῶς δεῖ ζῆν; 'How are we to live?' Not like Ajax, and certainly not like Menelaus.

Now Tecmessa and the child take their place as suppliants beside the body; it is the ultimate appeal of humanity, and it is rejected by Agamemnon, as it is by Creon in the other play, in the name of discipline and law. Again there are echoes. Agamemnon is scarcely less vulgar, and hardly more understanding, than Menelaus. He scorns Teucer for trying to champion one who is a man no longer, only a 'shadow' (1256); perhaps Sophocles thought we might remember what Odysseus had said: 'None of us who live is more than a phantom, an empty shadow.' Agamemnon says: 'It is not the strong and burly who prevail, but the wise ($oἱ φρονοῦντες εὖ$)'; perhaps we remember what Athena had said to Odysseus. Teucer can answer Agamemnon's insult with insults, not much more; but at least he commemorates the great deeds of Ajax and appeals to $χάρις$, 'gratitude' – and this also we have heard about before, when Tecmessa vainly appealed to $χάρις$, and to $αἰδώς$ mercy, in Ajax. We are all shadows; how should we treat each other?

These men leave us in despair. The great Ajax has met with the inevitable reversal that must come to one who cannot 'think human thoughts', and these lesser men have meaner thoughts. The catharsis that must come is brought by Odysseus, the man who stands closest to Athena. We are in the presence of death, the death of a great man, slain by his own hand; and Odysseus can respond worthily. He knows where hatred must end and pity begin; he knows that in the midst of change we must not be rigid, that enmity must not endure for ever, that we must remember benefits and forget injuries, that 'I too shall come to this', that the laws of the gods must prevail over transient human passions, or we shall all suffer. The final scenes are irrelevant to the *Ajax* as simply a tragedy of character; not to the *Ajax* as a Tragedy of Man.

3. The 'Antigone'

The *Antigone* is accused, though more gently, of the same fault as the *Ajax*: the heroine drops out half-way through and leaves us to do our best with Creon, Haemon, and their fortunes.[1]

We must recognize that if there is a fault it is a radical one, due to deliberate choice and not to oversight or to the inability of

---

[1] A critic of a Glasgow production of the *Antigone* in 1922 objected to the impressive cortège which escorted Haemon's body back to the stage because, emphasizing this shift in the centre of gravity, it underlined this fault in construction.

Sophocles to cope with a difficult situation. It is inevitable that
Antigone should disappear, but it is not inevitable that so little should
be said in the Exodus about her, that her lover's corpse but not hers
is brought back, that Creon should at such length lament his own
fate, least of all that Eurydice should be so unexpectedly introduced
in order to kill herself immediately. Why Eurydice? Sophocles had
no Elizabethan relish for corpses. She is relevant only to Creon.
Clearly the close of the play is all Creon, deliberately so, for there is
less of Antigone than might have been. Sophocles is not even making
the best of a bad job.

The difficulty that we feel arises from our regarding Antigone as
the chief character. If she is to this play what Oedipus and Electra are
to theirs (and the *Antigone* is often critized on this assumption), then
the play is ill-balanced, but if the *Antigone* is more like the *Ajax* than
the *Tyrannus,* the centre of gravity does not lie in one person, but
between two. The *Ajax* is second-rate Sophocles until we feel the
significance of Odysseus; the last part of the *Antigone* makes no
sense until we realize that there is not one central character but two,
and that of the two, the significant one to Sophocles was always
Creon. It is simply a matter of looking at the dramatic facts.[1] The
older criticism (for of late things have taken a turn for the better)
assumed that, of course, the play was about Antigone, and then set
about explaining away the last scenes. The most satisfactory proof
is performance. Creon can dominate the play; in the Glasgow
production he did, easily and naturally.[2] But even without performance, we may note that Creon's part is half as long again as
Antigone's, a point which is less mechanical than it sounds, and that
it is the more dynamic part. Hers is impressive and affecting enough,

---

[1] Purely formal criticism of Sophocles, by rule, is an impertinence. 'All arts aspire
to the condition of music'; what this means was illustrated by (I think) Schumann.
He was once asked by a man who had just heard him play one of his compositions
what it meant. 'I will tell you,' said Schumann, and he played it again. The form *was*
the meaning; and so it is with Sophocles – until it is shown that he was incapable of
expressing himself properly. Any fool could 'improve' the *Ajax,* but only by making
it mean something that Sophocles thought not worth saying. The disastrous notion
that the artist is one who makes pretty things has been 'the begininng of many evils
to the Greeks'.

[2] This was interesting. It was produced (Harrower's translation) in a large circus;
the ring became the orchestra and a narrow stage was erected at the back. Two
choruses were used, one to dance, the other placed on either side of the stage, to sing.
It ran for a week; on the first two nights the audience was all highbrow and paper
on the last two the populace was fighting to get in.

but his has the wider range and is the more elaborate. Her fate is decided in the first few verses and she can but go to meet it; most of the dramatic forces used in the play are deployed against Creon – the slight reserve with which the chorus receives his edict (211–14), the news that he has been defied, and that, too, by a woman, the opposition of Haemon, the disapproval of the city (691 ff.), the supernatural machinery of Teiresias, the desertion of the chorus (1098), the death of Haemon (foreshadowed), the death of Eurydice (unforeshadowed). Creon truly says

> Old sir, ye all like bowmen at a mark
> Let fly your shafts at me.[1]

Antigone is indeed opposed, but not like this. Her tragedy is terrible, but it is foreseen and swift; Creon's grows before our eyes.

This must have been the balance that Sophocles designed; whether this reading saves the play from fault is another matter. Perhaps modern minds make more of Antigone than was intended (though as the argument of Sallustius explains why the play was called the *Antigone* we may perhaps infer that ancients felt the difficulty too), perhaps Antigone upset Sophocles' plans as Dido is held to have upset Vergil's; it is most likely that Sophocles did precisely what he set out to do, and that in this play, as in the *Ajax,* he built on a double foundation.

As to this double foundation, in the change from the bipartite structure of the *Ajax,* through the much less prominent double interest of the *Antigone,* to the splendid unity of the *Tyrannus* and the *Electra,* it is natural for us to see a technical development; but something much more important than technique is involved, and it is not in fact easy to picture a Sophocles learning the rudiments of his art at the age of forty-five. As in the *Ajax,* it is a matter of finding the right point of view, the right distance. We have just spoken of the 'supernatural machinery of Teiresias' – but is it supernatural? He makes it plain that the unnatural behaviour of the birds and of the fat which would not burn – both contrary to Dike, the natural order – are the outcome and reflection of Creon's offences against Dike, 'the laws of the gods.' The gods are angry with Creon; their Erinyes will punish him; yet the punishment, as we saw above, descends on Creon as it were automatically, out of what he himself

[1] V. 1033. My verse translations from this play are taken from Harrower.

has done. The gods are not directing events as if from the outside; they work *in* the events.

This brings to life other details of the play. Haemon enters, doing his best to remain the loyal son. Creon insists that it is discipline and obedience that protect a family, and that Haemon's love for Antigone is of no account. So brutal is he that he threatens to kill Antigone there and then. When he has reduced Haemon to rage and despair, the chorus, the wise Counsellors who support Creon until Teiresias frightens them, sing about the invincible power of Aphrodite. Their meaning is that Love has betrayed the loyal son to such unfilial behaviour; but no Greek audience, believing in the reality of these gods, could fail to see the power of Aphrodite working against Creon at the tomb, when Haemon tries to kill him and then kills himself. Creon's inhumanity has served not to strengthen but to destroy his family.

Another point: it is a common error to suppose that in the burial of Polyneices the welfare of his soul is at stake. Not a word in the play suggests it. All the emphasis is laid on the mangling of the body (vv. 29 f., 205 f., 696–80). And why should the Guard, having mentioned the dust (256), go on to say that no bird or animal had touched the body? No 'dust' could be so effective – but this dust was. The chorus-leader thinks that the gods may be at work; Creon's furious reply shows that this may be the truth: 'What? Can the gods have any regard for the body of this traitor?' He has to learn later that they do care for it; they were working in what Antigone did. Are we not reminded of 'the god' who, out of season, froze the Strymon? This play, too, has its wide horizons. The conflict between Antigone and Creon is indeed vivid and poignant, but there underlies it a deeper one: that between Creon and the gods, between the tyrant and the ultimate realities. These the tyrant can defy, but they will recoil upon and crush him.

The *Antigone* has been variously interpreted. The transcendental philosophers, who, from Plato onwards, have never been at their ease with the tragic poets, have done their worst with it, and have been discomfited. It has been a problem-play, the poet's condemnation of contemporary statecraft, his confession of religious faith. What are the consequences of regarding it as primarily the tragedy of Creon?

First, I think we can afford to be reasonable about Antigone.

Hegel had to assume that there was something seriously wrong with her; later critics, rejecting this preposterous view, were nevertheless careful to maintain (partly out of deference to Aristotle) that Antigone was not spotless. People are never spotless, especially heroes and heroines of tragedies. Antigone's hardness to Ismene therefore was exploited to the full – but this, surely, was no very striking blemish, hardly enough to spoil a perfect figure. We saw, however, in dealing with Pelasgus that the ἁμαρτία doctrine must either be interpreted reasonably or amended; Pelasgus had no fault in the *Supplices* not because he was a perfect man but because his character was irrelevant; equally we need not be assiduous in looking for saving faults in Antigone, because only part of her character comes into question here, the part which impels her to defy Creon; and where the blemish is there, only Hegel can tell us. The play is not a full-length portrait of Antigone, in which, let it be granted, perfection would be a little uninteresting. Her part is to suffer, and there is no dramatic canon which demands that victims should have faults: hardness and decisiveness were given her to explain her rebellion and her suicide. The chief *agent* is Creon; his is the character, his the faults and merits, which are immediately relevant to the play. If Sophocles is really inviting us to watch Creon, Antigone becomes much more natural, relieved of the burden of Aristotelianism, no longer the standard-bearer of the Unwritten Laws. On this, the last day of her life, she can be spared faults, as she can be spared heroics. Why indeed does she defy Creon? From a sense of religious duty? To Ismene, in the prologue, she mentions religious duty once: in an attempt to shame her sister. Her real thought comes out in phrases like

> 'Αλλ' οὐδὲν αὐτῷ τῶν ἐμῶν μ' εἴργειν μέτα.—
> Τόν γ' οὖν ἐμὸν καὶ τὸν σόν, ἢν σὺ μὴ θέλῃς,
> ἀδελφόν.

He has no right to touch what is *mine*! –
Yes, my brother and – though you deny it – yours.

She has a passionate feeling of what is due to her brother, to her race. Face to face with Creon's legality she indeed answers legally, and nobly, inspired to her highest eloquence, but essentially she is doing much more than championing one code against another; she is giving her whole being for her brother's honour. This leads to the genuineness of vv. 911–30. The confrontation with Creon over, we hear little more of her religious faith; she protests her innocence indeed, but the burden of her defence is again that her brother is hers to honour. Her tone is noticeably more personal. As the end draws near her defences fail one by one, until, in that marvellously moving and tragic speech which was not to the taste of those who saw in Antigone chiefly a martyr to the Higher Law, she abandons everything except the fact that she did it and had to do it. Facing death, deserted by the Chorus, she has no confidence even in the gods, and doubts her own impulse. For a husband, she says, No; for a son, No; but for a brother –

Μητρὸς δ' ἐν Ἅιδου καὶ πατρὸς κεκευθότοιν
οὐκ ἔστ' ἀδελφὸς ὅστις ἂν βλάστοι ποτέ.

A frigid sophism borrowed from Herodotus? Yes, the finest borrowing in literature. This is the final tragedy of Antigone: *novissima hora est* – and she can cling to nothing but a frigid sophism.

If Antigone is more interesting than a mere antithesis to Creon, he is more than the stubborn fool who kills her. Sophocles was interested in his fate. He is, if not cruel, at least insensitive; like a tyrant, he is quick to suspect, and he does not know how to yield. But he has his own honesty, his own justification, and his own sense of responsibility. But what Creon is is not the whole of the story. We have this clear-cut issue between him and Antigone – itself a little too elementary to serve as the sole background for so subtle a thinker as Sophocles. We have, too, the clear-cut personal clash; it is noteworthy that from the beginning of her confrontation Antigone shows her contempt for this court. She wastes no time in trying to bridge what she knows to be an impassable gap. But behind all this there is the evolving tragedy of Creon. Creon may be what you like, but he is neither unintelligent nor irresponsible. He has his own field of action and his own principles; impulse, unwritten laws, are, he feels, not for him; he cannot move in this ampler region, and he sincerely feels he has no business to. In his own field he has thought things out and is confident of himself. We feel his confidence as soon as we hear his

Ἄνδρες, τὰ μὲν δὴ πόλεος . . .
Citizens, for what concerns the State . . .

He has tradition and experience on his side, his maxims are sensible. True, a native stubbornness is given him, that he may defend his position to the dramatic end, but it is not from folly or wilfulness that he originally takes up his position. But his confidence judgement was wrong; his reason betrays him. It is true that but for his obstinacy he could have escaped with a lighter penalty, but the bitterness is that his judgement was wrong, and that Antigone's instinct was right; and in the end he has less to cling to than she. She goes 'in the sure and certain hope That dear to thee will be my coming, Father';[1] he can say only

ἅπαντα λέχρια τἀν χεροῖν.
Everything is turned to water in my hands.

'By far the biggest part of happiness,' says the Chorus, 'is Wisdom (τὸ φρονεῖν).' And what is this? To reverence the gods, to respect, in all humility, those deep human instincts: respect for the dead, loyalty to one's kin, the love that joins a man to a woman – in a word, τοὺς καθεστῶτας νομους 'the laws established' (1113), for μέγας ἐν τούτοις θεὸς οὐδὲ γηράσκει,' a god is in them, and he grows not old' (O.T., 871).

4. The 'Electra'

This is a play which has troubled Sophoclean criticism more than any. As in the *Oresteia*, the central problem is a problem of δίκη, 'justice': what are we to think of the matricide? Very different answers have been given. Jebb held that it is to be accepted as right and glorious, as it was commanded by the god; that from the very first scene, in which the birds are singing their morning songs, 'it is the bright radiance of Apollo that prevails'; that Sophocles is inviting his audience to put itself at the Homeric standpoint, from which Orestes' act is seen to be one of simple merit.

This is quite impossible; all the dramatic facts are against it. The play does indeed open with dawn chasing away night, and with the cheerful songs of the birds, but from this point onwards it is sombre and unrelieved beyond any other play of Sophocles. The heroine, however much we may pity her, whatever her character may have been capable of, has become a harsh, unlovely

---

[1] Harrower's translation.

woman, a credit to her own mother, as she herself says (v. 609). There is no 'natural', like the Guard in the *Antigone,* or the messenger from Corinth in the *Tyrannus,* to relieve or at least vary the tension. There is no ecstatic dance, nor any other sort of ode that gives relief. The only cheerful scene, the Recognition, has for its undertone the passionate cry for vengeance, and is clouded by the terrible deed to come. The heroine's part leads logically and implacably to her last scenes: she stands on guard outside the palace while Orestes is killing their mother within, and when Clytemnestra's death-cry is heard, she shouts 'Strike her again, if you have the strength!' Then, when Aegisthus is confronted with his wife's dead body, and tries to parley, she cries 'In god's name, let him say no more. Kill him at once! Throw his body to the dogs! Nothing less can compensate me for what I have endured.' It is a grim and a bloody business, and Sophocles does not try to pretend that it is anything else.

This interpretation will not do – and those who respect Sophocles need not regret it; for had Sophocles, for once, nothing of importance to say to his fellow-citizens, that he should invite them to get into an archaic frame of mind, and pretend that the murder of a mother was a deed of simple merit, in order to enjoy some poetry, stage-craft, and character-drawing? We would rather suppose, if we can, that Sophocles once more had something of significance to say.

The exactly opposite view has been taken by Sheppard.[1] He argues that Apollo did not approve of the vengeance; that Orestes, in asking him not whether he should do it, but how – presuming on the god's compliance – was falling into an elementary blunder, like Glaucus in Herodotus; and that the indignant god lets the impious man go ahead and take the consequences. But this view is obstructed by as many obstacles as the other. Bowra has mentioned several,[2] but there is another which seems decisive – and just as decisive against the interpretation that was offered in the first edition of this book, that Sophocles carefully dissociates Apollo from the vengeance. Both of these interpretations disfigure what is perhaps the most important and exciting moment of the play.

Clytemnestra comes out of the palace to sacrifice to Apollo. She has been frightened, as we know, by a dream, the significance of

[1] *Classical Review,* 1927, pp. 2 ff.
[2] *Sophoclean Tragedy,* 216 ff.

which is perfectly plain: the rightful heir will recover his throne. This already shows how Sophocles is thinking; for if the dream does not mean that the gods are interested in the punishment of Clytemnestra, it is a mere coincidence – leading to nothing in particular, since its effect on the plot is slight. But if the gods are interested, then the dream and its results are momentous. For Clytemnestra comes out, intending to sacrifice to Apollo; but the harsh quarrel with Electra intervenes. 'Cannot you even allow me to sacrifice in proper silence, after I have let you have your say?' Electra promises to keep the silence necessary for the rite. Clytemnestra, with her attendants, advances to the altar. The audience, too, must observe a reverent silence; and the holy rite begins. Clytemnestra places her offerings on the altar and puts fire to the incense. As she does so she prays – a prayer of unexampled blasphemy; for she prays that she may continue to enjoy what she won by murder and has protected by adultery, and that her son may never return to avenge his father, but may die first – though this is a prayer that she shrinks from putting into words. Such is the petition that she thinks fit to offer to the god of purity. There is a pause; we watch the incense rising to Heaven with this prayer. The silence is broken by the arrival of a man with news: Orestes is dead, killed in a chariot-race – and at Delphi. Unless we can persuade ourselves that this impressive scene and its immediate sequel were contrived by Sophocles only as a piquant turn in the plot – and that he was so pleased with it that he used it twice, here and in the *Tyrannus* – we must see in it, as the original audience must surely have seen, the hand of the god. Apollo has heard the terrible prayer, and swiftly sends the fitting answer, a false message, designed to lure Clytemnestra to her death.

But the messenger was coming anyhow; his coming was arranged by Orestes in the prologue. Similarly in the *Tyrannus*: the messenger's arrival at that precise moment, as if in answer to the innocent prayer of Iocasta, seems to betray the agency of the god; yet Sophocles goes out of his way there to tell us that this man has come, post-haste from Corinth, entirely for his own profit. In both these plays, as elsewhere in Greek poetry,[1] the action is seen on two planes at once, human and divine.

A satisfactory interpretation of the play, then, must explain convincingly several difficult points. Besides – as always – accounting

[1] See Jaeger, *Paideia,* I, 52 (English edn.).

logically for the general style of the play – for the elaborate character-drawing for instance – it must explain this dual plane on which
the action seems to move. It must explain why an action which is
necessarily shocking, and which is presented so starkly, with no
attempt at glorification and no hint of future punishment, can be
countenanced by the god, and that, too, without any criticism or
defence from the dramatist. It must also, if we are to regard the
Electra as a first-rate play, make its religious or philosophical content
something of importance, and not leave it a mere exercise in
character-drawing and play-making. Finally, we would like our
interpretation to explain the conspicuous detail on which Sheppard
fastened, that Apollo does *not* command Orestes to kill Aegisthus
and his mother.

Bowra's treatment of the play, valuable though it is in many
ways, does not seem to satisfy these demands. It is, in brief, that
justice must be done; that this is sometimes a painful task to him
who has to do it; but that when it is done, in this play, and order is
restored, a new force of love arises. But, in the first place, had
Sophocles wished to show the re-establishment of order and of love,
he could not have ended the *Electra* as he did, with these two
grim scenes, with Electra crying 'Strike her again, if you have the
strength,' and 'Throw his body to the dogs'. Surely somebody, at
some time, must have told Sophocles that Greek tragedies end
quietly, somewhere beyond the climax. Had he meant this, he must
have added a quiet scene to show order and love gathering strength.
A concluding tag from the chorus cannot possibly efface from our
minds the grimness and horror of these final scenes. In the second
place, though the punishment of crime may sometimes be painful,
in no civilized society can it involve anything so hideous as matricide. With what intention then did Sophocles take this mythical
situation, without either condemning it, as Euripides did, or explaining it, as Aeschylus did, as an unsatisfactory but transient phase
in the struggle for justice?

Since the problem concerns a god, and Justice, we may remind
ourselves that the word θεός may have a very different complexion
from the word 'god', and that 'justice' may be a very indifferent
translation of the word δίκη. Ares, to take an extreme case, was a
θεός, but he was often spoken of in terms that we reserve for the
Devil. Certainly Apollo was no Ares, but for all that in thinking

of 'the god Apollo' we may unconsciously assume a degree of 'godliness' which is not there, so ingrained in us is the idea of a personal, beneficent god. As Grube has pointed out,[1] θεός always implies 'a power', and may imply no more than that. As for δίκη, whatever the origin of the word may have been, an early meaning of it was simply 'the way' of something, hence 'the right way'. In Aeschylus it is a moral and social word, 'retributive justice' in the *Agamemnon,* mellowing into 'justice' as things improve. But the Ionian philosophers could use δίκη and its opposite, ἀδικία, in an amoral sense, as when Anaximander said that 'things are continually paying retribution (τίσις) to each other' τῆς ἀδικίας, for their 'injustice'. Philosophers who did not make our sharp distinction between the physical and the moral could call δίκη what we call 'the balance of forces of Nature', 'the law of averages', and the like. If there is too much wet now, there will be too much dry later on; wet will pay to dry retribution (τίσις) τῆς ἀδικίας, for its encroachment; and so δίκη, the proper balance, will be restored.

What if Sophocles' δίκη has in it something of this conception? What if his θεοί, and Apollo, their intermediary with men, are conceived as 'the powers' who protect his δίκη? We will assume – in order to see what happens – that in the *Electra* δίκη means 'the proper and natural order of things', not now in the physical universe, but in human affairs, moral and social. If the proper order is disturbed by some violence (ἀδικία), it must, in the nature of things, restore itself, somehow; the restoration of the balance is an act of δίκη because it re-establishes δίκη. If so, we need not expect the act of δίκη to be agreeable in itself; the deluge that ends a drought may itself do harm.

Clytemnestra, in murdering Agamemnon, violently disturbed the natural order. This was an action bound, in the nature of things, to provoke an equivalent reaction – unless indeed all concerned should acquiesce in the ἀδικία. As the action was hideous, so there is no reason to expect that the reaction should be lovely. Why should it be? The ἀδικία caused a wound; δίκη may involve an amputation. To see that δίκη is re-established is the concern of the gods, as well as of men. In the *Electra* it is re-established – and how? By a perfectly natural process. We have three people to consider, the three surviving children of Agamemnon. Chrysothemis is no impressive

---

[1] *The Drama of Euripides,* pp. 41 ff.

figure. She can acquiesce; so far as she is concerned, ἀδικία can continue. The hero and heroine are not like this. Orestes cannot and
will not spend his life living in exile, on charity; he is determined
to recover his patrimony (as Sophocles is careful to tell us, even to
the point, apparently, of showing us a view of this patrimony on his
painted περίακτοι). He asks Apollo how he is to set about it; and
the reason why he is not commanded by the god, as he is in Aeschylus, is precisely that Sophocles wishes to represent the act of δίκη as
the natural, even inevitable, outcome of the original crime. A
disinherited son *will* do this, unless he is a coward. Action provokes
its reaction; this is δίκη, and the act of δίκη is conceived and carried
out entirely by the human actors, from natural motives and by
natural means. The third child, Electra, is like Orestes, unable to
acquiesce; and in her we see a different aspect of this reaction. Her
character, in her situation, makes it inevitable that she should live
for vengeance; that is the reason why this character and situation
must be described in such detail.

So, as these two are great enough to resent and resist ἀδικία, the
hour comes and δίκη is achieved. We are not obliged to admire the
deed – Orestes himself clearly does not – nor to see in it the institution of a new and better order of things – about which Sophocles is
silent. A violent disturbance of δίκη has been violently annulled.
It is the nature of things, and Sophocles invites us to see in this the
working of a natural law.

But what of Apollo, and the two planes? If the whole action is
complete on the human plane, is not the god a superfluous addition?
By no means. Apollo's part is of the utmost significance. He does not
affect the action in the least; he neither commands nor assists
Orestes; but he does, as it were, accompany the action on his own
plane. When Orestes has at last decided to act, Clytemnestra has her
dream – and it would be stultifying to suppose that this is mere
coincidence. Orestes is an autonomous agent; but the gods are
moving on a path parallel to his. Even more significant is the arrival
of the Paedagogus at that particular moment. On the human plane,
this is a move that we are expecting; but the fact that he comes just
when he does, as if in answer to that prayer, suggests to our minds
that Apollo is working here, independently of the Paedagogus and
of Orestes. In other words, what Orestes and Electra are doing,
though an action complete and intelligible in itself, is at the same

time part of a larger design, the will of the gods, the principle of δίκη, the universal law. It is not merely a private matter, a particular case (see below, pp. 167 ff.).

Now we can see why Sophocles could take this, the most questionable part of the Pelopid legend, and present it, by itself, as an action that needed neither defence nor sequel. He is as far as possible from being 'literary' and archaistic, asking us to make impossible assumptions for the sake of some trifling dramatic effects, like character-drawing and strong scenes. He is demonstrating a law in things, that violence must produce its recoil; and the fact that the δίκη here is so grim and unrelieved is a measure of the hideousness of the original offence. That the actual form of the vengeance here is one that could not occur in civilized society is immaterial; the underlying law that it illuminates is true for all time.

One point remains, the explanation given by Electra of the sacrifice of Iphigeneia.[1] It is conspicuously different from the explanation given by Aeschylus. In the *Agamemnon* Artemis holds up the fleet because, for pity, she objects to the expedition; she is 'angry with the winged hounds of her father'. She gives Agamemnon the choice between sacrificing his daughter and going home; if he is bent on playing the part of a devouring eagle, let him first devour an innocent child of his own, and take the consequences. In the *Electra* the position is entirely different. In the first place, Artemis is a Sophoclean, not an Aeschylean, deity; her motives are quite amoral. Agamemnon offends her by killing one of her stags and boasting about it. He was at fault, but the goddess hits back implacably and, by human standards, unreasonably. She acts as Athena does with Ajax, when he offends her; she acts as electricity does, if an incautious tinkerer makes a mistake. In the second place, Sophocles' Agamemnon had no choice at all, for we are told 'There was no escape for the army, either homeward or to Troy' (vv. 573 f.). Agamemnon therefore was to be pitied much more than blamed, and Clytemnestra has much less justification than she had in the *Oresteia*. The reason for this difference of treatment is clear. Aeschylus wanted her crime to be the direct result of the similar crime of Agamemnon, its punishment and its continuation; Sophocles wanted it to be a wanton and unjustified disturbance of δίκη, to be avenged, once and for all, by its inevitable recoil.

[1] Vv. 563 ff.

5. The 'Oedipus Tyrannus'

The story of the *Tyrannus* is of a common Greek type; something unpleasant is predicted, the persons concerned try to avert it and think themselves safe, but in some natural though surprising fashion the prediction is fulfilled. Next to the *Tyrannus* itself, the most elaborate example is the story of Astyages and the infant Cyrus in Herodotus. What does Sophocles make of this ancient motif?

At the beginning of the play Oedipus is the great King who has saved Thebes in the past and is their only hope now; no one can compare with Oedipus in reading dark secrets. At the end, he is the polluted outcast, himself the cause of the city's distress, through crimes predicted by Apollo before he was born. Is this grim determinism? Is Sophocles telling us that Man is only the plaything of Fate? Or does he mean, as Bowra suggested,[1] no more than that the gods have contrived this awful fate for Oedipus in order to display their power to man and to teach him a salutary lesson? Or is Sophocles simply making exciting drama, leaving the philosophical implications unexplored? There is only one way of finding out. Whatever Sophocles meant, he put his meaning into the play, and to get it out again we must contemplate the play – all of it, in all its aspects; not bits of it, and some of its aspects.

As in the *Electra,* the action shows a certain duality. In the foreground are autonomous human actors, drawn vividly, and complete. Oedipus himself, Teiresias, Creon, Iocasta, and the two shepherds, are all as lifelike as characters in a play can be; and so, in their degree, are the remoter characters who do not appear – the hot-tempered Laius at the cross-road, and the unknown Corinthian who insulted Oedipus when he was half-drunk. The circumstances, too, are natural, even inevitable, granted these characters. Oedipus, as we see him time after time, is intelligent, determined, self-reliant, but hot-tempered and too sure of himself; and an apparently malignant chain of circumstances combines now with the strong, now with the weak side of his character to produce the catastrophe. A man of poor spirit would have swallowed the insult and remained safe in Corinth, but Oedipus was resolute; not content with Polybus' assurance he went to Delphi and asked the god about it, and when the god, not answering his question, repeated the warning

---

[1] *Sophoclean Tragedy,* p. 175.

given originally to Laius, Oedipus, being a man of determination, never went back to Corinth. It was a coincidence, but not an unnatural one, that Laius was on his way from Thebes to Delphi. They met at the cross-road, and as father and son were of similar temper the disaster occurred. Even so, he could have arrived at Thebes safely, had he not been a man of high intelligence; for then he could not have read the riddle of the Sphinx. But again, though intelligent, he was blind enough to marry a woman old enough to be his mother, certain that his mother was in Corinth. The story is not moralized. Sophocles could have put Oedipus in the wrong at the cross-road; he could have suggested that blind ambition made him accept the crown and Queen of Thebes. He does neither of these things; Oedipus is not being given his deserts by an offended Heaven. What happens is the natural result of the weaknesses and the virtues of his character, in combination with other people's. It is a tragic chapter from life, complete in itself, except for the original oracle and its repetition. Sophocles is not trying to make us feel that an inexorable destiny or a malignant god is guiding the events.

But we are made to feel, as in the *Electra,* that the action is moving, at the same time, on a parallel and higher plane.

The presence of some power or some design in the background is already suggested by the continuous dramatic irony – which seems overdone, if it is regarded as only a dramatic effect. In the matter of the Plague this hidden power is definitely stated; and its presence is most imaginatively revealed, as in the *Electra,* in the scene containing Iocasta's sacrifice. She who has been so sceptical of oracles surprises us by coming out with sacrificial offerings. She lays them on Apollo's altar, puts fire to the incense, and prays for deliverance from fear. There is a moment of reverent silence, and this is broken by the arrival of the cheerful messenger from Corinth: Polybus is dead; fear is at an end; the prayer has been heard. But within the hour Iocasta has hanged herself. – And what of her offerings? Still there, on the altar, in full view of the audience; the incense, it may be, still carrying to the god a petition that he has so terribly answered.

This is no theatrical trick, but a revelation of the dramatist's thought. It is the action of the unseen god made manifest. But how does the god answer the pitiful prayer of Iocasta, the impious prayer of Clytemnestra? Not by any direct interposition. The Apollo of

Sophocles is nothing like the Zeus of Aeschylus, who works his will by freezing the Strymon or by blasting a fleet. It was not Apollo who incited the Corinthian to come, but his own eagerness to be the first with the good news, and his own hopes (as Sophocles is careful to tell us) of standing well with the new King; for besides the news of his succession to the crown he has another and a much more exciting tale to tell – in his own good time. He, like the Paedagogus, is completely autonomous, yet in the coming of each the hand of the god is seen. The action moves on two planes at once. Nevertheless, the whole texture of the play is so vividly naturalistic that we must be reluctant to interpret it as a bleak Determinism. These people are not puppets of higher powers; they act in their own right. Nor, I think, does this texture encourage us to accept Bowra's explanation.

In the first place, if Sophocles meant that the gods are displaying their power because they will, that they have ordained this life for Oedipus in order to read men a lesson, it was so easy for him to say so – to write an ode on the power and the mysterious ways of the gods. He conspicuously does not do this. Indeed, in the ode that immediately follows the catastrophe the chorus says not that the fate of Oedipus is a special display of divine power, but on the contrary that it is typical of human life and fortunes.

In the second place, although Oedipus is by far the greatest sufferer in the play he is not the only one. There are others who suffer, not by any means in the same degree, but in the same way; and we must take account of them too, not dismiss them as being parts of the dramatic economy but not of the thought. If we contemplate, as we should, the whole play and all its aspects, we see that Oedipus is not a special case, except in the degree to which he suffers; he is, as the Chorus says, typical; what has happened to him is part of the whole web of human life. Why for example does Sophocles introduce the children in the last act? Not simply because it is 'natural'; a good play isn't 'nature', but art. One reason must be that Oedipus may say to them what he does say: 'What a life must yours be! Who will admit you to the festivals? Who will marry you – born as you were born?' Such is life, such are the gods. The innocent suffer with the guilty.

We must contemplate also two other characters who form no inconsiderable part of the play – the two shepherds. It was not merely to liven up his play, or to indulge his talents, that Sophocles drew them like this, with their motives, hopes, fears, so sharply presented. The Corinthian, like the Paedagogus, makes no bones about expecting a tip; not for the reason that Headlam so oddly gave,[1] that it was the oriental custom to reward messengers (as if dramatists were only photographers), but because the point bears on the drama. The news that this man brings is great news indeed, but he has something much more astonishing in reserve, and the moment for producing it soon comes. 'Polybus? He was no more your father than I am. . . . Why, I gave you to him with my own hands. . . . A hired shepherd? Yes, my son; but that day I saved your life.' A hired shepherd – but this is a great day for him; he began by addressing Oedipus as 'My Lord', but now he can say 'My son'. 'No, *that* I cannot tell you. . . . You must find the Theban who gave you to me. . . .' Iocasta's last despairing shriek does not disturb him, for, as Oedipus says, probably she is dismayed to find that her husband is of low birth. The chorus is happy and excited; and when the reluctant Theban is brought in, our friend becomes even more bland and helpful, as he works up to his climax:

> *Here is the man, my friend, who was that baby!*

And this is his last speech. No reward for him; no glory in Corinth – only bewilderment and utter dismay; for in a moment he hears, from his old companion,

> *I pitied it, my lord. I thought to send*
> *The child abroad, whence this man came. And he*
> *Saved it, for utter doom. For if you are*
> *The man he says, then you were born for ruin.*

He sees his new King rush into the palace; and then – the final ode? Not yet. These two actors have to make their exit, by the long side-passages, in full view of the audience; some forty yards of exit. And as we watch them stumbling out we have time to reflect that this is the outcome, for them, of their merciful interest in an abandoned baby.

Is not this, too, the work of Apollo? Here, as in the greater case of Oedipus, is that conjunction of well-meant action with a situation which makes it lead to disaster. An act of mercy, tinged with a

---

[1] See G. Thomson, *Oresteia*, II, 69 (note to v. 591).

perfectly honest shrewdness, leads the Corinthian to the verge of what is, for him, greatness; as he stretches out his hand, eagerly and with confidence, it turns into horror.

The other shepherd, too, is one who refused to kill a baby. Part of his reward comes years later, when he sees the man who killed Laius ascend his victim's throne and marry his Queen – an event which sends him, for his own safety, into half-exile;[1] the rest of his reward comes now, when a sudden command brings him back at last to the city, to learn what he learns here.

These minor tragedies, of the children and the shepherds, are all of a piece with the major one. This is Apollo; this is life. An awful sin is committed in all innocence; children are born to a life of shame; virtuous intentions go awry. What are we to think of it? Of course, moral and prudential lessons can be drawn from it – though Sophocles draws very few – but what do we think of it? Where is the explanation? What, in other words, is the catharsis? That Oedipus accepts his fate? But when you are knocked flat, you must accept it; and if you cannot get up again, you must be resigned. There is little illumination in this.

The catharsis that we are looking for is the ultimate illumination which shall turn a painful story into a profound and moving experience. It has been suggested by Professor Ellis-Fermor[2] that the catharsis of plays like the *Tyrannus* and *Macbeth* lies in the perfection of their form, which, by implication, represents the forces of righteousness and beneficence, of which Aeschylus speaks directly, in his choric odes. This is manifestly true of the *Tyrannus*.

Let us go back to Iocasta's sacrifice, and Apollo's swift and devastating answer. In the corresponding passage of the *Electra* the point was clear. Clytemnestra prayed that injustice, ἀδικία, might triumph, and she got the answer she deserved. What of Iocasta? She has been denying the truth of oracles. Was Sophocles then so fiercely orthodox that he could equate Iocasta's scepticism with Clytemnestra's wickedness? Of course not; this was not the size of Sophocles' mind. He means much more than this. Iocasta has said 'Why should we fear oracles, when there is no such thing as forethought (πρόνοια)? Best live at random, as one may' – a doctrine

---

[1] For he, no bought slave, but reared in the palace (v. 1123), besought Iocasta to send him into the fields, as far as possible from the city (vv. 758 ff.).

[2] *Frontiers of Drama*, p. 133.

which would deny the very basis of all serious Greek thought; for while Greek life was still healthy and stable, the Greek believed, as if by instinct, that the universe was not chaotic and 'irrational', but was based on a λόγος, obeyed Law. The Ionian philosophers did not discover, but rather postulated, this λόγος.

The tragic poets too think in this way – as Whitehead saw, when he said that they, rather than the Ionians, were the first scientific thinkers. In Aeschylus we find moral laws which have the same sort of validity as physical and mathematical laws. The doer must suffer; ὕβρις leads to Atê; the problem there – a problem for gods as well as for men – is to find a system of Justice that will fit into this framework without disastrously contravening these laws. To the mind of Sophocles this λόγος shows itself (as we shall see more fully in the next chapter) as a balance, rhythm, or pattern in human affairs. 'Call no man happy until he is dead,' for the chances of life are incalculable. But this does not mean that they are chaotic; if so they seem to us, it is because we are unable to see the whole pattern. But sometimes, when life for a moment becomes dramatic, we can see enough pattern to give us faith that there is a meaning in the whole. In the *Antigone,* when Creon is overwhelmed, it is by the natural recoil of his own acts, working themselves out through the minds and passions of Antigone and Haemon, and we can see in this a natural justice. In the *Electra,* the vengeance that at last falls on the assassins is linked to their crime by natural chains of cause and effect. In the *Tyrannus* we have a much more complex picture. The same δίκη is at work, though this time the ἀδικία which it avenges was involuntary and indeed innocent. Oedipus – to repeat our image – is blasted as a man may be who inadvertently interferes with the natural flow of electricity. Δίκη here works through many apparently casual and unrelated actions – of the shepherds, of the charioteer who tried to push Oedipus off the road, of the man at the banquet. . . . Things fall out contrary to all expectation; life seems cruel and chaotic. Cruel, perhaps; chaotic, no – for if it were chaotic no god could predict, and Iocasta would be right. 'If these oracles are not manifestly fulfilled, why should I join in the sacred dance?' Piety and purity are not the whole of the mysterious pattern of life, as the fate of Oedipus shows, but they are an important part of it, and the doctrine of chaos would deny even this. The pattern may harshly cut across the life of the individual, but at least we know that it exists, and we may feel assured that piety and purity are a large part of it.

Every detail in the *Tyrannus* is contrived in order to enforce Sophocles' faith in this underlying λόγος; that is the reason why it is true to say that the perfection of its form implies a world-order. Whether or not it is beneficent, Sophocles does not say.[1]

---

[1] (Note to 3rd. edition). There is more than this to say about the *Tyrannus*, and it depends on a scrutiny of the structure of the play. See therefore pp. 174–185 below.

CHAPTER VI

The Philosophy of Sophocles

We found, in the *Electra* and the *Tyrannus,* the two related ideas of a δίκη that is not necessarily 'Justice', and of a rhythm or pattern in human affairs. Are these ideas peculiar to these plays, or are they found elsewhere in Sophocles?

We may begin with a special case of pattern. How often in Sophocles do we find the idea that the dead are killing the living? Of the seven plays there are only two in which this idea is not found – and they are the late plays, the *Philoctetes* and the *Coloneus.* Here are the five instances. Ajax and Hector, bitter enemies, exchange gifts (vv. 817 ff.). Ajax received Hector's sword – and kills himself with it. Teucer says (vv. 1027 ff.) 'Did you see how at last, even from the grave, Hector was to destroy you?' Then Teucer goes on to tell how Hector, for his part, was killed by means of the belt which he had received from Ajax – modifying the Homeric account in order to make the parallel. He concludes 'All these things, I would say, are contrived for men by the gods'; that is to say, we have much more here than mere coincidence. From the *Ajax* we turn to the *Antigone,* and there (v. 871) we find Antigone saying, of Polyneices, 'Ah, it is your dead hand that has taken away life from me!' In the *Electra* (vv. 1417 ff.), 'The dead live. Those slain long ago will drain from their slayers αἷμα παλίρρυτον' – literally, 'blood flowing in the reverse direction.' In the *Tyrannus* (v. 1451) Oedipus beseeches Creon to drive him into Cithaeron, 'which my parents, when they lived, appointed to be my tomb; that I may die at the hands of those who tried to slay me.' And finally, in the *Trachiniae,* we have a full-scale presentation. The Centaur Nessus, in mid-stream, insults Deianeira; Heracles, from the bank, shoots him with a poisoned arrow. It is this poison, innocently administered by Deianeira as a love-philtre, that kills Heracles and avenges Nessus – and not only Nessus, for the poison was in origin the blood of the

Hydra whom Heracles had slain. In this elaborate instance we may observe, first, that the whole course of things was darkly foretold by an oracle of Zeus (vv. 1161 ff.), and second, that it is significantly linked with what is, in this play, the weak spot in Heracles' character, his reckless passion for women. This double revenge of the dead on the living is, then, no mere coincidence; it is a pattern woven into the very fabric of things.

So that in all these five plays we find, more or less prominent, the idea of a rhythm or recoil. Things are not, in the long run, left unbalanced. In the *Electra* it is clearly Justice; elsewhere it may not be Justice – for why should Heracles not have killed the Hydra and Nessus? – but it is δίκη.

We may go a little further. The speech in which Ajax announces that he has changed his mind, and will submit to the Atreidae, is full of parallels from Nature:

> *All things doth long, innumerable Time*
> *Bring forth to light, and then again conceal . . .*

Winter gives place to summer, night to day, storm to calm, and the sleeper awakes. Why then, he says, should I, too, not yield? – That is, an eternal rhythm pervades the universe, and man is part of it. So, in the similar speech that Oedipus makes in the *Coloneus*,[1] nothing remains the same, either in Nature or among men. Πάντα ῥεῖ, everything is in flux; not in a straight course, but to and fro. Today's friend is tomorrow's enemy, and today's enemy tomorrow's friend.

This idea of a universal rhythm, ruling in the physical world and in human affairs, alike, appears, too, in Sophocles' formal similes, and gives them additional weight; as for example when Haemon reminds Creon that it is the branches which bend that are not broken. This is not mere illustration, but an appeal to Law. And it may not be too fanciful to see in this habitual way of thought the origin of what was surely Sophocles' favourite word, σύμμετρος and its congeners.

A correlative of this, most imaginatively enforced in the *Tyrannus*, is that the complexities of life are not due to chance. None of these other plays give us this idea so strikingly, but it is implicit in all. Every one of them has its oracle or prophecy which is fulfilled, and it is surely self-evident that what can be predicted is not directed by

[1] *O.C.*, 607 ff.

chance. The universe – including, again, human affairs – is rational, even though we may not be able to see the *ratio*, the λόγος, except imperfectly and rarely. As in the *Tyrannus,* the gods only predict; they do not compel.[1] As in the *Tyrannus* and the *Electra,* we have a conjunction of gods who predict and humans who are entirely autonomous. The denial of chance is implied in the prophecies; it is implied, too, in the last verse of the *Trachiniae*: 'Nothing is here but Zeus'; and it is very clear in the *Antigone.* For the Messenger, coming in with his news of the sudden overthrow of Creon's prosperity, remarks (vv. 1158 ff.), 'It is chance that exalts the lowly and overturns the prosperous'; but we, who have been in the play from the beginning, can see that it is nothing of the sort. It is not chance, but δίκη.

It is another of the strands that bind all these plays together that δίκη in the *Antigone* works exactly as in the *Electra,* not by divine intervention, but by the natural course of events. In each play, ἀδικία is committed; that Creon acted out of honest motives, Clytemnestra and Aegisthus out of guilty ones, makes no difference. Each ἀδικία might have continued indefinitely – perhaps – except that in each case there were those intimately concerned who were great enough to oppose it, at whatever risk; and in each play the greatness of the heroine is indicated by the contrast with a sister, an ordinary 'nice girl', who is willing to accept the ἀδικία. We have seen how impossible this was for Electra, with her temperament, and in her situation; impossible, too, for Orestes, whom every motive of filial piety, personal honour, and self-interest impelled to punish the criminals and recover his rights. So it is with Antigone. Natural piety, loyalty to her kin, love of her brother, everything that is in her character impels her to defy Creon's edict. Everything that is in his character impels him to exact his pound of flesh, and the fact that his son happens to love Antigone confirms him in his obstinacy, and becomes, too, the pivot on which the catastrophe turns. The admired logic of Sophocles' plots is not merely a dramatic merit; it is the reflection of the logic that he sees in the universe; this is the way in which δίκη works.

Before we continue, we should consider a question which the last paragraph suggests: what happens if there is not someone at

---

[1] In the *Ajax* Athena makes Ajax mad. This is the only case of direct divine intervention.

hand who is impelled to oppose the ἀδικία? Is δίκη then not attained,
the balance not restored? The answer to this question comes from
the *Tyrannus* and the *Antigone*. In the *Tyrannus* the ἀδικία – the
slaying of a father and marriage with a mother – was not even suspected, much less purged. Therefore it went on festering, as it were,
in the body politic, undetected, until at last it issued as a physical
plague. Something similar is suggested by Teiresias in the *Antigone,*
when he tells Creon that those cities will rise against him in enmity
whose hearths are being defiled by the birds and dogs that have fed
on the flesh of Polyneices. In one way or another δίκη must assert
itself; if not by the act of man, then by the compulsion of nature.
Human affairs, as we have seen already, are part of a universal
λόγος; the moral and the physical are not divided.

In the *Antigone* and the *Electra* we are concerned with that part
of δίκη which coincides with moral 'justice'; in the *Tyrannus* we
are in a region beyond, where δίκη is not exclusively moral.
Χρόνος δικάζει, Time avenges, things done by Oedipus in complete
innocence; an idea which no doubt offends our sense of Justice, yet
is true to our own experience of life: what we do, innocently or not,
may have its unpleasant consequences. This is the region of which
we ourselves say 'Life is cruel'; but in Sophocles, the fact that these
things come to pass in the way they do is itself an indication that
design of some kind lies behind them – but what is the design?
Why must these things befall Oedipus, for no fault of his, and
apparently for no particular end? We may well ask; but Sophocles
makes no attempt to answer our question. It is not one of the
achievements of the *Tyrannus* that it answers the ultimate riddle.
Oedipus does indeed say, in the *Coloneus,* 'Perhaps the gods were
angry with my family from of old' – a long-delayed recoil of δίκη.
But in fact this hint tells us no more than we knew already, that it
is part of a pattern, a λόγος.

The Aeschylean universe is one of august moral laws, infringe-
ment of which brings certain doom; the Sophoclean is one in
which wrongdoing does indeed work out its own punishment,
but disaster comes, too, without justification; at the most, with
'contributary negligence'. Oedipus would not have done what he
did had he been a little more prudent, a little less self-confident, nor
would Heracles have suffered if he had never given Deianeira cause
to use the supposed love-philtre. But this does not explain why,

in a given case, a comparatively small fault should have such consequences; still less does it explain why a Deianeira should be at one moment a loving, anxious but hopeful wife, and at the next a hanging corpse.

Sophocles' philosophy, so far as we have yet discussed it, is a confession of intellectual faith – a peculiarly Greek one. It should, perhaps, defend him against the charge of being a 'pessimist' – though certainly he understood the mood of black despair, or he could never have written that bitter ode in the *Coloneus*. But what else has Sophocles to say, whether to counsel or to comfort?

Of this pattern, which men call the Will of the Gods, a great part is piety and purity. Accordingly, no poet speaks more than Sophocles of the need for εὐσέβεια, reverence. But part of it lies beyond morality, and is incalculable. Accordingly, no poet speaks so much as Sophocles of the need for φρόνησις, 'wisdom'. 'Phronesis' implies knowing what you are, knowing your place in the world, being able to take the wide view, with a due sense of proportion – unlike Creon in the *Antigone* and Agamemnon and Menelaus in the *Ajax,* who could see only that Polyneices, or Ajax, was a dead traitor, and could not see the more important fact, that he was a dead man. This quality is almost personified in that impressive character Odysseus of the *Ajax*. Because he can see that 'All mankind is nothing but a phantom, an insubstantial shade,' he can pity his foe when he is mad, and not exult, and plead for his burial when he is dead, weighing his worth against the enmity he has shown, and remembering that 'I, too, shall come to this'.

But no piety and no wisdom can protect against those ἀναγκαῖαι τύχαι, blows of fate, of which Tecmessa speaks, twice involved in the ruin of others; and as for consolation, what can we say to an Oedipus? But even if we leave these sufferers, as we must, to face their sufferings with what spirit they can find in them, we can say that on the wider view Sophocles finds much to put into the other balance. No hopes indeed of a better world; only 'Hades that receives all' – though, as Electra says

τοὺς γὰρ θανόντας οὐχ ὁρῶ λυπουμένους
I see that the dead are not vexed.

But do not the grave beauty and dignity of Sophocles' own plays necessarily reflect the beauty and dignity that he found in human life? Man may be 'an insubstantial shade', without the διόσδοτος αἴγλα, the 'god-given glory', that Pindar sometimes saw playing around the head of that same shade; but for all that, Sophocles leaves us with a great sense of the dignity of being a man. To have been great of soul is everything. Ajax faces death proudly; he has been Ajax, and he can pray for his son nothing better than he should be like him, except in fortune; Antigone knows that she has done her duty, and will be welcomed by her kin among the dead. As for Oedipus, surely the Sophoclean image of Man himself, as he was the Aristotelian type of the Tragic Hero, his essential greatness (like that of Heracles too) impresses itself at last on the gods themselves:

When we had gone we turned round and looked from afar. Him we saw nowhere, but Theseus we saw, his hand before his face, as if to shade his eyes from some awful sight upon which he could not look. Then, a little later, we saw him do reverence to the Earth and to Olympus of the Gods in one and the same prayer. But by what death he perished no man could tell but Theseus only; for no blazing thunderbolt from heaven worked his end, nor any storm arising from the sea at that time, but either some escort sent by the gods, or some dark, yawning, kindly chasm of the Earth below. For not with lamentation nor pitiable with disease was that man sent forth, but wonderfully above all others.[1]

[1] *O.C.*, 1647 ff.

CHAPTER VII

The Dramatic Art of Sophocles

1. The Third Actor

We have seen what Aeschylus did in the *Oresteia* with this Sopho-clean invention. Sophocles must have seen it too, with some surprise, for assuredly it was not his conception that the third actor should be grafted on to Old Tragedy and used to extend the lyrical part. Why did Sophocles make this decisive innovation? Although the first twenty years of his dramatic activity are practically a blank, we can answer the question with some confidence: he wanted the third actor in order to do what Aeschylus resolutely refuses to do with him in the *Agamemnon*, namely to illuminate the chief character from several points of view. The Aeschylean conception implies the single-minded tragic hero, one who is all ἁμαρτία – or rather one in whom the ἁμαρτία is all that concerns us. Ὕβρις is done, and Heaven smites, through its chosen instrument. Sophocles sees not the simplicities but the complexities of life. Certain persons, because they are like this and not like that, and because their circumstances are these and not those, combine to bring about the catastrophe. Had any detail been different the disaster would not have occurred. The working of Law is seen in the way in which all these delicate complexities dovetail, to make a pattern which is suddenly seen to be inevitable.

The Sophoclean hero, because he is complex, not single-minded, must be seen from more than one point of view. We do not know our Creon or our Oedipus, we cannot therefore understand his tragedy, until we have seen how he behaves to a diversity of people and (equally important) how they behave to him. Oedipus' consideration for his people, his courtesy to Creon and Teiresias which quickly passes to suspicion and rage, Creon's attitude to Haemon – these are not decorations or improvements; it is essential to the tragedy that we should know our heroes like this. Similarly the Watchman's reluctance to face Creon is important as a sidelight on the King's character, not only sub-comic relief. Eteocles' colourless Spy is transformed, necessarily, into this attractive character of flesh and blood. This is not 'progress'; it is plain logic. This art of 'undercutting' is used in the *Tyrannus* as it has rarely been used since, when the supreme eminence of Oedipus is shown by the collapse of Iocasta's bold scepticism.

Here, we may be sure, we have the origin of the third actor, but there was an accessory cause and a development. No catastrophe can be self-contained; others besides the sinner are involved. To Aeschylus this necessary aspect of tragedy presented itself as a linear movement, hence the trilogy; either the tragic event is the result of inherited character, or it leaves a legacy of tragedy for the next generation.[1] To Sophocles this idea presents itself in a complexive way, as one immediate situation which involves others at once. Ajax' vanity ruins Ajax, but it endangers, too, his sailors, Tecmessa, Eurysaces, Teucer; Creon's stubbornness threatens the Watchman and destroys Antigone before, through Haemon and Eurydice, it involves Creon himself. Thus again more actors are wanted.

Further, if we may trust our scanty evidence, Sophocles began to lay more weight on the tragic interworking of circumstance with character, so that situation becomes more complex. In these four plays, as we shall see in a moment, there is a distinct 'improvement' in the manipulation of the three actors. The explanation is not that Sophocles is perfecting his technique, or not only this, but that his thought is taking a new direction. It is significant that as plot becomes more complex the hero's character becomes less catastrophic. Oedipus and Electra are very different from Ajax and Creon; we feel that these last are so ill-balanced that a slight push may upset them; the former are of such a nobility that only a most unlucky combination of circumstances can bring them low. So, against a more balanced characterization, we have a more complex situation, and the more complex situation brings the use of the three actors to its highest degree of fluidity.

Let us now consider this use in our four plays. In the *Ajax* the third actor plays a restricted but significant part. Between the Prologue and the last scene his only effect on the piece is that he

---

[1] This linear movement is very clear in the *Supplices*. (See p. 21.)

enables the not very dramatic Messenger[1] to give his news to Tecmessa as well as to the chorus. The use of the third actor is restricted in this way because the plot is such that the two chief actors, Ajax and Odysseus, cannot meet. This explains why Sophocles, who had for twenty years been writing for three actors, makes little of them here.[2]

The Prologue uses the three actors well. Athena and Odysseus give us, as it were, the common-sense attitude to Ajax' crime; they also give us a direct view of Odysseus which contrasts excellently with the uncomprehending way in which the Ajax-group always speak of him. But it gives more than this. It is an astonishingly imaginative piece of 'theatre'. It is assumed that Athena, who is invisible to Odysseus, is visible to the audience. Why? Nothing in the scene demands it, and if she is hidden, speaking from behind, 'like the voice of a brazen trumpet', we have the fine spectacle of Odysseus alone on the stage with his raving enemy – alone but for the presence of the unseen goddess.

In the last scene, too, there is imaginativeness. After Menelaus comes Agamemnon; the succession of scenes is perhaps a little lacking in subtlety, but not in point, for it makes clear that Teucer has against him not the whim of one leader only but something like public opinion, and that Teucer cannot find the grounds for over-turning that opinion. Now Odysseus, the arch-enemy, arrives, and while he prevails over Agamemnon with such magnanimity and good sense, Teucer stands by silent, astonished at this support from this source. He thanks Odysseus worthily. Odysseus asks to be allowed a part in the burial, but Teucer cannot rise to this height, and has no confidence that the spirit of Ajax could. Teucer and Ajax remain on the same level as Menelaus and Agamemnon, and Odysseus has to retire disappointed but acquiescent. Nothing could

[1] 'Not very dramatic' because (1) the account of Ajax's previous acts of hybris is what the tragic theme requires rather than what this man in this situation would naturally say; (2) the fact that Athena's anger will last only one day seems left in the air. If it is designed only to quicken the action it is artificial; if it has a deeper meaning, e.g. that the Greek commanders might be induced to forgive Ajax, we are given no clue to it.

[2] There is a superficial notion, which has been received with more patience than it deserves, that this and other innovations were used at first with a timid reserve. Criticism has discovered places in the *Ajax* where Sophocles would have given the third actor more to say if he had not been writing in 450 or thereabouts. Dalmeyda (*R.E.G.*, 1933, p. 2) has disposed of this. (See also Schlesinger, *C.P.*, 1930, p. 230.)

more finely indicate the intellectual loneliness of Odysseus among these men, and the point depends on this, that Teucer was present and heard Odysseus' argument. He was silent not because the play was written in 450 and Sophocles had not yet learned how to make him talk, but because Sophocles had more dramatic imagination than some of his critics.

The Prologue of the *Antigone* does not use three actors, but as it is a scene such as only three-actor tragedy would contrive we may consider it briefly. Like all prologues it outlines the situation; like all good ones it does also something much more important. As the prologue of the *Ajax* presented the situation from a point of view different from that assumed during the greater part of the play, so here the private, personal and feminine atmosphere contrasts sharply with the full light of publicity in which the action is to be played out. It is an admirable preparation for the jubilant hymn of triumph that follows it. The prologue of the *Electra* does the same thing: the practical and political considerations of the two men make an excellent foil to the desolation and the personal sorrow of Electra.[1] In all these juxtapositions there is a finely imaginative relevance; Sophocles makes half his effect by an architectural disposition of mass, and this was made possible by the fluidity which the third actor gave.

Two other scenes in the *Antigone* demand consideration. The first, that between Creon, the Watchman and Antigone, is extremely dramatic, a foreshadowing of the triangular scenes in the *Tyrannus*. The dramatic power arises from this, that each of the three characters has his private preoccupation, his own attitude to the central fact. Creon is faced with the incredible news that the rebel is no political agent but his own niece; Antigone, the deed now done, stands apart, out of touch with the scene, rapt in her almost mystic confidence; the Watchman, finding in the situation his own vindication and escape, is completely at his ease, struck with the wonderfully irrelevant idea that a man should deny nothing – this is the moral that he draws. How effective is his conversational τοιοῦτον ἦν τὸ πρᾶγμα[2] against this background. He, a person on the outskirts

---

[1] Those who like mechanical arguments might add this to the discussion (p. 124) on the centre of gravity in the *Antigone*. Both the *Ajax* and the *Electra* begin with two subordinate characters in order to prepare the way for the Hero. The *Antigone* begins with Antigone and Ismene; therefore the hero is Creon.

[2] 'It happened like this.'

of the tragedy, has escaped. That is how it affects him. It is only by
an effort of ordinary decency that he can remember what it means
to Antigone:

> . . . *partly to my joy, part to my pain.*
> *For to escape oneself from scathe is sweet,*
> *But sore it is to bring a friend to scathe.*
> *Yet nature bids me hold all else for cheap*
> *If so mine own deliverance I secure.*

Once more, this is not dramatic decoration; it is the mocking way
in which things do happen.

The second triangular scene of the *Antigone*, Creon – Antigone
– Ismene, is not of such importance as the first. Both differ from
Sophocles' later scenes of the kind in that the situation, though
dramatic, does not develop; and this second scene is less significant
than the earlier one, for Ismene does little to modify the situation
or to heighten the tragedy. It illustrates Sophocles' methods rather
than his philosophy. We saw Ismene in the prologue; it is the natural
fulfilment of that if we see her again now, and are shown the effect
on her of Antigone's deed. Her attitude in this second scene, an
attitude of pure emotionalism, is indeed a foil to the clear and almost
hard lines of Antigone's resolution, and Creon's utter bewilderment
adds a dramatic point, but the significance is really structural; it is a
link with the prologue and a preparation for the next theme – since
Ismene is obviously the best person to introduce the matter of
Antigone's betrothal to Haemon.

Coming to the two later plays we find an enormous advance in
technique. In the two great discovery scenes of the *Tyrannus*, the
situation is not presented practically complete before our eyes; not
only does it grow, but it grows in opposite directions for the two
chief actors. The conversation between Oedipus and the Corinthian
Messenger is itself painfully dramatic, but the addition of Iocasta
more than doubles the power of the scene. The progress of Iocasta
from hope, through confidence, to frozen horror, and that of
Oedipus from terror to a sublime resolution and assurance, the two
connected by the commonplace cheerfulness of the Corinthian (who
must be extremely puzzled by the tremendous effects his simple
message is creating) – this makes as fine a combination of cross-
rhythms as can well be imagined. Nor is the effect of the following

scene inferior to this. Here it is Oedipus who ends in horror, while the direct contrast lies between the Corinthian, even more cheerful and helpful this time, and the Theban shepherd whose life-secret is being torn from him. There is nothing in dramatic literature to match the peculiar and awful beauty of these scenes except the passage in the *Electra* between the Paedagogus, Electra and Clytemnestra. The long and harsh wrangle between mother and daughter culminates in Clytemnestra's blasphemous petition to Apollo, and immediately, as if in answer to that prayer, the Paedagogus comes in with his statement of Orestes' death. Electra's answer is a cry of anguish; against this Clytemnestra's excitement, now as later, is finely drawn:

$$\tau i \; \phi \acute{\eta} s, \; \tau i \; \phi \acute{\eta} s, \; \mathring{\omega} \; \xi \hat{\epsilon} \hat{\imath} \nu \epsilon; \; \mu \grave{\eta} \; \tau a \acute{\upsilon} \tau \eta s \; \kappa \lambda \acute{\upsilon} \epsilon.$$
What sayest thou, stranger? What? Do not listen to *her*!

Then comes the elaborate and vivid account of Orestes' supposed death: the most brilliant by far of Sophocles' speeches. In his *Ancient Greek Literature* Murray called it 'brilliant but undramatic' (and the whole play 'uncharming') – an interesting criticism, coming from so distinguished a Euripidean. The speech is harsh; like the Crisean plain which it describes, it is strewn with wrecked chariots; the traditional limpidity of Greek poetry is entirely missing. Exactly: the Paedagogus is not really a Messenger, he is playing at being a Messenger. We must not criticize him and the Messenger in the *Antigone* on the same principles. He is not charming: he has something else to do than to charm, and it is precisely because he is not charming that he is not undramatic. Look at the sweep of the speech. A quiet beginning leads to the ominous words $\mathring{o} \tau a \nu \; \delta \acute{\epsilon} \; \tau \iota s \; \theta \epsilon \hat{\omega} \nu$ $\beta \lambda \acute{a} \pi \tau \eta,$[1] and he begins again to work up, through his catalogue, to the beginning of the fatal race. The next few verses obviously lead to a climax, and we hear $\pi \rho \grave{\iota} \nu \; \mu \grave{\epsilon} \nu \; \mathring{o} \rho \theta o \iota \; \pi \acute{a} \nu \tau \epsilon s$[2] . . . and we are sure that this is the end – but not yet. Sophocles holds back; Orestes is still safe among the wrecked chariots. A second and a greater climax grows as the two remaining charioteers go round and round the course until the terrible end comes. It is good, but behind it all we can feel the fierce exultation of the Paedagogus in his skill, in his piling up of falsely convincing details, leading Clytemnestra through

[1] 'When a god sends hurt' (696).
[2] 'At first all stood upright' (723).

the divagations of his story to her death. It is a magnificent piece of bravura, and as we listen to it, watching the grimness behind it, observing its effect on the two women, who, fresh from their quarrel, hang upon every word, so that it comes to us through their minds, amplified – 'undramatic' is the last thing we should call it.

This long effort ended, a masterly scene follows. First the Chorus thinks of the royal line here ended:

> φεῦ, φεῦ· τὸ πᾶν δὴ δεσπόταισι τοῖς πάλαι
> πρόρριζον, ὡς ἔοικεν, ἔφθαρται γένος.[1]

There is limpidity this time. Then Clytemnestra thinks of herself, her sorrow, her relief. This Clytemnestra does not 'hide laughter in her eyes'; her grief is genuine, that she wins safety only in the destruction of her son. But in a moment she begins to realize how great her relief is. She is at last safe, and she gives us a terrifying glimpse into what has been going on beneath the surface:

> ὁ προστατῶν
> χρόνος διῆγέ μ' αἰὲν ὡς θανουμένην.
> νῦν δὲ . . .

Time in its course led me along always under the shadow of death. But now . . .

While she bares her soul like this, the Paedagogus stands by in apparent stupidity. What brings forth Clytemnestra's most intimate confession is his ill-timed and crude suggestion of his tip. Then there is Electra, aroused from her prostration only by her mother's natural and unnatural joy. Again we are recalled from a terrible passage between them by the old man's apparent nervousness about his reward. Messengers in Greek Tragedy, as he well knows, are allowed to be frank on this point. He has, perhaps, to be a shade insistent, but he has played his part well, and Clytemnestra takes him in.

This is a convenient point at which to consider what is in some ways Sophocles' masterpiece in the use of the three actors: the *Philoctetes*. It is very much of an actor's play; the subject offers little scope for lyricism, and the poet will not manufacture it. Ostensibly

---

[1] Untranslatable. A rendering is:
  'Alas! the long line of our kings, rooted out, utterly destroyed!'
It belongs to the company of:
  'He has no children. – All my pretty ones?
  Did you say all?'

the subject is the plot laid by Odysseus against Philoctetes, and its failure; the dramatic interest is to watch how the young hero comes to realize, with increasing shame, how false and intolerable is the enterprise into which Odysseus has entrapped him; the theme that underlies the whole is that the Greek commanders at Troy are suffering the natural recoil of their past inhumanity to Philoctetes. The action of the play moves forward, step by step, with a subtlety and a certainty not unworthy of comparison with the action of the *Tyrannus*. The three chief characters are brilliantly contrasted: the embittered and immovable Philoctetes, Odysseus the plausible villain, and the young Neoptolemus whose gradual transit from the side of Odysseus to that of Philoctetes is so absorbing a spectacle. The plot moves with the utmost freedom – yet, one is surprised to note, the *dramatic personae* in this quite unlyrical play are fewer than in any of the other six. They are in all only five, and of these one is only the conventional *deus ex machina,* who in fact has little to contribute to the plot. Apart from Heracles there is only one minor character, the Merchant, and he appears in only one scene. To contrive so fluid a plot under such a severe restriction evinces great technical virtuosity. One of the secrets is the bold and entirely successful reliance on that form of dramatic shorthand which is often called 'inconsistency' (see below, pp. 297 ff.); another is that the chorus is very subtly used (as at 169–90, 391–402, 676–717) to put before us the feelings of pity and indignation which, as we must realize, are working so strongly on Neoptolemus.

2. The Chorus

The different attitude which Sophocles brought to tragedy affected the chorus as much as the actors. It is indeed obvious – or it would have been had not Aeschylus written the *Agamemnon* – that more actor must mean less chorus. Indeed we began to suspect from the *Eumenides* that the chorus was about to disappear altogether. From this ignominy Sophocles rescued it: the chorus in Middle Tragedy – when Sophocles was writing it – held a position as logical and as secure as in the most choric of Old Tragedy. Like the Eumenides themselves, what it lost in power it gained in other ways.

It has been argued that the chorus was the natural and perfect frame for the Aeschylean quasi-religious tragedy. The atmosphere of vengeance and retribution into which Agamemnon emerges, the background of doom and battle against which Eteocles plays out his lonely drama, are created by the chorus. In the Sophoclean conception the background is tragic human relationships and the complicated web of circumstance, and these are matters for the actors to present. Thebes is a threatened city in the *Tyrannus,* as well as in the *Septem,* and a curse is there too, but neither of these is the most important theme in Sophocles' play. In his *Electra,* again, the primitive law of vengeance is an important motif, as it is in the *Choephori,* but in Aeschylus' play it conditions everything, and is kept before our minds by the enveloping chorus; in the *Electra* it is part of the mind of the protagonist. When Eteocles is killed the logical close is the funeral hymn of the chorus; when Oedipus finds his doom the chorus sings Ἰὼ γενεαὶ βροτῶν, but this is not enough. The actor has superseded the chorus, and the logical ending is that we should see Oedipus in his ruin. It is not an easy task for Oedipus to follow and complete that tragic ode, but he has to do it, and he does.

A further important change is that the tempo of the piece is now entirely in the hands of the actors. The logic of the drama is no longer that of dramatico-musical emotion, but, in some degree, that of real life. The chorus can, by convention, fill up gaps in time, but it cannot suspend time as it and Cassandra do in the *Agamemnon.* If past events have in the drama the significance which the sacrifice of Iphigeneia has in the *Agamemnon,* they must be presented through the consciousness of the actors on whom our attention is fixed. The drama is now theirs, and the chorus has to admit it. The chorus is limited to the present action – being in this sense more dramatic, more of a συναγωνιστής than the chorus of Aeschylus. We shall see how Sophocles accepts this limitation, keeps the chorus within the bounds set, and, as his drama increases in complexity, finds in this limitation one of his most powerful weapons.

How did he fit his chorus to these new conditions? First and most obviously, by making it always dramatic. It can no longer surround and control the action but it is always concerned in it. In the *Ajax* it consists of Ajax' own followers – a point of little interest in itself, but one which becomes significant when we realize that they may be the first victims of Ajax' fall. Their exhortations to him to arise and assert himself are no mere operatic platitude; they feel themselves to be in danger. The themes of the *Antigone* and the *Tyrannus* are essentially public themes, and the chorus is the public – though, as we shall see, the *Tyrannus* has an advantage in this respect. In the *Electra,* where the dramatic excuse for the chorus is less strong, Sophocles has nevertheless made it entirely relevant by a very deft link. Aegisthus is made to threaten to put Electra away; a point which, in the manner of these later plays of Sophocles' middle period, is made to serve three ends at once, one of them being that Aegisthus' reason, the subversive sympathy which Electra arouses in the city, is personified in this sympathetic chorus. In fact, while tragedy was based on these big general themes the difficulty of finding a suitable chorus and of connecting it with the action remained in the background. Sophocles' chorus was as easy to come by as Socrates' audience. It was when tragedy turned from public to private themes, like the intransigence of Medea or the frenzied behaviour of Euripides' Orestes, that the chorus became a nuisance.

Then Sophocles normally succeeded in investing his choruses with some individual character. The follower of Ajax come to life for us in their loathing of the war and longing for Greece, as well as in their devotion to Ajax and fear for themselves. More than this: Sophocles allows them always to have their own view, not the right one, of Odysseus and his doings. They are never the mouth-piece of the poet,[1] and in this play they are definitely not 'ideal spectators', holding even the balance between Ajax and the other Greeks. They are always pro-Ajax, therefore dramatically the more interesting. So, too, the chorus of the *Antigone*: personally sympathetic with Antigone, unlike Creon, yet disapproving of her action, unlike the ordinary Thebans. More than once Sophocles uses it with a kind of irony, making it say the right thing, but about the wrong person. But Oedipus' chorus is so far a personality that its character helps in making the cross-rhythms of the play. It is pious, and it is devoted to Oedipus. In the second ode it is its loyalty and its confidence in Oedipus which prevail; in language somewhat bold for a chorus it says 'God is certain, but that his prophets know more than another man, that is not proved'. When next it speaks it has had more shocks and its tone is different; now its instinctive piety asserts itself and leads it to pray for the fulfilment of the oracles.

---

[1] Kranz (*Stasimon,* p. 191) has observed that Sophocles begins his odes with a statement of fact, Euripides with an expression of opinion (cf. *Antig.,* 332 with *Alcest.,* 962): an interesting reflection of the greater plasticity of Sophocles' dramatic mind.

There is real reaction and movement here; it is not merely singing, not simply being an ideal spectator. In the second ode itself, still less: after Teiresias' denunciation of Oedipus, the chorus proceeds to picture the guilty man as a homeless outcast, slinking away from men's eyes. Not until the ode is half over does it mention the prophet. Has the chorus not fully understood him? Or has it understood so clearly that it is deliberately fighting down his disturbing suggestion? There is, perhaps, room for difference of interpretation; what is certain is that the chorus is behaving as a person, not as a machine, as Jebb suggested. It was his odd view that 'there was a canon that the Chorus comments, in order, on those things of importance which have happened since it last spoke';[1] Sophocles did not work like this.

Sophocles did not write to formulas, and the chorus of the *Electra* is the exact opposite to that of the *Antigone*. The latter makes itself felt as a dramatic force neither by taking a prominent part in the action nor by displaying any marked character, but rather by the veering of its sympathies – by the way in which, after its first slight recoil from Creon's edict, it steadily moves away from Antigone, and then suddenly deserts Creon. In the *Electra* its character is carefully assimilated to that of Electra, as its part is to be completely dominated by her, to become – after the slight reserve which they show at the beginning – practically an extension of the heroine's personality. The formal expression of this is the lack of a Parodos; the introductory anapaests are Electra's. During the following scene it is persuaded to accept Electra's view of Piety and Reverence, and so, in entire accord with her, it leads us right up to the grim end, τῇ νῦν ὁρμῇ τελεωθέν. Its complete confidence here is as dramatic as the cheerfulness of the introductory birds; a reserved or doubtful chorus would have ruined the fine reticence and irony of the close.

These points are, however, not much more than negative; Sophocles did not fail to do what obviously had to be done. Let us look more closely into his use of the chorus, first as actor, then as singers. 'The Chorus', says Aristotle, 'must be regarded as one of the actors.' So it is; but how?

It was said above (p. 29) that the acts of the individuals are bound to be more striking than those of a group. Sophocles saw that, and

[1] Note *ad loc.*

accordingly when his chorus takes part in the action it is normally before the more vivid dramatis personae have set to work. Its more generalized action prepares the way for, but can hardly follow, the more incisive action of the single person. So in the *Ajax,* it is the chorus which is presented as the first presumptive victim of Ajax' fall; Tecmessa is the second, because in her the pathos of the situation can be brought to a finer point.[1] Then the chorus and Tecmessa together, as minor characters, are used to prepare for the appearance of Ajax.

The *Electra* is built as a series of attacks on the resolution of the heroine: Chrysothemis, with the threats of Aegisthus looming behind her, Clytemnestra, the false Messenger, are successive moves in this attack; but before all these is placed the first slight reserve of the chorus, with its counsels of submission, before the more keenly edged attack of the actor begins Even the *Antigone* has its suggestion of their participation in the action (v. 215) before the real actors enter; and in the *Tyrannus* when we face the situation afresh after the Parodos and Oedipus' denunciation, the chorus makes its only direct contribution to the action (vv. 282–92) before the others start. The chorus never attempts to compete with the actors: if used as actors, it is always used before the others begin.

When it has shot this early bolt its part as actor is normally finished, except that, as it is always present and always relevant, it is freely used in minor ways to lend a hand when wanted – as to receive messengers, to announce new-comers, and in general to make transitions smooth. But these services to the plot are not always mechanical. When Creon, in the *Tyrannus,* enters in indignation, the chorus is there to receive him, but the scene gains enormously in effectiveness from the fact that it thus begins on a level of neutrality, from which it can gradually work up to its violent close.

The chorus has a third clearly-marked function in its part in the dialogue. It is perpetually saying things like

> *Oh king, give heed if sense be in his words;*
> *Heed thou thy sire too – both have spoken well.* (*Antig.,* 724–5.)

What is the point of these tedious remarks? Simply, I take it, that when one speaker had made an effective speech the beginning of the

---

[1] For this reason, too, as well as from the exigencies of staging, it is Tecmessa, not the chorus, who finds the body of Ajax.

reply was likely to be missed, if not because of a murmur of approbation and of physical readjustment, then because the minds of the audience were still on the speech just heard. These commonplace couplets are merely buffers, designed to give a moment of rest between speeches. Often, however, such a comment is used to give an effective cue to the reply (*Antig.*, 278, 471, 766, *Tyrannus,* 1073–5); with which minor service we may compare the habit of Sophocles' characters of addressing their reply to the Chorus when they are too angry to answer directly (*El.*, 612, *Tyrannus,* 429, 618, *Antig.*, 726).

As Actor, therefore, the chorus has its continuous share in the drama, and has, in one way or another, its contribution to make, due regard being paid to its somewhat indefinite character. Its most important function, however, is obviously the lyrical one, and this we now consider. We shall have to examine the plays in order, for a distinct development in this respect is discernible.

It is, I think, fair to say that the odes of the *Ajax* provoke neither censure nor any great admiration. There is the Parodos, appropriately composed in the Dorian rhythm, in which the chorus calls upon Ajax to arise in his might and dispel the rumours that are gathering around him. The first stasimon is entirely dramatic; here they think of their own homes which they are doubtful of seeing again, and of the ill news which is coming to Ajax' parents. Next we have the bright *"Ἔφριξ' ἔρωτι,* of which we shall speak later. The third stasimon is a natural and vivid expression of their loathing of the war. These worthy sailors do not soar, but what they say is always in keeping with the situation and with their own characters. However, it cannot be said that any of their odes (with the exception of *"Ἔφριξ' "ρωτι*) makes any considerable contribution to the play.

The *Antigone* is by far the most lyrical of the extant plays, as the use that Sophocles made of it is great in proportion. The Parodos this time is more than suitable; it is astonishingly dramatic, sweeping away the almost conspiratorial air of the prologue, substituting for the private sorrows of Antigone the joy of the city in its deliverance, making Polyneices not the unburied brother but the defeated traitor. It has also its ironical close, in its call for 'forgetfulness of these woes' and for night-long dances to be led by Dionysus.

As for the renowned second ode, the lyrical poem on the Ascent of Man, we obscure its dramatic point if we think of the Chorus as 'the mouthpiece of the poet'. The chorus in this play is very much of a dramatic character, and like any other character it can be mistaken. It begins the ode by tracing, in a few vivid pictures, the rise of civilization, achieved by the inventiveness and daring of Man; yet these qualities have their dangers: the city is secure only when 'the justice of the gods and the laws of the land' are observed – the implication being that the two coincide, and that the unknown rebel against Creon's decree is also a rebel against Dike. The chorus is to learn that in this instance they do not coincide; not the unknown rebel but Creon himself is putting Thebes in hazard. This idea is repeated later in the play. Creon, in his long speech to Haemon, insists that it is obedience and discipline that preserve a city, an army, a family; but it is precisely his own defiance of the laws of the gods – his own inhumanity to the body, to Antigone, to his own son – that bring down his house in ruin.

The third ode is hardly less notable than the second as a lyric poem, and is no less closely bound to the development of the tragic theme. Its opening, Εὐδαίμονες οἷσι κακῶν ἄγευστος αἰών, 'Blessed are they who have not tasted sorrow,' is the natural culmination of what has gone before, while its sombre close, 'Evil appeareth good in his eyes whom the god is leading to destruction', is an ironic and powerful shadowing of what is to befall the king.

The short ode to Eros also has its ironical tinge. To the chorus, it is Haemon who has been 'twisted into unrighteousness' by the power of Love; later we see what is the real manifestation in the play of 'invincible Aphrodite', when the maddened Haemon turns on his father to kill him.

The ode begins a long musical movement which continues, interrupted only by the two speeches, until the end of the fifth ode. In the *commos* it is Antigone who has the lyrics; the chorus, still believing her to be in the wrong, can offer only conventional comfort. The tragic power of the scene derives partly from the fact that Creon is present throughout, and is so entirely unmoved by it that he can at last intervene as harshly as he does. So Antigone, misjudged and friendless, goes to her death – a poignant moment which calls for lyrical relief more insistently than any other in Greek tragedy; yet the fifth ode, beginning with Danaë, seems artificial, even learned. So it is, if we attend only to the words, and forget the dance and music. Sophocles wanted to keep his wise political chorus firmly on Creon's side until Teiresias comes in to frighten them; he could not therefore make them give direct expression to what everyone in the theatre is feeling. Nevertheless, the expression is there: the ode is full of the idea of Darkness – Danaë, though innocent, was immured; Lycurgus, too, being guilty; and then, passing over the immuring of Cleopatra, Sophocles speaks of the darkness so cruelly brought upon her children's eyes 'that cried for vengeance', ἀλαστόροισιν. It is all there: savage cruelty, darkness, and vengeance to come. Not a word is said about Creon – but he is there on the stage for us to look at.

The last ode too is a splendid piece of lyric poetry, exciting in language and in rhythm, and firmly built into the play. When last the chorus invoked Dionysus (v. 154), it was in thanksgiving for deliverance; now they invoke him, more earnestly and passionately, to bring deliverance from the new evils that threaten the city – a prayer that is at once answered by the Messenger with his word Τεθνᾶσιν, 'Death'.

The *Antigone,* few will deny, shows a marked development in Sophocles' powers as lyric poet. The odes in the *Ajax* are by no means weak; Ὦ κλεινὰ Σάλαμις has the authentic ring; but in Πολλὰ τὰ δεινὰ, in Εὐδαίμονες οἷσι κακῶν, in Πολυώνυμε, there is a depth and a power which surpasses anything in the earlier play.[1] Nor in the *Ajax* is there anything so fine as the rhythmical effects in the *Antigone* – the brilliant variations on the Glyconic, for example, which opens the Parodos, the noble mating of rhythm and sense in the two couplets

> Ἀντιτύπᾳ δ' ἐπὶ γᾳ πέσε τανταλωθεὶς
> Ἀλλὰ γὰρ ὰ μεγαλώνυμος ἦλθε Νίκα,

or the astonishing

> κυλίνδει βυσσόθεν κελαινὰν θῖνα καὶ
> στόνῳ βρέμουσιν ἀντιπλῆγες ἀκταί.[2]

Nor does the *Ajax,* with the exception of the second stasimon, show the same dramatic imagination in the use of the lyrics as part of the structure of the whole. In the *Antigone* the chorus carries more of the

---

[1] One would, however, hesitate to say the same of the iambics, in spite of Antigone's speech to Creon.

[2] | ◡ — | (◡) — | (◡) — | ◡ — || ◡ — | (◡) — | (◡) — | ◡ —, etc.

burden of the tragic theme than in the later plays, though the odes in the *Tyrannus* are scarcely less impressive.

The prologue of the *Tyrannus* is based on three main ideas, the Plague, the obscure message of hope from Delphi, and the beginnings of the discovery in the first clues advanced by Creon. The purpose of this third part is evidently to prepare for the suspicions which Oedipus forms of a plot between Creon and Teiresias; the chorus has heard nothing about it. Their Parodos is based on the other two themes, the Plague and the Message. It contains nothing new, for all our attention is wanted for Oedipus and what he is going to do; nor is there any sense of repetition, as both of these themes, vividly though they were presented in the dialogue, become something much more immediate when presented through song and dance. It is not repetition, but fulfilment. But the most interesting point at the moment is not so much the substance as the arrangement of the ode. The two themes appear in the reverse order, the Message and then the Plague; not because Sophocles is obeying some obscure canon, but because this arrangement makes smoother the transition from the Prologue to the first episode. The chorus enters on the note of hope on which the prologue ended, and closes on the note of apprehension and prayer with which the next starts.[1] This method, continuation and preparation, we noticed once or twice in the *Antigone*; here and in the *Electra* it is always used, greatly to the advantage of the dramatic sweep of the plays.

The second ode, the first stasimon, we have already discussed (p. 159). It is immediately relevant to the situation, and it is highly dramatic, in that the chorus postpones as long as it can expression of the perturbation which Teiresias has caused. Further, the scene which is to disturb the chorus as much as the prophet has done is ushered in with the confident words

Τῷ ἀπ᾽ ἐμᾶς φρενὸς οὔποτ᾽ ὀφλήσει κακίαν.
Never will my judgement convict him of sin.

The long scene is broken by the entrance of Iocasta, and here the chorus is used effectively. The quarrel between Oedipus and Creon is devised to show how the quick intelligence of Oedipus draws

[1] Contrast the opening dactyls and the closing iambics. – Kranz (*Stasimon,* p. 193) makes the end a 'return' to the beginning. Certainly beginning and end are prayers – but in different moods.

inferences which are totally wrong, but so certain, for him, that he will kill an innocent kinsman. The furious climax must be allayed before the action can continue, but Sophocles does not wish Oedipus to admit error. Therefore, to Iocasta's plea he adds the lyrical appeal of the chorus, couched in the heavy cretic rhythm that Aeschylus applied to Pelasgus. So, plausibly and economically, Oedipus is induced to rescind his decree, though still maintaining his blind confidence in his complete misreading of the situation.

The third ode has been found difficult. The first stanza, on the majesty of the Unwritten Laws, seems as remote from the existing dramatic situation as does the ode on Man in the *Antigone*, for we naturally ask how observance of these laws could have saved Oedipus from marrying a woman about whom he knew only one thing, that she was not his mother? To this question there is no answer. Then the chorus sings of hybris: we think it will obviously be the hybris of Iocasta or of Oedipus – but which? Again there is no answer. We shall see below (p. 182) that it cannot be Iocasta. Certainly we have just witnessed an outbreak of tyrannical hybris in Oedipus, hitherto the exemplary king, but unfortunately Sophocles goes on to speak in terms that can only remove our thoughts from Oedipus: his man of hybris is ambitious, wins his gains unjustly, luxuriates in pride, is wantonly sacrilegious. The ode does resemble the one in the *Antigone*; our ideas of what is 'dramatic' need to be adjusted. We shall see later that here, as there, Sophocles is thinking not of the persons in the play but of its underlying idea – and in each case the chorus, for the moment, has the tsage to itself.

The next ode does more than usher in the catastrophe with an outburst of confidence; it takes up and enlarges what has become an important part of the tragic theme: the idea of Chance. It shows, too, that Sophocles was not always concerned to characterize his chorus consistently: he will sometimes use it purely as a lyrical instrument. Such it was in the previous ode, when despite its loyalty to Oedipus it had prayed for the fulfilment of the oracles; now it becomes once more the group of loyal Thebans. Oedipus has just declared himself to be the son of Chance; the chorus takes up the idea with music and dance: he will prove to be the son of some god and a mountain nymph. Then comes the Shepherd, to prove him the son of Laius and Iocasta. The last ode is lyrical relief, like the

G

Danaë – ode. Once more the order of the themes is important. Had the chorus sung 'Alas for Oedipus! Yet how like human life this is!' the effect would have been one of conscious moralizing, a little unnecessary and certainly undramatic. As it is, the effect is perfect. Ἰὼ γενεαὶ βροτῶν, coming immediately after the horrible discovery, is not moralizing but an immediate reaction. Dramatically, its very remoteness is a wonderful relief – provided, as always, that it is sung and not said.[1] Then, in the most natural way, to the general succeeds the particular. The personal cry 'Would that I had never seen thee!' by conveying so directly the dreadful revulsion that the chorus feels vividly expresses the peculiar horror of Oedipus' fate. This personal tone, drawing our minds away from the tone of philosophic reflection, is also an excellent means of transition from the catastrophe to its results, the blinded but not broken Oedipus.

In the *Electra* the chorus is deprived of its entry-song; the first music is given to Electra, and since her monody is composed in anapaests, the march rhythm, we may perhaps infer that during its performance the chorus entered one by one. This leads to the long lyrical dialogue between Electra and the chorus, and there is no question that she is the dominant party. Thereafter there are only three odes, two of them very short. It is not difficult to see why in this play Sophocles diminished the role of the chorus: Electra is to be the dramatic centre. The whole action rests on her passionate loyalty to her father, her longing for Orestes' return, her implacable hatred of the two murderers. It might indeed seem that the chief function of the chorus is to subserve Electra: that in the lyrical dialogue their comfort and counsel is designed to bring her determination into higher relief; that the first ode picks up and magnifies the excitement with which she has already acclaimed Clytemnestra's dream, much as the fourth ode in the *Tyrannus* takes up Oedipus' mood of blind confidence; that in the *commos* (820–70) the chorus does but show us into what despair Electra is fallen; that the second ode (1058–96) marks the height of resolution to which she has risen; and finally that the short and swift third ode (1384–97), though it does not further illuminate her character, does serve simply to mark the moment of her and her brother's triumph. Yet, though much

[1] For nothing can be more drab and miserable than a reciting chorus. – This arrangement of themes, the remote followed by the near-by, became a common formula (Kranz, *Stasimon*, p. 250); here we best see the dramatic reason for this.

of this would be true, it is far from being the whole truth. There are other agents in the drama no less important than Electra and Orestes: the gods also are concerned, and their concern is shown, partly in the structure of the play (as we shall see a little later), but to no small extent through the chorus.

It is true that the consolation and advice offered to Electra by the chorus in the first dialogue emphasize for us the strength of her loyalty and determination, but what thoughts will cross our minds when the chorus trustingly says 'Zeus will bring Orestes home in triumph' (160 ff.), and 'Zeus oversees all things' (173–84)? Since we have ourselves seen Orestes back in Mycenae, we are bound to reflect that it is Zeus who has brought him, that Zeus is concerned in the righting of this wrong. To the same effect, when in the *commos* the chorus cries 'How can the gods look upon this, and remain unmoved?' (823–6), we must reflect that the gods are indeed not being unmoved.

As for the third ode, what in fact is the chorus saying? The avengers have just entered the palace: the chorus identifies them with Ares the war-god and with the Erinyes, 'the unerring hounds on the trail of crime,' and declares that Hermes is with them to conceal their guileful purpose. In the same vein, it is the chorus that sings a little later (1417–21):

> The dead are stirring;
> Those who were slain of old now
> Drink in return the blood of those that killed them.

This is but the fulfilment of the first ode, in which the chorus foresees that Dike is coming in full power upon the criminals. No longer can we see this ode as only a reflection of Electra's excited hopes; it has independent authority. The Chorus enables the dramatist to enlarge the frame of reference, so that what is done by Electra and Orestes can stand free, entirely their own actions, and yet be seen by us as being also the concern of the gods.

Two of the odes raise interesting questions. The first consists of the two stanzas that proclaim the coming of Dike, and of an epode which harks back to the treacherous chariot-race of Pelops which brought death to Myrtilus and disaster upon disaster to the House. Why did Sophocles write the epode, and place it here? Elsewhere in the play we are concerned only with the crimes of Clytemnestra

and Aegisthus, never with those of Pelops, Thyestes, Atreus. Indeed,
Sophocles departs so far from the Aeschylean form of the myth that
in his play the Erinyes are with Orestes. The end of the play closes
an account that was opened by Agamemnon's murder; nothing is to
follow the vengeance, as nothing significant preceded the crime.
Why then in this one passage does Sophocles go right back, and to
the chariot-race, not for example to Thyestes' crime, or the crime of
Atreus? It seems irrelevant.

We can at least notice that the epode concludes an ode about Dike,
and is at once followed by the long scene in which a second chariot-
race is described – though indeed one which never happened; and
that the fictitious description of this race is an important part in
Orestes' plan for the vengeance which redresses the crime and
restores the House (1508–10). Are not these antistrophic chariot-
races another instance of that feeling for 'pattern' which seems to
have been part of Sophocles' conception of Dike?

The other point concerns the second ode. In the previous scene
Chrysothemis has rejected Electra's plan to kill Aegisthus, and
twice the chorus-leader took her side in the dispute. Yet in the ode
the chorus praises Electra without reserve. To us, it is an inconsistency; yet clearly it is one to which Sophocles was indifferent, and
presumably his audience too. It seems to involve the same considerations as the epode in the *Agamemnon* discussed above (p. 71). We
ought probably to infer that, in the theatre, the chorus-leader acting
as a minor character, as an individual, was so visibly distinct from
the chorus-leader leading his fourteen colleagues in dance and song
that no feeling of inconsistency arose.

In the sequence *Antigone, Tyrannus, Electra,* there is a steady
diminution in the part allotted to the chorus. How far this is true of
Sophocles' work as a whole during this period we can only guess,
having so small a sample; though when we take Euripides' into
account it does seem probable that the actor was gaining ground
at the expense of the chorus. What, however, is clear, and more
important, is that Sophocles, especially in these three plays, found in
the Chorus a most flexible and powerful dramatic instrument. He
was able, at any moment, to draw from it that contribution to the
development of the play, and of its theme, which it was from its
nature peculiarly qualified to make.

3. Structural Principles

There is a problem here. Some of Sophocles' plays exhibit a complete mastery of dramatic form; there is total unity, comprehensive and intelligent control, from the broad outlines of the plot down to the most minute details of diction or metre. There are other plays, notably the *Ajax* and *Trachiniae*, in which this power of control seems either to have deserted him or not yet to have reached him. The dichotomy is not indeed as sharp as the one we shall meet in Euripides, but it is remarkable enough.

The modern scholar is not surprised. He will say (wrongly) that it is unreasonable to expect from a dramatist plays without mistakes – just as, presumably, it is unreasonable to expect a professional cabinet-maker always to turn out tables with the correct number of legs, all of the same length. In fact, one regularly finds first-rate workmanship in second-rate dramatists – Sardou, for example. But in the case of the *Ajax* and *Trachiniae* it would be a question not of elegance of workmanship but of ordinary competence. We are told sometimes that Sophocles would have increased the unity of the *Antigone* and *Trachiniae* had he displayed the heroine's body in the final scenes: is it credible that so elementary a point could have escaped the notice of a dramatist who had been winning prizes for years – and in Athens, not among the Triballi? Sophocles was not – like some of his critics – desperately struggling with the rudiments of his art.

One popular argument must be disposed of, the argument *ad misericordiam*, that the Greek dramatist was not always in control of his material, being sometimes constrained by his myth, like Laocoon by the serpent. 'The structure of a play depends partly on the subject, and few subjects are without some flaw.'[1] The word 'subject' is an ambiguous one, as we shall see; here it seems to mean *myth*, or *story*. One might think that it is a foolish dramatist who takes a story out of which he cannot make a satisfactory play, but we have seen already, and shall see again, with what natural and intelligent freedom myth was handled by those Greek dramatists who have survived. In only one of the thirty-odd plays that we possess can I see that the dramatist was constrained by his myth, namely the *Philoctetes*,[2] if the account of the play given below fairly

[1] F. R. Earp, *The Style of Sophocles*, p. 167.

[2] The ironical endings of certain non-tragic plays of Euripides are no real exception. (See below, pp. 321 f.)

represents what Sophocles was thinking about; and there, if I am right, Sophocles was completely unconcerned: having said, through the story, precisely what he meant (and, incidentally, having shaped it very differently from Aeschylus or Euripides), he devised a conventional ending, with a *deus ex machina,* to square his plot with ancient history. A dramatist who could abolish the pursuit of Orestes by the Furies does not look like one hampered by his chosen myth. We must look for some more persuasive explanation of the surprising structure of some of the plays; neither incompetence nor *force majeure* will serve.

The word *subject* has been used. Clearly, if an artist has learned his craft, if he has something to say, or a clear notion of what he wants to do, and if he is not constricted by unsuitable material – unsuitable stone if he is a sculptor, an unsuitable but unalterable plot if he is a dramatist – then the object, the finished work, will correspond with the subject. When our criticism and appreciation go astray, the reason usually is that we have made certain assumptions about the subject that never were in the mind of the artist. The object does not correspond with what we assume the subject to be; therefore we blame the artist, and, in the sublimer instances of error, explain to him patiently what he should have done. Our instinctive assumptions are made, naturally, under the influence of certain local and temporary prepossessions; any history of critical literature will show how criticism and understanding of literature have been dominated by the 'taste' prevailing in each successive age. But we can be a little more objective than this, simply by studying the object and deducing from it what the subject is. In feeble work one cannot; in strong and competent work one can.

Here we will consider two plays, the structure of which has escaped serious blame, the *Electra* and the *Tyrannus*: the former in order to show how easily our conception of the subject may differ from the poets, so that we fail to appreciate fully or exactly what he was saying; the latter in order to establish what the subject is.

What is the subject of the *Electra*? The question may seem foolish. Is there another play of comparable length that presents a character-study like this one? For with the exception of the first scene and the brief final stasimon (1384–97), which can hardly have taken much more than one minute in performance, the heroine is on the stage continuously, always at the centre of things, placed in sharp juxtaposition with some other character, and in situations that are constantly changing. 'The whole arrangement of the plot – the Chrysothemis scenes, the long messenger speech, and the delaying of the recognition – is designed to give Electra's motives the greatest possible scope, so that we can see her in turn gloomy, scornful, elated, desperate, purposeful, sorrowful, joyful and triumphant.'[1] 'The interest depends primarily on the portraiture of human character.'[2] What can be more obvious? Taking this view I explained, in the previous editions of this book, that the play is built around Electra, as a series of dramatic attacks upon her, to illuminate different facets of her character and to show how its essential nobility has been twisted awry, hammered into hardness by her situation.

This is not untrue; it is simply inadequate. If this and nothing more was Sophocles' subject, then there are not a few passages where subject and object do not correspond. We then seek some other explanation of their existence, as for example that Sophocles was pious, and therefore made his characters pray from time to time. But if the prayers are an organic part of the structure, and we have not seen this, but explain them as if they were not, then during these passages the drama, for us, has been languid; we have thought that Sophocles was only being pious when in fact he was being dramatic – which is a pity. We will look at these prayers.

There are four of them. We can be fairly sure that their visual effect, on the stage, was not small; the third of them was obviously very impressive indeed. The reason for saying that they are organic, not a pious addition, is that they make immediate contact, in so many directions, with so much of the play. First (62–72) Orestes prays to his native soil and native gods that they will help him purge the house and regain his lawful station. Then (110–17) Electra prays to Hades, Persephone, the Curse, the Erinyes, that they bring back Orestes and help them both. The third is Clytemnestra's solemn sacrifice to Apollo, accompanied by the blasphemous prayer which receives at once its devastating answer in the arrival of the Paedagogus. Finally, as the three men enter the palace on their grim business, Electra, too, prays to Apollo; and surely Sophocles saw to it that she stood exactly where Clytemnestra had stood. She prays that Apollo may help them,

[1] T. B. L. Webster, *Sophocles,* p. 81.

[2] Jebb, *Introduction,* p. xxxviii.

> *And show mankind what chastisement the gods*
> *Inflict on those who practise wickedness.*

This prayer, too, Apollo answers. And when Electra, having offered this prayer, enters the palace, the chorus draws for us a picture of the Erinyes following the trail of crime into the house; the 'guileful' (δολιόπους) avengers are being led by Hermes, who shrouds their 'guile' (δόλῳ) in darkness. As for the 'guile', linked here with the avengers and with Hermes, it pervades the play. Apollo had advised Orestes to use 'guile' (37); Agamemnon was killed 'by deceit' (ἀπάταις) by Electra's 'guileful' mother (124–5); lust was the slayer, 'guile' was the plotter (197). Therefore, when at the end of the play Aegisthus is driven in to die on the very spot where he had murdered Agamemnon, we must surely feel that he dies not only on the same spot but also in the same way, by 'guile'. Certainly Electra has just used him with some irony.

On the assumption that the subject of the play is the character of Electra, all of this is peripheral, a source of interest no doubt, but not an intensification of the subject.

As we are considering structural principles we may legitimately ask why Sophocles began his play with the arrival of Orestes, and did not anticipate the *Elektra* of Strauss by reserving Orestes for a dramatic entrance later in the play. We should give a random answer unless we thought about it in relation with the structure of the whole. It clearly has such a relation, and the question is worth answering. We have in fact anticipated it, in discussing above (p. 167) those passages in which the chorus assures Electra that Zeus will bring her brother home. In the mouths of the chorus they are no more than an expression of faith; to us, because we have seen Orestes, they mean much more. Postponing Orestes' arrival, Strauss achieved a dramatic stroke; by not postponing it, Sophocles achieved a stroke no less dramatic, but very different. Zeus is active in this play, not Electra and Orestes only.

Then there is the dream. If any reader should be so malicious as to refer to my earlier analysis of the play he will find that everything in it so far mentioned was not noticed at all, and that the dream shows only how 'Electra, rapt in her dream of vengeance, clutches at any straw'. This illustrates what can happen when one has mistaken, and reduced in size, the subject of the play: an intensely dramatic moment is whittled down to nearly nothing. Orestes prayed to the gods of his race; Zeus, as we now know, has brought him home; Electra hears the bare news that Clytemnestra has had a threatening dream. Her response comes immediately in her cry:

Gods of our race! be with us now, at last.

We know that they are with her. Our sense of the gods' presence is reinforced when the chorus takes up the theme: Dike is coming upon the murderers, an Erinys in arms, 'springing on them from an ambush'.

With these clear directions the urn-speech (1126–70) takes on an extra dimension. To say, as I did earlier,[1] that it reveals a new aspect of Electra's character is true; now we see in her a tenderness which hitherto has been overlaid with hatred and hardness. But the scene was not designed for this only. Let us visualize it. Orestes has not recognized Electra; why indeed should the Princess Royal be out in public like this, and so ill-dressed? She is well forward in the orchestra; the men are now at the back, twenty or thirty yards away, surveying the entrance to the palace – a stage-direction which has no authority except common sense. Electra's speech is a soliloquy. As an expression of pure grief it is as moving as anything Sophocles ever wrote; it can stand up even to Antigone's *commos*. Had it survived only as a citation in Stobaeus it would have been used over and over again to illustrate Sophocles' profound pessimism: all Electra's tenderness, love, resolution, endurance, have gone for nothing, useless, ἀνωφέλητον, ἀνωφελές (1144, 1159). Fortunately we have the full context; as we listen we can also see, and what we see is the living Orestes, brought back by the favouring escort of Zeus. He is by the gateway, and presently he will enter through it. Here at least Sophocles is no pessimist.

Passing over much else we may consider the final scenes. Again, they certainly reveal more of Electra: no tenderness now! 'Strike her again, if you have strength enough!' (1415). There is the deadly irony with which she receives, and deceives, Aegisthus; there is the moment when he lifts the face-cloth, which I described (rightly, I think) as 'perhaps the most shattering *coup de théâtre* ever invented'; there is the savagery with which Electra cries 'Kill him at once, and throw his body to the dogs! Nothing less can compensate for what

[1] 2nd. edition, p. 173.

I have endured'. But there is something more. Aegisthus, when he sees the shrouded body, says:

> '*Zeus, here is one laid low, before our eyes*
> *By the anger of the gods.*'

The whole structure of the play enforces the thought that he is speaking the solemn truth – except in the one small detail in which he is mistaken. A *coup de théâtre* indeed, but 'theatrical' as, in *Hamlet,* the death by poison of Claudius the poisoner is theatrical.

With a play like this, with many Greek plays, and with some of Shakespeare's too, our difficulty today is to avoid both of two opposite errors. The one is to suppose that 'the whole arrangement of the plot is to give Electra's emotions the greatest possible scope'; the other is to expound it as an illustration of fifth-century religious ideas, and either to neglect its purely dramatic aspects or to discuss them separately, in a different chapter.[1] Sophocles, we should remember, was writing – like Shakespeare – at a time when religion and art, intellect and the imagination, had not yet said good-bye to each other. Neither did he write supremely good theatre and then give it a religious colouring, nor did he inculcate religious ideas by dressing them up in drama. The two are fused; so also are the particular and the universal aspects of the same action. What is certain is that he did not 'create' his Electra simply to show us what an exciting Electra he had created; such an interpretation leaves too much of the structure lying loose and flabby; the deeper interpretation makes everything taut and purposeful. He does indeed show (as I said previously) what effect the situation has had on the heroic and devoted nature of Electra, making her hard, even cruel; but this in turn illustrates how, in this instance, Dike works. Electra's passionate speech about her daily humiliations not only helps to explain what she has become; it also helps – like Orestes' references to his own dispossession – to explain why Dike comes upon the murderers and usurpers, 'springing on them from an ambush.' They have, themselves, created the situation which breeds their own destruction. So do the gods operate. The extreme dramatic vividness of everything is not an added merit; it is necessary. Sophocles

[1] There is, of course, a third possible error, to suppose that Sophocles was merely dramatizing myth, as best he could. I say nothing about this – but Johnson's phrase comes to mind: 'stark insensibility.'

will show something of the inner workings of life, the ways of
the gods; if the whole texture is not instinct with life, the exposition
of the inner workings will not carry conviction.

All our post-romantic, even post-renaissance, ways of thought
incline us to assume, perhaps without much thought, that Sophocles'
subject was simply Electra. Most of the play confirms us in that
belief. But when we begin to suspect that the real subject is something wider, something like the natural or inevitable working of
Dike seen within the Electra story, then everything in the play
springs into life, the whole structure becomes much more purposeful. This wider subject Sophocles might have added to a merely
personal character-study of Electra by means of reflective, didactic
odes or speeches, but that was not the Hellenic method; rather, the
wider meaning is built into the structure of the play – which is the
reason why it can escape our notice: we are not expecting so much
and see only what we do expect.

Some way back (p. 156) we were finding the *Tyrannus* rather
difficult: is it possible that here, too, our natural assumptions about
the subject may be too narrow, and that a steady look at the structure
might be a corrective? It is difficult for us to read the play as if for
the first time. However, we will make the attempt, trying to record
what Sophocles does, and trying not to bring in what he leaves out,
especially our own preoccupation with free will.

It would be wrong to say that the play falls into three parts: it
does not fall; it stands up. Nevertheless there are three evident
points of climax, which do mark out three areas within the play
which we may consider one by one: they are the condemnation of
Creon by Oedipus; the discovery, with the consequent self-blinding
of Oedipus; and the actual end of the play.

The first part moves, with steadily growing impetus, through the
Teiresias scene to its climax, and this is prolonged by the *commos*.
We say of it, perhaps, that it begins in a tentative and remote way
the process of discovery; that it builds up the character of Oedipus;
that, in preparation for the end, it presents Oedipus as the great
King, the sole hope of Thebes, himself so remote from the cause of
the plague; finally, that the Teiresias scene most ominously introduces the theme of blindness. All this would be true; now let us
record some more facts.

Of the first scene we could reasonably say that it puts before us a picture of Oedipus as the ideal king, devoted to the welfare of his subjects. Towards Creon, whose help he has naturally used, he is courteous. But at the end of this part of the play Creon is most unjustly condemned to death – or exile, for the point is not made precise – and the brief dialogue 626–30 may well call to our minds the tenor of the altercation between Haemon and Creon in the *Antigone* (740–56): Oedipus the King has become Oedipus the arbitrary tyrant; and Sophocles continues by making it clear that though he is persuaded to rescind his decree he is in no way persuaded that it was a monstrous error.

Such is the first of the three climaxes. It is not what we should have expected. The condemnation of Creon, so subtly prepared through a long chain of suspicions, hints, confident but quite erroneous inferences,[1] does not further the plot at all, except to the minor extent that it brings Iocasta upon the scene. Of course the process of discovery is being got under way, but for this purpose it was not necessary for Oedipus to be brought to the verge of a judicial murder. Of course it draws a strong portrait of Oedipus; but after all, this Oedipus was invented by Sophocles, so that the question is: Why did Sophocles want an Oedipus who goes to this length in tyrannical hybris? It cannot contribute to his doom: that is sealed already. It does not explain it, because Sophocles never suggests that it was through hybris that Oedipus fulfilled the prophecies. Yet it is a conspicuous part of the structure: if the plot did not require it, presumably something else did.

In the Teiresias scene there is the contrast, so emphatically made, between the physical blindness of the prophet and the real blindness of the king. The intelligence of the king had been emphasized by the Priest (31–9): now Oedipus is confronted by an incredible accusation. Being intelligent he puts two and two together. Suspicions of collusion between the prophet and Creon are the result. Perhaps we should not blame him for *that*: 'How all occasions do inform against me,' as Hamlet observed; the circumstances do look suspicious. (Similarly, we can hardly blame him for what he did at the Three Ways, or when he came to Thebes.) His conclusion is entirely wrong, but his reasoning has its plausibility. But what happens next? He is so certain of himself that he will not listen to Creon's own appeal to reason (577–602); still worse, he rejects out of hand a direct and

[1] Vv. 73–5, 124 f., 287, 345–9, 378, 380–9, 390 ff., 570 ff.

reasonable challenge that would at once have proved him wrong, namely that he should go to Delphi with the simple question whether the god had or had not given the response which Creon had reported (602–7); he also rejects Creon's solemn oath (664–6). In his complete certainty he sweeps all aside; but as chorus remarks (617), 'Swift is not always sure.' So is the good king betrayed into behaving like the unjust tyrant; he is too confident in his own judgement.

What is the point? Hybris explains neither his past actions nor his coming fall; there is, however, one patent link between the present action and the past: the blindness of the intelligent man, his false confidence, when circumstances are treacherous. He was certain that Polybus and Merope were his parents; it never occurred to him that he might be wrong. He is certain that Creon is conspiring against him. The earlier certainty betrayed him into disasters of which he had been explicitly forewarned; this one leads him straight to an outburst of tyrannical hybris.

We hear about hybris in the second part of the play, but let us first look at the last of our three climaxes. Even more than the first, it is not what the story dictates; it is no inevitable ending to a play about the tragic fate of Oedipus, but it does cohere logically with the first part and with its climax.

What could be more obvious, logical, and dramatic than that the play should end with the exiling of Oedipus? Teiresias has prophesied that Oedipus will become blind, an exile, a beggar, execrated by all. Oedipus himself pronounced his curse on Laius' murderer; now the curse has recoiled upon his own head: he it is who brought the plague upon Thebes. The stranger who once saved Thebes by his own intelligence must now, though Theban born, save it by leaving the city for ever. How did Sophocles come to miss such a dramatic ending?

We can make a guess: it was because of the *Coloneus*, which requires that Oedipus shall have remained in Thebes for several years. The worst of making such a guess is that it discourages us from looking and thinking any further. Even if it is correct, the question still remains whether this ending, so motivated, is or is not a real climax. Perhaps in any case it is not likely that Sophocles would have impaired the ending of this play for the sake of another which was not to be composed for some twenty years yet; but we have only to look at the structure calmly to see that the ending was contrived for the sake not of the *Coloneus* but of the *Tyrannus*.

Creon is brought back. All the materials are there for a 'strong scene' and for one of those contrasts in character at which Sophocles was so good. It is a heaven-sent *peripateia*: Creon, who had barely escaped death or exile at the hands of Oedipus is now King, and Oedipus is abased; the intended victim is now in control. Hitherto Creon has had a passive role in the play; now comes Sophocles' opportunity: he will draw for us a Creon who is vindictively triumphant, or greatly magnanimous. But Sophocles appears to be hardly interested. Creon does indeed bear no rancour – and the fact is dismissed in two verses (1422–3); he is not made noticeably kind to Oedipus, nor noticeably hard. What Sophocles does is to develop a situation perfectly antistrophic to the one at the end of the first part of the play.

No fewer than four times does Oedipus demand to be driven out; twice he demands it of the chorus (1340 ff., 1410 ff.), twice of Creon (1436–7, 1518). Once again Oedipus is quite certain: previously it was, as the chorus said, 'upon uncertain calculation,' ἐν ἀφανεῖ λόγῳ (657), now on a clear one, for the god has decreed it and Oedipus himself had confirmed it. But Creon refuses, twice. Not out of kindness: 'I would certainly have done it, but I wished first to learn of the god what should be done.' 'But the god has spoken clearly!' 'Yes, but in this pass it is better to inquire how we should act.' It is a contrast of attitudes rather than of persons. Had Sophocles wanted to give us a sharp image of Creon the man, he could have done it; he has not. Oedipus, earlier, would not consult Delphi to check his own inferences even though a man's life was at stake; Creon, though the case seems clear, will not act in a crisis, when better authority is available, until he has consulted that authority.

This link between the two parts of the play is reinforced by a verbal repetition. When Oedipus is drawing his desperately wrong conclusions, he asks Creon (562 ff.) 'When Laius was killed, did the prophet mention me?' 'No.' 'Why not?' Creon's answer is 'I do not know, and when I lack knowledge I prefer not to speak':

οὐκ οἶδ'· ἐφ' οἷς γὰρ μὴ φρονῶ σιγᾶν φιλῶ.

Towards the end, when for the second time Creon refuses to drive Oedipus from Thebes, Oedipus cries: 'But the gods hate no man more than me!' 'Then,' says Creon, 'you will soon have your wish.' 'You affirm it?' 'Ah no; when I lack knowledge I prefer not to speak at random' (1546):

α μὴ φρονῶ γὰρ οὐ φιλῶ λέγειν μάτην.

The contrast between certainty and caution is very much in Sophocles' thoughts, and we saw that in the first part certainty led to hybris.

Superficially, the end of the play seems undramatic and negative. Any one who cares may of course still say that he would prefer a more spectacular ending; it does however begin to appear that it is not simply negative.

The very last action too invites attention; it is by no means inevitable. The two children have been brought out (as is indeed natural, though not inevitable), and what Oedipus has said to them, and about them, is a most tragic addition to the picture of ruin and desolation that Sophocles is drawing. Now, when Oedipus is led into the palace, the children too must be removed from the stage. There is no need to make a dramatic point of it, but Sophocles does: they are removed from Oedipus' embrace, and when he protests Creon says, in the last genuine verses of our play: 'Seek not control (κρατεῖν) in all things; the control that you did have broke before the end.' Such is the terminus to which Sophocles has guided this long train of events.

Certainty, and control: both are illusory. Laius was given a warning, and was left quite unfettered. He made himself safe by destroying the child (and Sophocles imputes no blame) – except that, naturally enough, he did not do the nasty thing with his own hands. He did something else that was just as good – except that it wasn't. He thought he had taken control. So did Oedipus when, being warned what was to happen, he avoided Corinth where his parents were and went in the other direction. Being attacked, he defended himself: why not? Being offered the crown and Queen of Thebes he accepted them: why not? Sophocles does not blame him; he simply points out that human resolution and intelligence can easily go wrong and be defeated. But circumstances were singularly adverse? Agreed; it is an extreme case, but who will say that it is not poetically true to life? that chance does not sometimes defeat the best of plans? Human control is an illusion. Further, Oedipus' certainty led him into hybris. Now, it was becoming a fashionable doctrine among Sophocles' more progressive contemporaries that 'We are the masters now'; as Protagoras said, the gods may or may not exist: the question is difficult, and life is short. The clever and ruthless Athenians at Melos, in Thucydides' account, explicitly disowned archaic ideas about justice: the guide to life is intelligent calculation. Thucydides had his doubts; so too had Sophocles.[1]

Of the three climaxes, both the first and the third are unexpected on the assumption that Sophocles' subject was merely the tragic story of Oedipus; as in the *Electra,* the personal drama is surrounded by something more universal, and here that has a decisive influence on the structure. We have not yet found, nor shall we find, that Sophocles is concerned with the idea of an arbitrary and inevitable doom; in fact, he makes it clear that one prophecy at least had no compulsive power. Teiresias had prophesied that Oedipus would become blind; when Oedipus has blinded himself he explains at length to the horrified chorus why he *had* to do it (1369–90): it was what we, in our terms, might call a psychological necessity; in spite of which Oedipus can say 'It was Apollo who brought these sufferings to pass ($\tau\epsilon\lambda\epsilon\hat{\iota}\nu$), but the hand that struck was mine alone'. In the *Electra,* Apollo, with the other deities, manifestly prefigure what we might call the normal or even inevitable course of events; so, too, is the blinding 'inevitable', to Oedipus; the god foresaw it; he did not enforce it. The major prophecies of the play certainly do not predict what we can call a 'normal' course of events; the play could not bear the sub-title 'A typical day in Thebes'. Yet they do not compel. What is exceptional in the play, the unmotivated intervention of the god, which here is in no sense an enlargement of human motivation, does not mean that Sophocles is contradicting all that he implies elsewhere, namely that omnipotent gods do not arbitrarily interfere in our lives; rather, he is taking a limiting case: 'Human control? human calculation? Let these people be even explicitly forewarned: even so the complexity of things, the limitations of human knowledge, their own natural behaviour, will defeat them.'

Now we may look at the middle part of the play, the part which is to show, so terribly, that the incredible is true, that the impossible

---

[1] See Bernard Knox, *Oedipus at Thebes,* the last chapter. I reach the same conclusion as Knox, but by a different path.

has happened. The underlying structure is firm, though at first puzzling – to us.

With difficulty, the chorus and Iocasta have persuaded Oedipus not to kill or exile Creon; the episode is barely mentioned again, and seems to have no influence on what follows. Iocasta proves to Oedipus that one oracle at least has failed, but in doing this she terrifies Oedipus with the thought that he may, after all, be the man who killed Laius. Iocasta repeats: Even so, the oracle has failed; he was not killed by his own son. Then comes the ode, so often discussed: the chorus prays for purity, for the observance of the Unwritten Laws, for the avoidance of that hybris which breeds the tyrant and inevitably is overthrown; then, in unmistakably solemn fashion, it prays that the oracles may be fulfilled, since the verity of religion depends on it; religion is falling into disregard. This leads at once to Iocasta's sacrifice and the answer that it receives – an exact and a challenging parallel to the sequence in the *Electra*, except (and here is the challenge) that Clytemnestra's prayer was so abominable that she deserved the answer that she got, while Iocasta is a tragic and tortured woman who is praying only for deliverance. Why, in each case, should the apparently reassuring message be only the prelude to death?

At this point, the idea of $T\acute{v}\chi\eta$, Chance, is made prominent. While Iocasta is convinced that yet another oracle has failed, she asserts that human affairs are ruled by Chance (977–9). Hardly has she said it when her fancied security is shattered; all she can do is to go in anguish to her death. At once the pattern is repeated. Oedipus, once more drawing a wrong conclusion, supposing that Iocasta is suffering from no more than wounded pride, declares himself to be the son of Chance; and the chorus, taking up the theme in dance and song, speculates which roaming god begot their King from some mountain-nymph. Upon which, there enters the Theban shepherd, to prove that he is no son of Chance but of Laius and Iocasta.

What we are confronted with, therefore, is the sharp opposition between Chance and prophecy, and the close connexion, affirmed in the ode, of prophecy and religion – and not merely a formal religion, but religion in its deep sense: purity, the observance of the Unwritten Laws, the avoidance of hybris.

We find it difficult. If we suppose, as many do, that Apollo had decreed that the disasters *should* happen to these people, then, since Sophocles has not represented them as having been wicked or impure, we find a religion which is not only unintelligent but also inconsistent with what we find in the other plays, where, emphatically, disaster is the result of sin or folly, even though the disaster may involve the innocent with the guilty. But are we any better off if we assume what the play really indicates, that the prophecies do not compel but only foresee? At first sight, no. The situation will now be that the omniscient god, knowing all the complexities of character and circumstance, knows that if he warns them they will do precisely what they are seeking to avoid. 'Therefore,' says Sophocles, 'seek purity and avoid hybris; prophecies come true; religion is not a fraud.' But it is at least not clear that obedience to the Unwritten Laws would have saved these people, or that Sophocles ever suggests that it would have done. Is then his mind in a muddle about these important matters, he being only a poet? Or did he not care, being intent only on thrilling drama?

We have already looked at the beginning and end of the play, and have drawn certain necessary conclusions; this middle part coheres perfectly. The first part, perhaps to our surprise, led to a climax irrelevant to the actual story: Oedipus, in his intellectual self-reliance, drew what seemed the obvious conclusion, was entirely wrong, and, in his certainty, nearly committed a crime of singular enormity. Here was 'the hybris that breeds the tyrant' (892). As for the ode, some have thought that it refers to the hybris of Iocasta in denying the truth of the oracle. This cannot be maintained. Iocasta is merely relating what she *knows*: the child was destroyed; the oracle did fail. In any case she has safeguarded herself by saying that the oracles may not have come from the god, only from his human interpreters (711 f.); and if this is hidden hybris, then the chorus itself is guilty of it, for it said exactly the same thing earlier (498–504). On the other hand Sophocles has created and displayed at length a conspicuous example of hybris: it was Oedipus who swept aside all restraints, acted like a tyrant, and because he was so certain went to the verge of crime, Δίκας ἀφόβητος, 'undeterred by Dike' (904).

Iocasta's part is different. She also is certain, both before the ode and still more after it, when she learns that Polybus is dead and that a second oracle has failed. From this delusion, as we saw above, she infers that Chance rules. We should look at the passage more closely:

> *Why should we fear, seeing that man is ruled*
> *By Chance, and there is room for no clear forethought?*
> *No; live at random, live as best one can.*

Now we can understand why her prayers, that the oracle should not be fulfilled, meets with the same response as Clytemnestra's.

In the other plays the dramatic function of prophecy is to assert that life is not chaotic. If Iocasta is right, then Creon's downfall in the *Antigone* was a mere fluke, and the *Electra* is no more than a superior thriller; there is no such thing as Dike, Order; only chance. If she is right, we might as well all be 'undeterred by Dike'. We are back in Melos, or in the company of Plato's Thrasymachus and Callicles.

At this point another modern prepossession must be challenged. 'Order?' we say; 'Justice? But where are order and justice here, if these people destroyed through no fault of their own, only by improbable circumstances?' The fallacy is that we translate Dike 'justice', and then equate this with the eighteenth-century idea of 'natural justice', happiness for the good and misery only for the bad.[1] But neither Sophocles nor any earlier Greek poet pretended that this is the way in which the gods work; their 'justice' is not built to human specifications; it is not τὸ φιλάνθρωπον. The poets knew, and accepted, that the gods can be hard, indiscriminate, but they knew also that the gods are not on that account to be disregarded. Antigone was dismayed that the gods left her to perish, as well she might be. They did leave her to perish – but they visited their anger on Creon. It is no failure in logic to say that Oedipus is not being punished for any fault, but nevertheless the universe is not random.

Iocasta, being certain that the oracles have failed, will allow no place for πρόνοια, forethought, carefulness, scruple; similarly, Oedipus, being certain that Creon was a traitor, would observe no restraints. Surely the ode need puzzle us no more, beginning as it does with the Unwritten Laws and ending with a prayer for the fulfilment of the oracles. Sophocles is not tagging orthodox piety on to a story that makes no sense of it. It is obvious that observance of

[1] See above, p. 101.

the Unwritten Laws would not have averted this catastrophe – and it is Sophocles who has made it obvious. His point is quite different, and he makes it throughout the play. Life is so vast, complex, uncertain, that we delude ourselves if we think that we can control it; human judgement is fallible, over-reliance on it leads to hybris, and that always ends in disaster. Many things may be inexplicable, but life is not random; the gods do exist and their laws do work. If we think there are no laws, that we can take each thing as it comes, neglect the restraints and sin intelligently, we are only deceiving ourselves.

The dichotomy with which we began is not so sharp as it seemed. The difference in form between the *Ajax* and *Trachiniae* and the *Electra* and *Tyrannus* remains, of course, precisely what it was, but examination of the two latter plays shows that we must not be too simple-minded about any of them. The vital structural principles are the same in all, and we shall not fully understand any of them if we attribute to Sophocles principles which he never followed. In none of the plays did he set out, as we so easily suppose, simply to create characters or to dramatize a situation; always some much deeper conception shaped his work. Assuming the wrong principles we make little of the *Ajax* and *Trachiniae*; it may well be that in any case we shall not find them as satisfying as the other plays, but at least when we see what their real subject is they become much more impressive and intelligible than they had seemed to be. Nor do the dramatic power and excitement of the other plays diminish when we see that Sophocles was not simply making brilliant drama, but was at the same time, through this brilliant drama, talking good and important sense.

CHAPTER VIII

The Euripidean Tragedy

1. Introduction

If this book were being entirely rewritten, chapters VIII and X would probably change places. I had misunderstood the *Trachiniae* because I had not paid close enough attention to its form; therefore I ascribed it to a later period of Sophocles' activity, one in which his dramatic thinking was less intense, in which he had begun to exploit the study of character and situation for their own sake. The *Philoctetes*, which I joined with the *Trachiniae*, does indeed exploit these more than any other of the extant plays, but even so I would not now draw the distinction which I did between Sophocles' 'middle' and 'new' tragedy. However, it is perhaps no bad thing if we now consider some of Euripides' plays; the young reader, at least, will be reminded that Sophocles and Euripides did not exist end to end but were contemporaries. It is probable that most of the plays to be discussed in this chapter were produced before the *Electra* of Sophocles.

During the period with which we are now concerned, the last three decades of the fifth century, all Greece was convulsed by the Peloponnesian War. No extant Sophoclean play shows the direct influence of this except the *Philoctetes*; Euripides reacted to it more violently. A more permanent influence on Greek poetry was exerted by another contemporary event which goes, rather awkwardly, under the name of 'the Sophistic Movement'. It is as if the Greek mind, during this period, began to shift its weight from one leg to the other: from intuitive intelligence, based on a generalized reflection about human experience, and expressing itself through art and the traditional imagery of mythology, to a conscious analysis of experience which made use of new intellectual techniques and was expressed, inevitably, in prose. It is a change that has something in common with our own Enlightenment which set in during the seventeenth century: after that, in England, until the romantic movement brought revival, poetry was either witty or pitiful; in Greece, big-scale poetry of importance dies with Euripides and Sophocles. Exquisite poetry was still to come, but no longer did it even pretend to grapple with what matters most; that became the province of the philosophers.

What we will call New Tragedy shows the influence of the shift on serious drama. We shall find it in some of Euripides' later plays, and it seems a safe inference that Agathon's *Antheus* was of such a kind: Aristotle says that Agathon invented the whole plot: Agathon would not have done this unless he were writing drama of an essentially romantic kind, depending on surprise and novelty, not professing to say anything very important.

But before we can deal with this stage of Tragedy we must consider that development which took its origin not in a general change coming over the art, but in the individual outlook of Euripides. He, like Sophocles, had his great tragic period; it survives to us in the *Medea, Hippolytus, Heracleidae, Heracles, Andromache, Hecuba, Suppliant Women* and *Troades*. These plays are all tragic, all but the *Hippolytus* badly constructed, by Aristotelian standards; they have certain features in common, such as the prologue and 'episodic' plots, and in some respects, notably characterization and construction, they are as unlike the rest of Euripides' work as the *Tyrannus* itself. Yet the *I.T.*, even to Aristotle, was a model of construction, and the *Ion, Electra, Orestes, Helen,* are at the lowest estimate well-made. Why is it that in the tragic group there is hardly a single play which has not provoked the most serious complaints and the most desperate apologies?

The thesis of the following pages will be that as we were able to trace the characteristic features of the Aeschylean and Sophoclean tragedy to the nature of the tragic idea that possessed these poets, so all the new features in these plays can be seen to be the logical result of Euripides' tragic idea. We shall see him moving from a drama which he made as much like Middle Tragedy as possible to one which, however un-Aristotelian, was at least the powerful expression of what he wanted to say.

Our first task, once more, must be to try to catch the tragic idea, that tragic way of thinking about life which made these plays what they are; for we will not suppose, if we can help it, that a poet of Euripides' calibre made loose plots like those of the *Troades* and *Heracles* by mere inadvertence, or committed the structural sins which Aristotle censured in the *Medea* out of simple inability to do better. In fact we shall find, time after time, the Euripides does very much less than he might have done if Aristotelian perfection of form had been his aim, and intellectual loyalty to his idea of no importance to him. In the dramatic methods which we see developing from the *Medea* onwards there is a purposefulness, or at any rate a positiveness, which is not to be explained by mere absence of something, a mere lack of harmony between the poet and his form.

We have, to mislead us, important aspects of Euripides' thought – his scepticism, his impatience with traditional religion (as if Pindar and Aeschylus had not been impatient and sceptical), the misogyny which ancient critics regretted in him, the feminism of which some moderns accuse him, his liberalism, his pacifism. These things are important. Politics and religion are more significant in drama than in painting, for instance, because the raw material of drama is drawn from the sphere of social and moral ideas; but to understand the art of a dramatist it is not enough to expiscate and record his religious and political beliefs – nor indeed shall we know what they are until we have understood his art. These doctrines of Euripides' do not help us in the least; for they colour all his work, while we are faced with this cleavage between the tragedies and the other plays. The *I.T.* and *Electra* contain more religious scepticism, more realism, more satirical handling of traditional legend than the *Hecuba* or *Troades*, yet they are in the conventional sense infinitely better constructed and contain much more normal characterization. There is some force in the common statement that there was a deep disharmony between his thought and the traditional form of state tragedy, though Euripides did not handle this traditional form, whatever it was, much more freely than Aeschylus had done; yet the *Suppliant Women,* an 'encomium of Athens' as it is called by critics ancient and modern, shows little sign that the dramatist for once felt comfortable in his civic bed.

Is there one general explanation of Euripides' strange methods, or must we either resort to a kind of Secret Service like Verrall's or take undignified refuge in phrases like 'unevenness', 'lack of unity', and 'carelessness'?

Let us state the problem more fully. The *Medea* is twice censured by Aristotle: the Aegeus scene is illogical and is not even used properly, and the end is artificial and therefore wrong. Moreover, by implication he condemns the murder of the children as 'revolting' (μιαρόν), and the catastrophe, the escape of Medea and the death of the innocent, is hardly what he approved. Both the *Hecuba* and the *Andromache* have a sharply marked duplicity of action; the *Heracles* contains three actions (though with a more obvious connexion) and a character, Lycus, who seems to belong more to melodrama than to tragedy; the *Suppliant Women* offers one scene, Evadne-Iphis, about which a recent editor conjectures that it was put in to interest those spectators who were bored with the rest of the play; while the *Troades* is one episode after another, held together, we are told, by the passive figure of Hecuba – as if Euripides needed Aristotle to tell him that what befalls one person is not necessarily a unity.

In the later[1] series of plays none of these major faults are to be found. Euripides satirizes Apollo, he argues, he ridicules or condemns heroes of legend, he uses the realism and the modern music that Aristophanes disliked, he expresses 'advanced' views in religion, philosophy, and sociology, he commits all sorts of anachronisms, he does a dozen other things to which this critic or that may object, but at least he never commits again any of those elementary blunders in construction.[2] When we add that all of the plays in the first series are tragic and none of the second, or, if the *Electra* and the *Orestes* are to be called tragic, they are tragic in an entirely different spirit – then we are justified in asking if these peculiar features in the first series are not intimately connected with the nature of the tragic idea expressed in them.[3]

2. The 'Medea'

There is no need to make phrases about the terrific power of the *Medea*. In important respects it diverges from what we think normal construction, at least normal construction as understood by Aristotle,

---

[1] It is convenient so to describe them, though the two series overlap.

[2] The prologue to the *Ion* is a special case. (See below, p. 316.)

[3] From the discussion that follows I have omitted all but the briefest reference to the *Heracleidae*. In the present state of the text it is a play to be argued to, not from, and to do this would contribute nothing to my theme.

and yet it is one of the greatest of Greek tragedies. So one writes, almost automatically, but most of the implications of that 'and yet' are wrong; for had Euripides managed to put the stuff of the play into a beautiful Sophoclean mould, making a 'better' play of it, it would not have been a better play but a ridiculous one. The *Medea* diverges from the Sophoclean pattern because Euripides' way of thinking was different.

Aristotle expressly cites the appearance of Aegeus and the sending of the magic chariot as being 'irrational', not the necessary or probable result of what has gone before; but, lest we be tempted to think that these are only casual licences taken by the poet which can, with luck, be explained away, we ought to observe how fundamental is the divergence between the poet and the philosopher here. How, for example, does Medea fit Aristotle's definition of a tragic hero? Not at all. Aristotle's tragic hero is 'like' us, for we should not feel pity and fear for one unlike us. He must not be a saint, or his downfall would be revolting, nor a villain, whose downfall might be edifying but would not be tragic. He must therefore be inter-mediate, better rather than worse, and find his ruin through some ἁμαρτία. Medea is not like this; it would indeed be difficult to find a Euripidean hero who is, until we come to Pentheus. Medea is no character compounded of good and bad, in whom what is bad tragically brings down in ruin what is good, and we certainly cannot fear for her as for one of ourselves. In fact, treated as a genuinely tragic heroine she will not work; she causes at least one of her admirers to fall into a grave inconsistency. Professor Bates says (*Euripides,* p. 37), 'In the character of Medea . . . the tragic genius of Euripides reaches its highest pinnacle. In none of the other plays is there a character which can approach Medea as a tragic figure.' This is a possible view, but it is inconsistent with the judgement (p. 44), that all our sympathy is concentrated on the unfortunate children, 'for we have little sympathy with the cruel, savage Medea.' Then she is not tragic after all, only melodramatic? The poor children, the wicked mother, the heartless father – surely this will not do?

A comparison with Macbeth is interesting. He can be made into a recognizably Aristotelian hero. He is presented at first in a favourable light: 'For brave Macbeth – well he deserves the name.' 'O valiant cousin! worthy gentleman!' He is better rather than worse; but he ἁμαρτία of ambition, and circumstances, as is their way with tragic heroes, play upon it – first through his very virtues:

DUNCAN. No more that thane of Cawdor shall deceive
             Our bosom interest. Go pronounce his present death,
             And with his former title greet Macbeth.
ROSS.   I'll see it done.
DUNCAN. What he hath lost, noble Macbeth hath won.

It may be hazardous to claim Glamis Castle for a stronghold of Aristotelianism, but this ironic touch is very like Sophocles, and certainly it is an essential part of the tragedy of Macbeth that he has been noble, loyal, and gallant.

Medea on the other hand is certainly not all villainy; she loves her children, loved Jason (if that is a merit), and was popular in Corinth; but it is the essential part of this tragedy that she was never really different from what we see her to be. Euripides could easily have represented her as a good but passionate woman who plunges into horrors only when stung by deadly insult and injury. There was no need for him to rake up her past as he does – except that this is his whole point. She never was different; she has no contact with Aristotle.[1]

Neither has Jason. In him it is impossible to find anything that is not mean; not because Euripides is satirizing anyone through him, though he does use his Jason to mock the complacency of his countrymen, but for the same reason, whatever it is, that makes his Medea so extreme a character. We may notice here how little the other characters count – naturally, when the chief characters are drawn in such simple colours. The Nurse is this, the Paedagogus that, and Aegeus the other thing, but were they different nobody would be much the wiser. This is not characterization as Sophocles understood it; we have nearly returned to Eteocles' Spy. Sophocles drew his minor characters vividly because he needed them, not because he was good at it; Euripides refrains because he does need it.

From characterization we may pass to the general tone of the play. Aristotle, in a dry little analysis, examines the ways in which τὸ φθαρτικόν, the deed of violence, can be brought about: the worst but one is for kinsman to slay kinsman knowing who it is that he is

---

[1] Neither had Agamemnon. Both he and Medea are tragic figures rather than tragic characters.

slaying. This is 'revolting', and the *Medea* is full of it. The unrelieved baseness of Jason is revolting; revolting in the highest degree is Medea's great crime; and what of the Messenger-speech? The horrible death of Glauce and Creon is described exhaustively in the terrible style of which Euripides was such a master. It is sheer Grand Guignol. We have yet seen nothing like it in Greek Tragedy. We have had before scenes, described or suggested, of horror – the self-blinding of Oedipus, the murder of Clytemnestra – but always the horror has been enveloped in the greater emotion of tragic pity. It has brought with it its own catharsis. Where is the tragic pity here? In the destruction of an innocent girl and her father there is no possibility of tragic relief. We pity them, as later we pity the children, but as they have done nothing which in reason should have involved them in this suffering, as no flaw of character, no tragic miscalculation, no iron law of life has brought them to this pass, but simply the rage of Medea, our pity has no outlet; we are impotent and angry – or would be, if this assault on our nerves left room for such feelings. From these things we can turn to no grim but majestic universal principle, only back again to that terrifying murderess.

Supposing that Sophocles had given us a comparable description of Antigone's death agonies? It is unthinkable; but is this only to say that Sophocles was Attic, Euripides already Hellenistic? And supposing that Aristotle had had his way, and that Medea, having committed these crimes, had made her way under her own steam to Athens? Or if the dramatic law of the necessary or probable had asserted itself, and Medea had been stoned by an outraged populace? The play would have been no tragedy at all, but the emptiest of melodrama; after this terrific preparation the story would suddenly have relapsed into insignificance, a mere exciting tale about Medea of Corinth. In the matter of the ending Euripides is un-Aristotelian by inspiration, not by mischance, as we shall see in a moment; but before considering this fully we may complete our survey by noting how his use of the chorus and his dramatic style differ from Sophocles'.

The Chorus, Aristotle lays down, should participate in the action, as in Sophocles, not in Euripides. The chorus in the *Medea* finds itself in a famous difficulty at the murder of the children; it ought to participate in the action and may not. Fifteen women of Corinth stand by doing nothing while Medea murders her children indoors – or rather they stand by deliberating whether to do anything or not.

In meeting this improbability nothing is gained by saying that the Chorus was a body of Ideal Spectators and that a Greek audience would not expect them to interfere. They have, in fact, always taken part in the action when circumstances suggested it – in the *Eumenides,* the *Ajax,* the *Antigone,* later in the *Philoctetes,* to mention only a few cases – and Aristotle feels that so it is best. Moreover, Euripides himself feels that they should naturally interfere now, for if no thought of the possible intervention of Ideal Spectators could have arisen in the mind of the audience, why does he go out of his way to suggest that thought?

The question of Euripides' use of the Chorus will recur several times; he did, in the later tragedies, make it a body of Ideal Spectators. Here it is the solid, flesh-and-blood chorus of Middle Tragedy, women of Corinth who come to inquire about Medea and not to sing philosophy; and such a chorus, natural enough when the theme of the play is one which involves the city, as in the *Antigone* and *Tyrannus,* becomes more difficult to manage convincingly when the theme and setting are not eminently public ones, and is a positive nuisance when private intrigue has to be represented on the stage. In this respect the *Medea* is half-way between two conventions, and a certain uneasiness is inevitable.

This chorus is a little surprising, too, in the ode that it sings at one of the most poignant moments of the play, when Medea has finally resolved that her children must die, and just before we hear the horrible story of Glauce's death. If we have in mind the tremendous effects that Sophocles produced with his chorus at moments like these, it is a little chilling to find Euripides going off into his study, as it were, and writing, in anapaests too, on the advantages of being childless.

Such indifference in the orchestra to what was happening on the stage later became a powerful weapon in Euripides' armoury; here it is a little puzzling. The subject is germane to the context, but the treatment is not; such generalized reflection breaks the emotional rhythm of the play. When such desperate deeds are afoot, why does Euripides insert this pleasant little essay? It may be tentatively suggested that it is Euripides' method of preparing for the messenger's narrative, that he deliberately lulls our minds with this inconspicuous piece of pavement-philosophy in order to give the messenger's onslaught a fairer field. But whether this or something else be the true explanation of the passage, we can draw one deduction from it, and that is that Euripides' attitude to his tragic heroine is quite different from Sophocles'. To Antigone or Oedipus it would have been an unthinkable dramatic impoliteness to break off like this to say something interesting; not because Sophocles was a better poet and dramatist in this respect, but because he was writing a different tragedy. For all the sympathy and the tragic power with which Euripides draws his characters, and although he is 'the most tragic of the poets', it seems clear that fundamentally he is detached from them. He can, as Sophocles cannot, retire for a moment and invite us to think of something else.[1]

Wherever we look, therefore, in the *Medea* we find that Euripides differs from Aristotle's theory and Sophocles' practice, and that not merely on the surface but radically; and the more he works his tragic vein the greater does this divergence grow, until in the *Troades* we have a play in which no single incident is the 'necessary or probable' result of the preceding one, the characterization is slight and inconsistent, the chorus, far from being a co-actor, takes no notice at all of the action – and yet the *Troades* is magnificent tragedy. The method then must be a logical one, and the logic we must now try to find, so far as it is to be seen in the *Medea*.

Medea is a tragic figure, but we have seen that she is no Aristotelian tragic heroine. She is indeed possessed of a passionate nature, quite uncontrolled in love and hate; this makes her dramatic, but it is not ἁμαρτία: it is the whole woman. That certain virtues may plausibly be attributed to her is dramatically of little moment. As she betrayed her father and murdered her brother in her first love for Jason, as in Iolcus to serve Jason she contrived a horrible end for Pelias (exploits which are mentioned by Euripides and are therefore evidence), so in Corinth, when betrayed and insulted by Jason, she thinks first of revenge, not the comparatively honest revenge of killing Jason, but one that shall bring down in ruin Jason, his new bride, his children, his whole house. That they are her children too is unfortunate, but not enough to deter her from her plan; she has her struggle with her maternal feelings – a theatrical struggle rather than a psychologically convincing one – but the decisive thought is that to be laughed at by enemies is not to be borne. She is tragic in that her passions are stronger than her reason

---

[1] This same detachment is displayed in Euripides' characterization and in his proneness to argument: the little essay on music (*Medea*, 190 ff.) is typical. Euripides is not absorbed in his Medea and does not pretend to be.

(θυμὸς κρείσσων τῶν βουλευμάτων, 1097); she is drawn with such vigour and directness, everything that she says and does springs so immediately from her dominant motive that she is eminently dramatic; nevertheless she is no tragic heroine as we have hitherto understood the term; she is too extreme, too simple. This is not character-study as the picture of Neoptolemus in the *Philoctetes* is, for in every possible way the characterization is concentrated in the one overmastering passion, and the situation is manipulated to stimulate this to the uttermost. It is not melodrama, for Medea, though extreme, is true, and her character and deeds leave us with something more than the mere excitement of a strong story. It is tragic, but we must be careful to see what we mean by tragic.

The tragedy of a hero like Ajax is that such strength is nullified by such weakness; of Medea, that such a character should exist at all. She is bound to be a torment to herself and to others; that is why Euripides shows her blazing her way through life leaving wreckage behind her; that is why the suffering of others, of Glauce and of Creon, are not to be glozed over. That she suffers herself is a great and no doubt a necessary part of the drama, but it is not the point of the tragedy, which is that θυμός can be stronger than βουλεύματα, passion than reason, and so can be a most destructive agent. Destructive to whom? Here, to the children, Glauce, Creon, Jason, and to Medea's peace – but not to her life; in short, destructive to society at large.

It follows that Euripides had either to describe Glauce's death horribly or to enfeeble his theme; the sufferings of Medea's victims are as much part of the tragedy as those of Medea herself, possibly a greater part. Hence the contrast with Sophocles. The logical climax of the Sophoclean tragedy is that the hero is ruined; others may be involved, as are Haemon and Eurydice in the *Antigone,* but only as they intensify the hero's downfall or are subordinate to it. Even if Greek taste had allowed a detailed picture of Antigone's death agonies, Greek logic would have forbidden it – and Greek taste and Greek logic were the same thing. Antigone's loyalty to her duty leads to her own death: Creon's shortsightedness and obstinacy leads through her death to his own ruin. Horror would have spoiled the first theme and misdirected the second; we are to watch his error recoiling upon him, not to be made feel that he is a monster of cruelty. There is no contrast here between Attic and Hellenistic; both poets are Hellenic, doing exactly what the theme demands.

The catharsis of Glauce's horror comes when we feel that she, and all the others, are the victims of an almost external force. 'Love,' the chorus sings, 'when it comes in too great strength, has never brought good renown or virtue to mortals.' Medea is drawn stark as the strongest possible impersonation of this force; balance of character is necessarily denied her, and this means that we cannot lose ourselves in sympathy with her as we do with Oedipus. Euripides is not asking us to sympathize with her in this way, but to understand her, to understand that such things are, that Medeas, and Jasons, exist, poetically (οἷα ἂν γένοιτο) if not actually. He asks us to feel terror when we hear of what her passion leads her to do, pity for all who are broken, tragic enlightenment when we see that all are the victims of a primitive force. So we do feel pity 'for the savage and cruel Medea', but only when we regard her in the same objective way as Euripides.

It is perhaps possible to bring all this into relation with Aristotle's theory of ἁμαρτία, and it is worth while to make the attempt for the sake of generalizing the Euripidean method. Euripides, like most Greeks, is a rationalist in that he believes reason, not belief or formula or magic, to be the guide to life; but he sees, too, that we have in us, besides reason, non-rational emotions which are necessary but may run wild,[1] thwarting our reason and bringing calamity. In the last analysis Euripides' tragic hero is mankind. Some natural passion breaks its bounds, and the penalty has to be paid, either by the sinner or by those around him or by both. Within this dramatic cosmos the ἁμαρτία is concentrated in one or two people; they, Medea and Jason, are ἁμαρτία and not necessarily anything else at all; that is why they are so extreme and so unrelieved. The results of the ἁμαρτία fall on the group; perhaps on the sinners, perhaps not; for though Medea suffers here, Menelaus and Orestes in the *Andromache* get off scot-free.

The typical Sophoclean tragedy is one in which the natural order, Dike, is defied – as by the habitual pride of Ajax, the crimes of Agamemnon's murderers, Creon's misguided decree, the moral violence of Heracles. Dike will always assert herself, and of course in a 'natural' way; therefore the whole action – the persons, and what they do – must appear natural. Sophocles' Aristotelian virtues

---

[1] This point has been well treated by E. R. Dodds, *Euripides the Irrationalist, C.R.*, 1929, pp. 97 ff.

are not merely an aesthetic merit; they are also a necessity. But Dike, a basic norm, plays little part in Euripides' thought: it is for this reason that he is 'the most tragic of the poets'. He presents passions or follies as a constant source of misery. Therefore, logically, he draws characters who are extreme, and makes plots that are schematic. To him, the Aristotelian virtues would have been irrelevant. Sophocles' tragedy is rooted in the conception of a universe which in itself is orderly; Euripides' is one shot through with passions, blind instincts, lunacies. Zeus, a symbol of unity and underlyng harmony for Aeschylus and Sophocles, tends in Euripides to evaporate into metaphysics: is he perhaps Mind, or Aether?

This approach to tragedy, which becomes clear later, is in the *Medea* only partly worked out. It may seem absurd to say that Medea, with her tremendous driving-force and sharply accentuated character, is essentially or theoretically a heroine of the same kind as Hecuba, a purely passive figure. It is not absurd. Hecuba and those around her are regarded as the helpless victims of villainy or cruelty, Medea and those around her as the victims of Medea's disastrous temperament. Unless we feel Medea in this way, a tragic victim rather than a tragic agent, we shall try to sympathize with her in the wrong way, and waste valuable time working up emotions about the poor children.

But even if this analysis is correct, is it necessary to our appreciation of the play? Not in the least, the play makes its effect directly, without the help of theory. But the analysis is necessary if we are going to criticize the play. Let us begin with the Aegeus scene, which so glaringly offends against the reasonable Aristotelian law of necessary or probable sequence. How far is this law valid?

In the Sophoclean tragedy of character its validity is absolute. The formula there is that a hero of a certain kind is placed in circumstances such that the play between character and circumstances is bound to result in disaster for the hero. Evidently the whole point of such drama depends on this, that the character shall be a convincing one and that the circumstances, though they may be exceptional, shall develop normally, and always in significant relation with the character of the hero. It would be stultification if the dramatist had to produce a railway-accident without which the hero's doom would not be achieved. But Aegeus comes out of the blue, like a railway-accident. If the *Medea* were really a tragedy of character, if, that is, we were being invited to see how she, a woman of a certain character, was placed in a situation in which her character was inevitably her ruin, and if an Aegeus had to be introduced after all in order to bring this to pass, then the play would be meaningless, as meaningless as if Eteocles had gone to the seventh gate because the champion already chosen had broken his leg on the way. But Euripides is not doing this at all. He is presenting to us his tragic conception that the passions and unreason to which humanity is subject are its greatest scourge. This implies no tragic interlock between character and situation; the situation is nothing but the setting for the outburst of unreason, the channel along which it rushes. What matters now is not that the situation must be convincing and illuminating, not even that the heroine must be convincing as a person; but that her passion must be, in however extreme a form, a fundamental and familiar one. If Medea is in this sense true, we shall not stay to object that she is not likely.

The situation then being only a setting, Euripides is philosophically justified in manipulating it in order to present his tragic thesis in its strongest colours. Sophocles cannot say, 'For the sake of working out my tragic clash between character and circumstances we will here assume that a quite unexpected and unrelated thing materially alters the situation, or that my hero will here do something out of character.' But Euripides can say, without destroying his whole point, 'Excuse me; here is a partial impediment in Medea's course. Let me remove it; you will then have far finer view of what I mean.' Medea was in any case certain to work some ruin; Aegeus only allows her, and Euripides, to go to the logical extreme.

This, incidentally, is the reason also why Jason can be so unrelieved a villain and yet not undramatic. If he stood to Medea as Creon does to Antigone, one whose character fatally interlocks with hers, he would be impossible; being so extreme, he would, as it were, prove nothing. If the dramatist simplifies his characters far enough, he can demonstrate anything. As it is, Jason is not intended to prove anything. He is a ready-made villain, easily assumed as part of the setting, and if, regarded as a dramatic character, he is a 'possible improbability' that matters nothing.

In fact, Aristotle's law is concerned really with two separate things, philosophical cogency and artistic effect. The former is not affected in the least by the 'irrationality' of Aegeus; the latter

H

undoubtedly is. In the later tragedies the artistic unity of the plot is not so obviously impaired by such intrusions (as of Evadne and Iphis in the *Suppliant Women*) because plot there has become frankly diagrammatic instead of organic. Here the plot is made to depend on Medea's will, in the manner of Middle Tragedy, and has that kind of unity and organic growth that comes from this, so that Aegeus, who is quite independent of that will and of the crisis of Medea in Corinth, is felt to be a blemish. Nevertheless, as this is not strictly a play of character, Euripides is logically justified in not making his plot depend on his characters. He may, logically, manipulate the plot himself, or, if you like, arbitrarily interfere, in order that his creations may work out his tragic idea to the end. Our analysis may have seemed far-fetched, but it was correct. The difficulty with Aegeus is that Medea is so nearly an Oedipus and the play so nearly Middle Tragedy that we may reasonably take offence. We are in the middle of a transition from one kind of tragedy to another.

As to the end of the play Aristotle's words are:

> In the characters as in the composition of the plot one must always aim at an inevitable or a probable order of events, so that it will be either inevitable or probable that such a person should say or do such a thing, and inevitable or probable that this thing should happen after that. It is obvious therefore that the ending, too, of the plot must arise naturally out of the plot itself, and not, as in the *Medea,* by external contrivance (ἀπὸ μηχανῆς).

This is not an objection to the *Deus ex machina* as such, only to such employments of it as we have here. The *Philoctetes* ends with a Deus, but the appearance of Heracles there is to some extent[1] a natural result of the action of the play; it has at least been prepared for by the importance in the play of his magic bows and arrows. In the *Medea,* there has been nothing of this magic background; on the contrary, the background has been at times painfully prosaic. We have had a scene of bitter domestic strife in a setting of ordinary social life – children, nurses, curious neighbours, old men gossiping around the spring. Medea may be the granddaughter of Helios, but for all that we are dealing with ordinary life and never feel that the gods are within call. Medea quite rationally, and to the detriment of

[1] This is, of course, not the whole explanation. See p. 308 f.

the play, provides herself with a refuge; why then is an unnatural means of escape provided for her at the end?

It is, of course, some answer to say that Medea is a barbarian princess and a magician; she is descended from Helios, and she is in possession of certain mysterious powers, or more strictly poisons, which ordinary women know nothing about. We are the less surprised therefore at her miraculous escape; less than if a magic chariot should come for the Second Mrs Tanqueray. This may be true, but at the most it is only a palliation; it made Euripides' error possible.

But if we look carefully into the last scene we shall see more than dramatic convenience in the chariot. Medea has done things which appal even the chorus, those sympathetic neighbours who had said, earlier in the play, 'Now is honour coming to womankind.' Their prayer now is 'O Earth, O thou blazing light of the Sun, look upon this accursed woman before she slays her own children. . . . O god-given light, stay her hand, frustrate her . . .' (1251 ff.). In the same vein Jason says, when he has learnt the worst, 'After doing this, of all things most unholy, dost thou show thy face to the Sun and the Earth?' (1327). Sun and Earth, the most elemental things in the universe, have been outraged by these terrible crimes; what will they do? how will they avenge their sullied purity? What Earth will do we shall not be told, but we are told what the Sun does: he sends a chariot to rescue the murderess.

Is this illogical? Could anything be finer, more imaginative? We shall soon see, in the *Hippolytus,* that although reason must be our guide, the primitive things in the universe – Aphrodite and Artemis there – are not reasonable. The servant of Hippolytus (v. 120) thinks what Jason and the chorus think, that 'Gods should be wiser than men'. Perhaps so, but these gods are not. They exist; as well deny the weather as deny Aphrodite; but they are not reasonable and can make short work of us. Zeus, 'whoever he is', is another matter. There may be a *Noûs,* a Mind, in the universe; but there are other powers too, and these we may worship in vain. The magic chariot is a frightening glimpse of something that we shall see in full force in the *Bacchae,* the existence in the universe of forces that we can neither understand nor control – only participate in.

The end of the *Medea* does not come out of the logic of the action by the law of necessity and probability, but is contrived by Euripides, deliberately, as the final revelation of his thought. When we begin to see Medea not merely as the betrayed and vindictive wife but as the impersonation of one of the blind and irrational forces in human nature, we begin to find that catharsis for which we looked in vain in the messenger-speech. It is this transformation that finally explains the 'revolting' and deepens a dramatic story into tragedy. Had Euripides been content with a 'logical' ending, with the play remaining on the mundane, Corinthian level, the 'revolting' would indeed have needed justification. This makes demands on our tolerance which cannot be met if the only profit is the news that barbarian magicians who are passionate and are villainously treated do villainous things. There is in the *Medea* more than this, and to express that Euripides resorts to a manipulation of the plot, an artificial ending which, like Aegeus, would have been ruinous to Sophocles. This imaginative and necessary climax is not the logical ending to the story of Medea the ill-used wife of Corinth, but it is the climax to Euripides' underlying tragic conception.

This is a conception which does indeed call for and receive purely dramatic imagery; we need not be silly and call the *Medea* an illustration of a theme. Nevertheless the conception is not so immediately and completely transfused into drama as is Sophocles' tragic conception; Medea is not quite to Euripides what Oedipus is to Sophocles, completely and utterly the focus and vehicle of his tragic thinking. Euripides remains a little detached. We can go beneath his Medea – for criticism we must, in appreciation we do unconsciously – to the greater conception underlying her; and in the last resort it is this, not the imagined character of Medea in these imagined circumstances, that moulds the play.

As Euripides develops his method, in particular as the war forced his thoughts more on the social aspects of tragedy, we shall find this gap between the stage-drama and the tragic conception, non-existent in Sophocles but perceptible in the *Medea,* growing much wider. Already the strict logic of plot, the Aristotelian doctrines of the tragic hero, the Sophoclean tradition of characterization and the use of the chorus are receding, and they will recede much further. Unity of interest, that is of tragic conception, remains; but how far that conception is to be presented through one hero and one action, how far through a diversity of heroes and a multiplicity of actions, is a matter to be decided privately between Euripides the tragic poet and Euripides the playwright.

3. The 'Hippolytus'

This play was produced three years after the *Medea,* and in several respects it differs widely from it. Its structure is much more regular, for we have no Aegeus scene or magic chariot to explain away, and the characterization is more normal. In Phaedra we have a rounded character who is by a long way the most complete and the most tragic character in any of this series of plays, and though the Nurse has parallels in Euripides' later plays, in the tragedies she stands alone. While Phaedra is on the stage the drama is quite Sophoclean. Her desperate struggle between her passion and her virtue, her tragic realization whence her passion comes (vv. 337–43), the complete contrast between her and the revolting but very natural old Nurse, the Nurse's well meant and cunning desire to help, the tragic but inevitable outcome of this, and Phaedra's resolve to save her honour by leaving the lying letter to Theseus, make an absorbing drama which Sophocles could never have written but which, as a dramatist, he must have admired.

But at this point a number of questions begin to arise. Why is Hippolytus so chilly a figure? As a recoil from Phaedra he was very dramatic, and the romantic atmosphere he brought with him from the hunt was very picturesque, but as the chief actor in the second part of the play is he not rather a disappointing character? Is he not too negative, protesting his pre-eminent purity a little too much? And why is Phaedra forgotten? The dramatic motif of the opposition between his nature and Phaedra's disappears. There is no suggestion that her personality, so prominent in the first part, remains active in the second; no suggestion that her death works at all in his mind; no pity or remorse or hatred is seen in him. In fact, Phaedra's letter seems to be no more than a mechanical link between her tragedy and his. Having in Phaedra so tragic a subject, why did not Euripides base his whole play on it? As it is, not only does the *Hippolytus* lack real unity, but its rhythm goes the wrong way, from the very dramatic Phaedra to the less dramatic Hippolytus; and even that useful body the chorus, by saying nothing about Phaedra in the second part, does nothing to conceal the division of interest. Finally, what are the goddesses for? Is Euripides taking all this trouble only to tell the Athenians that in his opinion Aphrodite and Artemis are not worth worshipping?

It is quite evident once more that this is no tragedy of character. It was never Euripides' idea to make the tragedy out of the opposition between Hippolytus' nature and Phaedra's; if it had been the play would have been closer knit, and there would have been no room for the goddesses. We have, perhaps a little rashly, attacked the dramatic character of Hippolytus. In fact he is extremely successful as a figure in the play – but because the drama is one of tragic victims rather than of tragic actors, at least as far as Hippolytus is concerned. Again Euripides shows a certain detachment from his hero. He is not for the time being lost within him, but uses him in the interests of a further tragedy, and this time that further tragedy is made explicit. We have here a play within a play. The prologue is not a confession by Euripides that he finds the task of properly expounding a dramatic situation beyond his power; it is the dramatic embodiment of his real tragic idea. In the *Medea* we had to infer this from the treatment and in particular from the 'irrational' ending; in the *Hippolytus* the two dramatic planes of thought are made formally distinct. On the one plane Aphrodite is the tragic agent. What she is we have known perfectly well since Aeschylus wrote the Danaid-trilogy, even if we did not know before. She is not a mythical being whose existence Euripides is trying to disprove, not a cult whose observance he is trying to discredit; she is one of the elemental powers in nature, to Euripides as to Aeschylus. To both poets she and Artemis are complementary forces which have to be reverenced. Aphrodite says here explicitly that she has no quarrel with Hippolytus for his devotion to Artemis, but 'I destroy those who are haughty towards me'. Hippolytus therefore is introduced to us not as a tragic actor but as a tragic victim; his part is not to have in his soul a tragic contradiction or complexity, but a tragic singleness. Like Aeschylus' Suppliants, he is to be one-sided, utterly denying Aphrodite, and like them, to pay for this one-sidedness. To Aeschylus the law of Zeus does not tolerate partial adherence; Euripides puts the same idea into psychological rather than moral terms and will show us that there are laws of nature that demand obedience as well as laws of morality.

Aphrodite goes on to destroy all possibility of dramatic surprise in the play by telling us exactly what is to happen; she will inspire with a fatal passion the virtuous Phaedra. Phaedra will die; that, Aphrodite calmly says, cannot be helped and is immaterial; and in

her death she will destroy Hippolytus. Now we know exactly where
we are. The fate of Phaedra and Hippolytus will be seen by us
always in the tragic frame that Aphrodite has made. It will not be in
their own hands, as is the fate of the Sophoclean hero, and it will not
arise from any complexity of their own characters, but from their
singleness. They will be drawn as extreme characters – like Medea
– for in Hippolytus at least nothing matters but the fanaticism of his
virginity. Hence the complete contrast between Hippolytus and
the Suppliants. The Suppliants are from first to last passionate and
exciting dramatic characters – which no one would claim for
Hippolytus. This does not mean that there were certain things in
drama that Aeschylus could do and Euripides could not; the reason
is that the one-sidedness of the Suppliants was only part of Aeschylus'
tragedy. He thinks first of people of a certain kind who between
them make a tragic situation; of incompatible claims which result
in violence and involve others in mischief. Wrong-doing, and a
resistance that goes too far, are of the essence of his thought; the
opposition between Artemis and Aphrodite is the expression but
not the substance of his thought. Therefore, to put it crudely, in
Aeschylus it is tragic characters who grapple, in Euripides it is tragic
specimens of humanity who come to shipwreck.

But have we not said that Phaedra is a rounded character, not a
specimen or an extreme? She is indeed, and it is interesting to see
why. Phaedra is tragic because virtuous; a struggle takes place
within her such as Hippolytus can never know. She is made virtuous
because if she is not, the theme will inevitably become something
other than what Euripides has in mind. His theme is, obviously, that
an unbalanced mind or temperament like Hippolytus' is unsafe; if
Aphrodite attacks, Artemis cannot defend, only promise to destroy
one of Aphrodite's darlings in return (1420–2). By implication, too
much Aphrodite is as unsafe as too little, but unless Phaedra, too, is
virtuous, the parallel between her and Hippolytus will not exist,
and the point will be destroyed that Aphrodite is a natural force,
quite indifferent to human morality, one with which we have to
make terms. Moreover, if Phaedra were a follower of Aphrodite as
Hippolytus is of Artemis, she would necessarily become a passionate
and a wicked woman, a Medea, and Hippolytus we should feel to
be simply her victim, not Aphrodite's. This, apparently, had been
the theme of the first *Hippolytus*. Phaedra there was a woman who,

like Medea, Stheneboea, and Phthia in the *Phoenix,* was prepared to
do anything to gratify her passion, a direct example of the terrible
power of human unreason; Hippolytus was simply her victim, as
Glauce and the others were Medea's. In such a play Phaedra's
passion was inevitably the dominant motif, and Phaedra the dominant character. In such a situation Hippolytus' own one-sidedness
would have little scope. In making Phaedra virtuous here, therefore,
Euripides was not revising his first play to placate the stupid,[1] but
taking a step which the difference in outlook demanded.

There is an interesting refinement in Euripides' treatment of
Phaedra. His basic drama demands, and states, only that Phaedra is
to be made a victim and tool of Aphrodite, a monument to the
irresponsibility of these cosmic forces; but when the outer drama
is played through, we find Phaedra herself giving a new and tragic
interpretation of her passion, for she recognizes in it a hereditary
taint (337–43). This in no way conflicts with that; it is the same fact
as it appears on the different plane, a pointer to what Euripides
means by his Aphrodite: not a member of the Pantheon of whom
Euripides disapproves, but a potentially disastrous element in our
nature.[2]

But although Phaedra is so Sophoclean a figure, we see behind
her the shadow of Aphrodite. This shows very clearly the difference
between the tragedians; there are no shadows standing behind
Oedipus or Electra. Sophocles puts all his thought into these;
Euripides uses his creations to bring on to the stage a tragedy that
is being played behind the scenes. We said that an inner tragedy
was the real controlling element in the *Medea,* in spite of Medea's
tragic will; now that inner drama is brought into the open. Even
so tragic a character as Phaedra is but a figure in it, not a heroine
who in her own right claims all our attention.

It is therefore no real violation of unity when Phaedra disappears
and leaves us with Hippolytus. But for the prologue we should be
at a loss, for we should necessarily expect her character and personality still to count for something; as it is, we know that the real unity
lies not in her fate but in what Aphrodite is doing, and in fact the

---

[1] At least, if he was, the fact is of biographical, not critical, interest. The assertion,
in the second Argument, that he was doing this is not a statement of fact but a critical
inference – possibly a silly one.

[2] It is, of course, because Aphrodite is this, an internal not an external tyrant, that
the *Hippolytus* is tragedy. She is not a 'goddess' who torments us for her sport.

last thing that we look for is to see her passion and death prolonging itself in Hippolytus' mind. The logic of the plot and the unity of the action obviously reside in the underlying conception and not in the tragic mind of either Phaedra or Hippolytus. So it was in the *Medea,* only there we had no Aphrodite and Artemis to help us. We had indeed a unity derived from Medea's own will, but since this was not the real centre of the tragedy, the unity it gave was incomplete.

But even with the goddesses to show us how to look at the action of the *Hippolytus,* Euripides does not seem to be entirely at his ease. He has reconciled his un-Sophoclean conception of tragedy more nearly with the Sophoclean form of drama, but if we look attentively at the second part of the play we shall perhaps see signs of strain, and these may explain why Euripides did not again use this regularity of structure until he gave up writing tragedy.

First, from the purely dramatic point of view, Phaedra's tragedy has a quality which makes Hippolytus' something of an anticlimax. We should not insist on this overmuch, for the less absorbing Hippolytus is as a tragic character, the more do we feel the unseen presence of Aphrodite. Nevertheless, however much he is a tragic victim driven before the storm, we can hardly be oblivious of the fact that he addresses Theseus as if Theseus were a public meeting,[1] and can state quite objectively that he is the most virtuous man alive. This is not untragic; on the contrary, it is the whole point; but it is awkward that the point must be made in this way[2] – especially after the perfect drama of the first part. We have to keep our minds on the tragedy and leave the drama a little out of focus; to weigh the tragic fact that Hippolytus, though virtuous, is being destroyed, and to overlook the dramatic inconvenience that it is Hippolytus himself who tells us of his virtue. Above all do we have to refrain from asking why the chorus, despite its oath, allows Hippolytus to be destroyed when a hint of the truth would at least make Theseus pause a while.

Secondly, the messenger-speech is not really dramatic, as Greek

[1] Putting into Greek verse the formula 'Unaccustomed as I am to public speaking'.

[2] In suggesting here and elsewhere that there were logical reasons for Euripides' handling of the tragic form I am not suggesting that their existence automatically turns bad drama into good. Every art has formal principles which cannot be successfully defied, and sometimes no doubt Euripides went too far. But we can understand his methods without having to approve of all their results, and the critic's mere approval or disapproval is not a matter of public interest.

Tragedy understands the word. Hitherto the great messenger-speeches have noticeably quickened the pace of the drama by introducing some new factor of tragic importance; if the messenger has not had this function to perform he has been brief. We recall the Herald in the *Agamemnon*, how his announcements increase our sense of forboding; the terrible irony of the Corinthian's news in the *Tyrannus*; the swift reversal of our hopes and the unexpected blow of Haemon's death in the *Antigone*; the poignant situation in the *Electra* (with which we may compare the illumination of what Orestes is that we get from the brilliant messenger-speech in Euripides' *Electra*); the horror of the *Medea*. The two messenger-scenes in the *Septem* are interesting. In the long scene, in which the messenger has a lot to say, his part goes with the movement of the whole play, and is very dramatic; when he returns to announce the death of Eteocles and Polyneices he is reporting a single fact, which has been half-foreseen; accordingly he is brief, for long description of the manner of the event (highly impressive in the *Antigone*, where it shows the hatred with which Creon has inspired his own son) would have been irrelevant.

The death of Hippolytus is even more inevitable than that of Eteocles and Polyneices. We doubt neither the efficacy of Theseus' curse nor the power of Poseidon to destroy. All that the drama demands is this destruction, and the speech adds nothing to this simple demand. Sheer horror, effective in the *Medea*, where it illuminates Medea, is not wanted here, where it can only advertise the power of a god; a long and complicated narrative, effective in the *Electra*, where it serves half a dozen dramatic ends, would here be false. As pure narrative the speech is very good, but as drama it is something less than the best. It really marks time.

Thirdly, is there not a slightly artificial ring in the ending? Artemis is necessary and very dramatic, but the treatment of Theseus is perhaps in one respect what the play needs rather than what the tragic idea demands. Artemis balances Aphrodite, structurally and morally, and she was also the only plausible way of informing Theseus of the truth. She completes the revelation of the inner tragedy – in a rather obvious way, one would think, had it not been so often misunderstood.[1] She points out to the unhappy

[1] As surely by M. Méridier, when he speaks of 'un rayonnement de transfiguration', une sérénité céleste'.

Theseus that he has fallen, a supplementary victim, into Aphrodite's trap, and she paints Olympus as a place of moral chaos – which can indicate only that what these deities represent, instinctive passions, is independent of reason and morality. She says, 'We gods destroy the wicked, with their children and all', but Theseus is not ruined because he is wicked, and Hippolytus is presently borne in protesting his complete innocence. Artemis is powerless to help; she cannot even shed a tear. She can, however, promise to destroy someone else, to annoy Aphrodite, and she can promise Hippolytus that honour of perpetual worship which he enjoys in common with several other of Euripides' broken heroes. Hippolytus has his *Aufklärung*: εἴθ᾽ ἦν ἀραῖον δαίμοσιν βροτῶν γένος[1] and we breathe a little more freely when this sub-human goddess has taken herself off, leaving the stage to the reconciliation between father and son.

All this is fine; but how genuine is the ἁμαρτία on which Artemis insists? She blames Theseus bitterly for his haste in calling down the curse on Hippolytus (ὦ κάκιστε σύ), and this has to bear the weight of the ending. Is this fair? It is not a mere matter of dramatic realism, whether Theseus was not in fact bound to believe the lying letter in face of Hippolytus' not very convincing defence and the general conspiracy of silence; though certainly we ourselves should not have raised the question of Theseus' guilt if Artemis had not. Beyond this there is the question of tragic relevance. Theseus' part in the tragedy is quite clear, and is indeed described accurately by Artemis. He is one of those tragic figures who stand at the cross-roads of disaster and get overwhelmed with the rest. That is the essence of his position, and any ἁμαρτία he may show is purely instrumental. When we see him confronting and cursing Hippolytus we do not feel him as a man who is doing something foolishly or wickedly wrong, but as one who can do no other; when we see him being railed at by Artemis and brokenly confessing error we are surely justified in assuming that this is being done to tighten the construction of the last scene and to give a weightier tone to the reconciliation. For this is an ending that needs some contrivance. The end of the tragedy is the destruction, by Aphrodite, of Hippolytus; the tragedy demands nothing more. But the play within the play does not end there very easily: Theseus has been involved, a third victim. To end simply with the second and third victims looking at

[1] 'Would that mortals could bring mischief on the gods!' (v. 1415).

each other and talking it over would have been weak; to have made Hippolytus die 'off', the prosaically logical course, and to end with the third victim alone, was a sacrifice of form to logic which Euripides was not yet (or at any rate not here) prepared to make. Hippolytus (unlike Andromache later) is brought back, and the ἁμαρτία, which even if justifiable is not logical, is introduced in order to stiffen the scene between the two.

The *Hippolytus* is justly renowned for its tragic beauty and power, and it is not suggested that the inconveniences just discussed are as prominent in reading or performance as they are in analysis. There is, however, the question why this play is strict in form while the later tragedies are not, and in these few discrepancies between the logic of the tragic idea and the demands of plot and symmetry of form we may see the answer to the question. A consideration of the *Troades* and *Hecuba* will suggest that later Euripides might have been content with presenting to us his three victims in bare juxtaposition with the minimum of logical connexion and formal unity. At all events, from now on, until he turned from tragedy to melodrama and tragi-comedy, Euripides sacrifices this external tidiness to directness of expression, being in this truly Greek; for surely the greatness of all Greek art lies not in its ability to achieve beauty of form (never the first aim of the great artist), but in its absolute sincerity to the underlying idea. We have to wait a century or more to see the rise of 'classicism'.

4. The 'Troades'

When the plays of Euripides are considered one by one, without distinction of kind or purpose, it is impossible not to be baffled by the vagaries of form and style in the tragedies which we now approach. Plot becomes chaotic, characterization uncertain, the use of the chorus unsteady, and undramatic speech-making endemic. When we find Euripides flouting our conception of dramatic form and yet being 'the most tragic of the poets', we tend to take refuge in general ideas about the clash, the *Spannung,* between Euripides' intellectualism and the religious background of his art, or we cleverly discover an *ad hoc* explanation of each problem. But as soon as we do distinguish kind and purpose the problem becomes simpler – or at least very different.

Euripides wrote tragedy, and he wrote several kinds of non-tragic drama. They must be kept distinct. In this chapter and the next we will consider the remaining tragedies (all but the *Bacchae*), first inquiring what kind of dramatic idea underlies them and how that moulds the dramatic form, then trying to see the logical connexion between the dramatic idea and the dramatic style of the plays. If we were making a critical study of Euripides himself, of his poetic and dramatic personality and the development of his views, we should have to take the plays in chronological order; but as we are considering his structural methods, and as these are the same in the whole group of war-tragedies but clearest in the last, we may begin with the last.

There is no need to assert that the *Troades* is a tragic unity; we feel it or we do not, and no analysis will make us feel it more; but in order to criticize we must see where the unity is. To appreciate this, we have first to remember that the play is unique in the later drama in being part of a genuine trilogy. The first play, the *Alex-andros,* dealt with Paris. His parents, warned that the child would be the ruin of his country if he reached manhood, shrank from killing him, as did Laius and Iocasta, and Paris did reach manhood. We know the plot; what Euripides put into it we do not know. The point of the second play, the *Palamedes,* is clear. It dealt with the judicial murder of Palamedes by his own Greek leaders before Troy – the act of treachery which Nauplius his father was to avenge by lighting beacons to wreck the Greek ships on Euboea as they sailed home. In these two plays the tragedy of two nations is started; in the third it is consummated.

In the prologue, shared by Athena and Poseidon, the capture of Troy is announced, and Athena asks Poseidon to destroy the Greek fleet on its way home; she had been their champion, but their ὕβρις, both to Cassandra and to the temples of Troy, has made her their enemy. A reference to the coasts of Euboea reminds us of the *Palamedes,* and the gods retire, leaving the stage to the prostrate Hecuba, to whom is presently added a chorus of captive Trojan women awaiting their captors' pleasure.

The action that follows consists of four scenes. Talthybius the Herald comes for Cassandra, the virgin-priestess, whom Agamemnon is taking; as Andromache with her infant son Astyanax is being borne away to the Greek ships Talthybius comes again to announce the decree of death against the child; Menelaus comes to carry off Helen to execution, and there is a set debate between Helen and Hecuba, Menelaus, as umpire, condemning Helen; lastly Talthybius returns with the body of Astyanax to give it to Hecuba for burial, to announce the burning of Troy, and to lead the captives to the ships. There is added incidentally to this list of miseries the fate of Polyxena, the slavery in Ithaca decreed for Hecuba, the snatching away of Andromache before she can even attend to the burial of her child, and the terrible plight of the Chorus. Everything, except the Helen-scene, is contrived to be as unhappy as possible, and not one of the incidents (the Helen-scene apart) is considered except in its effect on the Trojans. No contrast is aimed at, no explanation of the Greek point of view. As if deliberately to make the actions of the Greeks simply impersonal decrees and to discourage us from interesting ourselves in their motives, the Herald is used throughout – not for example Odysseus, as in the *Hecuba* – coming in like a series of telegrams.

Considered superficially the play lacks both unity and a tragic idea. As for the unity, little is gained by pointing to the continuous presence of Hecuba; what happens to one person is not necessarily a unity, and in fact the centre of interest is successively Hecuba, Cassandra, Andromache and Helen. Certainly the presence of Hecuba helps; without her the play would seem more episodic. We may fairly call her a symbol, but if she is that, and if the unity of the piece is seen in her, it must really lie in that which she symbolizes, the sufferings of the defeated.

And what of the tragedy? The spectacle of the strong trampling on the impotent, though it may be salutary propaganda, is not tragedy; but we remember the general course of the trilogy, and there is the illuminating prologue. The Greeks are under sentence of death for ὕβρις, but before retribution descends on them they make it clear, by their further outrages, how much they deserve it. There is a moral structure not unlike that of the *Agamemnon*. The first ode there reminds us of Agamemnon's great sin, and starts the play in an atmosphere of doom; then we have the ominous aggravations of his guilt – the sufferings inflicted on Greece, the sacrilege committed in Troy, the purple carpet, Cassandra. It is an oppressive series, made the more oppressive by Agamemnon's blindness; only the carpet makes him feel uneasy. In our play the function of the great ode is discharged by the prologue. The Greeks are doomed from the start, and proceed to pile up the count before our eyes, the more awfully because it is done so impersonally. This series of outrages, episodic and merely pathetic if we look only at the Trojans, is cumulative and tragic if we look at the Greeks, and it is to ensure that we shall take this point of view that Euripides writes his otherwise unnecessary and unusually impressive prologue. The Greeks are the collective tragic hero or tragic agent, the Trojans the collective victim.

The comparison with the *Agamemnon* can be carried a stage further. There is no Aristotelian connexion between the killing of Iphigenia and the trampling on the purple carpet except that the same man did both, and out of the same moral blindness. So in the *Troades*: the connexion between the rape of Cassandra and the murder of Astyanax is simply that both proceed from the same ὕβρις in the Greeks. Aeschylus might have chosen other instances of Agamemnon's blindness; Euripides might have chosen other incidents to illustrate the cruelty of the Greeks – or have put these in the reverse order. Aristotelian cause and effect do not apply. The *Troades* completes a movement whose beginnings we saw in the *Medea*. It is now apparent that we have the tragedy not of the individual hero but of the group. In the *Medea* Euripides could logically interfere in his plot to make his tragic idea clearer; now the whole plot is constructed, as it were, by Euripides and not by the will and actions of a hero; it has become quite inorganic. We ventured to suggest that Medea, in spite of her dramatic qualities, was not a character in the Sophoclean sense, and that Euripides is slightly but definitely detached from his creation; in the *Troades* this schematic rather than naturalistic treatment of character is carried to its natural limit. Since the character that is tragically significant is the collective one of the Greeks, Hecuba's is left an outline only. Her part in the tragedy needs, and receives, no more detailed characterization than Pelasgus' in the *Supplices*; she shows such character as the play demands, nobility in suffering, and that is all.

The Helen-scene shows us how far Euripides was from regarding this as a play about Hecuba; it shows, too, on what principles he is now making his plots. Helen pleads *force majeure*; it was Aphrodite who caused the whole affair; she herself is innocent. This plea Hecuba easily demolishes: 'It was not Aphrodite but Aphrosyne –

your own wantonness.' Euripides will not abate his doctrine of
personal responsibility. Menelaus, as judge, agrees with Hecuba;
Helen deserves death and shall be put to death – only not just now,
but in Sparta, without fail. In a play about Hecuba's sufferings the
point of this scene would not be very clear, but such as it is it would
surely have been more effective had Menelaus given Hecuba another
insult by acquitting Helen there and then. But Euripides is not
thinking first and foremost of the stricken Queen; she may be the
symbol of his tragedy but she is not its incarnation – if she were, this
scene would have been more of a dramatic contest and less of a
debate; for Euripides does not use the forensic style simply because
he cannot help it.

The scene is there not for Hecuba's sake but because, like the last
scene of the *Medea,* it embodies part of Euripides' thought. When
he has given up tragedy we shall find him saying (*Helen* 38 ff.) that
the gods caused the war to relieve over-population; the essence of
this social tragedy is that mankind, or some men, are directly responsible for these miseries. In the *Suppliant Women* a Socratic
elenchus makes Adrastus admit that the basis of the war of the Seven
was reckless folly; here Menelaus decides that Helen is guilty. This
means – whatever the man may or may not do later – that this war,
too, was misconceived, its basis the worthlessness of a woman. The
scene interrupts the plot but it illuminates Euripides' thought – and
the play itself does no other.

If we consider how Euripides treats the episode of Polyxena we
shall understand clearly the principles on which he constructs these
plots. At v. 260 Hecuba asks Talthybius what is to be Polyxena's
fate. The reply is so evasive that it ought only to have provoked a
further question, but Hecuba accepts the evasion and passes on. The
Scholiast expresses surprise: Why does not Hecuba either lament or
ask how 'she is released from sorrow'? If she knows, she should
lament for her; if she does not know, she should ask and find out.'[1]
A recent editor, M. Parmentier, remarks, 'Euripide évite de revenir
sur le sujet de l'*Hécube.*' But why should Euripides be so self-conscious about a play ten years old? If he was, why did he mention
Polyxena at all? And in fact, far from avoiding the subject, he raises
it here, only to drop it rather awkwardly and then to treat it at some
length later (622 ff.). If we assume that Euripides is simply following

[1] As emended by Schwartz.

a course of dramatic events at Troy, making of them the best plot that he can, we can offer no explanation of this procedure – unless some Verrallian comes to the rescue with a theory of private performance, *contaminatio,* or something else just as convincing. When we see that Euripides is not putting together a play but presenting a tragic idea, the explanation is obvious. The incident is used not logically, like an incident in Sophocles, but suggestively. Polyxena's fate is even more terrible than Cassandra's, therefore must come after it; moreover the effect of its announcement is more poignant coming from Andromache than from Talthybius. Yet the pathos of the Cassandra scene is greatly strengthened if we, the audience, know that Polyxena lies behind it; therefore the veiled reference is introduced to assure us that Polyxena will not be forgotten. It is once more a deliberate manipulation of the action, now independent of the characters, contrived (at the cost of a momentary awkwardness) to increase the tension; and for such a solid advantage Euripides was well content to puzzle a scholiast.

For even if the logic of a steadily evolving action is now abandoned, the dramatist is not without his principles of plot-construction. The principle to which he now owes allegiance is that the successive scenes must bear upon his central tragic idea with an ever-increasing power; in fact we are back again, by a roundabout way, at the law of increasing tension which we noticed in the *Prometheus.* Here, as there, scenes could be transposed without any violence to the logic of fact, but we cannot say, in Aristotle's phrase,[1] that there would be no difference; the logic of fact might be as good, but the logic of the inner tragedy would not.

The law of increasing tension we saw to be essentially lyrical in conception, even if not in origin too; and its reappearance here coincides with a remarkable revival of the lyrical part of Greek tragedy. We shall have to discuss the Euripidean chorus in detail later, but something must be said here, as without the chorus neither the *Troades* nor Euripides' methods are fully intelligible.

The Chorus had been threatened with extinction more than once – notably by Euripides himself when he found it such a nuisance at certain points in the *Medea* and the *Hippolytus*; but its inherent vitality (that is, the fact that the Greek poets were not conservative) found a new use for it again and again. If this Trojan chorus had

[1] Which perhaps was not aimed at these plays in particular.

been taught to behave 'as in Sophocles', to follow and comment, either directly or philosphically, on the action, it would necessarily have sung a series of odes on the rape of Cassandra, the captivity of Andromache, the murder of Astyanax, and the wickedness of Helen. But this, though beautifully Sophoclean, would have been ruination to the play; it would have unnecessarily emphasized the schematic nature of the plot, and it would have given to the events that kind of dramatic significance which they are not meant to have. This chorus does not obey dramatic canons; it recognizes facts. Whatever may happen on the stage, the chorus takes no notice of it. Polyxena may be sacrificed, or Astyanax' bleeding body brought back, but the chorus says not a word about it. It has one theme only, Troy – why it fell, how it fell, and what is to happen to them, the survivors. Nothing can move it from this mournful *ostinato*.

In this Euripides was not being merely negative, avoiding what would have underlined the hazardous features of his dramatic method. The chorus sticks to the fall of Troy positively. Its lyrical nature enables it to penetrate more nearly to the inner tragedy than the actors. The actors can sharply present certain facets of the human tragedy which is Euripides' real theme; Hecuba, no real heroine, can be an impressive individual symbol of this on the stage. The chorus sings of ruin and death – not the ruin of Hecuba, which is but a shadow, but of Troy; thus in its own way, as Hecuba in hers, prefiguring the inner tragedy. This symbolic use of plot and action has, in fact, broken down the recently won supremacy of the actors, but we do not return to the earlier drama in which the Chorus enfolded the action; rather are Chorus and actors now co-ordinate forces, each in its own way presenting the inner drama of the poet's own conception.

5. The 'Hecuba'

The material of the *Hecuba* is taken from two legends which have no connexion except that both come from the Trojan cycle and both intimately concern Hecuba. A purely formal unity is given by the continuous presence on the stage of Hecuba and the chorus of Trojan captives, but there is no causal unity that links the sacrifice of one of Hecuba's children with the murder of another. Like the incidents that make up the plot of the *Troades,* they remain separate;

in the *Troades* indeed there is the nexus that all the action proceeds from one side, the Greeks, but in the *Hecuba* even this mechanical help is missing. The Greeks have sacked Troy and enslaved those that they have not killed; they now sacrifice Hecuba's daughter Polyxena to the shade of Achilles; then the Thracian Polymestor is discovered to have murdered Hecuba's remaining son Polydorus, to get his treasure; finally Hecuba takes a terrible revenge on Polymestor. Such is the scattered material that makes up the plot. That kind of unity that we find in the *Troades* is wanting, but in compensation we have here more character-interest; in the *Troades* Hecuba is only a helpless victim, while here she does retaliate on one of her oppressors. It is indeed commonly maintained that the aim and purpose of the play is to study the character of Hecuba. Is the view tenable?

We may first note the chief features in the play for which we must try to account. There is the prologue spoken by Polydorus' Ghost, the obvious purpose of which is to hold together the two separate actions of the play;[1] no hint here, as in the prologues to the *Troades* and *Hippolytus,* of what the underlying idea is. There follows an interesting inversion of an ancient practice when Hecuba is lyrical and the chorus acts as Messenger. They announce to her the impending sacrifice of Polyxena, and presently announce it to Polyxena herself. This occupies 150 verses of lyrical dialogue, and is a scene clearly designed for its misery-value, since in it action, characterization and διάνοια[2] are reduced to a minimum.

Next the demand for Polyxena is sent to Hecuba, through Odysseus. Why Odysseus and not the regular herald Talthybius? Obviously because Odysseus is under a peculiarly deep obligation to Hecuba;[3] Hecuba consented not to denounce him when Helen recognized him as a spy inside the walls of Troy. Out of this obligation Odysseus tries to wriggle by saying that he is indeed bound to Hecuba, but not to Hecuba's daughter. This point, of which much is made, is (compared with the loss of Polyxena) negligible in its effect on Hecuba's sufferings, still more so in its effect on her mind and character, which in any case have hardly begun to interest us.

---

[1] It is in fact rather more subtle than this; see p. 282.

[2] What is the English for this? Bywater translates it 'thought'. In this context perhaps 'intellectual interest', though clumsy, would sound more natural.

[3] Euripides seems to have invented this.

If Odysseus is preferred to Talthybius merely for the sake of this extra dramatic piquancy, it is a second-rate device; legitimate enough in quasi-melodrama where piquancy in the turns of the plot is one of the chief elements of the play, powerful in tragedy if the added point deepens the tragedy (cf. the Watchman in the *Antigone*). Here it makes a strong impression, and if the misfortunes of Hecuba and her reaction to them are our chief interest, that impression is beside the point.

When Hecuba's plea to Odysseus fails, Polyxena is asked to plead for herself. She refuses, and accepts death – that is murder – willingly, her reason being that she has nothing to live for. The interest we have in her therefore is purely pathetic; Euripides has not made her an Antigone, who has everything to live for. Hecuba nobly offers to die in her stead, but the nobility is conventional rather than dramatic, as she, too, has nothing to live for. Euripides in fact is not seriously trying to interest us in these two women as characters; rather in the Greeks who do these things. This feeling is reinforced when we come to the next choral ode. The chorus says not a word about Hecuba and Polyxena; their theme is 'What will be *our* fate?' Is this only selfishness on their part and the waste of an opportunity by Euripides? If we are to watch Hecuba with all our dramatic imagination, it is odd that our attention should now be directed away from her agony.

Then we have to consider Odysseus' argument, that a state in order to flourish must honour its benefactors. Odysseus is in grave danger of appearing dishonourable; is this plea a mere excuse, rhetorical *inventio,* or is it sincere, containing some tragic point? There was no need to send Odysseus; if he is sent only in order that, being sent, he may extricate himself by a piece of sophistry and so enable Euripides to make a hit at politicians, we may properly accuse the poet of debasing his art – for this is tragedy, not melodrama, like the *I.T.* But Odysseus' reasoning – granting the premisses – has force. We must remember, too, that the decision to sacrifice Polyxena was not made unanimously or easily. Agamemnon was against it – for the sake of Cassandra; the two sons of Theseus were in favour; so was Odysseus – who received from the chorus hard names not accorded to the two Athenians (vv. 123–33). We must, I think, be prepared to find the tragic point of the sacrifice as much among the Greeks as among the Trojans; the more so when Talthybius arrives, first to start back in horror at the misery he sees, then, in describing the sacrifice, to give us the impression that the Greeks are, after all, very decent people.

This scene ends with a remarkable bit of philosophizing from Hecuba,[1] and is followed by an ode which, dealing with the origin of the war and the misery it has brought to Trojan and Greek alike, has again no reference to the action on the stage.

Now, by an obvious link, we pass from Polyxena to Polydorus; the servant sent to fetch water to purify the one body finds the other on the shore, as the prologue predicted. We wait to see what Euripides is going to do with this artificial addition. There is the necessary interval for lamentation, and Agamemnon is brought in. Hecuba, in a series of conventional asides, brings herself to ask his favour – not for the freedom which he, ironically, is so ready to offer, but for his acquiescence in a proposed retribution upon Polymestor. There is movement of character and mind here; Hecuba is prepared to go to any lengths to win over Agamemnon. He has his purely political difficulties, but matters are at last arranged. Hecuba assures us, by citing the Lemnian Women, that she and her helpers between them will be able to encompass revenge, and the messenger is sent to Polymestor.[2]

Still this obstinate chorus refuses to take any notice of the action. It is as far as possible from being an Ideal Spectator. It sings a marvellously vivid ode, not about the Lemnian Women or just retribution or anything else connected with the present action, but about the night on which Troy fell; 'My husband lay on his bed . . . I was arranging my hair before the mirror . . .' Sometimes the Euripidean chorus finds itself in a position where it can hardly say anything both relevant and lyrical; here it could and will not.

In the last scene there is no lack of dramatic movement. Hecuba easily traps the barbarian into convicting himself of treachery and murder, and, by playing on his cupidity, entices him into the tent. But if we expect to hear of his death, we are disappointed. Hecuba, a second Medea, does something far more revolting, blinding him and killing his two sons; and to ensure that we shall be revolted and not edified Euripides causes the wretched Polymestor to come out

---

[1] 592–602. See p. 270.

[2] Incidentally, it appears from v. 898 that the sacrifice has not availed to raise the favouring wind.

of the tent on all fours. He does not, in his tragedies, use such 'realism' merely for the sake of being lively.

In most of these tragedies there comes a point at which the critic may profitably ask himself how he would have finished the play. This seems to be one. We should naturally try to contrive an account of the actual revenge, and, whether or not we were taking the line that Hecuba was justified, we should make our Hecuba dominate the last scene beyond any question; heroine or fury, she should at last stand before us fully revealed. Or, remembering our Oedipus,[1] we might have allowed Polymestor to prophesy the approaching end of Hecuba, as Euripides has done here; but only in order that she might rise magnificently over even this. What we should never have thought of is what Euripides does. Polymestor, practically, steals the thunder, and the secondary figure of Agamemnon is made as prominent as Hecuba, if not more prominent. We have a trial-scene, with Agamemnon acting as judge, the inevitable and horrifying account of the actual revenge, the evident revulsion of Agamemnon, but his judgement that Polymestor has got his deserts. Then the barbarian turns vicarious prophet, and prophesies not only Hecuba's end, but also the murder of Agamemnon, so that we finish not with a final revelation of Hecuba, but with the seizure and banishment of Polymestor.

It is perfectly true that in Hecuba we see first an unresisting victim, then a victim who gathers all her strength to hit back. This change gives a great impetus to the second part of the play, but to call the play on that account a study of character or psychology is a mistake. We need not underrate the character-interest, but we cannot suppose that what drove Euripides to construct this rather odd plot was the desire to portray a tragic Hecuba. This does not, to begin with, account for the ending. Then, as a character-study, it would be altogether too simple and too violent. To put this play and the *Philoctetes* in the same category is to do an injustice to both. When Polydorus' body is found, our conception of Hecuba's character is to vague that she might do anything without surprising us. We can hardly say that in Hecuba we have a woman driven mad by suffering, because we have not seen what she was like in normal circumstances. Further, Euripides cannot have contrived all this misery and this awful barbarian merely to play on Hecuba's

[1] i.e. how at *O.T.* 1076 ff. he adds climax to the climax of Iocasta's exit.

character, to illustrate her reactions; it would be too uneconomical and too shocking for a Greek. The *Philoctetes* will show us how such a study should be set – in a situation which may be serious, but in which a satisfactory outcome is assured. If it is objected that the *Tyrannus* is a study of character which, however, is tragic through and through, the answer is that the tragedy of Oedipus was his character, whereas the tragedy here is first what is done to Hecuba, in which her character has no part, then in what she does to others, not in what she suffers. Fourthly, this view leaves unexplained the prominence given to Polyxena's sacrifice and to the Greeks; it also fails to explain Odysseus and the behaviour of Agamemnon, and finally it would make of the chorus a sustained irrelevance.

We have noticed that the chorus here is not the background of the action. It most remarkably keeps aloof from the action, as if it were playing out a tragedy of its own – which in fact it is doing. It keeps to its theme, the fall of Troy; and this has nothing to do with Hecuba's character or with her revenge on Polymestor or with Odysseus or with the later dilemma of Agamemnon. The only way in which we can bring into one focus all the strands of the play and find a theme which is worthy of the magnitude of the events related is to suppose that here, as in the *Troades,* the separate actions are meant to point to one overriding idea, the suffering which the human race inflicts upon itself through its follies and wickednesses. We start, as it were, with a central heap of desolation in the ruin of Troy and the misery of the Trojans. This is continually kept before our minds in the series of choral odes. To it the action of the play makes one addition after another, each proceeding from a different source. The Greeks are not cruel, but their superstition and the political wisdom of their leaders throws the body of Polyxena on to the central heap. Political necessity is one of the three sources of evil used during the play. Odysseus was honest in his plea of honouring benefactors; it is a political necessity – and here it involves murder.[1] Odysseus was chosen as the messenger, that political necessity may be shown to involve him in private dishonour. This theme reappears with Agamemnon. He, personally, is a well-meaning man, willing to give freedom to Hecuba, sympathetic to her on all counts, anxious, too, that she should be avenged on the barbarian – but

---

[1] A theme used with Lycus (*H.F.*, 165 ff.) and with the murder of Astyanax (*Tro.,* 1159 ff.).

unfortunately the barbarian is an ally, and Hecuba is not exactly popular in camp. The poor man hedges, with the result that the punishment which the King admits is deserved becomes a frightful revenge.

But war and political necessity are not the only causes of the misery of this play. After Polyxena comes Polydorus, victim of the comparatively simple crime of greed, and after Polydorus, more additions to the central heap, perhaps the most pathetic, the two boys. The pitiful victim of oppression herself turns oppressor, giving way not to blind rage but to calculating cruelty. Agamemnon did not blame her; perhaps we need not; nevertheless, when the bereaved mother slaughters the two sons of Polymestor we shall not applaud her, nor merely congratulate Euripides on a powerful stroke of psychological development or a fine dramatic climax.

When all is done, when superstition, politics, lust for gold, and blind cruelty have done their worst, there remains as a grim finale the death that awaits both the well-meaning Agamemnon and the ill-used Hecuba. This finale, like the chorus, is a pointer to the meaning of the whole. It is not, as we have seen, a reasonable ending for an orthodox play on Hecuba as a tragic heroine, for Agamemnon is too prominent in it; it is a most imaginative ending for a play whose tragic idea is one that embraces both the Greeks and Hecuba as wrongdoers, and both the Greeks and Hecuba as the victims of wrongdoing. During all these scenes of increasing misery the chorus pursues its monotone, not because the fall of Troy had an essential connexion with the events on the stage, but because it is made the symbol of that whole – the sufferings of humanity – of which the events on the stage are parts and vivid illustrations. The chorus is not indeed the hero of the action, for Euripides does not now give us heroes, either morally or dramatically speaking, but it is the focus of the tragic thought.

It might be possible to devise a formula which would express the essence of the *Hecuba* more accurately and fully than this. I do not insist on the formula. The play, taken quite simply, makes its own impression, and that is its 'meaning'; only when we begin to criticize does it become necessary to put that meaning into words – a task certainly much easier and more natural, but sometimes hardly less grateful, than trying to put into words the 'meaning' of a piece of music. What must be emphasized is that this 'meaning' is not the character, action, and fate of Hecuba herself, but something deeper and more general. She is a symbol in a way in which Eteocles and Oedipus are not, and the play derives its unity and power not from the symbol, but from the thing symbolized.

6. The 'Suppliant Women'

With the exception of the *Heracles* no play of Euripides is more baffling and 'unsatisfactory' than this one, yet into few has Euripides put more of himself.

> Le style en est particulièrement soigné. Les *Suppliantes* abondent en formules saisissantes, en maximes, en vers bien frappés; les morceaux brillants sont nombreux, et ce n'est point par hasard que la tradition indirecte nous en a conservé tant de citations, souvent alterées, comme il convient à des γνῶμαι qui étaient dans toutes les bouches.[1]

These are perhaps superficial merits, but they are merits, and we can go further. Few plays, even in this group, surpass this one in tragic feeling and imagination – one has only to think of the conception of the mourning chorus, of the half-demented Evadne, of the whole scene at the pyre. Yet, dramatically, the play seems helpless; the action seems to reach its proper conclusion at v. 975 at the latest – even so we could willingly spare the Funeral Speech of Adrastus – and, besides being scattered, it is very inconsistent in tone, for the Socratic confutation of Adrastus by Theseus, not to mention the set debate on democracy, do not, at first sight, consort well with the tragic features we have mentioned. No Euripidean play atones for more numerous irritations by more evident excellences.

The usual estimate of the *Suppliant Women* seems to be that of the Argument, 'an encomium of Athens'. It is a patriotic play, in which the disinterested nobility and the sagacity of Theseus are contrasted with the folly of Adrastus and the boorish presumption of the Boeotian Creon; just as the democratic constitution of Athens, though criticized, is favourably compared with autocratic constitutions. The play, too, gives to Athens a glorious part in one of the great actions of the mythic past; it reflects recent events to the credit

[1] M. Grégoire, ed. Budé, p. 99.

and comfort of the Athenian people, and it tells the enemies of
Athens what Athens thinks of their behaviour.

It is indeed obvious that much of what is said in the play would
gratify the Athenians, but this does not mean that 'eulogy of
Athens', 'patriotic piece', are satisfactory descriptions of it; they do
not explain enough. They certainly do not explain the tone of the
play, for in spite of Theseus' optimist philosophy – and Theseus
here, we must remember, is a young man – the general tone of the
play is surely one of almost unrelieved pessimism. In eulogies,
pessimism is best omitted. Nor is it easy to cast the tragic dramatist
who wrote the *Hecuba* and the *Troades* in the role of patriotic poet.
In these plays we see Euripides as the poet of humanity, loving
Athens without a doubt, but not finding even Athens big enough
for him. In these plays he is what we should call today a good
European, and the *Suppliant Women* only confirms this impression.
Further, if this is a eulogy in purpose, what are Evadne and Iphis
doing in it? Are they really introduced only to interest spectators
bored by the rest of the play?[1]

In a play in which the characters say so much about so many
things it is unusually dangerous to base an interpretation on quota-
tions, but in this play three things are said[2] which at once arrest the
attention. 'If Death were visible in the casting of the vote, Greece
would not be destroying herself by her war-lust' (484–5). 'Empty-
headed mortals . . . you yield not to the persuasion of friends but
only to facts. . . . You cities, who could remedy your troubles by
reasoning, prefer to settle matters by slaughter' (745 ff.). 'Unhappy
mortals, why get spears and make slaughter among yourselves . . . ?
Life is a short thing; we should pass through it easily, with as little
trouble as we can.'

That this pacifism (which has been often noticed) does not lie on
the surface, like the debate on democracy for example, is indicated
by the fact that it touches the form of the play at several points. In
the first place, it explains Evadne and Iphis. Iphis we have met before, as Theseus in the *Hippolytus,* and we shall meet him again, as
Peleus in the *Andromache.* Evadne is a recognizable descendant of
Cassandra in the *Agamemnon.* These two characters are not melo-

---

[1] M. Grégoire, ed. Budé, pp. 100–1.

[2] Characteristically of Euripides, it is immaterial who says them. The first is said
by the Theban Herald, the other two by Adrastus.

dramatic ornaments, but more examples of Euripides' abstract or
suggestive use of plot. The theme is the same as that of the *Hecuba*
and *Troades,* the communal suffering that comes from communal
wrongdoing and folly. The wrongdoing and folly here are the
remarkably stupid behaviour of Adrastus and the impious arrogance
of Creon; the suffering is typified in the mourning of the mothers
and sons, and is brought suddenly to a sharp point in the frenzied
grief of Evadne – just as Cassandra suddenly brings into a focus all
the horrors of the house of Atreus. Of Iphis M. Grégoire remarks
(p. 145 of his edition) that he goes home to die in despair, being in
this no Heracles. But why is he not a Heracles – or a wild blasphemer, or something else really interesting? Why, if Euripides was
at his wits' end to stimulate his audience, did he make Iphis simply
an inconspicuous old man? Because that was precisely what he
wanted. Iphis is the type of ordinary humanity that suffers because
of the follies that this play exposes, suffering not greatly and
romantically, like Evadne, but dumbly and uncomprehendingly.

This 'pacifism' explains, too, Adrastus. 'Adraste visiblement
agace Thésée.' Why? Theseus so pitilessly lays bare the foolish
behaviour of Adrastus not because he wants some kind of stick with
which to beat contemporary Argos – that we may believe when we
are convinced that Euripides was not a great tragic poet – but for
strictly dramatic reasons, to make it quite clear that this expedition
of the Seven against Thebes was not something vaguely inevitable,
not some misty but glorious emprise. The real purpose of the
elenchus we do not see at first, naturally; we see only what it does.
There was the strange oracle, that Adrastus should marry his
daughters to a boar and a lion; two exiles turn up, the one a homicide, the other a man cursed by his father, ruffians both, for they
start fighting at once. Confident in his brilliant identification of these
two with the boar and lion, Adrastus passes over the natural circle of
suitors,[1] Argives, and thrusts his daughters upon these two fortunate
men, and they (aided by 'the clamour of the young men' which
overbore him) at once involve the silly man in the war. He began by
reading an oracle; he asked for no confirmation, and sought no
more mantic aid. Indeed, such as came unasked he rejected. This
extremely foolish, not to say impious, behaviour he describes later
(734), after the manner of his kind, as 'the will of Zeus'.

[1] 133 f.

Plainly the motive of this passage is not a simple-minded desire to draw an Adrastus who should be different from Aeschylus' (Euripides must have spent very few of his working hours in trying to be different from Aeschylus), nor to ridicule ancient stories in the easy manner of 'A Yankee at the Court of King Arthur', but to establish the terrifying fact that the misery which fills this play has an origin so tragically foolish. So, when Theseus says, 'What of that Argos of yours? Big words, and nothing else?' (135), he is not covertly expressing Athens' irritation at the profitable neutrality of Argos during the Archidamian War. It may be true that Euripides would have avoided such an expression at a time when Athens was trying to get Argive help; it is possible that, in spite of the poetry and the music and the remoteness of the Athenian stage, the Athenian dramatist could not use 'Argos' poetically without being understood politically. That is another thing. His point here – and he returns to it at v. 737 – is a purely dramatic one, that military strength is no safe substitute for ordinary prudence. In fact, if there is a direct contemporary allusion in this part of the play we should see it in vv. 738 ff. Here we find a detail which Euripides seems to have invented: 'When Eteocles offered a composition, making demands which were moderate, we rejected it . . . and then we were destroyed . . . O empty-headed mortals . . . you settle it by slaughter.' The Spartans offered terms to Athens in 425 B.C.

The expedition then was an act of criminal stupidity. Adrastus' ἁμαρτία is brought out clearly – and we may again notice that the ἁμαρτία is of importance in the life of the community rather than in the life of the wrongdoer. Here it is not its first function to illuminate Adrastus, nor is it of the first importance that it recoils upon him. In fact, it does – Menelaus in the *Andromache* is luckier – but the dramatic results are those which affect the mothers and sons, Evadne and Iphis.

To Adrastus Theseus behaves as a man of pure intelligence: 'Since it is your own doing, mend it yourself.' He uses that σύνεσις, intelligence, which is the first gift of God to man (203). But Aethra points out that there is something else, the claims of humanity, religion and honour; these cannot be laid aside. To Adrastus Theseus will not yield, to Aethra he must. His expedition is one undertaken in defence of law and humanity – that is why he will allow Adrastus no part in it. It is of the nature of a sacrifice freely offered by the city,

with no hope of gain – not even of mandates – and when he is
victorious Theseus refuses to enter Thebes. The theme demanded
that Creon should turn the potential sacrifice into a real one, a point
to remember when one is considering whether the play reflects the
refusal of the Thebans to restore the Athenian dead after Delium. In
Aeschylus' play on the same myth, the *Eleusinians,* the Thebans yield
to persuasion. If there were no dramatic reason for their refusal to
yield here, the inference that Euripides was thinking of Delium
would be irresistible; as there is such a reason Delium may be
concidence.[1] Here Creon must refuse Theseus' reasonable request
in order that Euripides may make clear his contrast between a just
and a stupid war. The horrors of the new battle are not passed over,
but from it no new misery is drawn. We return to the original
theme, the waste caused by the expedition of the Argives, without
the addition of new Athenian mourners whose dead did not die in
the cause of stupidity.

So far as Aristotelian unity goes, the play obviously might end
with the return of the dead. Logically, Evadne and Iphis are an
entirely fresh development; if they come in, why not uncles of
Parthenopaeus, or cousins of Hippomedon? Evadne and Iphis are
introduced in order to develop the tragic idea. Euripides in fact is
not merely dramatizing the legend of the Suppliant Women and
filling it out with maxims, discourses, and debates on democracy;
he is expressing a tragic vision and using the legend for that purpose.
If conflict arises between the development of the idea and the smooth
conduct of the action, it is the action that has to give way. The
development of the idea demands that after the generalized suffering
and grief of the Mothers and Sons we should see an intenser expression of grief in a single person; that the ruin which has already come
about through Adrastus' folly should be brought to a focus in the
ruin of Evadne's life, and, through her, of Iphis'. There is provided,
naturally, a formal link – the prominence in the first part of
Capaneus; the real link is in the idea.

When these two have sounded their very personal note and have
gone, Euripides introduces, with the Sons, a new and, to my
thinking, an even more tragic development. It is not that orphaned
children are more pathetic than bereaved mothers; the Sons raise the

[1] See Parmentier's judicious remarks about the *Troades* and the Sicilian expedition.
(Ed. Budé, pp. 13 ff.)

question, 'What of the future?' Here, unless I have entirely mistaken my play, Euripides has small comfort to offer. The Sons do all that is accounted virtuous – they dedicate themselves to vengeance, but the Mothers sing, 'The evil sleeps not yet.'

This hint of vengeance to come is either a perfunctory way of preparing the wind-up of the play, or it is an intensification of the tragedy. Perfunctory because if the theme is simply and solely that of the Suppliant Women it is already finished; the addition of the Sons can be only a stage-effect, and statements about a happy revenge were best left to the conventional *Deus ex machina* – who indeed does arrive to make them. If this is all, there is no point in the intervention of the Sons, except a certain pathos; still less is there real development. If on the other hand the play is what we take it to be, there is both. The boys will avenge fathers who died in a war which should never have been begun, one from whose results the prudent Theseus – until won over by Aethra – had held strictly aloof. The Sons, unquestionably, are showing nobility – but ʽΕλλὰς δοριμανὴς ἀπόλλυται – the destruction goes on. The more noble their aspiration, the more awful the tragedy. This is development, logical and powerful, the last turn of the screw.

Here is the end of the tragedy; it remains only to append a formal conclusion, a perfectly artificial scene in which – seeing that it has no tragic tension whatever – we may find allusions to our heart's content. This time it is, naturally, Athena who arrives, and she arrives with a remark which is surely intended to jar: 'Hearken, O Theseus, to the words of Athena . . . Give not these bones for the Sons to convey to Argos, letting them pass so lightly from thy hands. In return for thy labours, and the City's, first exact an oath . . .' What? A goddess less generous than Theseus? A mandate after all? We can find reasons in plenty for ending the play with oaths of friendship, but why is Athena so very blunt about it? There is Euripidean precedent for deities who are morally inferior to men; what is the reason here? Athena winds up the *Ion* because, as she hints, Apollo is ashamed to show his face. The Dioscuri end the *Electra* partly because it is so ridiculous for a woman like Electra to have uncles in the sky, partly because it is so damaging for the newest of divinities to say what these say about Apollo. Athena ends the *I.T.* because Apollo, who is responsible for Orestes, does not exist. Apollo ends the *Orestes* because nothing could establish his

non-existence better than the impossible solution he gravely pro-
pounds. Euripides liked to produce gods, especially Apollo, at the
end less to cut the knot than to cut their own throats. Athena here
is certainly not spoof; for one thing the play has not been melodrama
but serious tragedy. We may, however, be prepared to see a certain
tinge of irony in the treatment she receives – unless indeed the play
is simply an encomium of Athens. She is less generous than Theseus,
as Artemis was less noble than Hippolytus, Aphrodite than Phaedra.
How are we to interpret this touch of acidity? That the romantic
expedition of Theseus against Thebes is not practical politics? That
Theseus does not after all represent the political wisdom of Athens?
It is difficult to say.

That the *Suppliant Women* has as much tautness and austerity as
the other tragedies of Euripides we cannot maintain. It is discursive –
and Euripides is aware of the fact (cf. the apologies in 427–8, 461–2,
567, 584). But apart from the loosely appended passages like the
debate on democracy, the funeral-speech, the criticism of the conventional messenger-speech (846 ff.), it is a coherent and well-
designed presentation of a single theme. It obviously is a eulogy of
Athens in that it contains a great deal that would appeal to Athenian
sentiment, but, like the *Persae*, it is as much a national warning as a
national eulogy. Theseus is the great man of the piece and Theseus
was an Athenian. Excellent. But Theseus' ordinary prudence was
against the war; he yielded only to Aethra's plea of religion and
honour, and when he defeated Creon he refused to enter Thebes –
more disinterested than Athena. Let the Athenians congratulate
themselves on their Theseus when they are sure that they are equally
disinterested in their war-making. Meanwhile the new detail of
Eteocles' offer of peace remains in the memory – and certain warn-
ings about politicians and the ruin of Greece.

That the play is a *piece d'occasion* in the ordinary sense, a work
inspired by one particular event or situation, it seems quite impossible to believe. The war dominated Euripides' thought for years,
completely filling this group of plays. Except for the *Heracles,* we
have no tragedy of his, after the *Hippolytus,* on any other theme.
He could escape into melodrama, and he could escape into Macedonia and write the *Bacchae*; in Athens he could write only about
the war, and as a tragic poet, not as an interested onlooker. The behaviour of Sparta could rouse him to the specifically bitter outburst

of the *Andromache*, but he did not attack the Spartans as enemies, hardly even war as war. In his mind these things were linked with the central tragedy of man, his capacity for intelligence and self-control, his domination by unreason and folly. The events of Delium may have suggested to him the theme of this play, or may have decided him to use it now and not later, but this is not to say that he was still thinking of Delium in the play; for with Euripides, as with any other creative artist, the original incident would grow into something entirely different and peculiarly his own.[1] Adrastus and Creon are no longer Argos and Thebes of 424 B.C., nor Theseus Athens of 424 B.C. These belong not to current politics, but to poetry, morality and tragedy.

7. The 'Andromache'

The *Andromache* illustrates very clearly Euripides' present method, and as the play shapes itself as a straightforward play of intrigue the very nearly complete break which occurs half-way through the plot is the more surprising. This hard and brilliant tragedy is, not incidentally but fundamentally, a violent attack on the Spartan mind, on *Machtpolitik*; in particular on three Spartan qualities, arrogance, treachery and criminal ruthlessness. These are portrayed in three separate characters, Hermione, Menelaus, and Orestes, and in two separate actions; for in the first half of the play Andromache and her child, attacked by Hermione and Menelaus, are saved by Peleus, and in the second half Orestes appears, out of a different legend, to carry Hermione off to Sparta and to murder Neoptolemus on the way. We are then left to manage as well as we can with Peleus, Thetis and the body of Neoptolemus. Andromache does not appear again.

Nowhere is it more evident that the unity of the play lies in its idea and not in the story. If we will not integrate these separate actions, and the epilogue, into one general impression we shall find no explanation of Euripides' behaviour, only a 'lack of unity' which, as Verrall truly declared, is a euphemism for downright insanity. It is useless to say that 'the second action grows out of the first', for it does not 'grow', and it remains a 'second action'. This is a method of making trilogies, not single plays. Méridier points out

[1] See Henry James's prefaces *passim*

to us an equilibrium, and in this way tries to impose a formal unity on the work; Hermione, humiliated in the first part, is victorious and takes her revenge in the second; Peleus, successful in the first, is overwhelmed in the second. But in the second part Hermione does not take a revenge, unless it is revenge to clutch at the first man who presents himself, and triumph to elope with an Orestes; nor can we congratulate Euripides if the gallant Peleus is overwhelmed not for some sin but for the sake of an equilibrium. The chiasmus does not work, and if it did it would be no explanation, for the principles of dramatic construction are not those of landscape-gardening.

The orthodox defenders labour under a grave disability: Euripides refuses to give evidence on his own behalf. He might easily have tempered this 'lack of unity', but he does nothing. There is a prologue; why is it not used, as the meaningless phrase goes, 'to bind the play together'? There is an epilogue; was it impossible to make room in it for Andromache? Why is Orestes' name not once mentioned before his surprising arrival? There was opportunity enough and need enough. Had Euripides made efforts to disguise the 'lack of unity' we could perhaps believe in theories of ineptitude, but there are no signs of uneasiness.

The answer to the questions we have just asked is that Euripides never concerned himself with them. He was not merely telling a story and making a play, and had no interest in concocting an artificial unity; as always, he is trying to embody an idea. Why does he not display Andromache in the epilogue? The impression that the epilogue is designed to make is that of the ruin and misery which Spartan *Machtpolitik* creates. To symbolize this the dramatist needs a figure central to all the events of the play – Peleus; one who has lost his son, now loses his grandson, and nearly loses his great-grandson. Andromache might have been introduced, but though she would have secured for the play a superficial symmetry she would have blurred this impression. Peleus represents the stricken house; she would have been only the ill-used captive.

Similarly no preparation is made for Orestes' coming. The deliberate avoidance of his name suggests that Euripides meant to challenge our minds by the shock of his arrival. The dramatist was willing that his play should stand or fall by its intrinsic effect; it is, we might say, a severely functional work of art which disdains pretences. Certainly we must not think of the *Andromache* as if in it

Euripides were deftly combining legends and throwing in some anti-Spartan venom as a make-weight. Drama can be made in this way, but such drama must above all be neat and workmanlike. The *Andromache* is animated and explained by one burning idea which, with its separate aspects, incorporates itself in a plot better suited to a trilogy than to a play; and because the play means so much to Euripides, so much more than the *Ion* or *I.T.* meant, he cannot find the time or inclination to tinker with it and give it a false unity which would in no way assist the idea.

In these important respects the *Andromache* resembles the *Hecuba* and *Troades*; in others it is very different. It has a vigour of action, a sharpness in characterization, which those plays conspicuously lack; on the other hand its chorus is less effective. These differences are not accidental.

The theme and feeling of the *Andromache* are not universal, as are those of the *Hecuba* and *Troades*. The play is a denunciation of Sparta, not a tragedy of mankind. The dramatic results of this are important. Since Euripides wishes to arraign specific aspects of Spartan morality he presents Spartans in action rather than their victims in misery; the plot therefore is much less passive than those of the other plays. To swiftness and decisiveness in action is added, from the same cause, a much more detailed characterization; obviously the Spartans, if not also their victims, must be drawn in the hardest of outlines. Moreover, we need not expect the light and shade of tragedy; in fact, both in action and in characterization the *Andromache* has the hardness and the glaring colours of melodrama. Euripides has not to keep within Aristotelian limits of the probable, the broadly human; his special and limited aim compels him to make his action and characters as extreme as he can. He must be definite, for vagueness in denunciation will not do, and he can be as extreme as he likes.

In these respects therefore the *Andromache,* though it verges on melodrama, is more normal than the *Hecuba* and *Troades,* but because it is so particular and brings everything to so sharp a point its chorus is not so happy. The lyrical background which the Trojan chorus holds up to a more poetically conceived action would here be incongruous; this time what Euripides wants to say he says in the action. These harsh and violent deeds do not permit themselves to be enfolded by music and the dance, and because the plot is schematic the chorus cannot be consecutive in the Sophoclean manner.

These points will be developed in the next chapter; meanwhile we may notice how clearly the style of the play is dictated by its indignant purpose.

In the early scenes the revolting cruelty and treachery of Menelaus are displayed with all possible emphasis in the plot against Andromache. Her child is used as a bait, and then, with an indecent show of formality, Menelaus proposes to murder both. These events produce a scene between Neoptolemus' unpleasant wife and his tragic concubine; also one of Euripides' statutory scenes of self-sacrifice. The former is often called a psychological study; but what does the term mean? If it is one that can be properly applied to the *Philoctetes*, or even to Euripides' own *Ion*, then we can hardly use it here, nor are we complimenting Euripides if we do. It is a good and effective scene, but for a study it is altogether too easy. There is a dramatic clash between opposed characters, but there is no movement of mind, no action and reaction beyond that of blank opposition. Even their relations to Neoptolemus are touched on only in the most objective way; there is no sign that either of them has any affection for him, or he for them, except that he finds Hermione intolerable, Andromache not. Euripides, we may be quite sure, would learn with dismay that such a scene was being held up as an example of his 'psychology'. It has the 'psychology' of melodrama, nothing but white and black; and rightly so, for Hermione is nothing but Spartan arrogance and narrow-minded cruelty, and Euripides draws her pure and strong not to make a domestic study but to denounce Sparta. As the stage-complement of such a figure, Andromache herself can hardly be subtly drawn, nor is she. She is middle-aged, and is a very tragic, or more accurately a very pathetic figure, but the incessant complaint that she is unsympathetic and argues like a barrister misses the point. Euripides drew his Phaedra, and his Helen, and he could have drawn a subtle Andromache – but the play did not need it and would not tolerate it. Her part is to be as unlike Hermione as possible and, by talking sense, to show what nonsense Hermione has delivered.

To Andromache's character we shall return; we may now consider the sacrifice-scene, the pathos of which, according to Hyslop's remarkable Introduction, is one of the qualities which save the play from worthlessness. There is pathos, and the scene is very moving – but how did Euripides intend us to be moved? Antigone's self-sacrifice is tragic; Andromache's is not tragic but monstrous, designed not to display Andromache in the quality of tragic heroine but to make our blood boil. Andromache, of course, puts her child before herself; she is heroic and noble – but our blood is boiling. The villainy of Menelaus, not the nobility of Andromache, has the first claim on our emotions. This is what Euripides intended and this is what he has done. When Andromache begins her speech with 'O Reputation, Reputation . . .' is she marring the situation, chilling its dramatic warmth, giving way to Euripides' love of rhetoric and sophistry? If we suppose that Euripides thought he was writing another *Antigone,* such must be our verdict; but in fact Euripides thought the matter of this speech before he thought of Andromache. She is there not to be herself but to say what she was invented for. The whole incident is conceived melodramatically, as the theme demanded. Andromache is simply caught in a trap; she can be noble or ignoble, that is all. There is no room for any but the most elementary character-drawing, and that is all Euripides offers.

After the arrogance, cruelty and treachery of Sparta comes Spartan stupidity. Menelaus has come to defend his daughter's conjugal dignity and happiness; he so acts that he must infallibly destroy both. What he cannot see for himself Andromache points out with clarity and force (hence her cleverness), that when Neoptolemus returns he must drive her out of his house, and who will take her then? The answer to this question is Orestes, but we do not know that yet. Menelaus is stupid and overreaches himself; he crumples up before Peleus, and Hermione, left unprotected, tries to commit suicide. 'I am tired out,' says the Nurse, with Euripidean humour, 'trying to keep her from hanging herself' (815).

'Avec le vers 765 on s'attendrait à voir finir le drame', remarks Méridier; but the real drama is the Spartan mind, not the exciting story of Andromache and her son, and Euripides has more revelations to make. There was another legend about Neoptolemus which made it possible (with enough invention and determination) to bring in Orestes as a mean schemer and murderer. His name has been carefully kept back; suddenly he enters, telling lies. First he pretends that he is on his way to Dodona and is only paying a friendly call on the cousin who was once betrothed to him, but quite soon (911 ff.) his questions begin to run with a surprising aptness in the direction of a possible murder. Hermione clutches at him like a drowning person at a straw; now he blandly informs her that he knew about it all the time; he has been waiting about, with a bodyguard, to see whether she would remain in Phthia or, 'terrified with the murder of the captive woman', would prefer to run away, in which case 'I will take and deliver you to your father. Kinship is a strangely powerful thing; when one is in trouble there is nothing better than a friend in the family'. Menelaus' stupidity has given Orestes a chance to blackmail him, and Hermione's hysterical jibe (170 ff.) that Andromache lives with the man who slew her husband is savagely turned against herself.

So Orestes disappears into the murk from which he came, and the completion of the picture of Spartan ways is left to the Messenger. The recital of the murder is a masterly piece of work, fit to be compared with the description of the gallant slaughter of Aegisthus by the same hand in the *Electra*. No element of the sinister and hateful is wanting; it is a fine climax to a deadly play.[1]

A play, however, cannot end with a messenger-speech, and the time has passed when it can end with a funeral hymn. Moreover, that would sound very incongruous after this exceedingly unlyrical drama. To bring back Andromache would be no true solution of the problem; she is not the heroine and centre of interest of the play, only the first victim of the Spartan machinations. We are left, when Orestes hurries after Menelaus, to contemplate the wreckage they have created, and the symbol of this wreckage must be Peleus. The war fought for Menelaus' wife robbed him of his son; now Orestes has murdered his grandson, and Menelaus very nearly his great-grandson.

But by this time our blood has boiled sufficiently. There is indeed no catharsis, but there may be a quietly conventional ending; there is no justice, but – in a play – there may be consolation prizes. So, as there is no catharsis, that is finality, in the emotions evoked by the action, finality is secured externally. Thetis is brought down to comfort Peleus with hopes of golden immortality and to make permament arrangements for Andromache and the child.

In some respects this is one of the most interesting of Euripides' plays, composite in plot like the other tragedies, but vigorous in

---

[1] I cannot understand how Mr D. L. Page (*Greek Poetry and Life*, p. 227) can be moderately friendly to Orestes and excuse this slow and intelligent murder as a *crime passionnel*. In Mediterranean latitudes passion, surely, is expected to work more swiftly.

action and definite in characterization like the later melodramas: a tragedy in essence but a melodrama in execution. Unity of action is always an artistic virtue, but it is a philosophical necessity only when the springs of the tragic action are concentrated in a single tragic hero, whose action is to be the tragedy. Here we have composite wickedness and composite suffering which allow, logically, a composite plot. They do not, however, compel us to admire that plot, and as the *Andromache* does rely on its action much more than the other tragedies of this group, the 'lack of unity' is correspondingly more obtrusive. It falls between two stools, and there is force in the ancient criticism 'The play is of the second rank'.[1]

It has, however, its own logic. Mahaffy called it a tragedy which 'has the air of a political pamphlet'; we might more correctly call it a political pamphlet which has the air of a tragedy. It would be an exaggeration, but it would save us from the error of labelling as 'faults' – and most inexplicable ones – features that were essential to Euripides' purpose. He did not set out to write 'a Greek Tragedy' and then spoil it by crude characterization and untimely political references.

But although in this play Euripides' indignation burns so fiercely against Sparta, he does not become a propagandist nor cease entirely to be a tragic poet. We shall deal with the chorus later, but we may note here that the first stasimon, on the Trojan War, and the fourth, on the miseries which that war brought to each side impartially, are much more general in their tone than the play as a whole. They establish contact with the poet of the *Troades*.[2]

[1] Second Argument.

[2] On the date of the *Andromache* I have not thought it necessary to say anything here. The political references in the play are too vague to produce anything but discussion, but it is perhaps permissible to advance two general considerations. (1) If we assume (as we well may) that it was some particular act of inhumanity, villainy or bad faith in Sparta that produced this explosion, the treatment of the Plataean prisoners (cf. Menelaus' treatment of Andromache) is antecedently far more probable an occasion than the campaign of Brasidas. The bad faith of Brasidas was of the kind that irritates politicians; Plataea of the kind to rouse poets. (2) The Scholiast, whom Méridier still prefers to follow, put the play 'at about the beginning of the War'. That Euripides should first have written this anti-Spartan play, and then, with deeper experience of the war should have written the deeper anti-war tragedies, is a development as convincing as such things can be.

Pohlenz, in an interesting passage (p. 304), argues for the campaign of Brasidas (though the evidence from Tharyps is a little exiguous) and suggests that Euripides refrained from putting the play on the stage. If we were certain that the play was published but not produced, it would be a tempting guess that the name Democrates which Callimachus found inscribed as the author's name was a *nom de guerre* chosen by Euripides. It would not be unsuitable to the occasion.

8. The 'Heracles'

This is certainly the most puzzling of the plays of Euripides which have reached us undamaged, so puzzling that it is surprising that it has reached us at all. We owe its preservation, probably, to the astonishing force of the madness scene. There is no question that this is the most powerful thing of the kind that Euripides ever wrote, and that the last part of the play is, in a very different way, equally impressive; but what is the meaning of the play as a whole? Is it a whole?

The plot is more orthodox than that of the *Hecuba,* in that it is based on one story, not two, but (like the plots of the *Troades* and *Suppliant Women*) it is not a dramatic unity. Between the peril of Heracles' dependants, with which we start, and the madness that descends on Heracles, there is no connexion but juxtaposition, and the last scene, introduced by the opportune arrival of Theseus, has no strict causal connexion with the previous one.

Since the plays falls into three distinct parts, it is not surprising that attempts have been made to find, in the play itself, a dramatic theme which will make it both a unity and a logically developed action. It has been put forward that the play is a study of a genius that is close to madness; that Heracles is subject to delusions which turn great but not superhuman achievements into miraculous 'Labours', and that the madness scene presents us with the tragic results of the last of these storms. Abnormality indeed had a fascination for Euripides. We find it already in the *Medea,* and the thread can be continued through the *Electra* to the *Orestes.* There is then nothing inherently improbable in some form of the delusional theory here, especially as Heracles himself recognizes (vv. 1258 ff.) a taint in his blood which might point to an unbalanced mind. Nevertheless such an explanation of the play involves real difficulties. Lycus, who alone expresses doubt of the genuineness of the labours, is presented as so preposterous a character that it is difficult to think that Euripides intended him to represent the normal sane man. The natural interpretation of what Theseus says and does is that Heracles did rescue him from Hades. Heracles' outburst of rage against Lycus might be accepted as an indication of frenzy in one known to be insane, but I agree with M. Parmentier that it cannot of itself prove insanity; it proves only that Heracles was not the man to remain calm and reasonable under extreme provocation.

If, provisionally, we look for another explanation what can we find? Of the straightforward view M. Parmentier makes an excellent exposition in his introduction (ed. Budé). Euripides' idea was to purify the crude popular pictures of Heracles, to give a Heracles who 'n'est pas seulement le bienfaiteur qui met sa force au service de l'humanité; il est bon fils, époux fidèle, père tendre, ami devoué, et enfin capable de supporter noblement une souffrance morale plus cruelle que toute douleur physique'. The madness comes – not from Hera, for that is a 'poets' lie – but from fate. After his life of labours Heracles finds himself at a cross-road where he has to choose between a life of torture and salvation through suicide; he has the greatness to choose life. The sense of the tragedy is given in Amphitryon's words (106) τὸ δ' ἀπορεῖν ἀνδρὸς κακοῦ – 'ne point persévérer est d'un lache'. The last victory of Heracles is the most heroic of all, a fitting climax to the play.

This interpretation accepts the labours as real, and it gives to a play which makes a purely tragic impression a purely tragic meaning, but it hardly goes deep enough, and it does not seem to account for the whole play. This conception of Heracles is, I think, the right one, but is the play then substantially only a portrait, its catastrophe only a means of heightening its colours, and its theme that a great hero is a great hero? This is perhaps to put it crudely; it may be urged that the *Tyrannus* is only a portrait. Perhaps so, but it is one whose frame is nothing less than Sophocles' conception of human life and human destiny; what conception underlies this picture of Heracles? Secondly, it is a little difficult, on this view, to see the bearing of the first part of the play on the whole. M. Parmentier calls it 'the first panel of a kind of triptych', which is just enough, if one remembers that it is restating, not explaining, the difficulty; for a play has no business to be a triptych.

If we accept the reality of the Labours and all that goes with them, we shall have to look for an interpretation that will explain the connexion between the first part and the rest, and will give a reasonable account of the 'Hera' whom Heracles himself appears to rationalize out of the play. If there is no logical connexion between the first part and the rest – and certainly none is obvious – if, that is, the play really is a kind of triptych, we must look for some tragic and dramatic idea which makes it a unity in thought and not merely by juxtaposition – such an idea as makes a unity of the Hecuba diptych.

We may begin by asking what can be made of the first panel. It is indeed a strange affair, the stranger in that it is practically all free invention. Lycus and his usurpation were created for the occasion, but to what end? Euripides has rarely invented so freely, yet is there in the whole of Greek drama a set of scenes that can rival these in debility? For consider what they contain – remembering that aphorisms like that of v. 106[1] may adorn but cannot create drama. Once more the play begins with suppliants at an altar, a situation that is explained in an elaborate prologue. The prologue we easily accept as a convention, and after recent experiences we do not perhaps expect much movement in the first scene. Megara follows Amphitryon. Her first twenty verses are moving – the description of the excitement when someone knocks at the door is one of the best things of its kind in Euripides – but the rest of the scene is flat. If we hope that the chorus will introduce some decisive motive, as it does for instance in the *Hecuba,* we are disappointed. Amphitryon has called himself a 'useless old man', hardly to be counted among men, and the incoming chorus is no better; indeed their two strophes are nothing but a description of their physical feebleness Was Euripides really so obsessed with old age as this?

At last a man appears – but he is only Lycus, a melodramatic swashbuckler, in whose mind and character we can take no very prolonged interest, whatever may be the case with his actions. But even as a strong man Lycus is disappointing.[2] He begins rather weakly by assuring the suppliants that their hopes in Heracles are ill-placed; Heracles was only a boaster and a liar, and now he is dead; no hero – only a coward with a bow. Such an imputation from such a man might well be disdained as not a thing to take seriously, and Amphitryon does in fact take a high line with Lycus. A great speech on the Labours would be beyond Lycus' deserts, and in any case the substance of it is being reserved for the chorus. Amphitryon has therefore little to contribute to the drama. The debate on bowmen and spearmen keeps us going for a time; the subject is just relevant, and it was topical, so that if dramatic movement had to be manufactured, it was good enough raw material, but obviously it is manufactured. We have (165 ff.) a tragic idea,

---

[1] 'Ne point persévérer est d'un lache.'

[2] Compare his entry with the impressive first appearance of Creon in the *Antigone*.

characteristic of this group of plays, that political necessity is held to excuse murder: 'Not cruelty but caution' is very like Thucydides on the Corcyrean affair; but still the scene as a whole seems to be groping after something dramatic.

At first it seems to be Lycus' part to be the *contemptor divom,* to trample on the rights of suppliants and the sanctity of altars, but though he may be Menelaus' equal in wickedness, he falls far short in resourcefulness. Once more, if we are looking forward to a strong scene of treachery or violence, even of bluster, we are disappointed. Lycus summons his men, he is very angry and very wicked; he will burn the suppliants out of their refuge to show them who is King now – and to do this he sends some of the men to Helicon, some to Parnassus, to find firewood. Even so, instead of making an effective exit on this not very high note, he remains on the stage looking fierce, until, seventy verses later, it occurs to Amphitryon to address him again. After the forceful-feeble gesture of Lycus the chorus is defiant but quite impotent; it has lost the strength of its good right hand. Still, it can boast of one achievement – it puts in twenty-two verses instead of the usual couplet between the one actor's speech and the next. After the chorus, Megara holds the breach for thirty-five verses. She despairs of Heracles' return, and Verrall made much of this, but we need see in it nothing more than the barest minimum of dramatic movement. If both she and Amphitryon were optimistic, how could dialogue go on? There is no sign of firewood yet, and none of a new dramatic motif, such as the comparable scene in the *Andromache* enjoys in plenty. After Megara, the chorus is feeble again, and turns to the feeble Amphitryon. He asks that he and Megara may at least be slain first, to be spared the sight of the children's death, but Megara is more helpful to a dramatist in difficulties: may they be allowed to enter their own house to put on funeral garb? Lycus, who has been standing feebly by for nearly a hundred verses, gives permission, Amphitryon makes a bitter attack on Zeus, the stage is cleared, and the chorus comes to our rescue with an ode on the Labours – and surely, when a Euripidean chorus goes on for a hundred verses, it is a portent. After the ode Lycus' victims reappear, dressed for the grave – a grisly effect which would remain long in the mind; a dramatic thrill at last. Against this horrible background Megara makes a long and not ineffective speech of farewell, Amphitryon, a supreme appeal to Zeus – and at length Heracles appears, putting an end to five hundred verses of drama which few, I imagine, have re-read for pleasure.

Surely dramatic feebleness like this is a remarkable thing in the poet of the *Medea* and the *Andromache*? It is quite clear that had Euripides merely wanted a dramatic scene or two to make a first panel he could have done much better with the same material. Amphitryon is conspicuously impotent among all Euripides' old men, and he is joined with a chorus of other old men whose chief part seems to be to explain that they would like to have one but are too weak. Why, for example, could Amphitryon not have borrowed some of Teiresias' impressiveness? Why need Megara remain so shadowy a creation? Lycus, too, is made not only completely wicked, so that he can have no moral struggles with himself, but also completely secure, so that he can find no opposition except from those unable to oppose. How easy it would have been, if a dramatic scene had been the object of Euripides' lavish invention here, to threaten Lycus with heaven's wrath, to make him uneasy but defiant, Amphitryon powerless but impressive.

This absence of the dramatic is clearly the result of deliberate choice; it contrasts with ordinary dramatic incapacity as the contrived ugliness of many an 'architect-built' house does with the result of a mere builder's inspiration. If Euripides has made Lycus much less interesting than he might have done and the action much less arresting, the only explanation can be that he did not want our minds to be intent on Lycus and his doings. Verrall (a sound destructive critic) was impressed with the dramatic emptiness of much of these scenes, and held that Amphitryon talked merely to gain time. This is not enough; everyone in the play does, and Lycus connives at it by sending his men to the confines of Boeotia for wood. It looks as if it was Euripides who wanted to gain time, or rather as if he were writing to a programme, as it were, one which (as happens with programmes) does not at the moment suit his medium.

We are bound to look for some explanation of this 'panel' which will make it a real though possibly a discrete part of the whole play – using, in fact, the assumption that the play is a triptych, but only as the old trilogy was, or the *Troades,* each part contributing clearly and decisively to one unifying idea. If our general theory of Euripides' present method of construction is true, it will not dismay us to find no organic, Aristotelian connexion between this part and what follows, but it will dismay us if we cannot see in this part a contribution to the whole comparable in importance to the madness scene itself. Moreover, as we are going on the assumption that Euripides was both a sincere artist and a competent dramatist, our explanation must explain, too, not only what he does here, but also what he conspicuously refrains from doing. It must show us (as simply calling it a 'first panel' does not) why Euripides is found fighting with one hand tied behind his back.

I cannot see that a delusional theory helps us. This would demand that the believers in Heracles, themselves deluded, should be offset by someone else who is clear-sighted, a Lycus who may be as cruel as you please but who is at least shrewd and worthy of credence – a Creon in fact. If, too, we had a chorus sympathetic but capable of independent judgement which was not deluded either, we should have a group natural to the idea and capable of a dramatic development far different from what we have. If the true explanation is one which should demonstrate that Euripides had to do what he did, and nothing else, it does not seem to lie here.

It is not plain that Euripides is, in some sense, doing here what he did with his Adrastus, namely making his point as absolute as he can, pushing it to the logical extreme? The villainy of Lycus, the impotence of both Amphitryon and the chorus – to say nothing of Megara and the children – are made as extreme as possible; obviously in order that the danger they stand in may be unqualified. Lycus is nothing to Euripides but imminent danger; that is why he is so baldly characterized. The others are nothing but persons dear to the hero – his tenderness to them is mentioned more than once, and soon will be strikingly displayed; that is why they are no more than sketched in. The impotence of the chorus, the sheer physical difficulty they find in reaching the place of the action, the indifference of the rest of the city, the inaccessibility of Lycus to all scruples or fear, the fact that these weapons are barely used against him – all these things, each a nuisance to the mere making of drama, are designed to underline this danger. The scenes are flat because, we may say, Euripides is really dramatizing a negative, the absence of the great man. During his absence Thebes has fallen to a buccaneer; for lack of his strong arm his father-in-law the King has perished, and soon, too, will his father, wife, and children. They are entirely defenceless and their danger is absolute.

What is the point? That Heracles is in fact no hero? That he has been neglectful towards his dependants in leaving them so unprotected? But he left them in Creon's care; why should he foresee his overthrow? Besides, he trusted to Theban gratitude (558–69); he is surprised to find his house so unbefriended. Are we then to blame not Heracles but Thebes? Perhaps the continuation will help us to decide.[1]

In a short series of questions Heracles learns the meaning of the horrible sight that confronts him. The extremity of the danger is emphasized, the barbarity of Lycus and the indifference of the city – all leading to that passage (562 ff.) which has been taken to be the beginning of a frenzy.[2] The threats are violent, but are they more violent than the extreme provocation would warrant, if we take Heracles to be a man of 'temperament' whose genius ran to heroic, not to intellectual achievement? Χαιρόντων πόνοι – 'Farewell, my Labours! I was wrong then to give myself to you rather than to these.' Heracles may, in the past, have been subject to delusions, but at this moment he must be clear-sighted; he sees, tragically, that if the safety of those he loves is to be his concern, his whole course has been a disastrous error.

This critical passage continues with Amphitryon's account of the revolution that has taken place in Thebes; Lycus came in with the help of a faction of ruined aristocrats whose object was to plunder those who were still wealthy. The brevity of this – it is dismissed in five verses – warns us that it is only explanatory, of no significance to the play as a whole. It explains Amphitryon's caution; Lycus has many supporters, so that it is not merely a question of cutting off Lycus' head and delivering Thebes from an oppressor. Heracles' first instinctive threat (565 ff.) would really embroil him with the dominant faction in the city, and this neither Amphitryon nor Heracles is prepared to face. Heracles is willing to take the cautious line; indeed

---

[1] Admittedly, the audience – if the play is a good one – should not have been as puzzled as we are at this point, but the audience would have had the advantage of seeing this part of the play presented by one who did know what was to come and had interpreted the first part accordingly.

[2] In v. 575 Heracles refers to Amphitryon as γέροντα ('old man' instead of the expected 'father'). Murray, rightly defending the text, remarks, 'Videtur iam delirans mortalem abnuere patrem, tum monitu Chori se comprimere.' But then, since in v. 1365 he more explicitly refers to Zeus as his father, he must be still mad; which is absurd. The monitus of the chorus is only a general remark that a son should protect 'his aged father' (πατέρα πρέσβυν), and 'se comprimere' is obtained from the simple verse, 'In what way am I being too hasty, father?'

he has already done so, in entering the city privily. Not the act of a
fairy-story hero, one who, we are told, with his own hand routed
the forces of the Minyans? We need, perhaps, take no offence at the
contrast between this caution and the threat which he uttered at the
height of his rage, that he would kill Lycus and all the Thebans who
had proved themselves ungrateful to him, but the contrast with the
Minyan story (220–1) is more serious. Is the latter therefore untrue,
or is it enough to say that Heracles was a hero who would not run a
greater risk than he need, or is there some further meaning in this
detail? We must bear it in mind.

Amphitryon's advice is followed by ten lines of dialogue which
hold up the action somewhat. In them we are told (a) that Heracles
did go to Hades and did find Cerberus; (b) that Cerberus is left at
Hermione (a natural place, as it was the seat of a chthonian cult, and
of an entrance to Hades); (c) that Eurystheus, far from possessing
Cerberus, does not yet know of Heracles' return from Hades; and
(d) that Heracles was so long in Hades because he added to his
original mission the rescue of Theseus. Theseus is not indeed still
with him, having gone home to Athens.

If we accept the story at all, these details, and the interruption of
the action that they entail, are easily explicable; (d) is wanted to
prepare for Theseus' arrival at the end of the play, (b) is wanted to
explain (c), which is itself necessary for the madness-scene, where
Heracles imagine himself to be at Argos attacking Eurystheus. This
visit to Argos is very much on his mind.

The following fifteen verses, with which Heracles leads his family
into the house, are not easy to reconcile with the *iam delirans* theory.
Οὐ γὰρ πτερωτός, 'Do not grasp my robe so; I shall not fly away!'
'Come – like little boats towed by a big one.'[1] Here surely we have
the very accents of gentle and understanding comfort, homely
pleasantries designed to banish acute terror. If this is not enough,
῏Ωδ' ἔβητ' ἐπὶ ξυροῦ; 'Were you then *so* near to death?' A moment
surely of utter clarity and peace.[2]

The ode that follows this scene is a disjointed composition, and
the most irrelevant to be found in this group of plays.[3] It closes,
however, successfully on Heracles, and the tone is important. 'He

[1] Tragically echoed at v. 1424.

[2] We must, no doubt, be prepared to hear medical testimony that madness does
come and go like this, but medicine is not drama.

[3] See below, p. 264.

is Zeus' son, but his worth[1] surpasses his birth; his labours have freed men's lives from danger, for he has destroyed the monsters that terrified them.' We may choose between this, supported as it is by the second ode, and Lycus' vulgar insinuations. If Lycus is meant to be right, Euripides has made it difficult to choose correctly.

The slaying of Lycus need not detain us. It is straightforward and effective, particularly in the rasping irony of Amphitryon's exit. The fourth ode expresses the unrestrained joy of the loyal chorus in the triumph of Heracles; 'The new King is gone, the old King reigns.'[2]

Now comes the third part of the play, and the third puzzle. With a kind of second prologue Iris appears, a female counterpart of Hermes, leading Lyssa, Frenzy, to attack Heracles. Lyssa herself is reluctant to do so horrible a thing; she goes so far as to say that she would like to turn Iris from this wicked path, but she must obey.[3] Heracles is driven mad, and, imagining himself in the house of Eurystheus, he slays Megara, his children, and very nearly his father The fit passes; Heracles sane contemplates with horror what he did mad, and would have killed himself forthwith but for the sudden arrival of Theseus. In the end, however, he takes the finer course; he will endure to live, and, Theseus offering him a refuge and honour, he goes with him to Athens.

What view are we to take of these extremely unusual and moving scenes? If we knew Euripides to have been a simpleton, we might perhaps say that he was giving a dramatic version of a current legend and leave it at that; but Euripides was not a simpleton. If he were a minor dramatist, we might say that he was concerned to rehabilitate the character of a national hero. who had been badly used, especially in vase-painting; but the motive is too small for Euripides, especially for the *Heracles*. To call attention to the nobility of the characterization and to the sublimity of the Heracles who emerges from these fires is just, but it does not explain the connexion with the first part of the play. Moreover, Sophocles gives us a hardly inferior picture of moral grandeur in the close of the *Tyrannus* – but how much more than this there is in it!

Fortunately the poet himself has taken care that we should not

[1] Ἀρετή – conjectural but sound enough.

[2] This, coming immediately before the catastrophe, reminds one of the hyporchemata of Sophocles.

[3] This inevitably recalls the merciless deities, more cruel than man, in the *Hippolytus*.

adopt here the most simple of the possible interpretations. The last scene in which Theseus wins Heracles from his first thoughts of suicide, is more than a conventional epilogue. Theseus is a highly intelligent as well as a generous man; the ordinary taboos that surround homicide mean nothing to him; he knows that a mortal cannot pollute the gods, that human threats cannot affect them. His chief concern is that his hero, Heracles, should not admit defeat like an ordinary man, that the benefactor and mighty friend of Greece should not die ἀμαθίᾳ, from blind folly (vv. 1248–54). Heracles' reply to this is to give an outline of his life-story, showing how it has been one long persecution by Hera,[1] culminating in the present disaster; he may no longer live in Thebes, and no other city will receive him. It is a speech which, like this whole part of the play, implicitly, and in several passages explicitly,[2] assumes the truth of the Hera-story. Theseus accepts it too (1311–12) – indeed, his first words were 'This is Hera's work' (1191); but he comforts and tries to strengthen Heracles by saying, in his character of intelligent man, that it is τύχη, Fortune, a power to which even the gods are subject; the gods commit crimes of all sorts – so it is said; why then should you, a mortal, think too much of this?[3] And as for the hopelessness of the future, Theseus is willing to repay the debt he owes Heracles by giving him a home, honour, wealth. 'When the gods favour a man he has no need of friends, for the god's help is enough, when he gives it.' To which Heracles remarkably answers, 'That, alas! does not touch my fate; but I do not believe, nor ever shall, that the gods commit crime, for if God is really God he needs nothing. These are poets' miserable tales.' But Heracles is a very imperfect Platonist, for he does not draw the obvious conclusion – nor does Theseus, less acute here than he is in the *Suppliant Women* – for the speech ends, 'We are all, by a cruel fate, victims of one blow of Hera's'.

This is magnificent. For once, at least, Euripides' intellectualism is put entirely at the service of his dramatic invention. His point, instead of being made in an uncharacteristic speech, is made the

---

[1] A contrast to what he says and implies at vv. 575 ff. ('Farewell, my Labours,' &c.), but there is no real contradiction. Events have now taught him to think bitterly and angrily about those imposed tasks whose performance had, in fact, interested him.

[2] E.g. 1127 f., 1253, and of course tne Iris-Lyssa scene.

[3] This is essentially the same argument, though couched in a different tone, as that urged by the Nurse to Phaedra.

basis of a most lifelike contrast of characters. The fine and intelligent
Theseus is intelligent only to a certain point, instinctively intelligent
rather than intellectual – for example, he has never thought clearly
about the gods. Heracles, on the other hand, is right where Theseus
is wrong, but again by instinct, a moral instinct; he has never tested
his instinct by his intelligence, for although his moral instinct makes
him disbelieve the crude legends that Theseus refers to, he goes on
believing in his 'Hera'. The contrast between the two great men is
absorbing.

But what does the passage mean to the play? It forces us to the
conclusion – which in any case is obvious to anyone who knows his
Euripides – that to call such a Hera a Deity is a contradiction. But
this conclusion is kept out of the play. In the *Heracles* Hera is as real
an agent as Aphrodite and Artemis are in the *Hippolytus*; in that
play the goddesses appear in person, therefore, dramatically, they
must unquestionably exist. No one supposes that Euripides believed
in a 'Goddess' Aphrodite who adorned the sky with her ravishing
beauty and visited Cyprus, yet Aphrodite is terribly real, both in the
play and in Euripides' thought. Zeus and Hera, too, are dramatically
real. The co-paternity of Zeus is accepted by Heracles sane (1263) as
by Heracles under suspicion of madness (575), and the chorus also
believes in it (805).[1] But if the co-paternity of Zeus is dramatically
real, the hatred of Hera is mythologically inevitable. Heracles is of
more than mortal birth, as also he is of more than ordinary genius
and achievement. The genius derives, dramatically, from Zeus; it
follows almost automatically that Hera must wish to destroy it.
While Heracles, driven by his flaming genius, is performing his god-
given task of taming the earth for mankind 'Fate protected him, nor
would Zeus allow Hera or me (Lyssa) to do him injury'. But genius
of this order is, it seems, more than Nature can long endure; the gift
from Zeus carries with it the inevitable hatred of Hera, and destruction comes. He who was to the chorus the benefactor of humanity,
to Lyssa the one who subdued land and sea and upheld the religion

---

[1] See Masqueray's note *ad loc*. – The double paternity, naturally, involves slight
confusion, and rationalists who read Euripides as if he were Bradshaw will not fail to
point out that the story is improbable, that Euripides could not have believed it, and
that Heracles contradicts himself about his fathers. If Euripides had invented a second
comic character, like Lycus, to point out lucidly that a man is unlikely to have two
fathers, we should have to take the rationalism seriously. But Euripides does nothing
of the kind; he means something by his Zeus, and the literal difficulties he simply
ignores.

of the gods, to Theseus his rescuer and 'the mighty friend of man'[1]
– such a one, deserving a twofold honour, one from men and one
from the gods, meets a twofold betrayal. While he is absent from his
labours those dearest to him are thrown into the extremity of danger;
when the Labours are finished, his 'destiny' ceases to protect him,
and Nature destroys what she has produced and used – or would
have destroyed him had he not met, in Theseus, a man nearly as
great as himself, one who successfully challenges him to show that
the greatness of a great man can triumph even over the blind hostility
of 'the gods'.

In so tragic a conception lies the unity of the action, and from this
point of view we may find relatively insignificant certain details
which, if the play is wrongly treated as realistic, are certainly obtrusive and difficult. We should observe that a play, even one of Euripides', does not become realistic merely because it may mention
spades or wheelbarrows. Orestes' Nurse does not make the *Choephori*
a realistic play, nor do we find it difficult to believe in the Furies
because she has just been talking of babies' napkins. The political
reference in this play similarly does not mean that the whole play is
to be considered politically, and the very decrepit arrival of the
chorus is not a piece of amusing but quite meaningless realism; on
the contrary, it is a most non-realistic abstraction, defencelessness
made manifest. Euripides removes himself from the realism of
Sophocles not by lyrical intensity (like Aeschylus) but by his abstract
and schematic handling. The method may not be so good or harmonious – that is another question; it is his method. It is, I think, in
this light that we must consider the Minyan exploit (see above, p.
242). Take the play literally and it is almost an impossible contradiction – but then, if we take the play literally it makes very little sense
at all; it is surely a figurative statement of Heracles' unqualified claim
to Theban gratitude, conventionalized as the character of Lycus and
the whole opening situation is conventionalized. So, too, with

[1] Vv. 698 ff., 849 ff., 1221 f. – It is this aspect of Heracles that is emphasized in the
long ode (348 ff.). The Labours are held up not as feats of strength and endurance but
as a purification of the earth from noxious monsters. Heracles freed the precinct of
Zeus from the lion, slew the Centaurs that ravaged the fields of Thessaly, slew the
horses of Diomed 'that devoured men', Cycnus 'who killed strangers', the Lernean
Hydra that 'slew many', and he 'entered the recesses of the sea, assuring calm for
men'. There is no word spared for the intensity of the struggles, the heroic strength
displayed, the miraculous nature of the achievements. This is not the highly personal
Heracles who interested Sophocles.

Heracles' secret return; it does not mean that Heracles is to be taken as the discredited leader of the Liberal party in Thebes, but it is the expression of one half of his tragedy. Instead of returning from his last Labour in triumph to an enthusiastic city, he slinks home privily, already, so far as Thebes is concerned, the outcast which soon, by Hera's vindictiveness, he does become.[1]

---

[1] (Note to 3rd. edition.) By the courtesy of its author, Mr. H. H. O. Chalk, I have seen an article on this play which is to appear in the *Journal of Hellenic Studies*. Mr. Chalk makes some pertinent criticisms of this chapter, and proposes a reading of the play which some, I fear, may find more convincing than my own.

CHAPTER IX

The Technique of the Euripidean Tragedy

1. Introduction

In the last chapter we tried to show that the structure of the Euripidean tragedy differs radically from that of the Sophoclean because Euripides saw the tragic in a totally different way. He saw tragic ἁμαρτία and tragic action not as part of the character of the individual, leading to the downfall of the individual, but, in a more abstract way, as a disastrous element in our common human nature which leads to suffering, in which the guilty person may share or not. The tragedies fall into two groups, the *Medea* and *Hippolytus,* and the war-plays or social tragedies. Even in the *Medea,* a play which seems to depend entirely on Medea's own will and tragic personality, we saw that there is, at least in analysis, a perceptible distinction between Medea's personal tragedy and Euripides' tragic conception; we saw that if the wider tragic reference is not apprehended, the heroine and the play become rather difficult – not far from melodrama, the making of drama for the sake only of dramatic excitement. In general, the characters are regarded as tragic figures in the grip of something greater than themselves, even when, as in the first group, this something is an instinctive passion in the highest degree personal. Medea's jealousy and vindictiveness are not made objective in a goddess, but for all that Euripides is thinking of them as he thinks of the love of Phaedra and the fanatical anti-love of Hippolytus: as psychological forces which take entire possession of their victims and drive them where they will. There is not, except by dramatic accident, any struggle in the soul of the victim between this passion and another, no suggestion that the passion is the one thing that ruins a nature otherwise excellent; to Euripides it is a universal force which shows its disastrous power through this victim, something which the end of the *Medea* suggests and the prologue to the *Hippolytus* declares to be an external dramatic agent. This, and not the character, begins to direct the action. In other words, the poet, no longer working out the inevitable action of a tragic character from the first conjuncture of situation with character to the catastrophe, can himself step in to manipulate the plot in the interests of his real tragedy. Hence the 'irrational' in the *Medea*, and in the *Hippolytus* the complete supersession of Phaedra by Hippolytus.

We saw that in the second group this distinction between the outer and the inner tragedy becomes greater and more explicit. The tragic beings of Euripides' stage are now victims in a more literal sense, victims of cruelty and oppression; and as cruelty and oppression may be exercised in one play by several people – as by Odysseus, Agamemnon and Menelaus indifferently – and endured by several persons indifferently, the plot becomes more schematic than it was when the victimizing force at least was one that proceeded through only one person, a Medea, or was made objective in an Aphrodite. Now the poet may manipulate his plot still more freely; still greater is the necessity, if we wish to explain the tragic unity that we feel, to look through the action to the underlying idea.

On such a basis not Euripides' structure only, but also the whole of his tragic technique becomes intelligible. He can never be explained on Aristotelian grounds because he was writing an un-Aristotelian tragedy, and unless we see what his real approach to tragedy was, we shall have to call him incompetent, with Schlegel, or suppose that he was so busy dropping warm tears that he could not stay to make decent plays.[1] The discovery of a logical method in Euripides will make no difference to the appreciation of his plays; those who cannot feel the essential unity of the *Troades* will continue not to feel it. The business of criticism is not to help us to feel, but to explain how the artist contrives to make us feel. It can show us, for example, that the unity of the *Troades* does not depend on the constant presence of Hecuba, but on something much more important.

---

[1] A recent writer on Euripides has found it possible to attribute the Euripidean prologue to nothing more profound, or convincing, than carelessness.

On Euripides' use of plot enough was said in the last chapter. In this one we shall resume and expand what we have seen of his characterization, and then consider his use of the Chorus, his rhetoric and dialectic, his dramatic style, and those famous prologues and epilogues.

2. Characterization

As with plot, so with characterization; the second group of tragedies develops tendencies already noticeable in the first. We have argued that the extreme character of Medea or Hippolytus, which we should have to call overdrawn in any other type of drama except Old Comedy, is in these plays logical, because the character is wanted by Euripides only as a vehicle for the passion of which it consists; and convincing, because the whole trend of the play forces us to contemplate these people as victims in a tragedy greater than their own. Sophocles could not have used Medea, for she would have simplified his tragedy to vanishing point; Euripides can, because he is projecting one tragic element of human nature into Medea and making it the ἁμαρτία which ruins not her only but the social group.

In the second series of tragedies his analytical or schematic treatment of character is given wider scope. The tragic theme is, if we may so generalize it, the social suffering which follows social wrongdoing – the dramatic antithesis to Sophocles' method, an individual fault which leads to individual suffering. Accordingly we have on the one hand the wrongdoers, on the other the wronged, and as the tragic point lies in the suffering rather than in the oppression, the drama concentrates on the victims. This is the reason why we have so many suppliants at altars, defenceless women, children; many of them but slightly characterized, since their situation is not usually the outcome of their character and is not to be developed or affected by their character. This, too, explains the high proportion of old men, extremely old and decrepit old men, not as Teiresias or Oedipus of the *Coloneus* are old – Peleus, Amphitryon, Iolaus, Iphis, and the chorus in the *Heracles*. To account for this feature of these plays it has been supposed that Euripides had at his disposal a certain actor peculiarly potent in representing impotence. Did he then have other actors who were very good at being children, others good in women's parts, and none who could play the normal vigorous man

– these being all commandeered by Sophocles? No; Euripides, at least in these tragedies, was more than a theatre-man, and we must look for other than mechanical explanations.

Opposed to the victims are the oppressors. As with Jason, so with these; the tragedy, normally, demands only that they be wicked. Their wickedness is not one significant element in their characters, as it is in Creon's, but, so far as we are concerned, it is the whole man. Hence men like Menelaus and Orestes, Lycus, Polymestor, the incredibly silly Adrastus. Certainly we have vivid sketches when the drama demands it – of Agamemnon, the leader who cannot lead for fear of what the army will say, of Odysseus, the politician in difficulties; but then, nobody can read the *Ion* and suppose that Euripides could not make a situation or character when he wanted to. In these plays he did not want to; nothing else can explain the contrast between the vivid full-length portraits of Electra, Orestes, Ion, Creusa, and the shadowy, floating population of the tragedies. Except for Heracles, and for Theseus in the *Suppliant Women,* there is no character who fills a play, and no character who is a normal man, even as normality is understood in drama.

But we can go further: Euripides not only simplifies his characters to a melodramatic degree, all black or all white, but also he can show a disconcerting aloofness from them. This, of course, because he is in fact not writing melodrama. Lycus as the very wicked man, Polyxena as the unspotted victim, do not really fill his mind; he has a vision beyond these, and he is liable to forget them – a fact which perhaps leaves him just as disconcerting as before, but if we are to censure, it is as well to understand first.

Of this aloofness we saw signs already in the anapaestic choral interlude of the *Medea*; in the second group it becomes common. Euripides, to our great surprise, will round upon a sympathetic character in the last act: Hecuba turns fiend, and the vague but intensely sympathetic Alcmena turns oppressor while the dreadful Eurystheus very nearly becomes sympathetic. Elsewhere characters who ought to be sympathetic are treated with an undercurrent of irony which is a little upsetting. Iolaus in the *Heracleidae* is to all appearance a noble and devoted champion of the oppressed; he is entitled to a dignified position in any play. Yet Euripides is not above suggesting that he is a prosy old man (unless, which God forbid, we suppose that the stream of platitudes with which he begins

was intended by Euripides to be a contribution to moral philosophy);
Iolaus makes us smile by climbing into armour which he can hardly
support, and finally rides gallantly, a Greek Quixote, clean out
of the play into fairyland. So much for Iolaus. Peleus is treated,
though not so thoroughly, in the same spirit. He totters notably, yet
makes stout work with his staff; he, with all philosophy, morality
and tradition at his call, condescends to obscure abuse against
Menelaus (590 ff.), and elsewhere (693) to demagogic claptrap –
unless again, with some commentators, we suppose that Euripides
really believed this nonsense about generals and common soldiers,
and did not see that v. 702, 'If only they had courage and ability
together,' gave away the whole case.

Such treatment of respectable dramatic personages we can, of
course, call realism. We can make it characteristic either of a sour
unromantic strain in Euripides, or of a readiness (which he shared
with the rest of Athens) to make fun of legend. The interesting
point, however, is not that he does these things, but that he does
them here; and unless we are prepared to think that he simply could
not help himself, like the inveterate 'humorist', we are bound to
look for some specific justification or dramatic purpose. For the
moment we are suggesting only that the irony must be seen as part
of Euripides' attitude towards his characterization; it is an offshoot
of his aloofness. The aloofness goes with the simplification of
character, and shows itself in one or two other ways.

We may consider the remarkable series of scenes of sacrifice or
self-sacrifice or attempted self-sacrifice that these plays offer; there
are Polyxena and Hecuba, Macaria, Andromache, Iolaus. All are
treated with dignity and sympathy, but a certain air of conventionality is felt. An entirely unmerited sentence of death is passed, or the
heroine is placed in a situation in which she must act either nobly or
ignobly; she acts nobly, and that, virtually, is the end of it. We
admire her motives, but we look in vain (if we insist on looking for
the wrong thing) for an intensity of feeling which we can compare
with the dramatic thrill of Eteocles' leap to death, or of Antigone's
tragic choice, or of Electra's self-dedication to her task. Antigone
and Antigone's audience can contemplate her imminent death only
tragically; Polyxena and Macaria make fine speeches about it. Here,
in fact, Euripides is careful to do what he was careful not to do in the
Medea, namely to avoid 'the revolting'. The sacrifice of Polyxena –

like Macaria's – is in Polyxena's own life nothing but a blind blow of fate; it is, to speak strictly, pathetic and not tragic. Only in the inner tragedy is it tragic, when we see the incident as part of the price which humanity exacts and pays for its superstitions. Hecuba must lament, but nothing would be gained by sending Polyxena to her death screaming; we should think of the Greeks as bloodthirsty monsters, when the whole point is that they are quite ordinary people who are persuaded to do a dreadful thing by the supposed demands of the political situation. They therefore are presented in a rather favourable light, and their victim is made to go to death willingly, preferring death to life. These all declare – all but Andromache, whose persecutors we *are* to regard as monsters – that they have comparatively nothing to live for; Antigone has everything to live for, nothing to die for – except her sense of duty. For the same reason Macaria comes forward to offer her life as someone quite unknown to us. Again the tragic value of the incident lies elsewhere – in the disturbing fact, apparently, that Demeter, whoever she is, should have made Demophon's difficult duty harder by demanding such a sacrifice. It is to prevent our taking an interest exclusively in her personal fate that Euripides keeps her in the dark before he needs her.[1]

As for Andromache, she is the victim of Spartan treachery, and in this lies the dramatic value of the scene. In giving her life for her child she is acting nobly. In morality, her nobility is the same as Antigone's; in drama it is entirely different. We must look past her to the villainous Spartan, so that again the scene has a slight air of conventionality; or, if this is too strong, it has at least a dramatic value quite different from that of Sophocles' scene. Andromache must be simply noble or simply ignoble, and the characterization is limited to this.

This logical refusal of Euripides to engage himself without reserve in the personality of these tragic victims shows itself sometimes, even more strikingly, in downright inconsistency of portraiture. Of this the clearest example is Cassandra. Within the compass of a hundred

---

[1] It is this consideration which makes me doubt if we have lost a scene from the *Heracleidae* in which the sacrifice was described.

With this method it is perhaps not altogether out of place to compare the practice of detective-story writers. They like to open their tales with a ready-made corpse because a murder is simply their datum and the detection of the murderer their sole interest. The tragic implications of murder they must avoid.

verses, Euripides gives us two distinct characters. First, we see through the wall of the tent the waving light of her torch – a most imaginative and quite unexpected scene. In a moment the crazed prophetess is before us, singing a wild song through which madness peers as terribly as it does through Ophelia's. Here is a Cassandra who will easily bear comparison either with Ophelia or with Aeschylus' Cassandra; yet Euripides does not in the least lose himself in his remarkable creation, for presently she is arguing as closely as an Odysseus or an Andromache. If only the speech had been preserved, without its proem, we should not have the slightest idea what sort of a character was making it, still less be able to attribute it to a crazed prophetess.

But we must notice that Euripides is not doing this out of habit or mere inadvertence. He does not treat his Ion like this, nor his Electra; to their characterization he remains faithful, and if he is unfaithful to his Cassandra it is because he has something more important to do than to be consistent with his characters. It is part of his tragic idea that the lot of the victors is no happier and much less glorious than that of the conquered; that Troy not only has more honour than Greece, but also less suffering. Someone must sustain this theme; not the chorus here (although the chorus was given something similar to say in the *Andromache*)[1] because this chorus is dedicated to a special purpose and cannot make the point clearly enough. Cassandra is chosen. It might possibly have been Andromache or Talthybius, but in fact it is Cassandra. This may be illogical like the irrationality in the *Medea,* but to maintain this tragic paradox was to Euripides vastly more important than to obey the rules of someone else's drama. If we can share in the tragic vision we shall not object to the inconsistency; if we cannot accept the inconsistency at any price, we had better not read Euripides.

It is idle to cite the Athenian love of disputation to explain such a scene. To the Athenians it would obviously have been interesting to listen to Cassandra arguing through this speech like Socrates defending a paradox against a Callicles; but we can hardly doubt that it would have been even more exciting had Cassandra continued as she began, mad, torch-waving, and disturbing. Equally idle to attribute the inconsistency to mere force of habit in Euripides. He is conscious of it, so conscious that (as often) he slips in an apology,

[1] Vv. 1028–46.

here a singularly awkward one (365 f.): 'I am indeed possessed, but to this extent I can control my frenzy.'[1]

The same can be seen in the *Andromache*. Is the heroine drawn as a hard, forensic woman, so unlike Homer's noble Queen, merely because Euripides took a morose pleasure in not being romantic? Not in the least. It is indeed obvious that it was no part of his plan to make her a vision of loveliness; her hardness towards her serving-woman (v. 87) might have been avoided; but in general she is what she is for Euripides' dramatic convenience. He did not begin thinking out his play with a certain conception of Andromache as the kernel of the tragedy; not, that is, as Sophocles obviously started thinking out the *Ajax* with a conception of a certain Ajax and a certain Odysseus. Why indeed should he? Andromache is only to a small extent an agent in the play; she is in the main a victim, and, as such, her character is irrelevant. She becomes barrister-like by accident, as by accident Cassandra becomes philosophical. Someone has to analyse the situation for the benefit of Menelaus, and that someone can be only Andromache. She must make her points with the utmost clarity and force; it is not necessary to the tragic idea that she should be like this, but it is necessary that the points should so be made.[2] Again as wife she has to be the antithesis of Hermione; we cannot see her as the devoted wife in action, as we do in the *Iliad*; therefore we have to be told about it, and that forcibly. Hence that passage about her improbable tenderness to Hector's bastards, a rhetorical point rather than a convincing piece of character-drawing. Does all this make a consistent portrait? Does the elegiac lament fall inevitably into place? We may prefer consistency; we may even find it here, with enough determination; but if we are unconvinced, the play is not ruined. It will mean only that Euripides thought it better to be vital than academic.

From the later, non-tragic plays we see that Euripides had no difficulty whatever in creating both good plots and consistent characters. If in the tragedies we find neither regular plots, nor a normal assemblage of characters, nor a normal treatment of these characters, it seems reasonable to look for one general explanation; not to explain the extreme lunacy of Adrastus by referring to contemporary

[1] For similar dramatic apologies cf. *Med.*, 473-4, 522-3; *Andr.*, 91 ff. (for the elegiacs), 333; *Hec.*, 603; *Suppl. Women*, 427-9; *Tro.*, 634-6, 898-913. How different these are from the self-revealing apology of his Electra, (900 ff.).

[2] See also on Hippolytus, p. 207.

politics, the prevalence of old men by assuming the existence of a certain actor, the prevalence of argument by invoking current taste, the intrusion of Evadne by accusing Euripides of a desire to brighten up his play, and the treatment of Cassandra by nothing at all. There is a fundamental difference between the two sets of plays; the later ones are self-contained, the tragedies are not. The story of Ion, Creusa and Xuthus is, quite apart from any light it may throw on the habits or existence of the god of Delphi, a complete and a coherent whole; the mere story of the *Troades* is not the whole, and the plot does not cohere without reference to the tragic idea that inspires it. In the later plays therefore, whether they present, to the discredit of Delphi, the exciting adventures of Ion or Iphigeneia, or the savage stories of Electra and Orestes (with a politico-social background), Euripides crystallizes the dramatic idea in the characters and actions of his *dramatis personae*. We have again actors and not victims; again actors who are regarded purely as individuals, not in any degree as types, or tragic and exemplary embodiments of some universal passion; again the action is self-contained; no longer are we expected to integrate separate part-actions in the light of one enfolding tragic idea. The dramatic idea, of whatever nature it may be, is completely realized in the action, limited to the play and filling the play. Therefore these plays are constructed according to the normal 'logic'. The tragedies, which do not in this way distil all their meaning into one consecutive action and one significant character or group of characters, use a different logic, deriving their unity not from some point within themselves, but from something that underlies them. They are meant to suggest something of which the people in them and what they do are only part. They do suggest this; that is why they are read. 'The best in this kind are but shadows,' but the shadows differ greatly in apparent solidity.

We may now return to a question raised but not answered just now. Even if, to serve his inner tragedy, Euripides interfered with the natural behaviour of Cassandra, as he interfered with the natural flow of the plot in the *Medea,* why does he treat Peleus and Iolaus as he does? The plays are tragedies, not tragi-comedies: how can he place the guying of Iolaus side by side with the self-sacrifice of Macaria? How treat Peleus so that we can hardly disagree with Menelaus when he says 'You are altogether too fond of abuse'?

A thoroughgoing melodramatist would have made great play

with Peleus. The gallant old man, chivalrous, wise, generous, utterly regardless of self, unhesitatingly fronts the villain in defence of an ill-used woman, who is little better than a slave, though a Queen, if everybody had had his rights. The noble mother and her poor orphaned son are snatched out of the wicked man's very grasp . . . The *Andromache,* on the surface, is perilously close to this kind of nonsense. It would not do for Peleus to raise a lump in our throats in this way, and Euripides sees to it that he shall not. The unromantic treatment seems really to be a form of stylization; we must actually be prevented from taking too literal and exclusive an interest in the stage-action. This necessity we shall meet again in another con-nexion;[1] meanwhile may we ask what the melodramatist would have done with the chorus of the *Andromache*? The question is no sooner asked than answered; he would have used it, as the serialist of today uses his weekly silences, to intensity the excitement of the plot. Nothing would be easier than to write the choral ode which ought to be sung upon Orestes' exit; it is so easy that only the end is worth recording: 'Soon, soon shall we see our lord returning in peace to these halls, having set right his previous affair with Apollo, who, saving him from the wicked preparations of the Argive, will make it plain to all that God pardons those who repent, and keeps safe the pious against the guiles of the wicked.' *Enter the Messenger.*

But neither here nor at any other crisis in the play does the chorus do anything so sensible and dramatic. The reason is not this time that it has a drama of its own to play out; it is at liberty to give all its attention to the play. It avoids doing this because to attend on and accentuate the turns of the plot in this manner would give the plot a degree of importance and, as it were, of reality which Euripides does not wish it to have; it would turn into melodrama what is to be felt as tragedy, but not as the tragedy only of Andromache and Peleus.

3. The Chorus

The tragic Chorus passed through some awkward vicissitudes before it emerged in the *Hecuba* and *Troades* as the keystone of the mature tragic style of Euripides. In the *Medea* and *Hippolytus* it is used, as we should expect, in the manner of Middle Tragedy, with necessary modifications, and these, like the other modifications which the

[1] Below, p. 282.

theme of the *Medea* entailed, are from the formal point of view no improvements.

We must first mention again that the change from the public themes with which Sophocles had been dealing to private, psychological subjects inevitably made the chorus more difficult to manage.[1] Creon's edict in the *Antigone,* the plague in Thebes of the *Tyrannus,* Ajax' crime, were matters that concerned the community, and the Chorus was that community; the story of Medea (as distinct from the tragic conception) is one that concerns Medea, Jason, their family circle and no one else. From the start the chorus here is an intrusion, dramatically as much out of place as in the private stories on which New Comedy was built; later in the play it becomes a dramatic nuisance. It has to apologize for its arrival (131 ff.), just as Medea has to apologize (214) for coming out of the house instead of nursing her grief within; and presently, much more awkwardly, it has to apologize for not helping the children. So in the *Hippolytus*; the Parodos, a charming ode, is in essence an explanation, and the improbable presence of fifteen women at what is a very delicate and private death-bed scene puts Phaedra to the conventional necessity of binding them by an oath of secrecy, and them to the conventional necessity of keeping it.

But these inconveniences are not serious. We would readily accept the Chorus as a dramatic convention and think no more about it, if Euripides had not, by his self-consciousness, directed our attention to the inconveniences.[2] As we have suggested already, these were plays of transition, which more than once betray a clash of styles, and no doubt Euripides was debarred from making the chorus a pure convention by its dramatic, realistic character in the contemporary drama of Sophocles.

What is much more interesting is the positive use of the Chorus. Apart from the slight awkwardnesses, and the chilling anapaestic interlude, the chorus of the *Medea* behaves like that of the *Antigone* and *Electra*. Like Electra's chorus, it is filled with the spirit of the heroine: 'Men are treacherous, but now is honour coming to womankind.' Like the chorus of the *Antigone,* it increases the dramatic momentum by changing sides. As it begins to realize what it is

[1] We have already seen something of this in Sophocles' *Electra*; see above, p. 168.

[2] As Roman Comedy sometimes does with the conventions of the Greek stage. The use of these by Menander, Plautus, and Terence is discussed with very interesting results by A. W. Gomme, *Essays in Greek Hist. and Lit.,* pp. 252 ff.

that Medea is proposing to do, it veers from sympathy to protest until, in its last ode, it sees in Medea a defiler of Heaven and Earth.

The chorus can attend on Medea in this way because, although she is perhaps in theory a victim as much as Andromache, she is the victim of a very personal passion which is so concentrated in her that she becomes dramatic as the later victims are not. Her will animates the play and her actions become the tragic issue of the play. The chorus, therefore, in following her closely is sticking close to the tragic theme, and when at the end it shrinks from her in horror it does much to illuminate this theme for us. A chorus which defended Medea's actions throughout would have left us completely at a loss.

Few of the later choruses resemble this one, but this principle remains fast, whether in Sophocles or in Euripides, that the chorus sticks closely to the tragic theme. For we must remember that the mature Sophoclean chorus, which this one resembles, was not a clever device for strengthening the unity of the play; it, like Sophocles' characterization, takes its origin from much further back. The Chorus attends closely on the hero, his actions and their outcome, without philosophical or decorative excursions, because all the poet's tragic thought is expressed through the hero, his character, and his situation; little is left over for the Chorus to play with. In Euripides there is always something left over; the tragedy is always perceptibly wider than the sum of the persons in the play. In the *Medea,* since the tragedy is to a very large extent, though not completely, distilled into the heroine, the chorus, attending to the inner tragic idea, does in fact remain close to her; this is the one extreme. In the *Hecuba* and *Troades* we find the other. The tragedy here is infinitely wider than the particular events of the play; and by waiting upon them, by commenting on the successive blows that fall upon Hecuba, the chorus would be deserting its station. Here it stands closer to the heart of the tragic conception by remaining aloof from the actors and pursuing its own monotone of mourning for Troy. Hecuba, Cassandra and the rest are but part heroes in a tragedy of nations or of humanity; the successive scenes, each an 'action' in itself, do not form a whole but are suggestive aspects of a whole. The Chorus, by neglecting these, not dedicating itself to the part-heroes and the part-actions as if they were complete and self-sufficient, performs in fact exactly the same function as it did in

Sophocles, but in the exactly opposite way. And not only does it perform this, its truest, function of conveying lyrically the tragic idea, but also, necessarily, it serves the more superficial purpose of making the play a unity. If Euripides, instead of being logical, had allowed his chorus to run about in pursuit of the action, the integration which he asks our apprehension to make would be impossible and the plays would be chaos.

Between the extremes are gradations. The chorus of the *Hippolytus* is further from orthodoxy than that of the *Medea,* and this for the obvious reasons that the play has not one hero but two, and that the tragedy, as we are told in the prologue, is somewhat wider than the unhappy history of Phaedra and Hippolytus. There is more left over, and we can see the consequence if we compare the ode to Eros (525 ff.) with any mature Sophoclean ode. That it should start, not with the unhappy Phaedra, but with an invocation of the mighty love-god is natural enough. Sophocles, however, would have worked back from Eros to the tragic hero who was prefiguring his thought, the general only a preparation for the particular. The ode in the *Hippolytus* does not work back to Phaedra; it remains general because Euripides' thought is general, illustrated by Phaedra but not totally transmuted into her.

One of the difficulties peculiar to this type of drama shows its head in the next ode. Phaedra, betrayed by her Nurse, goes in with the express intention of ending her life and so bringing ruin to Hippolytus. What is the chorus to say? Our minds are entirely taken up with the sudden fulfilment of Aphrodite's threat; she is going to strike, as she said, but only in order to be able to strike at another. We, having heard the prologue, know more about the real meaning of it all than the chorus; what can they say that will tighten this inner tragedy for us? The tragic transit enabled the chorus always to augment the dramatic rhythm; it passed from triumph to fear, or from sympathy to opposition. Now, with foreseen catastrophes and external agencies, this effect is impossible. Here the real agent and the real tragedy is invisible to the chorus, and the theme of the power of Eros has already been used. What the chorus does here is to use, not for the last time, the formula εἴθε γενοίμαν, Would I were somewhere else. In their first two stanzas, which are largely decorative, they wish themselves elsewhere, and in the last two they reflect, quite simply, on Phaedra's coming to Greece and the fate that awaits her now. The ode is, without being undramatic (for we may read anguish in their desire to be elsewhere), as far as possible from attempting what Sophocles did; as if Euripides were purposely making the chorus stand a little on one side, not to obscure our vision of the inner drama.

In the *Andromache* and *Heracles,* necessarily, we move still further from the classical treatment of the Chorus. Each of these plays involves difficulties which make Euripides use the Chorus in a rather indeterminate way. To use it as in Middle Tragedy was impossible, for in neither play has he a hero whose will or actions are the driving-force of the drama. In the *Andromache,* as we argued above, Euripides deliberately keeps his chorus slightly detached from the action,[1] while in the *Heracles* the ostensible action is so disjunct, and the first part of the play so schematic, that any attempt to bind the play through the chorus, besides being false, would only call attention to the absence of formal unity. And once more the unifying idea is such that the chorus cannot stand nearer to it than the actors do, as it can in the *Troades.* This idea, in the *Andromache,* resides in the action, in the ruin of the house of Peleus, of which the chorus is only a spectator; in the *Heracles* it resides in Heracles himself. These choruses have no drama of their own to play out, one that should underlie and reinforce the drama on the stage.

Accordingly in both plays there are odes in which the chorus says what it can. The *Andromache* has four odes. The first, which deals with the origin of the Trojan War, is entirely relevant to Andromache's position. The second stands apart from the action, considered as tragic action; it treats the situation between Andromache and Hermione intellectually, as an example of the truth that polygamy and divided royalty are both bad things. The third also begins reflectively, praising high birth, with Pindaric reminiscences in thought and language and rhythm, and it ends with a solemn affirmation of belief in the legendary history of Peleus. There is surely irony here; not the tragic irony of Sophocles which would have bidden us rejoice in the victory of Peleus just before we see that the victory is a hollow one, but the slightly mocking irony which we have already noticed in Euripides' drawing of Peleus. The Phthian maidens are sincere enough, but how are we to take seriously this Pindaric tone and this solemn Credo after the scene

[1] P. 259.

K

which has passed? In both the second and third odes therefore there is a certain feeling of detachment which we do not find, except in the anapaests, in the chorus of the *Medea*; but the last ode, the one which we ventured partially to rewrite above, is most remarkably detached. Why does the chorus, at the most dramatic turn of the plot, abandon the House of Peleus and return to Troy? Desire for symmetry, balancing the first Trojan ode? So mechanical an explanation we will not easily accept. 'Troy,' sings the chorus, 'was abandoned by the gods and destroyed. Agamemnon was slain, and his wife. Greece mourned many dead, slain in the war; not on Troy alone did the scourge fall.' What can this be but an indication where we are to look for the tragic bearing of the play? Beneath this story of Spartan intrigue is the further idea that such wickedness destroys victims and perpetrators alike. The Gods hold themselves aloof; Trojans and Greeks alike were slain, and Agamemnon was murdered. Here, then, we have the same use of the Chorus as in the *Troades*; in the second and third odes little more than a conventional curtain.

The chorus of the *Heracles* is again a band of sympathetic spectators. It has two important lyrical contributions to make, namely to present the picture of Heracles the Benefactor, a picture essential to the comprehension of the whole, and the expression of its joy at his return. Its elaborate parade of weakness in the parodos and its disjointed second stasimon (637 ff.) reflect its indeterminate position. It is made physically weak to reinforce the idea that Heracles' dependents are entirely defenceless; it takes part in the action, but the action is inaction. In the second stasimon it is difficult to see anything but an undisguised intrusion of the poet's own personality, such as we have not yet encountered.[1] It combines a complaint against old age, rather artificially worked out with regret that the virtuous cannot live twice, with a truly Pindaric stanza in praise of Song, from which it returns, not very convincingly, to Heracles. Neither is the ode itself a unity nor has it any connexion with the action or the

---

[1] For although the essay on childlessness in the *Medea* may state Euripides' own opinion, and the remarks in the *Andromache* on monarchy and democracy no doubt do, they have just so much dramatic relevance that we need not suppose these not very remarkable sentiments to have been brought into the play for their own sake. The artificiality of the old-age passage here suggests that we should not take it too seriously as Euripides' own lament, but as material plausible enough in this chorus; the noble stanza to Song is, however, altogether different; undoubtedly personal and not dramatic.

thought. We may perhaps conclude that Lycus and his inevitable destruction did not merit the attention of the chorus twice, and that since an attempt to read the action of this play as a logical unity could only be confusing, and since the chorus is in no position to point to the underlying tragedy, Euripides preferred something quite neutral, something to remove our attention, at least for the moment, from the action. There has to be a pause, and he fills it.

In these plays the chorus is not completely in the action, as it was in Middle Tragedy, nor close to the heart of the tragedy, as in the *Hecuba, Suppliant Women* and *Troades*. In the *Suppliant Women* it virtually becomes protagonist once more.[1] Its suffering sums up the tragic bearing of the play, and its appeal begins and controls the action, overruling the worldly prudence of Theseus and succeeding where the guilty Adrastus failed. Here is no uncertainty, no turning to moral or social disquisitions for the sake of a curtain. In these three plays the Chorus takes as natural and apparently inevitable a place as it had in the oldest of Greek Tragedy, the representative or the symbol of suffering humanity.

4. Rhetoric and Dialectic

It is clear that if Euripides' attitude to tragedy implied a restricted use of characterization, this in its turn must affect the manner in which the dramatic action is presented, what we may call the dramatic style. In Middle Tragedy we are interested in action as the outcome of character as much as for its own sake; the person behind the action always gives it its particular dramatic value. Creon's decree is both something that will affect Antigone and something that reveals Creon and will affect him in turn; Electra's long struggle is more than a series of events; it is a continually developing revelation of a will and a mind. Events are qualitative. In the mature Euripidean tragedy they are often only quantitative. When a Menelaus or a Lycus does something, what is done does not interest us as a reflection of the spiritual or mental balance of the doer; he was invented to do this and for no other purpose; having done it he is exhausted. It is not now the case that the person behind colours the action; in fact it is the action that creates the person behind it. When Creon acts as he does to Teiresias, in the *Antigone*, or Oedipus

---

[1] And Aeschylean in form, as Kranz points out (*Stasimon,* 176, 208).

to Creon, we say 'Ah! Creon and Oedipus *would* behave like that'. When Lycus explains why he proposes to put to death the children of Heracles we do not think 'How entirely characteristic of Lycus', but we do think of Thucydides and politics. Tragedy, in fact, is being presented through Lycus but not in him; he has no independent existence and meaning which can lend further colour and significance to what he does.

Nor are these events regarded as critical in the characters of the victims. These are presented only as victims, and even when Hecuba hits back, this, although an ironic point, is not regarded as the result of suffering upon character. Injuries in fact are inflicted by ready-made characters whose motive is nothing more complex than one of the general follies of mankind, and are received by victims whose part is only to exemplify what mankind suffers at its own hands.

The pathetic therefore predominates, and gives to the action its characteristic flavour. Instead of that strenuousness of thought and action which makes so powerful a rhythm in the Sophoclean drama, we find, on the whole, a series of violent actions, not essentially connected; and these, actions which cannot provoke counteractions. Therefore, not only does the play as a whole lack that organic growth which we find everywhere in Sophocles, and to a large extent in the *Medea* and *Hippolytus,* but the individual scenes, too, tend to be static. What can Hecuba do but cry to Heaven and lament her wrongs? She must mourn, and when the pathetic force of her mourning is spent, nothing remains but to wait for the next blow. Even resistance is ruled out; Euripides cannot have Polyxena dragged struggling to the altar.

This is, as we have said before, a tragedy lyrical in conception, and it cannot be set upon an actors' stage without considerable adjustment. Since Euripides has a dramatic rhythm which is not a steady growth, but one which (so far as the action is concerned) consists of periods of slackness slung between moments of violence, like the rhythm of telegraph-wires seen from the train, he is committed to what Aristotle vividly called ἀργὰ μέρη, passages, quite literally, in which there is nothing doing – nothing, that is, so far as the action is concerned. Of this we had an extreme example in the opening scenes of the *Heracles*; other scenes of dramatic emptiness could be cited if the ungrateful task were necessary. Aristotle's practical advice was 'In slack passages elaborate your style'. Euripides was not reduced to this (though the messenger-speech in the *Hippolytus* comes close to it) because he was not play-making but presenting tragedy, and there is always tragedy and tragic thought to be followed in his mind even if the actors, for the time being, have nothing in particular to do; still, something had to take the place of Sophocles' steady development of character and situation, and this was very largely rhetoric, dialectic, and sheer theatrical contrivance.

It is a commonplace that argument, dialectic, rhetoric, were Euripides' most frequent resources, and they are often spoken of as if they were deliberately or consciously adopted. This does not seem to be true, if it is taken to mean that Euripides, having settled on his theme, put in often, or fairly often, speeches that are rhetorical and argumentative rather than 'ethical', because he or his audience or both found them stimulating. If our general theory of Euripides is sound, he was committed to this intellectualism in dialogue and speech from the start, just as he was to his restricted characterization and non-organic use of plot. Consider Medea, for example. Jason comes (v. 446) to inform her blandly that it is all her own fault; she replies, most convincingly, by blazing at him: 'What? You dare to come to me? This is not courage or boldness, but utter lack of decency.' But does she continue by loading the miserable man with reproaches and contempt? Not in the least. With the standard dramatic apology she begins to state a case: 'You have done well to come, for I shall both unburden my own heart and wound yours by speaking ill of you. Now, I will begin from the beginning. I saved you . . .' The chilling thing here is not the rehearsal of history; that is relevant and dramatic. It is the formality of the procedure. These claims of hers ought not to be so calmly arranged in chronological order. There is a lyrical method, which disdains logic; there is a dramatic method, which follows the course of thought and emotion; there is a prose method, which is objective and follows the facts. This is the prose method.[1]

It is no answer to say that Euripides intended to present Medea as a woman of such self-mastery and clarity as would naturally lead her so to control her rage. This defence may be attempted with Andromache, but here the rest of Medea's behaviour contradicts it; and since most Euripidean heroines speak like this, it would imply

[1] Contrast Oedipus' speech to Creon, *O.C.*, 960 ff. (p. 382).

that this was the only type of woman in whom he was interested. Still less just is it to invoke mere habit or a personal idiosyncrasy in Euripides, unless we are prepared to say that Medea speaks intellectually because the whole play is conceived intellectually. That indeed seems to be near the truth. Euripides did not follow and reflect dramatically the natural rush of Medea's emotions as Sophocles would have done because the course of Medea's emotions at this point does not matter. What matters is that we should clearly see the utter baseness of Jason; this is one of the chief ingredients of the tragedy. We have to see Jason as he is; not as he momentarily appears to a desperate Medea but as Euripides wants him to be. Conversely, Jason's reply might have been a torrent of abuse, a shifting of the blame upon the convenient gods, possibly something else. It is, in the main, a calm analysis of Medea's record; cynical, revolting, but not false. That Jason should state his case so clearly is not undramatic, but this is accidental. He is doing exactly what Medea did, for exactly the same reasons; not first and foremost being Jason, but giving us Euripides' picture of the essential Medea, the woman who has always been at the mercy of her passions. Certainly Jason is dramatically fortunate that in doing this he does give a picture of himself. He is dramatic while Medea, Cassandra, Andromache are in the same circumstances non-dramatic or even inconsistent. Rhetorical dialectic happens to suit Jason, but all are like this because it is more important to Euripides' theme that they should say what they say as clearly and forcibly as possible than that they should say it in this way or that.

Hippolytus is in the same case. Are we tempted to think him somewhat of a prig when he expounds his virtue? If we do, we are thinking of him as a tragic character instead of what he really is, a tragic figure. His purity is the whole point of his tragedy, consequently of his character too. Euripides must insist on it; nothing else in him counts. As Hippolytus speaks we must see him as the tragic victim of Aphrodite, going to his death because of her wrath. He speaks, like the others, out of the inner tragedy and not out of his own personality, and if we cannot take him simply as a tragic figure whose personality, except in this one respect, never comes into consideration; if, that is, we feel him to be priggish, that must be written off as one of the inevitable inconveniences of the whole method.

Examples of this dramatic rhetoric or dialectic can be found in all these tragedies. Neither in substance nor in form is the examination of Adrastus by Theseus an amusement; it is the exposition of the basis of the tragic situation and of its underlying idea – exactly comparable, therefore, to Creon's first speech in the *Antigone*. It is not that Euripides' style has been affected by influences which Sophocles escaped; in the difference between Creon's speech and the cross-examination of Adrastus we have nothing less than the difference between two antithetic minds; both dramatic, both tragic, both, at the moment, working with similar material – character and politics – but the one synthetic, the other analytic. The basis of the tragedy of the *Antigone* is the character of Creon as it issues in his statecraft, and that is what fills this speech. The basis – or an important part – of the tragedy of the *Suppliant Women* is the sheer folly which leads to the bereavement of the Suppliants, and the examination establishes that. To move on to the *Troades* and its formal debate between Helen and Hecuba before Menelaus: is this merely a brisk imitation of the law-courts? Realism of this kind has nothing to do with it except maybe in a few quite superficial details; the logical refutation of Helen belongs to the inner tragedy as much as the self-confidence of Oedipus to his or the practical incapacity of Deianeira to hers. It must be shown that the Greeks cannot plead the will of Heaven; this is a tragic, not a decorative point. How more simply and directly could it be made than by the set debate, with Menelaus accepting Hecuba's argument? This part of the tragedy cannot be shown in action, only in dialectic.

But debate and dialectic in these plays are not always as necessary and dramatic as this. The two extremes can be illustrated from the *Heracles* – the discussion on the nature of God, which is so dramatic, and the discussion on bowmen, which is only a fill-up. Between these there are many gradations. In most of the plays can be found moments when, because the actors in the drama are passive victims unable to do anything important and not endowed with the character that would make action significant, an intellectual movement is created, or, failing that, a rhetorical one. When Creon, or Oedipus, comes to grips with Teiresias there is a clash of opinion indeed, but that is incidental to the impact of the prophet's attitude on the King; when Theseus meets the Theban Herald there is no such impact; that Theseus should behave as Creon or Oedipus did, bringing up all the reserves of his personality, is impossible and would be meaningless. He must demand the return of the bodies; the Theban must say No. There would be no point in making these argue as do Creon and Antigone, in flashes that reveal the soul of each. The souls of Theseus and the Herald do not count. Therefore, in so far as the issue is argued it must be argued on its own merits, dialectically that is and not passionately. On these terms there is not a vast deal to say about it, and in any case it is incidental to the chief theme of the play, the suffering of the Mothers. The discussion on forms of government is not very much more remote, and can be brought in to extend a scene which the first question is not enough to fill. There is a lack of tragic tension on the stage; the stage accordingly embroiders the tragedy which broods in the orchestra.

Debate then may be a direct expression of some aspect of the tragic idea or it may be a substitute for action and the revelation of ethos. We may now turn to reflective, 'sophistic' passages, some of which seem otiose, perhaps distinctly out of character. Here, too, we have to distinguish. Not to waste time I take four instances only, Theseus on σύνεσις, Intelligence (S.W., 195 ff.), and on Life (ibid., 550 ff.), Hecuba on heredity and education (Hec., 592 ff.), and the fragment of dramatic criticism in the Suppliant Women (846 ff.). Of such passages it is not always enough to say that Euripides was given to thought and did not mind interrupting his play to say something interesting; some of them, notably the first two cited above, have a deeper origin. That intelligence is God's greatest gift to man is not simply a stray thought that occurs to Theseus (or to Euripides), which Theseus develops regardless of his context; it is part of the tragic thinking from which these plays arise – our intelligence overborne by our folly. So is the second idea, that we should show circumspection in our conduct. Comments like these – and not comments only, but full statements of a philosophical view – illustrate again the difference between Euripides' mind and Sophocles'; they are, as it were, parts of the original thought or emotion that do not find themselves transmuted into dramatic imagery.

But though this is true of some of these passages it is not true of all. Hecuba's inquiry and the dramatic criticism of Messenger-speeches do not belong to the original stuff of the drama; they are another indication of the external way in which Euripides approached his characters and situations. If the Hecuba were really a character-study the former passage would be impossible: the mind that it implies is inconsistent with the Hecuba who revenges herself on Polymestor. This is not to say that Hecuba has no character, only that her characterization is intermittent. Not being conceived – why should she be? – as a person whose precise blend of character is significant, she becomes, between whiles, a neutral personage who can be used rhetorically. Further (to anticipate our next point), what is Hecuba to say here? Lamentation, invective against the Greeks, or a sheer breakdown in grief – any of which would be a natural result of the sacrifice of Polyxena – would be comparatively uninteresting: lamentation we have had in plenty; invective or a 'natural' outburst of grief would force us to take the incident as tragedy, which would underline the 'shocking' element. Therefore what we have in this speech, the serious treatment of a serious and appropriate theme is, as it were, an intellectual stiffening to a situation which is in danger of running to melodrama or still more lyricism.

This brings us to a third noticeable result of this kind of dramatic action, the specifically rhetorical nature of the typical Euripidean speech. We may say in general that his preoccupation with an inner drama and his detachment from the persons on his stage make these speak in a standard accent. Euripides is as far as possible from creating an Oedipodean or a Creontic style for a single character; he could have done it, but it would have meant nothing. It is easy to see that such a standard accent, in Athens and at this period, might easily become rhetorical, yet it does not seem inevitable. But perhaps we can go further. We may recall the position of Hecuba in the scene just quoted, or we may consider Andromache's position in the *Troades* when the decree of the Greeks is announced. What is Andromache to say? It is in some ways a comparable moment when the Paedagogus announces the death of Orestes in Sophocles' play. Euripides gives us nothing like the utter limpidity of the Chorus there, the revealing directness of Clytemnestra, the noble simplicity of Electra's speech; not because Sophocles was better at doing these things than Euripides,[1] but because his situation was tragic (though feigned) while this is μιαρόν; tragic – like Medea's murders – only when we can relate it to the underlying idea. As the situation is, tragically speaking, unreal, so must Andromache's speech be to

---

[1] No doubt he was, but the comparison is meaningless without the reason.

some extent unreal, rhetorical like Medea's murders. Simple, moving
and tragic accents belong to simple and tragic situations, to Antigone
facing death; not for instance, to Polyxena. The character of
Polyxena we hardly know, nor does it affect her situation; Euripides
does right to intellectualize her speech and let her set out with a
πρῶτον μέν.

Or we may take a rather different moment. Hecuba makes a
speech in the *Troades* (466 ff.) when the situation is that Cassandra
has just been led off captive and that nothing else (except a choral
ode) is destined to happen until the next blow falls, the appearance of
Andromache, captive. The whole interval cannot be filled with
lyrics; Hecuba has been lyrical for nearly two hundred verses
already. She therefore is given a speech (cf. Soph., *El.*, 254 ff.), but
since nothing matters, dramatically, but the next blow – not
Hecuba's 'reactions', her character, possibility of counter-action –
the moment is quite static; there is no forward movement and
Euripides does not pretend to make any. This time there is no
debate or philosophical reflection to replace dramatic by intellectual
activity. Hecuba is given a reminiscent speech, and this consequently
must be interesting as a speech, that is, rhetorical.

5. Dramatic Surprise and Ornament

We have tried to show that debate, 'sophistry' and rhetoric were
natural results of this schematic treatment of plot and character,
whether springing directly from the theme, or introduced because
other interest was not easy to come by. We will now briefly consider two further consequences, 'theatre' and decoration.

Euripides' dramatic style is noticeably thin in texture. Not only is
his poetic style simple and limpid, as strong a contrast to the weight
of Aeschylus' style as to the infinite subtlety and richness of Sophocles', but every other part of his drama is in keeping. As his
characterization is schematic, his speeches lack ethos; as his plots are
schematic, they lack the incessant change of rhythm which Sophocles offers. Action that reveals the depths of a complex personality,
those triangular scenes, cross-rhythms and tragic irony that are an
illumination of the mechanics of life, play no part in Euripides.
Pathos and lamentation replace energy and tragic action, static
scenes illuminated by intellectual analysis take the place of the ever-

changing drama of Sophocles. And even intellectually Euripides does not make greater demands than Aeschylus or Sophocles; it would be a bold man who would assert that his stichomythia was more difficult to follow than Sophocles', or his speeches more packed with thought than Aeschylus'. Even here Euripides' texture is relatively thin.

This not because he was addressing a different or less intellectual audience. The thinness is desirable as well as necessary; it is not for nothing, or from accident, that Euripides hands out his drama in large pieces, easily to be grasped, while Sophocles demands every moment all the percipience we can muster to penetrate his subtleties. We can do one thing or the other. Sophocles does not expect us to integrate his *Tyrannus*; all that he means is there. That is the reason why it is so rich and so difficult, with something significant happening every moment. Euripides does demand that we shall make some effort of the imagination (not necessarily of the intellect; that is the critic's business) to integrate his *Troades,* even that we shall feel the tragedy of the *Medea* to be something more than the ruinous conduct of a slightly improbable woman. Therefore the simplicity which is the logical result of his dramatic method becomes an advantage. It allows us, as Sophocles never does, to lean back and ask ourselves what it is all about. If Euripides were really as simple as he appears from the pavilion in which sit those who edit him for schoolboys, it would indeed be difficult to account for his greatness. He is the most tragic of poets, not for the Hecuba and the Medea whom he made, but for the tragedy that lies behind these.

Still, the texture of the actual drama is thin, and Euripides, having sacrificed so much to the logic of his social tragedy, is prepared to find compensations elsewhere, in bold theatrical strokes and in sheer decoration. Of the compensations, some arise as it were automatically out of his method; others are by no means so inevitable.

Looseness of plot and emancipation from the law of the necessary or probable, though it deprived Euripides of the effects which Sophocles drew from his impressive ordering of events, made possible, and legitimate, certain effects which Sophocles could never use. Euripides was always ready to take advantage of his schematic construction by contriving turns of plot which were theatrically effective as well as contributory to his tragic idea. The chariot of Medea, whose tragic significance we have seen already, makes a splendid finale which Sophocles might have applauded though never imitated; the transformations which come over Hecuba, and over Alcmena and Eurystheus in the *Heracleidae,* transformations which are possible because the characterization has been slight and the plots not rigidly logical, legitimate because they underline the tragic idea of the plays, are at the same time very good theatre. The *Troades* similarly exploits its legitimate possibilities. Its singularly impressive ending Aristotle would no doubt have accepted as logical, but the scene between Helen, Hecuba and Menelaus comes from Euripides' logic, not Aristotle's. It is strictly a part of the theme, but what good theatre it is too! After the scenes of misery, and the impersonal Talthybius, we suddenly see face to face the ruined Queen (with the desolate Trojan women in the orchestra), Helen the lovely paramour and faithless wife, and Menelaus the betrayed husband and victorious general – a striking scene and a marvellous setting for Euripides' tragic argument. To these effective turns we might add the horrible but necessary effect of Glauce's death, the mysterious arrival and ominous departure of Orestes in the *Andromache,* the wild and romantic Evadne. None of these would be possible in Sophocles, but all belong as strictly to Euripides' theme as do Sophocles' complications of plot to his.

The conventionalized character-drawing too, though it has its inconveniences, brings its compensations. It makes possible sharply accentuated contrasts like those between Medea and Jason, Andromache and Hermione. Because he is pushing his characterization to extremes Euripides gets an almost melodramatic strength of effect impossible to Aeschylus and Sophocles, because their contrasts, though they may be complete, are more complex. Again, since Euripides is interested in these persons as figures in a drama rather than as rounded characters to be studied from the inside, he can make a sudden and effective stroke out of what, to a different dramatist, would have been a slow process, or at least a complex one. Hermione will illustrate this. In the first part of the play she is arrogant, sure and successful; when next we hear of her it is to be told that she has been trying to hang herself all over the palace. Euripides can short-circuit all her mental processes and present us with the startling result because she is a figure rather than a character; it is necessary that she should now see clearly, but how she comes to see clearly is no concern of ours. Or we may compare Hecuba before Agamemnon with Antigone's Watchman before

Creon. The Watchman's hesitations are naturally and dramatically reflected in a speech, for the whole nature of the drama demands that he shall be a real person and that the action shall look like life; Euripides is giving us something that is more like a diagram than a picture of life; there is much less need for Hecuba to speak like a Queen than there was for the Watchman to speak and think like a common soldier; therefore he renders the hesitations in a stagey manner (to use the word in a neutral sense). Hecuba is given a series of 'asides'; her doubts are not conveyed ethically, but made the opportunity for an effective bit of 'theatre'. Sophocles, not Euripides, is the realist here. Euripides, in his tragedies, has a degree of abstraction reminiscent of those mathematical personages A, B, and C who used to plough fields for us at such convenient rates. It is theatrical that the work they did should be so neatly mensurable; Sophocles gives us the real ploughman.

The slight but definite degree of detachment which we have observed Euripides showing towards his creatures opens the door to interesting effects. We have suggested that his sub-ironical treatment of Peleus may have been a defence, deliberately adopted, against a thoroughgoing melodramatic acceptance of the *Andromache*. Whether this is true or not, it is certainly a legitimate consequence of the general method, and quite an effective one. Euripides is not wholly wrapped up in his Peleus, and a conflict between a villain and one who is not quite a sage is certainly more interesting than one between pure black and pure white. Much more obvious is the effect in that puzzling play the *Heracleidae*, where Euripides allows the gallant Iolaus gradually to dissolve into fantasy.

All these effects, major and minor, are logical, and the best of them assist the theme, not the play only, as rigorously as Sophocles' very different effects always do. Some contrivances, however, do not seem so successful.

Hecuba (*Tro.*, 701 ff.) is consoling Andromache, and ends by telling her that at least she has Astyanax; Talthybius enters to announce the sentence of death on him. Why is the tragic irony rasping, not impressive and frightening like Sophocles'? Because it is not really tragic. Sophocles makes Oedipus welcome circumstances which in fact are big with disaster because he sees life, when it is tragic, as a stage on which character is at the mercy of circumstance, one on which even just calculation can lead to ruin. Because this is an essential part of his thought, even touches of irony which individually we could hardly justify in logic become transcendentally relevant. In the Euripidean tragedy circumstance plays no essential part; the whole foundation is rationalistic – οὐκ Ἀφροδίτη ἀλλὰ ἀφροσύνη. Such a view of life, though it might be rich in irony as we understand the word – something nearer to comedy than to tragedy – is not obviously a source of Aeschylean or Sophoclean irony, which indeed Euripides seldom imitates. In the Astyanax incident he does; and what does it reveal? Not that life, or indeed the Greeks, were particularly cruel in choosing this moment for the announcement; not that some mysterious and malevolent Power lies behind human action.[1] It intensifies but does not enlarge our sense of Hecuba's and Andromache's suffering. It is a stroke very like the ending of the *Hecuba,* a kind of rhetoric of action, not indeed to be reprehended, but not to be compared with the Sophoclean irony.[2]

This looser dramatic structure is naturally more tolerant of pure decoration. Certain rhetorical ornaments have been already noticed, and the additions which we can make to the list are not many. The Chorus of Huntsmen which attends on Hippolytus may be regarded as a decoration, by no means an illegitimate one, as it reinforces the Artemidian element in the play. When it reappears, the antiphony which it sings with the real chorus is effective, but it hardly adds to the tragedy – not as the Sons do in the *Suppliant Women.*

A much clear use of pure decoration is Andromache's Lament. This is a pure show-piece, whose undercurrent of self-pity, lack of suggestion of energy, independence and hardness, is set in striking contrast with the Andromache of the scenes that follow. If the Prologue had seriously engaged our interest in Andromache as a tragic heroine, as we are interested in Antigone, or if the action to come were felt to depend on her character as does the action of the *Antigone,* this interruption or suspension of interest would be quite

---

[1] We can imagine Hardy revelling in this incident.

[2] Only in one case (and that a curiously unimportant one) does it seem fair to accuse Euripides' contrivance of being artificial. It is the slight preparation for the Helen scene. Andromache (766 ff.) speaks – naturally enough – of Helen, and the succeeding ode devotes a stanza (841 ff.) to Eros. At 850 the chorus mentions the φέγγος ὀλοὸν which now looks upon Troy and at 860 Menelaus enters greeting the καλλιφεγγὲς ἡλίου σέλας which will witness his revenge on Helen. As the Helen scene is really disjunct it is perhaps permissible to criticize this preparation as artificial; at all events its value is less than that of similar preparations in Sophocles.

intolerable. Sophocles' Electra begins with a monody, but this is not decorative; on the contrary, it gives us the key to Electra's character and situation – things which are the basis of the whole play. It is because Andromache is important to Euripides' theme as a significant victim and not as a significant agent that he can stand back for a moment and pity her, objectively, in elegiacs.

In general, then, the most conspicuous strokes of Euripides' stage, his strong contrasts and his imaginative or at least effective juxtapositions, are the logical outcome of his method. The method has certain weaknesses in its slight or even inconsistent characterization, its disjointed plots, its uniform style: but it has its compensations, even if we limit ourselves to the purely theatrical. Unable for the most part to use the powerful dramatic rhythms which Sophocles mastered, he could not always prevent single scenes from sagging except by the extra-dramatic means of rhetoric, but to the play as a whole he could give a great impetus by calling upon one of these major effects. Because in these diagrammatic plots Sophocles' crescendos and cross-rhythms were impossible, the sudden stroke becomes characteristic – as of Heracles' children dressed for the grave: strokes which, like Glauce's death, have a perceptible tendency to address themselves to our nerves rather than to our poetic imagination. In fact, we see growing here the dramatic technique which made Euripides such a master of melodrama and tragicomedy – his sure instinct for a piquant turn or telling juxtaposition, his fertility of invention, his command of the rhetoric of action, the macabre, and the ironic. When he became content to make plays that were self-contained and complete in their immediate appeal, he is at once placed by Aristotle on the level of Sophocles.

When this happens, it is interesting – and seems inevitable – that it is Euripides, the tragedian of the sudden stroke, the manipulated plot, the slight characterization but sharp contrasts, who begins to write exciting melodrama; Sophocles, the tragedian of the close texture and complex rhythm, who produces the close and complex study of the *Philoctetes*; a play which, even if we should consider it only as a dramatic intrigue, has a subtlety of movement as characteristic of Sophocles as the breathless sweep of the *I.T.* is of Euripides. But while Euripides is still writing tragedy, he makes these strokes of his so subordinate to his tragic theme that it is in the highest degree unjust to think of him as a mere theatre-man. If he had been, his plays would have been better made and himself not the most tragic of the poets. Yet so tellingly are these strokes made that it is equally unjust to think of him as a great tragic poet indeed but hardly of equal rank as a dramatist.

It is, I suppose, a common experience for a reader to pass from Sophocles to Euripides with the feeling that he has gone from a cathedral into a dynamo-house, but if we find Euripides' thinness disappointing and some of his inconveniences irksome, we should probably do well to reflect that in his tragedies he has come down to us stripped of more of his essentials than Sophocles. Each has lost the stage-spectacle and the music, the movement and colour of the Chorus, but while in Sophocles these were important indeed but accessory to a tragic idea primarily realized in the characters, the plot, and the drama, in Euripides they were much more. In the *Hecuba* and *Troades* the chorus, with its communal tragedy, embodies more of the essential meaning of the play than ever it does in Sophocles, and that meaning is gravely attenuated to us, who have only a bare text. We have, in fact, most prominently before us those elements in which this Tragedy is not particularly strong – the stage-action and the discussion – and have lost the greater part of what was designed more immediately to present the tragic idea. The mere physical presence of one of these choruses – for example, of the Mothers with their grandchildren during some of the debates in the *Suppliant Women* – must have given to the scene an atmosphere which we cannot now recover, except by proper performance. The dialectic, so prominent to us, would be less prominent if the chorus had its true stature, and would no doubt take on a tragic hue now invisible. In fact, in so far as this Tragedy is a communal one, it lives most in the orchestra; the stage gives a sharper but an incomplete and diagrammatic picture of it. The reader has lost much of the total impression of what proceeded from the stage, but very much more of what proceeded from the orchestra.

6. Prologues and Epilogues

We come finally to these most characteristic and most puzzling features of the Euripidean drama. The formal narrative prologue has very little wherewith to recommend itself to a reader whose ears are full of the great choral odes with which early Tragedy opened, or whose dramatic sense has been excited by the way in which the *Agamemnon,* the *Antigone,* or even the later *Philoctetes* began. No wonder that Aristophanes laughed at such stiff and undramatic first scenes. Why did Euripides, and apparently no one else, write them?

It is no answer at all to call the prologue a playbill. Perhaps it is that, but why is playbill confused with play? Euripides, we are told, innovated so freely in myth that it was necessary to warn the audience beforehand that the story was to be not quite what it might be expecting. Did then Aeschylus and Sophocles not innovate? Was Aeschylus' Prometheus the Prometheus of Hesiod, or Sophocles' Philoctetes the same as Euripides' or Aeschylus'? Even if the myth was being severely rehandled, was the audience now so lacking in wit that it could not follow a new story in the play itself, and was the dramatist so helpless that he could not make his story intelligible as he went along? Had Sophocles written the *Tyrannus* in vain?

We must remember what the Euripidean plot is, and consider what were the alternatives to the not very exciting prologue. The plot is never in essence and rarely in fact a logical story in which certain characters inevitably work out their ruin, but a series of incidents, necessarily related but not necessarily a logical whole, chosen to illustrate or point to some overriding tragic idea. The plot of the *Troades* is nothing but a selection of incidents from many which followed the capture of Troy, one section of our line of telegraph-poles, one which does in fact end at an obvious terminus (unlike the series in the *Hecuba*), but is not itself a unity. Clearly the logical way of introducing this is to begin at some satisfactory *terminus a quo* and to summarize rapidly until the section under review is reached. Plot in fact has taken a decisive step towards narrative. Aristotle objected to Aegeus on the grounds that strict construction cannot allow such incursions from outside. We have defended Aegeus as being allowable in theory, though certainly not free from fault in practice. But if Euripides' tragedy had been cast in narrative form, a form which can afford to be looser in construction, Aegeus would hardly provoke any objection. So, too, the plot of the *Hecuba* is perfectly good as a section of narrative; only as drama does it raise questions. To such narrative plots a narrative introduction is the obvious beginning.

Further, these plots are not regarded as being within the control of the chief characters (the *Medea* excepted). The Trojan victims can do nothing; Euripides' Suppliants are far from being the determined Suppliants of Aeschylus; even Phaedra and Hippolytus are presented as victims of a power greater than themselves. Therefore, when we begin to consider alternatives to the prologue we meet a difficulty at once. The typical opening scene of Sophocles is not a mere purveying of information. If this were a legitimate excuse for such a beginning, Euripides need never have done anything different. Sophocles begins decisively, showing the action as already started, producing one of the significant characters at once, because such action and such characters are the essence of the drama. This is the ideal beginning for a play in which the character and the separate interests and motives of everyone in it are significant, one in which we are to see the outcome of the joint actions. But the Euripidean drama is nothing like this. Never is the dramatic point an interlocking of character and interests, nor, in this second group, is the real interest of the play the action of the chief characters, but rather their passion. To illustrate the first point it is sufficient to ask how Euripides was to begin the *Medea*. Had the play been conceived as a tragedy of character, like the *Antigone,* a study of the disastrous opposition between Jason's self-seeking and Medea's passionate jealousy, then nothing would have been simpler to contrive than a strong opening scene between the two, or between Jason and Creon, or between Medea and Glauce; no need to begin with the Argo cleaving the dark Symplegades – all this could have been taken for granted, or slipped in later. But as the play is not this at all, as the motives and character of Jason are accessory and those of Creon and Glauce immaterial, such a scene would, in fact, be mere pretence. What matters is not the quality of Jason's acts, nor the action and reaction that pass between him and Medea, but simply what a woman like Medea will do in this now complete situation. The logical beginning therefore is a plain narrative statement of this complete situation, not dialogue between two persons whose characters are a matter of indifference.[1] If this is true of a play so near to

[1] That the prologue is in fact spoken not by an indifferent person, like a god, but by the Nurse, who puts something of her own inconspicuous personality into her narrative, is a sign that in this play of transition Euripides has not gone to this logical conclusion.

Middle Tragedy as the *Medea,* how much the more true of the later Euripidean tragedy?

But if a dialogue-opening is false, why not begin with the Chorus? The plays are lyrical in feeling, and to say that choral openings had gone out of use is only to say that Euripides did not use them. To this question there is a decisive answer. The problem we are really considering is how to bring in events past. To Sophocles, the past was significant chiefly as it affected the actions or motives of the actors in the present; to his Electra the murder of Agamemnon was a past event which coloured the thought and conduct of the present Electra, therefore it is given to her, and to Orestes, to tell us of it. So, more strikingly, with the complicated past history of Laius and Oedipus. We are told nothing about it at the beginning in order that Oedipus may appear before us without a shadow, and the story is, as it were, dragged out of the past by Oedipus himself for the sake of the tragic effect and the light it throws on his character. That this is also a neat way of disposing the material is a bagatelle. On the other hand, the past in the *Agamemnon,* notably the sacrifice of Iphigeneia, is no part of Agamemnon's present mind, nor, though it is part of Clytemnestra's, is this of importance to us at the beginning of the play. First we are to see this past as a living element in the present, as a debt Agamemnon has to pay; that is the reason why it is dealt with first, and by the chorus. But in these Euripidean tragedies the past, usually, is nothing, once the play has begun. It works neither as a controlling element in the conduct of the actors nor as part of the tragic atmosphere of the whole.[1] Neither actors nor chorus therefore can work it in without a considerable amount of pretence.[2] Its only significance is that it has, in fact, produced the present; it is quite formal, and is formally dealt with. Nothing prevents either chorus or actors from harking back to the past when it is relevant to the present theme, but they may not recapitulate it as a way of starting the action, or talk merely to give us facts; yet the play, not being an organic growth, can hardly begin without a summary, so that the 'playbill' prologue becomes inevitable.

Once established, the prologue could be put to some remarkable

[1] The *Troades* is a manifest exception to this, but obviously the tragic quality with which the past is invested in this prologue could not be entrusted to the chorus, still less to the actors.

[2] There is a reminiscent ode on the capture of Troy in the *Hecuba* (905 ff.), but this is no exception. In this terrible ode the past is brought in not for our information – we could do without it – but as part of the tragedy of the chorus.

uses. We see how in the *Hippolytus* it gives the cosmic framework to what would otherwise be an exciting but not particularly significant story. Similar, but much more powerful, is the double prologue to the *Troades*. It might have been possible to open this play with the chorus; the play is, however, not merely a pathetic picture of cruelty to the conquered, but also a tragic picture of the results of wickedness and folly both to conquered and conquerors, and it is the prologue that directs our attention to the tragic blindness of the conquerors; serving, as we have suggested, the same end as the first ode of the *Agamemnon*.

The prologue to the *Hecuba,* spoken by the ghost of Polydorus, is put to a different but equally significant use. This prologue, in conventional narrative, tells us the antecedent circumstances, and then proceeds to 'bind together' the two unrelated themes which are to make up the play, the sacrifice of Polyxena and the discovery of Polydorus' own body: perhaps a necessary, but hardly a brilliant device. Yet we may suspect, when the Ghost goes on to tell us when, where, and by whom the body will be found, telling us in fact what we must in any case learn from the play itself – we may suspect that in this prologue Euripides has a deeper motive than merely starting the play, and a more respectable one than tying together a shaky structure. Why does he virtually make Polydorus say 'At verse 657 my death will be announced by Hecuba's servant'? The detailed foreshadowing reminds us of the way in which Aeschylus' Suppliants foreshadow their threat of suicide, and of their reason for doing so – to discount the purely theatrical thrill of the incident (p. 29). Here we are so precisely told what is going to happen in order that, being set free of all excitement over the facts, we may have minds at leisure to take in the real tragedy. The inner drama here, unlike that of the *Hippolytus* and *Troades,* is hardly such as can be put into dramatic shape in the prologue; still, the way can be prepared for it.[1] Such foreshadowing is quite inconceivable in a Sophoclean play; not because these are 'better constructed' and do not need underpinning before they are built, but because the meaning and the function of action in Sophocles are radically different; they are so intimately connected with character and thought that they may be

---

[1] Note that the climax, the revenge taken by Hecuba, is not foreshadowed. This is intended as a shock. A further point in this prologue, a separate and secondary advantage, is that our foreknowledge of Polydorus' death increases for us the pathos of Polyxena's.

regarded as character and thought made manifest. If Sophocles told us what Oedipus was going to do, it would be equivalent to telling us what sort of a man he was.

Nothing could more clearly indicate the illustrative nature of these plots. We are not to concern ourselves dramatically and emotionally in the actual events, as we do with the events of the Sophoclean stage; these do not reveal the character and thought which is the essence of the tragedy; they are chosen as a convenient means of conveying an inner tragic idea. These characters are the dramatic counterpart of the mathematical ploughmen A, B and C; we were never expected to follow them homeward plodding their weary way when the field was ploughed, nor here are we expected or desired to enter passionately and exclusively into the heart of Hecuba and to follow these events only through the tearstained eyes of the tragic Queen. The prologue, with its foreshadowing, slightly but definitely detaches us, as Euripides himself is detached.

In complete contrast stands the prologue to the *Andromache*. It has been felt that the connexion between the two separate stories here is somewhat slight. Had then Euripides not yet thought of the masterly device of using the prologue as string? It would have been perfectly simple to start with a prologue spoken by the god of Delphi, or his apologist Hermes, or the Dioscuri, to pull the play together and to state the connexion between the first part and the second. This, however, is exactly what Euripides does not want. This time his tragic idea does depend on the element of surprise and shock in the narrative. He wants Orestes to take us by surprise; his Hermione and his Menelaus have not, as we innocently supposed, exhausted Sparta's genius for doing evil. To tell us even the barest outline of the plot beforehand would leave us only the secondary interests of the play – the discussions and debates, the 'psychology', the realism and the rest.

Later parallels to the *Andromache* enable us to say that when Euripides is writing any kind of drama in which the movement of the plot is an important source of interest, he is careful not to foreshadow; indeed, if anything is foreshadowed, it is something that is destined not to be fulfilled. Thus Dionysus in the *Bacchae* threatens a salutary lesson to Thebes – this in the tragic manner. As in the *Hecuba*, we are told roughly what is to happen in order that we may receive it, when it comes, tragically and not melodramatically; we are not told the full extent and nature of the lesson, because the shock of that surprise is necessary to the poet's theme. The *Helen, Electra, Phoenissae,* on the other hand, being melodramatic rather than tragic, have prologues which confine themselves strictly to past events; the course of future events is one of the main interests of the play and is therefore kept dark. The prologues of the *Orestes* and the *I.T.,* plays of a similar kind, look forward to the future – but incorrectly, for the sake of enhancing the surprise;[1] while in the *Ion,* for the sake of making the plot still more piquant, Euripides makes Hermes prophesy events which Apollo fails to bring off properly.

The Euripidean prologue was then in origin a convention adopted out of artistic honesty. His tragic plots were never the self-contained interactions of a group of people, like the Sophoclean. They con-sisted rather of a series of typical events, bound together not by any strict law of causality, sometimes indeed by none at all, but by the fact that the poet could use them to convey a single tragic vision. It was logical, therefore, to start from some satisfactory ἀρχή (which in three of these plays was the Trojan War) and by simple narrative to continue until the section was reached which contained the events of the play. This was the origin of the prologue; its use became something much more subtle. It could be used as in the *Hippolytus,* to close the gap between the ostensible and the inner drama; or it could be used, as in the opposite examples of the *Hecuba* and the *Ion,* as a powerful means of controlling the story-element of the play, either by removing our interest from the crude events, all or some of them, or by directing our attention to them more closely.

It seems evident that the same circumstances which led to the prologue must lead also to the epilogue, that we shall both enter and leave the chosen section of the story by narrative. In fact, the narrative epilogue becomes standard only in the next group of plays; the *Andromache* may end in a narrative summary, but the *Troades* can be brought to a full close by the crash of falling walls. Still, we can see in this group the difficult of finding a convincing way of finishing a diagrammatic plot.

Here, as in the matter of continuity, the old trilogy had had little trouble. Its third play, like the first and second, dealt with a self-

[1] In the *I.T.* Iphigeneia infers from a dream that Orestes is dead, and in the *Orestes* Electra places her hopes of safety in the arrival of the useless Menelaus.

contained, though related, situation; its plot was a logical story and a logical story has a logical end. Plays like the *Hecuba* have no end of this kind, no inevitable pause; for if three symbolically related scenes, why not four or five? There is no reason why the *Hecuba* should end with the vengeance on Polymestor except that nothing else is wanted and nothing could well be grimmer. The real end of the story of the *Andromache* is the death of Neoptolemus, but this neither makes a satisfactory dramatic close nor completes the poet's idea. The chorus can no longer end the play of its own authority with a funeral hymn (as it does in the *Septem*) nor, so far as concerns the idea, can it be the symbol of the community. For this, someone nearer the heart of the story must be chosen; Euripides chooses Peleus, but nothing in the play makes this inevitable. So, too, the *Suppliant Women*; the story would find its natural close in the recovery of the dead, or their cremation or removal to Argos. Iphis and Evadne are not what the story demands but what the poet wants; the natural point of ending the story would not have given Euripides the material he wanted. Therefore, in the absence of a logical climax, there must be more or less of deliberate contrivance in the ending; a feeling of finality has to be created.

To meet this difficulty was the function of the *Deus ex machina*. The simplest case of the Deus is Thetis in the *Andromache*. There, the action leads to a situation in which nothing more can happen, but which is not a satisfactory close. We can only watch Peleus mourning, and reviling the Spartans; and to this there is no obvious term; moreover there are loose ends lying about – Andromache for example, and, if the play is not to leave the wrong impression, a purely melodramatic one, Peleus must receive his consolation-prize for the sake of avoiding 'the shocking'. When the futures of Peleus, Andromache and Molossus are arranged for, when in fact the victims of this human accident are made comfortable, then the play can end.[1]

---

[1] This kind of ending goes naturally with any form of story in which all our sympathies and all our attention are not absorbed by the hero or heroes. At the end of the *Tyrannus* Sophocles does not have to pension off the two shepherds or tell us what happened to Teiresias; he does not even have to arrange for Oedipus' daughters, although they are deliberately introduced, to show us more of Oedipus' character. With Thetis we may properly compare Jane Austen's charmingly conventional endings, in which minor characters are married off or otherwise provided for; this because her comedy of manners is wider than her heroes and their fortunes. Thus the Euripidean Deus, already, it is admitted, a 'faded' version of the Epiphany in which the earliest Tragedy ended, fades further into a mere last chapter, the god at length identified with the author – a confused situation which cannot be investigated here.

But as with the prologue, so with the epilogue; a simple necessity is turned to powerful uses. The *Hecuba,* like the *Andromache,* leads to no inevitable end; a god, this time at second hand, is introduced to prolong the story until finality is reached in the transformation of Hecuba and the murder of Agamemnon. But how much more than this there is in Polymestor's prophecies! This epilogue, like the prologue of the *Troades,* suggests in dramatic form the tragic thought which underlies the whole play; not a mere ending but an illumination of the whole action. Later we shall find the epilogue put to a markedly satirical use; not in the tragedies, unless indeed we see satire, or perhaps irony, in the treatment of Athena at the end of the *Suppliant Women.*

Two more devices may be noticed, the first a point we have discussed, the transformation of the Heroine. To see Eurystheus and even Polymestor on our own side of the fence as it were, to find them not exactly in the right, but at least persons to be considered with interest and some sympathy, is not in itself a climax, but it does not help to produce a sense of finality. 'He was after all . . .' we say to ourselves; it is clearly the end.

Finally, there is the *aition,* the linking of the story to some actual rite, monument or natural feature. Medea refers to an existing ritual at her children's supposed grave. Hippolytus has his worship, Hecuba becomes a rocky promontory, and so on. These serve the same end as the Deus and wee ursually associated with him.

Now aitia are universally popular, but especially with story-tellers and anthropologists. Why the story-teller likes them is perhaps a question for the psychologist rather than the critic. It may be that they lend an air of veracity to the story, for the audience will argue, by Aristotle's παραλογισμός, that since the thing explained does exist the story must be true; or it may be that the aition forms a convenient half-way house between the fictive world of the story and the real world that will resume its sway when the story ends – a half-way house which has obvious advantages when the story does not end in a blaze of transfiguration. But whatever may be the psychological explanation, it is clear that when an aition turns up the play is over. It reinforces our feeling of finality, and is used when a play does not reach an Aristotelian end but merely stops.

To the anthropologist, on the other hand, the aition has been a matter not of stopping a drama but of beginning it. He has argued that since the aition comes in strongly at the end of Greek Tragedy it must have been there at the beginning: the Euripidean play ends with a reference to a rite because it originally *was* the rite; the *Deus ex machina* represents an original Apotheosis. It may be so; it is possible that we have before our eyes the awful spectacle of Euripides destroying himself, like the suicidal lemming, in blind obedience to an ancient instinct. Nevertheless as his aitia, like his gods, are so useful in his structure and so consonant with the diminished stature of his characters and the different significance of his plots, it seems safer to ascribe them to literary judgement, not to historical survival or antiquarianism. The one surviving play of Aeschylus we have that ends with anything like an aition, namely the *Eumenides,* is also the one which is intellectualist in tone. To his other plays, as to Sophocles always, they are quite foreign, simply because the quality of the dramatic thought in these plays could not endure them. Sophocles has one *Deus ex machina* – and it is in the *Philoctetes.*

CHAPTER X

The 'Trachiniae'
and the 'Philoctetes'

1. The 'Trachiniae'

None of the seven plays has been more variously assessed than the *Trachiniae*; the verdicts range from 'good' to 'downright bad'. Broken-backed, double-yoked, *zweispaltig*, are epithets that have been applied to it. Jebb explained lucidly where Sophocles went wrong, and what he should have done in order to achieve 'artistic unity': he should have made less of Deianeira, since her humanity steals too much of our attention from the heroic sublimity of Heracles. The great difficulty has been the structure of the play: there are two central characters, and they never meet. When at last Heracles enters, Deianeira is already dead, and little reference is made to her. Indeed, it seems that Sophocles was so determined to write a bad play that he did not even bring on Deianeira's body, in order to give the semblance of unity to his plot.

A current fashion is to call the play a diptych. This is well enough, provided that we do not think that a new name is also an explanation. A diptych may be a good or a bad one: which is this? If a medieval diptych displayed in one half the horrors of a saint's martyrdom, and in the other his eternal bliss, not many of us would be seriously worried about its unity. The form of a composition is a function of its meaning; if we entirely mistake its meaning, as I think Jebb did, and many other scholars, including myself in the earlier editions of this book, we are not likely to understand its form. It will be argued here that the form is intelligible and significant – as soon as we have relieved our minds of the modern idea that in drama character-drawing comes first. It is, of course, important, but let us at least set it alongside other things which seem to have been more important to Sophocles, in order to see them all in their due proportion.

Once more, a good deal is said or implied in the play about the gods, especially about Zeus. Is this only a generalized piety, or is it part of the fabric of the play? On our answer to this question will depend, very largely, our understanding and estimate of the whole composition.

It has often been pointed out that the *Trachiniae* is quite unlike the other six plays not only in its form but also in its background and its material. Jebb remarked:[1] 'The play is, in fact, an exceptionally difficult one to appreciate justly; and the root of the difficulty is in the character of the fable.' Did Sophocles then not make the plot clear? Or did he fail to make it significant? The contrast between this play and the others has been vigorously asserted by Mr Letters in these terms: 'Heracles belongs to another race than the simply human, his myth to an era more primitive and daimonic that that of Ajax or Oedipus'; monsters and marvels abound in the play; primitive magic, especially in the nightmarish idea of 'the ghostly Centaur living on in his slayer's tormented flesh', figures here as nowhere else in Sophocles. 'Wherever we place it in a chronological table of Sophocles' plays, it will be in violent contrast with its neighbours'.[2] In these respects, certainly – but how important are they? These are on the surface; everything below the surface is familiar and thoroughly Sophoclean, especially this matter of the participation of the gods in the human action.

There are the frequent references to Zeus, who, for the obvious reason, is more prominent here than in the other plays: he is the father of Heracles. There are the oracles: the life of Heracles, as of Oedipus, is encompassed by them; and their fulfilment in each play has the same quality of mocking irony. There is, too, that peculiarly Sophoclean feeling for pattern in human events, which here, as in four other of the plays, takes the form of the dead reaching out to kill the living (p. 143, above). The venomous blood of the hydra, says the chorus (834), was created by death and nurtured by the hydra. Heracles killed the hydra, and with its venom he killed the centaur – in each case justly. Now the same venom kills Heracles. It is exactly parallel to what we find in the *Ajax*: the story, three times

[1] In the *Introduction* to his edition, p. x

[2] F. J. H. Letters, *Life and Works of Sophocles*, pp. 176, 185, 194.

mentioned, of Hector's belt and Ajax's sword. The two men had been bitter enemies (*Ajax*, 662, 817). In the famous story in the *Iliad* they met in single combat, and having fought each other until nightfall they exchanged gifts. Each gift brought death to the recipient, for Hector was strangled in Ajax's belt (in Sophocles' version of the story), and Ajax dies on Hector's sword. 'Death,' says Teucer (*Ajax*, 1034 ff.) 'made the belt, the Erinyes forged the sword; the gods brought this to pass, as all else.' The mention of the Erinyes certifies that this is the work of Dike, in one of her remoter and more mysterious manifestations. So, too, in the *Trachiniae*: Death created the venom, the envenomed robe is called by Heracles 'a snare woven by the Erinyes', and Hyllus ends the play by saying: 'Nothing is here but Zeus.' Heracles, no doubt, means by the Erinyes Deianeira's vengeful spirit – for he does not yet know the truth – but we, the audience, shall certainly see in the Erinyes here the agents of that same Dike. The tide turns, a pattern completes itself, all according to the dispensation of Zeus. We must not lose ourselves in the analysis of Deianeira's character, or in the personal contrast between her and Heracles, and take no notice of this; nor on the contrary must we disregard the vivid character-drawing as only decoration, give our chief attention to the divine agents, and turn the human actors into puppets, which manifestly they are not. We must at least use the assumption, until it breaks down, that Sophocles meant these two aspects of his drama to cohere and make sense.

> There is an ancient proverb among men
> That no one's fortune can be rightly judged
> As good or bad, until his life is ended.

Rather a dull opening to a play? Certainly it does not show the dramatic qualities of some of the other openings, but perhaps we had better get the whole play into the correct perspective before we censure it as undramatic. Sophocles' standards, after all, may not be the same as ours.

Deianeira goes on to describe her monstrous suitor the River-god, and the struggle between him and Heracles. We can easily find something incongruous in the picture of this gracious lady in such a setting; yet the whole play ends with a protest against the cruelty of the gods who have destroyed both Deianeira and Heracles: what if the real theme of the play is nothing less than the human situation

itself, Man and the gods? In that case our first judgements might have
to be modified a little; the Athenian audience might not have been
expecting what we instinctively expect, and Sophocles may have
been more in tune with them than with us.

Let us anticipate. Just before the end, Heracles delivers a long
speech: what do we make of it? Jebb, one of those critics who look
at Greek drama through a literary haze and suppose Sophocles to
have been rather a bookish character, not really a man of the theatre,
thought that Sophocles was consciously drawing a Homeric
Heracles. Does Sophocles avoid all reference to the hero's apotheosis?
The reason, says, Jebb, is that there was no apotheosis in Homer.
Therefore the long speech is 'a magnificent recital' in the epic
manner, and it leaves Jebb 'comparatively cold'. Naturally. Do the
final scenes give Sophocles' own conception of the mind and
character of Heracles – just that, and nothing more? If so, they do
not much move us. Naturally. But if we suspect that the real theme
of the play is the baffling and tragic uncertainties of human life, and
some of its laws which are neither baffling nor uncertain, then the
scenes escape into a new dimension and become much more
impressive and intelligible. Now we have only to listen to what
Heracles is saying, to realize that every single thing is directed to one
end: life, the gods, are treating him, as he sees it, with a cruel,
mocking irony. This is what he says: He was making thankoffering
to Zeus for his triumph; at that very moment Zeus requited him
with this agonizing pain (993–6). He has spent his life serving
humanity, yet now his Greek followers will not do him the service
of putting him out of his agony (1010–14). 'Never did even my
enemies Hera and Eurystheus make me suffer as now my wife has
done, with this robe of the Erinyes that is eating away my flesh.
No foe in arms, no host of giants, no monster, has done to me what
this unarmed woman has done – my wife. Never before have I
shed a tear, but she, a woman, makes me weep like a child. Look at
my tortured body! Look at my poor arms, my back, my chest!
Where now is the strength that destroyed the Nemean lion, the
hydra, the Amazons, the Erymanthean boar, Cerberus, the dragon
of the Hesperides, the other monsters? Never was I defeated, until
now. Bring her to me, that I may strangle her!'

No possible irony of circumstance is wanting; in particular, the
oracles seem to have been deliberately mocking him – and there is

no apotheosis to come. The significant thing in the speech is not that it is Homeric: it is that it is so eminently Sophoclean, for it makes Heracles a close parallel to Oedipus. He, too, seems, in the end, to have been continually mocked by circumstances; he, too, was beset by oracles, which he himself fulfilled; he, too, had been a saviour of his people, but was suddenly cast down from an almost godlike pre-eminence to utter shame and ruin; and as here the glory of Heracles' physical strength and endurance appears to have been singled out for mockery, so there is the intellectual strength of Oedipus: the man of pre-eminently clear vision is seen to have been blind, and blinds himself when he learns the truth. Such, it seems, are the ways of the gods.

We will return to the beginning of the play; we shall find that the apparently cruel ironies of life prevail throughout.

Life, says Deianeira, is an uncertain affair. She, for example, had been beautiful (24) – and Sophocles was not the only Greek poet who knew that beauty can be perilous. From the horror of her monstrous suitor she was delivered by the favour of Zeus, 'if indeed it was favour,' εἰ δὴ καλῶς (27). But from her life with Heracles she has had little happiness, much anxiety, and her present year of anxiety has been the worst. But the chorus encourages her, and in very Sophoclean terms, for it appeals to the great rhythm of nature: 'As night and day succeed each other, so in the life of man do joy and sorrow. To nobody does Zeus give unbroken sorrow; nor will he be neglectful of his own son. Therefore have good hope.' That is, life owes Deianeira some happiness, and will surely pay the debt.

So it seems. A messenger runs in with great news: Heracles has returned. This means, as Deianeira knows from an oracle (166–9), that his last labour is safely over; henceforth peace is assured for them both. She thanks Zeus; she calls for a hymn of triumph, and the chorus sings to Paean, the Healing God. But, as so often in Sophocles, the happy excitement is only the prelude to disaster. Lichas arrives, the official herald. He confirms the news: Heracles has indeed returned, he has just captured Oechalia, the city of Eurytus, and Lichas has brought with him the captive women. 'And is this the reason for so long an absence?'

Lichas' reply costs him, and us, forty-three verses – a dull speech, from the wrong point of view. Certainly he had to explain that

Heracles had suffered a year's enslavement, and he had to explain why then he had attacked Oechalia, but why does Sophocles make him spend about twenty-five verses on the details of the death of Eurytus' son Iphitus? They cannot interest Deianeira very much, at this moment. If we think that Sophocles was a dull plodder, we will say that he found the story in his sources and did not have the sense to keep it within bounds. If on the other hand we think that he was not quite so prosaic as this criticism is, we shall be seriously perturbed by the incident. Heracles, Lichas tells us, had been gravely insulted by Eurytus; to avenge the insult he had caught his son Iphitus when he was off his guard, and had hurled him to his death from a high place. Had he killed Iphitus openly, the gods would have pardoned him, 'for the gods, too, have no liking for hybris' (280), but since he had killed him treacherously, Zeus punished him, by having him sold as a slave for one year. Then, says Lichas, Heracles vowed that in return for his own enslavement he would enslave Eurytus and all his family, and he has done it: he has destroyed the city, killed all its men; and here are the women, captives. He will soon be home; he is making a thankoffering to Zeus for the conquest.

Not exactly a pretty story, even as Lichas tells it. Zeus directly punished Heracles for an act of treacherous violence; will he then accept thankoffering for the destruction of a city, an act of vengeance for the punishment which Zeus himself had inflicted? 'The gods, too, have no liking for hybris': the destruction of Oechalia looks very much like hybris.

The chorus bids Deianeira rejoice. Her reply is interesting, and not only as a piece of character-drawing:

> *I do indeed rejoice, with all my heart.*
> *To learn of this good fortune of my husband*
> *Calls forth in me a joy that runs to meet it.*
> *And yet, the cautious cannot help but fear*
> *At great success, lest it be overthrown;*
> *For I am moved with pity, as I look*
> *On these unhappy women, driven from home*
> *And parents on to foreign soil; once free,*
> *Condemned henceforth to lead the life of slaves.*
> *O Zeus, great Arbiter! may I not see*

> *Thy hand so fall upon a child of mine;*
> *Or, if it must fall, may I be in my grave!*
> *To see these women here so terrifies me.*

What has given check to Deianeira's joy is not simply the instinctive feeling that great success is not to be trusted. There is more: the feeling that something is gravely wrong, when such misery is inflicted upon the innocent, particularly on one of them, the one who most arouses her pity.

But Lichas, for creditable reasons, has dissembled. When he is out of the way for a few minutes the Messenger intervenes, and his honest intervention proves to be a turning point in the tragedy. The Messenger knows more, and unlike Lichas he cannot keep his mouth shut. He knows, and presently makes Lichas admit, that it was for the sake of this girl that Heracles destroyed the city: Heracles had demanded of Eurytus his daughter, to be his concubine, κρύφιον ὡς ἔχοι λέχος (360). All this ruin, therefore, because Eurytus would not grant a dishonouring request! Heracles at this moment is offering thanks to Zeus for his destruction of the city; how will Zeus receive it? For neither have the gods any liking for hybris.

The whole of this passage forcibly recalls the *Tyrannus*: the intervention of a typically Hellenic opportunist, who sees and takes the chance of doing himself a good turn; the emergence of the truth in spite of efforts to keep it back (*O.T.* 1146); the disastrous effect of well-meant action (*O.T.*, 1177 ff., above, p. 139) – especially in what Deianeira now proceeds to do. Does this mean that human affairs are bound to go wrong, as if on some malignant principle? Not in the least; Sophocles has been careful to indicate the major cause of it all. We expected sunshine at last, in accordance with the natural rhythm, but a great cloud of hybris has appeared in the sky. The killing of Iphitus as an act of revenge the gods would have forgiven; his murder they punished. Now Heracles has done something far worse – and we are to see how Zeus will punish this: not, this time, by direct intervention, but, as in the *Antigone*, by a perfectly natural working-out of the complexity that we call Life.

As for what Deianeira does, it is natural for us to treat it as an Aristotelian ἁμαρτία: she has many virtues, but she is too simple-minded, and has to pay the tragic penalty. Having said that, let us see how Sophocles treats it. In the first place, he makes her win the cautious approval of the chorus before she uses the love-charm; this already makes her mistake more than an individual one, something more like a typical one: 'impetuous action taken in un-certainty,' as she herself says later (670), 'a dreadful thing done in good hope' (667); 'I learn the truth too late, when it cannot help' (711). In the second place, he does exactly the same thing with Hyllus: he makes Hyllus curse his mother for a murderess, and then (932 ff.) reproach himself bitterly for driving her to her death, in his ignorance and hastiness. Again, it is what Oedipus did, more than once; it is typical of the blindness which is the inescapable lot of humanity.

Something else comes into play here, the power of Eros (354, 441, 490, 497 ff.). It is important not to misunderstand this. It is emphatically not the case that if Eros or Aphrodite is called re-sponsible, then Heracles is not; still less that the god will pay for the damage that he causes. Even we can say of a man 'Drink was his ruin', but we do not thereby absolve the man and throw the blame upon Drink; men should not give way to Drink. So here: Eros is a universal passion, and Heracles gave way to it beyond all reasonable measure. Eros is an explanation, not an excuse. Deianeira is under-standing; she knows that Heracles has had many women, and bears no resentment; she says, with pathetic irony, that it is idle to fight against the gods. But then she sees that Iole is different; Iole will live in the house, and she herself will be pushed on one side. This is more than she can bear; therefore she thinks of using the charm that will win back for her Heracles' love. The legend may be dealing in magic, unlike Sophocles' other plots, but it is also dealing with much more familiar things.

Another god, too, is mentioned, Ares, the wild frenzy of battle, the lust for destroying (653 f.). The chorus says that 'Ares, mad-dened, Ἄρης οἰστρηθείς, has ended sorrow for Deianeira'. No Greek audience would for a moment believe that Ares could ever do anything so constructive. If Heracles gave way to Ares, or was helped by Ares, nothing but trouble can be expected.

The news about the robe is brought by Hyllus. He, like Lichas earlier, has a long speech in which there are apparently inorganic passages. He is describing to his mother, whom he thinks a mur-deress, the death-agonies of his father: would he then naturally spend fourteen verses in describing the details of Lichas' death? Of

L

course not – but then, Sophocles was not a naturalistic dramatist. Shall we then say that it was in the legend, and that Sophocles either could not or would not leave it out? But he could and did leave out something much more important that was also in the legend, namely the apotheosis. He was the master, not the slave, of his sources. Or shall we say that it is the conventional messenger-speech, about which the Athenian audience was quite uncritical? Even if the audience was, Sophocles was not; nowhere else do we find him dealing in such second-rate clichés of composition. Or shall we do something which some scholars seem to think slightly indecent, namely respond imaginatively to what an artist has constructed? If we do, we notice an interesting fact: the killing of Lichas is an exact replica of the killing of Iphitus: both are innocent men, flung to their death from a high place. The one is meant to recall the other; untamed violence is characteristic of this otherwise great hero.

So, too, is his total disregard for others. Sophocles might have made him cry: 'Stand away, my son, lest you share my death'; or he might have omitted this detail altogether, since it does nothing to advance the plot. Instead, he makes him say: 'Raise me, my son, even if you must die with me.' The possible death of his son deters him no more than did the feelings of the loyal wife to whom he offered such outrage. What he is suffering now is the direct outcome of that; so do the gods work, here, as in the other plays.

Now we can move on to the last act, remembering how it emphasizes the apparently cruel ironies of Heracles' fate, and imagining as best we can the visual impact of it: that glorious physical strength so ravaged. We can see now that no malignant gods have brought it to pass.

It is a stroke of Sophoclean power that while his hybris is coming home to him like this it continues in him with undiminished strength. Hyllus at last succeeds in telling him the truth about Deianeira; he is as indifferent to her death as he was to her feelings when he acquired Iole to supersede her. His indifference to others continues to the end. He makes two demands of Hyllus: one, that Hyllus shall place him, still living, on a pyre and burn him; the other that Hyllus shall marry Iole, in order that no other man shall have her. From both demands Hyllus recoils in horror. The first one, therefore, Heracles will modify, but on the second he is adamant, although Hyllus regards Iole as the slayer of both his parents. Why does Sophocles contrive this? To the question there is a perfectly good scholiastic answer: in history, Hyllus and Iole were the ancestors of the Dorian tribe, the Hylleis; in the play Sophocles has departed from the main line of the tradition in making Heracles demand Iole not to be Hyllus' wife but his own concubine – Sophocles' reason for this being obvious. Therefore he must now rejoin the main line: Hyllus must marry Iole. But this would imply that Sophocles was a fool. Any competent dramatist, if all that he wanted was to rejoin the main line, would do it unobtrusively: 'Father, I cannot refuse your dying request; yes, I will marry Iole.' But Sophocles makes him protest vehemently and give way only with repugnance. An engine-driver who could not rejoin the main line with less jolting than this would soon find himself off the footplate. Sophocles is not merely satisfying the myth; he is making it work for him to the very end. Heracles' great services to humanity meet with this reward because in his personal relations he had no consideration at all for anyone else.

To Hyllus, everything has happened at once, with both parents so suddenly and cruelly destroyed. 'This is what Zeus has done to us!' he says (1022); 'Zeus is the cause of it all' (1278). 'The gods beget mortal children, and then let things like this happen to them' (1268 f.). 'The gods are cruel,' he says (1265 f.) – and we should notice that his word ἀγνωμοσύνη, 'cruelty', by rhyming with συγγνωμοσύνη, 'forbearance', points the contrast: Hyllus may reasonably ask humans to forbear with him in what he is about to do, but the physical and moral laws of the universe cannot 'forbear', or make special allowances, without destroying themselves. In this sense only are the gods 'cruel'.

The play puts before us the apparent malignity of things. Everything goes wrong. Deianeira could not have done worse, nor fared worse, had she been a vindictive murderess. Every good intention seems to be frustrated, every casual event big with disaster. Why then should we even try to behave ourselves? What is the use? The play began with Beauty and the Beast; the handsome hero vanquished the beast, but as it turns out the beauty might have had a more tolerable life with beast than with the hero. The only constant principle seems to be that nothing will ever go right.

If this is really Sophocles' picture of the human condition, then it is absurdly overdrawn, and if the ironic oracles mean that it is all foredoomed, then it is unintelligent as well. But over against the apparent chaos and malignity are set Zeus, Dike, her agents the Erinyes, and oracles that do not determine but only foresee. The Erinyes will destroy: it was they that wove the robe, and the suicide of Deianeira moves the chorus to declare: 'The new bride has born her child, an Erinys for the house.' But they destroy as the agents of Dike; what Heracles did has had its natural result. There is no malignity. A violent outbreak of hybris on the part of Heracles, a typical one, burst upon this Trachinian world; it created chaos and punished itself. But why should it punish others too – Deianeira, and Hyllus? Is this just? Antigone asked the same question: 'I am being punished for acting rightly; why then should I look to gods any more?' To this question there is no answer – for Antigone. It is not 'just', but it is Dike; it is the way in which the universe works. The conditions of life are what they are, precarious at the best: we cannot foresee the results of an innocent action, and a casual event – the coming of a well meaning messenger, for example – may have disproportionate effects. Gods could not help Antigone, precisely because the universe is *not* arbitrary. Creon's moral violence destroyed Antigone and Haemon, but it inevitably came home to him – no comfort indeed to Antigone, but we are talking of Law, not of comfort; only if there is Law can we begin even to plan for comfort. There is Law; 'nothing is here but Zeus.' Take life at its worst, as Sophocles does in this play, with Hyllus protesting against the gods: we can still see that human wrongdoing is a major cause of human suffering. In an irrational universe we could lay aside all responsibility; but there *are* gods, and they are not capricious; therefore we may not. But we should remember the human condition and not hope for too much. When the Nurse has told of Deianeira's death she continues (943 ff.):

> Therefore it is folly
> To count upon tomorrow: there is no
> Tomorrow, until we have survived today.

2. The 'Philoctetes'

There is, indeed, much that is new in the *Philoctetes*. Compared with its predecessors it is very much of an actors' play. The role of the chorus is diminished not only in extent, but also in significance, for the chorus remains firmly embedded in the immediate action, and says nothing to set it in a wider perspective. Essentially, it is a minor character in the piece, an Assistant Conspirator. What the chorus loses, the actors gain. The play might fairly be said to resolve itself into a struggle between Odysseus the schemer and Philoctetes his embittered victim, with Neoptolemus first doing his best to serve Odysseus, then, after humiliating experiences, going over without reserve to the side of Philoctetes. This, in turn, means that the part of Neoptolemus has a much wider range than any other in extant Greek Tragedy; not vertically indeed, but horizontally: there are those – Electra and Oedipus for example – who rise higher and sink lower; there are those, like Creon, who are suddenly made to see that their whole course of thought and conduct has been based on error; but in no other play is a character so treated that he enters upon one course of action, finds it more and more intolerable, abandons it, and finally does the exact opposite. Indeed, the greater part of the play, from the moment when Neoptolemus has committed himself to Odysseus, may be reasonably described as a long and inexorable turning of the screw on him in his false position. If any Greek play can be said to show development of character, it is this one. From which it follows that we should be suspicious of any interpretation of the play which does not take full account of the importance of this role. If the spiritual journey which befalls Neoptolemus is not very close indeed to the real theme of the play, Sophocles has miscalculated badly, for we cannot imagine that any responsive audience would have been disposed to give its most serious attention to something else.

There was, perhaps, some reason for treating the play as a serious but self-contained study of character and situation with no wider, religious, reference. But it was a mistake, and my mistake has been well criticized by Mr Letters,[1] who points out that we must not leave out the gods. True; but what does Sophocles mean by the gods in this play?

If only an audience could witness a play backwards, then we could accept one of two interpretations, or indeed combine them. We could say that the gods have their own plan for the capture of Troy; that this plan is obstructed first by Odysseus, who thinks that the city can be taken on his terms, and then by Philoctetes, who

[1] F. J. H. Letters, *Life and Works of Sophocles*, p. 274.

will not go to Troy at all; and that both have to learn how vain it is to try to oppose the gods. Or we could say that Sophocles is dealing with the mystery of human suffering and divine providence: Philoctetes is a hero who, inadvertently trespassing on holy ground, incurs an incurable malady; but after years of suffering, in the gods' good time, and upon his submission to the gods' will, not only is he healed but also is given undying glory in recompense.

The reason why we should have to read the play backwards in order to reach these satisfying results is that Sophocles does not give us a clear statement about either the divine plan for Troy or the origin of Philoctetes' malady until the play is nearly over (1326–47). So far as Philoctetes' sufferings are concerned, up to this point all the emphasis is laid on the brutality of the Atreidae and Odysseus, who for nearly ten years have abandoned a disabled comrade on an uninhabited island either to linger on in misery or to perish, and are now proposing to filch from him his only means of remaining alive. As for the divine plan, during most of the play we are not quite sure what it is, and the interpretation mentioned above would reduce the play to intellectual and artistic chaos; for we should have to reflect that when Neoptolemus is manfully doing his best to serve the villainous Odysseus he is helping to obstruct the gods' will in one way, and when he renounces his own hopes of glory in order to regain honour and self-respect he is only helping to obstruct it in another. Not easily will we credit Sophocles with so arid a theology.

This is a play in which, more than ever, it is necessary for the modern critic to observe quite simply what Sophocles does, and when he does it; for he does several things which, on careful analysis, prove to be very odd. In performance they escape notice – naturally, for the dramatist knew exactly what he was doing. The reason why we, today, have to be careful is that we, not being Greeks, have to reconstruct the general theology from the plays themselves, while to the original audience it would have been familiar.

At the beginning of the play it is assumed that Neoptolemus does not know that Philoctetes is to have any part at all in the capture of Troy: 'What? Am *I* then not to capture it, as I was told?' (114). Yet at the end of the play he knows in detail how the prophecy was given and what it was. Even more strangely, the poet decides that Neoptolemus shall impart this information (though it is not at all

clear how he has acquired it) just before the omniscient god appears,
with the natural result that Heracles has little to say, except to fill in
the details. Again, this is the speech in which Neoptolemus makes
his last unsuccessful attempt to persuade Philoctetes to go with him
to Troy, and he can now tell him, most impressively, not only what
the origin of his malady was, but also that it can be cured only at
Troy; yet earlier, though both Neoptolemus himself (915–26) and
Odysseus (980–1000) were desperately anxious to persuade Philoctetes, and though Odysseus knew all about the prophecy, it occurred
to neither of them to make use of this very strong inducement.
(Neoptolemus indeed says, at v. 919, that one of his purposes is
σῶσαι κακοῦ τοῦδε, but this need mean no more than 'to relieve
you of all this misery', and can mean no more than this to Philoctetes. In fact, as I have shown elsewhere in detail,[1] all these attempts
at persuasion, including the one made by the chorus in the *commos,*
are very carefully graduated by Sophocles, to the end that we shall
always accept their total rejection by Philoctetes as being, in the
circumstances, not unreasonable; Neoptolemus actually admits, at
v. 1373, 'What you say is natural.' Further, the arguments which
are used on Philoctetes are carefully limited, as we shall see; no
appeal is made in the name of the ordinary Greek soldiers who are
suffering before Troy, nor does Neoptolemus even make the
obvious point to Philoctetes that if the gods have decreed that Troy
shall fall in this way during the coming summer it is quite idle for
him to refuse.

These, and all the other details of the plot, we should expect
Sophocles to have considered carefully and to have arranged with
intelligence, in order to make on his audience the precise impact
which he wanted.

Presumably the first scene was devised with this in view. It
presents us, very forcibly, with a serious problem in political morality. If the Greeks are to capture Troy, and if Neoptolemus, the son
of Achilles, is to enjoy the glory which has been promised him, a
certain dishonourable thing must be done: the bow must be stolen.
The intelligent Odysseus explains convincingly that persuasion and
open force are both impossible; equally impossible is it for Odysseus
to show himself openly, since it was he who had marooned Philoctetes on the way to Troy: Philoctetes would naturally shoot him at

---

[1] *Form and Meaning in Drama,* pp. 121 ff.

sight with his unerring bow. Only young Neoptolemus can approach him with any hope of success; with a few deft lies he should be able to steal the bow. The σόφισμα, the 'clever stratagem', is admittedly a dirty trick, especially in the eyes of a son of the chivalrous Achilles; unfortunately, if the Greeks are to take Troy and return home, there is no alternative. For one single day Neoptolemus must be a blackguard; he will have the rest of his life in which to be an honourable man (81–85).

Such is the dilemma, one imposed by harsh political necessity, to which Neoptolemus feels obliged to capitulate; such is the opening scene, the one through which Sophocles chose to approach his audience. It will surely be strange if so challenging a problem, put before this very political Athenian audience, proves not to be near the centre of Sophocles' thinking: an honourable and necessary end cannot be attained except through inhuman treachery. Having established this, Odysseus takes himself off, with a prayer to Hermes the Crafty, and Athena goddess of the City and Giver of Victory. In the *Electra,* as in the *Choephori,* Hermes the Crafty is invoked by Orestes, with great effect; in this play neither Hermes nor Athena will do anything to help Odysseus.

Now the Chorus arrives, men from Neoptolemus' own ship. It receives its instructions (135–60); then Neoptolemus briefly indicates the wretched life that Philoctetes has been leading – of which we have been already given some pitiful details: the home-made cup and the stinking rags. The chorus might have answered: 'Poor man! Still, if we can get the bow we shall bring the war to an end.' Instead, Sophocles gives it two stanzas to sing, full of pity for Philoctetes. In reply, Neoptolemus says: 'None of this surprises me. The gods caused his sufferings – cruel Chryse; the gods did not wish him to capture Troy before the time appointed.'

As to this, we must make up our minds whether Sophocles was a bad theologian or a good dramatist. How seriously are we to take the suggestion that the gods had to inflict such misery on a man in order to prevent him from upsetting some divine time-table? Sophocles did indeed know that life comprises much that seems inexplicable; we need look no further than to the *Oedipus* and *Trachiniae.* But the whole point of these two plays is that what the hero suffers is at least not unconnected with his character and with normal human behaviour; what Chryse did to Philoctetes is quite arbitrary, and it is not until we reach the end of the play that we are told why she did it – and even then there is no suggestion that Philoctetes is anything but an innocent victim of sheer mischance. Further, if Sophocles proposes to interest us in the vast theme of unexplained suffering sent to man by the gods, he will surely do something which *will* interest us in it. In fact, from this point onwards he carefully keeps it out of sight; Philoctetes (265–7) tells us quite simply that he had been bitten by a snake, and we hear no more about it until Neoptolemus is allowed to tell the whole story at v. 1326 ff. What we do hear about, all this time, is the monstrous behaviour of the Atreidae and Odysseus; this it is in which Sophocles tries to interest us, and we should do well not to frustrate him.

Let us suppose instead that Sophocles was being intelligent. Nothing whatever was said about the origin of the wound by Odysseus: the man was disabled, he was a serious nuisance, they left him behind – that was the situation as Odysseus describes it, and that is all we know. Neoptolemus is not a brute; he has seen the horrible things in the cave, and he has the imagination to realize, in part, what Philoctetes has been enduring (163–8). Now Sophocles writes these two stanzas for the chorus, and it is in reply to them that Neoptolemus blames Chryse – and then keeps her well out of sight for over a thousand verses. Surely the dramatic purpose is obvious? It is not a matter of 'exposition', since the dramatist does not continue to expound; it is simply that Neoptolemus is desperately uneasy about the unpleasant task that Odysseus has given him, and in blaming Chryse is only trying to reassure himself; not yet will he face the fact that he is serving a trickster. It is by design that his theology is made so naïve. To Sophocles, Chryse and her holy snake have only a conventional value, as being the point from which the story begins; that is the reason why he does not even mention the snake here, or Philoctetes' inadvertent trespass. His theme is to be not the way in which the gods treat man, but the way in which men treat each other.

The screw has begun to turn on the young hero. From this point onward, all the details are so contrived as to make what he is doing seem more and more repulsive to him. We note how carefully Philoctetes' entrance is prepared, his cries of pain being heard long before he appears; how Neoptolemus has no ready answer to his first appeal: 'Do speak to me! It is not right for you to refuse me this, nor if I should refuse it to you.' It has been made clear already that if the bow is stolen, Philoctetes must perish miserably; it is a telling stroke that the man whom Neoptolemus has agreed to condemn to this fate turns out to be an old friend of his father's. The long dialogue in which Philoctetes inquires about his old comrades-in-arms is not only pathetically natural: Sophocles so directs it as to make Neoptolemus observe that war always takes the good and spares the bad – a sentiment which may well have sounded a sombrely topical note in 409 B.C., but is in any case directly dramatic, for the implication is that those whom he is now serving are not of the noblest.

He seems on the point of doing more than he hoped – of not merely stealing the bow but of abducting its owner too – when Odysseus' man arrives in the guise of a trader. This intervention is contrived by Sophocles with masterly skill. Neoptolemus' credit with Philoctetes is increased by the tale that he is being sought by such honourable characters as Phoenix and the two sons of Theseus; the true story that Odysseus is looking for Philoctetes not only makes it clear, very soon, to Neoptolemus how bitterly Philoctetes hates Odysseus, but also makes him the more eager to set sail with Neoptolemus. But there is much more than this: the pseudo-trader makes a statement about the prophecy that goes much further than anything we have yet heard: the significant new details are that Philoctetes himself, not the bow alone, must be brought to Troy if the Greeks are to succeed, and that he must be 'persuaded'.

If we are to give any credit at all to what this man says, the situation is transformed. *Must* we believe him, seeing that he is a professed liar? Perhaps we are not sure. But events are so directed that two hundred verses later Neoptolemus has accomplished all that he set out to do: Philoctetes is fast asleep, Neoptolemus has the bow; he need only walk away with it. The clever stratagem has succeeded brilliantly. Unfortunately, it is no good. When the chorus urges Neoptolemus to make off at once, Sophocles cleverly causes him to reply in hexameters, the metre of the oracles; so that if we can take a hint, we shall know that what he is saying is indubitable. 'True, he can hear nothing, but I can see that our pursuit of the bow is vain, if we sail without him. His is the glory; him the god has told us to bring. It is shame, indeed, if we must confess both to treachery and to failure.'

This is what it has come to: he has humiliated himself and brought dishonour on the name of Achilles, and success is as remote as ever. Soon he has to face realities – though not before having to endure the further humiliation of listening to Philoctetes' pathetic expressions of gratitude. There is talk of the 'loathsomeness', δυσχέρεια, of Philoctetes' foot; Neoptolemus' reply is 'Everything is loathsome, when a man is false to himself and behaves unworthily'. Briefly and bleakly he tells Philoctetes the truth. Nothing is done, by Sophocles, at this moment to make the truth sound inviting to Philoctetes. He wants to turn the screw still harder on Neoptolemus, and incidentally on Odysseus too; therefore he does nothing which might make us feel that Philoctetes is being unreasonable in refusing, for this would divert some of our attention from the clever men's predicament to the unreasonably obstinate Philoctetes.

This calculation, that we are to accept Philoctetes as a brick wall against which the others bruise their heads in vain, explains the substance of the one independent ode, which we have passed over in silence. Here only has the chorus got the stage to itself. If Sophocles thought that his play was concerned with deep theological matters, here was the opportunity of giving his audience the necessary clue. No need to pretend that his fifteen sailormen were philosophers; he need only give them a few simple reflections on the mysterious ways of the gods, or on the folly of trying to oppose them. But instead, he fills the first three stanzas with what we know perfectly well already: that Philoctetes has been suffering abominably, and alone – and we know who it was that abandoned him to suffer in this way. (In the fourth stanza, when the two men are again within earshot, the chorus resumes its role of Assistant Conspirator.) All the time, and in every detail, the emphasis is laid on the callous way in which the Greek commanders have treated Philoctetes; therefore, when at last Neoptolemus baldly says 'You have to come to the Greek army, to the Atreidae; there is no help for it' (921: πολλὴ ἀνάγκη), we are not surprised when the answer is 'I will *not* come; I will stay here and die'. So that Odysseus and Neoptolemus will have done nothing with their clever stratagem except commit a peculiarly revolting and pointless murder. No wonder that Neoptolemus says (969) 'Would to god I had never left home!'

He seems on the point of giving way when Odysseus leaps in. The next hundred verses offer a brilliant example of Sophocles' skill in the use of a silent actor; for the young man has to hear how he, in his inexperience, has been used as a catspaw by a villain in difficulties, and at the end of the scene he is reduced to such humiliation that he cannot bring himself to answer directly Philoctetes' last appeal: he can speak only to the chorus.

Odysseus had heard the prophecy given by Helenus; it would be 'logical' therefore if in his anxiety for the Greek cause he now sought to overwhelm Philoctetes' resistance by using its authority to the full. He does not; he says not a single word about the healing of Philoctetes; and what he says about the glory that will accrue to him, and about the will of Zeus, being said at such a moment by such a man, will carry no weight either with Philoctetes or with anyone in the audience; for it is a capital point in the structure of the play that we, the audience, know very little yet about the divine plan (since we are not witnessing the play backwards), and therefore are not bemused by any feeling that Odysseus is saying less than he might. When he declares 'It is Zeus, let me tell you, Zeus the lord of this earth, Zeus, who has decreed this; and I am his minister', we shall treat his assertion just as Philoctetes does: reject it with scorn. 'Disgusting creature!' he says; 'what blasphemies you invent! You make the gods your pretext, and turn them into cheats.' Something said by him a few verses later (1035–39) sounds more like Sophocles' normal theology than what Odysseus has said: 'Ruin take you all! And it will, for your treatment of me, if the gods have any concern for Dike. And I know they have, for you would never have sent a ship for a wretched man like me unless some divine compulsion were driving you to it.'

So much for the stern political necessity with which the play opened, and the consequent need to do evil in order to produce good. It now appears that the Greek commanders are caught in the recoil of their own inhumanity towards Philoctetes, and that the astute plan of Odysseus has only made things worse for them. Conceivably Neoptolemus, acting honestly, could have prevailed on Philoctetes; this new revelation of cunning and treachery has so worked on him that he tries to dash himself to death rather than go to Troy; and the swift way in which Odysseus forestalls him proves that his talk of using the bow himself is only bluff.

The *commos* that follows is like that in the *Antigone*: the chorus plays a minor part, and what it says is unconvincing. It says 'You have brought this upon yourself' (1095–1100); 'It is Fate, not any treachery of ours' (1116–22); 'Our master is only serving his friends' (1140–5); 'Accept the escape which your friend offers you' (1163–8). There is nothing here to move a man driven frantic by cruelty, a man who is now stalked and hunted as if he were an animal. Someone's resolution will break; we are not encouraged to think that it will be, or should be, Philoctetes'.

It is Neoptolemus who breaks. He returns, followed by a very anxious Odysseus. He denounces Odysseus to his face; he tells him that his cleverness has not been clever enough. He will do what is right, and defy the rage of the Greek commanders – and Philoctetes, later, assures him that they will be helpless, since the divine bow (657) will protect them both. Righteousness, it seems, is not without its strong defence.

We come to the speech in which Neoptolemus tells us things that have hitherto been kept out of sight. Since, on analysis, it is not clear why he should now possess information which he seems not to have had earlier in the play; since Odysseus, who must have had it from the beginning, was not allowed to use it when he was trying to persuade Philoctetes; and since it could now come more naturally from Heracles, because he is a god, it is evident that for some reason Sophocles wanted the information to be given at this precise moment, neither earlier nor later, and that it was relatively unimportant who should give it. It is a matter of timing. The reason why Heracles should not be chosen is clear: Philoctetes could not say No to a god without being both blasphemous and foolish; he can say No to a man, if he chooses. Therefore Sophocles wanted Philoctetes to say No, in the face of every possible inducement. On the other hand, if the full disclosure had been made earlier, before Neoptolemus had made his choice and Odysseus had been confounded, our attention would have been split. As it is, we have been entirely absorbed in the inner struggle of Neoptolemus and the total failure of Odysseus, but had we known then what we know now, we should have become preoccupied also with the extreme and hopeless obstinacy of a Philoctetes trying to oppose the gods. Sophocles has, in fact, been careful to add buttress after buttress to Philoctetes' resistance: to the sickening effect on him of his young friend's duplicity is added the sudden appearance of his arch-enemy, and to that, the indignity of being seized like a criminal. He is to remain, until the last possible moment, a brick wall, rejecting everything, arousing our pity indeed but not our censure.

Two other facts must be noticed, and they point in the same direction. It is 'illogical' that Neoptolemus should first declare the prophecy and then continue as if it could be neglected. He does do this; for he agrees to sail to Greece with Philoctetes and leave the Greek commanders to their fate without once reflecting that if this is contrary to the divine plan it cannot be done. The other fact is that the arguments which he does bring to bear on Philoctetes are all of them personal and prudential only. The theological argument, if used, would be unanswerable; he does not use it. It prepares the audience for the *dénouement,* and then is simply put into cold storage. There is another obvious argument which Philoctetes could not oppose without forfeiting much of our sympathy: that by consenting, he would be setting free thousands of Greek soldiers from their long miseries. Neoptolemus does not use it. The arguments that are used Philoctetes is entitled to reject, at his own cost, if he feels like it. He does reject them – and we should observe his reasons: the emphasis, once more, is laid on the treachery of the Atreidae; they have done such things to him that he cannot trust them; he will endure to the end rather than help them. To the last possible moment Sophocles insists on the idea that the Atreidae and Odysseus are caught in the natural consequences of their own cruelty, and that no degree of cunning will extricate them from it; while the son of Achilles, pushed to the logical extreme, is ready to renounce everything and to risk anything in order to do what is right. Neoptolemus therefore makes ready to escort Philoctetes to his ship, in order to fulfil honestly the promise which he had made dishonestly. We cannot blame Philoctetes for his obduracy, and our admiration for Neoptolemus must be unbounded; while as for Odysseus, his immoral astuteness has led to a result which is the exact opposite of what he hoped.

But for several reasons matters cannot be left like this. For one thing, Troy did fall. For another, the real theme of the play is now concluded, with the total discomfiture of political immoralism, and it would be both aesthetically and philosophically objectionable if we were left to contemplate a Neoptolemus who had to pay so heavy a price for being honest, and a Philoctetes who was left in pain for the rest of his life as the result of a mischance which was no fault of his own, and has been, throughout the play, no more than a datum. It would cause nothing but confusion if now we had to consider the problem of inexplicable suffering inflicted by the gods, when throughout our thoughts have been occupied by suffering inflicted by men. Therefore, here only in his extant plays, Sophocles employs a *deus ex machina*.

Several points claim attention. The use of the *deus*, like the realism with which Philoctetes' misery is presented, is commonly held to show the influence of Sophocles of Euripides. Perhaps it does; perhaps Sophocles would never have done these things if Euripides had not done them first. We cannot tell, nor does it matter. The important thing is to see *why* he does them here. As for the realism, it is obviously no mere dramatic effect, sought for its own sake; it is an essential part of the screw-turning. As for the *deus,* since it has been said very often, though not very intelligently, that Euripides used it in order to extricate himself from his own plots, it is not irrelevant to notice that there was no difficulty whatever in finishing this play without a *deus*. When Odysseus has been dismissed Neoptolemus could appeal to Philoctetes not only in his own interest but also on behalf of the Greek army and of Greece at large to swallow his just resentment and to end the war – a plea which the chorus could naturally reinforce, thereby finding something to say. Philoctetes could be brought to accept this, and we could reflect that generosity and humanity have triumphed where cunning and force had failed. If Sophocles rejected so obvious an ending in favour of one which involves artifice, the only reason can be that the obvious ending would have meant one thing, whereas he wanted to say something different. The ending which he did prefer, the one which takes us to the point where we see Philoctetes and Neoptolemus departing for Greece and leaving the Atreidae and Odysseus to face ruin, is one which pushes as far as possible, even beyond what was historically possible, the typically Sophoclean conception of injustice generating its own disastrous recoil. For this, he was prepared to pay the necessary price. He certainly was not using the *deus* merely because the *deus* was becoming fashionable.

The last scene then is conventional: the plot must be reconciled with history, the conventional datum of the snake-bite must be disposed of appropriately, and the two heroes must not be allowed to suffer quite irrelevantly. Sophocles accordingly makes the scene quite conventional in style; critics who find illumination and climax in the speech of Heracles pay small compliment either to Sophocles or to themselves. If we compare it with any of the considerable speeches in Sophocles we have to admit that it is singularly unexciting. As a spectacle, no doubt, the appearance of Heracles was impressive; what he says is not; no scholar in his right mind would include any of it in an anthology. It begins well enough: after all his suffering Philoctetes, like Heracles himself, is to be recompensed with glory – a satisfactory statement, but no revelation of a divine mystery. The next seventeen verses are purely factual – and the interesting facts have been anticipated by Neoptolemus. The final warning, that the conquerors of Troy should respect the holy places, is not out of place, considering what happened in the *Agamemnon* and *Trojan Women,* but it has no obvious relevance to Philoctetes and Neoptolemus. If we insist that Sophocles was trying to say something profound, we must conclude that he was getting tired; if we assume that he was not trying to do this, but only to conclude his play with a *tableau* which should set all right and satisfy τὸ φιλάν- θρωπον, our sense of natural justice, then he succeeded admirably.

CHAPTER XI

New Tragedy:
Euripides' Tragi-Comedies

This term, not altogether a satisfactory one, is intended to describe the *Alcestis, Iphigeneia in Tauris, Ion,* and *Helen,* four plays which are essentially akin, even though the *Iphigeneia* ought perhaps to be called romantic melodrama and the *Helen* high comedy. There is, indeed, ancient precedent for inability to classify these plays convincingly. The second Argument to the *Alcestis,* in a passage which is a perfect example of rule-of-thumb criticism, calls the play σατυρικώτερον, 'in the manner of the satyric play,' and states, simply on the ground of its happy ending, that it is comedy rather than tragedy, like the *Orestes.* Strange reasoning leads to strange results. There is something common to the *Alcestis* and the *Orestes,* but it is hardly comedy, and certainly not to be detected by a comparison of endings.

Needless to say, in the urbane and sophisticated *Alcestis* there is no trace of the satyric; the slightly tipsy Heracles is at the most a touch of low comedy. The play is pure tragi-comedy, like the *Ion.* Twenty years later Euripides could put a non-tragic play in the honourable part of the tetralogy; in 438, within five years of the *Antigone,* this seems to have been impossible, so that the *Alcestis,* a play more tragic and less comic than the *Helen* (which ranked as tragedy), was put in the position normally occupied by the farcical satyric play.

The differences between these four plays are considerable, but what they have in common is more fundamental. In sharp contrast with Euripides' tragedies these tragi-comedies have plots whose construction is not only free from fault but even deft and elegant to a remarkable degree; the character-drawing is no longer inconsistent, but is neat and entirely unembarrassed; and no longer are we puzzled or irritated by untimely rhetoric and sophistry. The dramatist who has been accused of utter helplessness suddenly becomes a model of virtuosity. But for all that there are problems, problems which again unite the four plays. It is not altogether easy for us to take up the correct critical attitude to them. We find, in disturbing proximity, the grave and the gay, or what is worse the grave and the flippant. Alcestis' death is sandwiched between a flippant treatment of the grim figure of Death and a scene between Admetus and Pheres which is never far from comedy or satire, and the burlesquing of Heracles is to follow. Calling the play 'satyric' may stand for an explanation of the burlesque, but it does not explain the tragedy. The *Ion* offers on the one hand the anguish and the mortal danger of Creusa, and on the other the broad comedy of Xuthus. The *Helen* is comedy from beginning to end, yet its messenger-speech costs the death of fifty or so innocent Egyptians, and its first formal ode (1107 ff.) touches a purely tragic note when it deals with the Trojan War.

If Euripides is a good and consistent dramatist, one worthy of his fame, there should be one explanation of these features, or at least a critical point of view from which they appear logical and coherent. Or can we, time after time, only shrug our shoulders and say 'Oh! Euripides again'? Pearson, a discreet critic, remarks – in the introduction to his *Helen* (p. 22) – 'It will be observed how Helen, in referring to the story of Leda, qualifies her reference by the expressions "if this story is true" (21), "as they say" (259). No reasonable excuse has been, or can be, offered for this defect.' In these points, then, details indeed but obtrusive ones, was Euripides quite insensitive? It is possible; it is possible, too, that the critic is looking from the wrong viewpoint. It is a simple matter to see that these plays are tragi-comedies, but it is also necessary to draw and apply the correct critical deductions from this.

Verrall, as often, helps us with one of his illuminating mistakes; he could not bring himself to believe that these plays, or at least the *Ion,* were not deadly serious: 'If the speech of Athena is really the Poet's last word . . . then Euripides cannot be acquitted of trifling and paltering with everything that deserves respect . . . then indeed, for such a purpose and to such an end, he had no right to drag us through the windings of such a labyrinth.' His Introduction to the *Ion* suggests that tragi-comedy is perhaps one of mankind's intermittent tastes. Certainly this criticism of Verrall's might be aimed with as much effect against Shakespeare. Is it possible that the awful scene of the wicked Jew sharpening his knife against Antonio is contrived only to excite the audience? Portia holds the ace of trumps all the time, and Shylock has committed himself irretrievably; why does she hold it back? Why is Antonio put to the agony of baring his breast, of seeing his vindictive enemy stretch out his hand to him? Surely nothing but the most intense tragic conception can justify this? But the tragic conception is not there. The play proceeds to the comedy of the rings, and ends with a passage which school editions discreetly omit. The agony of Antonio serves only to give the audience its thrill – yet the *Merchant* is a good play, not a monstrosity to be excused by the plea of Elizabethan taste. The reason is that it is composed within the conventions proper to tragi-comedy, which are by no means the same as those of tragedy. One important difference is that the plot of a tragedy must appear real, but the plot of a tragi-comedy may be, and normally is, entirely artificial. The crucial point seems to be that the existence which Antonio enjoys is considerably less real than that of a tragic hero; for, to go no further, the single and improbable fact that on this particular occasion all Antonio's argosies are wrecked demonstrates of itself that we are moving in a world of make-believe different from the more serious make-believe of tragedy. Antonio has his being within the conventions proper to tragi-comedy, and we can accept the momentary agony because we know that these conventions will somehow prevent the knife from cutting.

In considering these four plays of Euripides' we must begin, as always, by asking ourselves what the dramatist was trying to do. We have seen even the admired Sophocles laying himself open to the charge of faulty construction because he was concerned not with making impeccable plays but with expressing a tragic idea; we have seen, from the *Medea* onwards, that Euripides' loyalty to his tragic conceptions led him further and further from academic standards of dramatic form; more than once we have seen our dramatists disdaining a stroke that would have been superficially effective because it was not the stroke that the idea demanded; the word 'effective' belongs not to the classical but to a late stage of the art.[1] That stage has now arrived. Hitherto Tragedy has been religious – not necessarily in the sense of being pious, but of trying to

[1] See above, p. 35.

see the world of gods and men as one, and of expressing, in the traditional Greek way, all that is permanent in it as θεοί, gods. Drama now ceases to be informed, and therefore controlled, by some dominant tragic conception, whether that be religious or not. For when all allowance is made for the serious, critical strain in the *Ion* and *Iphigeneia*, it is evident that the first purpose of the dramatist in writing these plays was to create an effective stagepiece; to exploit the resources of his art for their own sake, not for the sake of something bigger.

Therefore the dramatist, for the first time, is free to attend entirely to his 'form', unhampered by any tragic conception working its imperious will on the play. He can devote himself completely to excellence of workmanship; in fact he must, for this is now his whole 'meaning'. In this respect only, we may compare these plays with minor poetry; it is when the poet has nothing in particular to say that he must be most elegant and attractive.[1]

Because these plays have a more limited scope than the tragedies we have entirely to change our critical premisses. Alcestis and Antonio are less real than Oedipus and Macbeth; theatrical reality takes the place of tragic, that is to say universal, reality. It is to be noticed that all these plays are founded on an impossibility, and that not a 'probable impossibility', like the evocation of Darius, but one which is presented as a fiction. By cheating the Fates Apollo prolongs Admetus' life – if he can find a substitute; the *Iphigeneia* and *Helen* start from a miraculous substitution; the *Ion* is based on a divine parentage and miraculous rescue which – told as they are here – nobody would believe. But the whole basis of serious Greek tragedy has been reality. The supernatural could readily be admitted as a dramatic accessory – a probable impossibility – but the essence of the whole thing, from the Suppliants down to the Greeks of the *Troades*, was that real persons in a real situation act and suffer in a real way. Medea's chariot is no exception to this principle; it is not a mere accessory, and it is miraculous; but it is used symbolically, a pointer to an even higher reality. Greek tragedy is always in immediate contact with the conditions and problems of life. Even

[1] The critic of Euripides has much to complain of, but in one important point he is fortunate. We know the date of two of these well-made plays; the *Alcestis,* 438, and the *Helen,* 412; the ill-made plays come between. The critic is not therefore under the obligation of refuting a theory that at one period of his career Euripides made good plots, at another bad ones. Here at least it is evident that date explains nothing, dramatic purpose everything.

the *Tyrannus,* in spite of its double interference by the god in the normal course of human affairs, derives all its significance from the fact that it faithfully reflects the conditions of human life as we know them to be. It is firmly based on realities.[1]

This basis is now cut away. From artificial situations like these there can grow no tragic $\mu\hat{v}\theta o\varsigma$, no action which will show us, as it develops, what are the terms and conditions of mortal life. Instead of the tragic reality which we have been studying we have what we may call a theatrical reality – for Reality, like the gods, has many forms. Euripides expects us to be moved by Alcestis' death, but not as we are moved by Antigone's or Polyxena's The emotion is limited to the play and to the moment – like our emotion in the presence of Antonio's peril; we feel (if we choose to examine our feelings) that the emotion is temporary because the whole situation, is fictive and unreal; it is tempered by our assurance that the outcome must be a happy one – for otherwise there would be no point at all, since the death of Alcestis cannot prove, illuminate or reveal anything in particular. The happy ending in fact takes the place of the tragic catharsis.

Further, although if we are wise we shall make the most of the delicate sentiment of the scene, what we make of it is necessarily modified by what we have heard in the prologue – by Apollo's remark to Death for example: 'What? You among the intelligentsia?'[2] Our deepest emotions can be engaged only lightly; the appeal is by turns to our sentiment, to our intelligence, to our curiosity. In the *Iphigeneia,* Orestes and Pylades stand in deadly peril which they, like Antonio, have done nothing to deserve; Euripides thrills us with the peril, but obviously only that he may also thrill us by the escape. These emotions have no roots in the eternal order of things; they are lightly engaged, and can therefore be lightly transferred to something else, to comedy, satire, criticism, burlesque. In fact, they must be, for the dramatic material in these plays is not such as to bear the weight of long concentration on any one point.

In this new world of theatrical convention the scenes of pathos are delicately edged with conventionality. Helen's seventeen years of widowhood are not funny – for tragi-comedy means not that everything is comic, but that nothing is tragic – yet it would be silly of us

[1] See above, p. 139.

[2] Only a slight over-translation of v. 5

to grow indignant with the gods about them. We must not play the game by the wrong set of rules. Creusa's suffering and Iphigeneia's grief come nearer to tragedy, but, between ourselves, these things are not real. We must indulge our sentiments only within the convention; in five minutes we shall be smiling again – the show-man will be showing us the amusingly pious cowherd or a ridiculous scene between Ion and Xuthus. How real these scenes of pathos are to be, each spectator must decide for himself. No doubt there were those in Athens who found the death of Alcestis infinitely tragic and beautiful, so much less disturbing than that terrible affair of Anti-gone; but for all that the distinction between tragedy and pathos is a clear one.

It appears then that the absence of a tragic theme is the direct explanation both of the regular form and brilliant execution of these plays, and of the blend that they present of the pathetic, the amusing and the melodramatic. But intellectual profundity is as alien to this tragi-comedy as is moral profundity; we look in vain for any serious purpose beyond the serious purpose of creating such elegant drama. What we do find is flashes of satire and criticism such as we can take in our stride; passages of serious moralizing, common in the tragedies, are altogether absent. The *Ion* is full of obvious criticism of Delphi, but it is conveyed easily, never allowed to stand for long in the foreground. Ion may briefly expound the doctrine that if the gods are not just they are not gods, but the interest of the passage lies in the manner rather than in the matter, in Ion's delightful 'I must speak to Apollo. What is he thinking of?';[1] and in his conclusion that if they do not mend their ways the gods will find their temples empty. The play indeed contains more ridicule than criticism; the keynote is given by the ludicrous behaviour of Hermes in the pro-logue – hiding in the laurels in order to see the play not proceeding according to plan. Nowhere do we find serious passages like those of Hecuba on education or of Theseus on democracy. It is true that we have from Menelaus an abundance of solemn adages, and from the messenger in the *Helen* views about divination,[2] just as in the *Electra* we have the advantage of hearing Orestes, the honest Peasant, and the Old Man successively on True Nobility, but in none of these passages is Euripides saying anything which he con-

[1] *Ion*, 436–7.

[2] On which see below, p. 317.

siders to have any but a purely dramatic value. The plays are a constant appeal to our intellect, but in order that we may appreciate the intrigue, the wit, the irony, not in order that we may grasp a thesis.

Indeed it is a capital point in the estimation of these plays that in them Euripides is not a minority poet, as Verrall supposed. Euripides makes fun of legend, exposes divination, attacks Delphi, ridicules Heracles, the Dioscuri and Hermes – but how? Much as Aristophanes did, and certain vase-painters before him. 'Belief' is a complex thing. Athenians who would believe heartily at the Panathenaea were obviously prepared to laugh just as heartily when a comic poet asked what would happen to the estate when Zeus died, whether Athena would be married off as an ἐπίκληρος. The Greeks, never having had much personal reverence for their anthropomorphic gods, were ready to take them (in Homer as well as in the fifth century) seriously or comically. Because, for serious political, ceremonial or artistic purposes, they could take them seriously, we are not to suppose that they could not also see their funny side – or call them remarkable people because they did. They were ready to laugh when Aristophanes supplied Prometheus with an umbrella, and with obscene jokes against the upper gods, or when Euripides makes Hermes hide in the shrubbery. This does not mean that the Athenians had 'outgrown' the serious treatment of the gods, such as Prometheus and Hermes received in the *Prometheus Vinctus*. Euripides guyed Heracles in the *Alcestis,* but a dozen years later he could treat the same Heracles with a splendid earnestness in the *Hercules Furens*.

Euripides offends his critic by making Helen cast doubt on the story of Leda's egg. But he is not, with a maladroit solemnity, informing Athens that in his opinion this ancient story is not true. Nobody believed that it was true, so that everybody found it extremely funny that Helen herself should share their scepticism. Euripides 'attacks' divination (*Helen,* 744 ff.). And how does this attack compare in tone with the attack on the war-spirit in the *Suppliant Women*? The passage is introduced by the laughable dismay of the Messenger at finding Helen on the stage after all; it is delivered after the sententious fellow has been ordered off on important business by Menelaus; then, when he has declared his views, the Chorus emphatically corroborates (being also among the elect); and Helen remarks, upon his exit,

Ε̃ἶεν· τὰ μὲν δὴ δεῦρ' ἀεὶ καλῶς ἔχει.

Very good. – So far then all is well.

If all this contained the serious publication of an important view, it would be incredibly inept; if, however, the poet is so sure that the audience is with him that it will laugh at rationalism when it is untimely, then the comedy is exquisite.

Athens had experienced enough in recent years to warrant mistrust of superstition and divination, and there was Aristophanic precedent for laughing at oracles; Delphi, however, as a powerful corporation, was a different thing and had to be taken more seriously. Yet here, too, it is evident that Euripides felt himself going with the tide. In the *Iphigeneia* he suggests that in sending Orestes to the Tauri 'Apollo' was trying to rid himself of an awkward client – having failed to buy off more than half the Furies. In this, Euripides is serious; but how serious? If the suggestion was one which he felt would not be accepted without resistance, one which he would have to maintain strongly, he must have put it in the forefront of his play, free from the distractions of an exciting plot. If, on the other hand, it was a view which the audience, or a sufficient part of it, would be ready to accept with satisfaction and without advocacy, the treatment of Apollo takes its place naturally as an intellectual stiffening in a play which is essentially one of incident and romantic colour.

In the *Ion* the point seems clear. Creusa was ravished by Apollo, bore her child in secret, laid it where the god had taken her – and nobody was any the wiser. Obviously Euripides does not believe the story; is he trying to suggest to his audience that it is not true and would be discreditable if it were? No; he solemnly pretends that it is true. It is Ion, not his creator, who is the simple-minded rationalist, who points out that the god will not answer questions to his own discredit, who warns Zeus against bankruptcy, who at the end takes his mother aside and says, 'Look you, Mother; are you sure you are not doing what so many women do, throwing the blame on to the god?' But Ion's suspicions are wrong. As Athena says (1595 ff.), 'Apollo hath done all things well. First, he brought thee to the birth without sickness, so that none of thy friends knew . . .' This must be accepted as dramatically true, not because a goddess says it, but because it is an assumption necessary for the whole play. Besides, the supernatural machinery must stand or fall together; if there is no

Apolline paternity there can be no Gorgon's blood, no Erichthonius sprung from the soil, no miraculous olive. But the wit of the whole piece lies in the conspiracy which Euripides makes with the audience; the conviction that these things are false was held so widely in Athens that there was no point in insisting that they are false, but great amusement in pretending that they are true. So with the respectable old legend that Delphi was the centre of the earth:

CHORUS. And there is another thing which perhaps I may not ask
        of thee ...
ION.   Speak: what wouldst thou know?
CHORUS. Doth the house of Phoebus in very truth stand upon
        Earth's navel?
ION.   Yea, girt with garlands, and around it are Gorgons.
CHORUS. So have I always heard.

It is the perfect picture of the awe-struck tourist.

In the *Ion* Euripides is not earnestly protesting and perpetually uncertain whether it is comedy or tragedy that he is writing. The actual untruth of the story of Creusa removes it from the world of tragedy to the world of pathos; but the pretence that all is real – and that Hermes is looking on – is an inexhaustible source of dramatic interest, from delicate insinuation to broad farce, one mood swiftly succeeding another until, after many thrills, checks, surprises and disappointments, Athena appears, to build a magnificent structure on some very shaky foundations, and to assure us that from this very bewildered Ion will spring the detailed heroes of the Ionian race, and that for the sake of Greece at large Xuthus and Creusa also will have their ancestral sons. This, of course, we receive in reverent silence; and it all goes to prove (as the chorus points out) that the good prosper and the wicked don't.[1]

Such then are the most important of the conditions which

---

[1] It is surely a mistake to take this antiquarianism seriously (as does M. Grégoire, ed. Budé, pp. 168 ff.). The Attic legends are handled in exactly the same sly way as the Delphian one above. As soon as Ion hears that Creusa is from Athens he says, with the eager *naïveté* just shown by the chorus, 'Was your father's grandfather really born of the soil?' 'Did your father really slay your sisters?' Again, Creusa cannot bring herself to mention the Gorgon's blood without telling the whole tale from a ridiculously long way back. Is all this the pious commemoration of national legends? No; the manner is all wrong. Even in matters of patriotism style counts for something. If Attic patriotism is connected with these passages (as may well be the case), it is surely that other tragedians were patriotically antiquarian, while Euripides reserved to himself the humbler role of laughing at their efforts in this good-humoured way.

governed tragi-comedy: absence of a tragic theme, avoidance even of an intellectual theme such as would demand serious advocacy, the adoption of a new standard of reality which, by reducing the tragic to the pathetic, made it possible to combine harmoniously into one theatrical whole a wide range of emotional effects. It is unnecessary to examine the separate plays as fully as we have done the separate tragedies, because the form is very similar to that of Middle Tragedy, and in these plays it undergoes no essential development. We may, however, consider some points in which the style of tragi-comedy differs notably from that of Middle Tragedy.

We have seen already that the Euripidean tragi-comedy reverts to the normal type of plot. Formally, the *Iphigeneia* obeys the same Aristotelian canons as the *Tyrannus*; a fact which Aristotle duly acknowledges. But though these plots obey the laws (a fact that we need not stay to demonstrate) they obey them in a new spirit, and the new spirit causes interesting changes in technique.

The impetus and the real unity of the typical Sophoclean plot comes from the purity and force of the original tragic inspiration. Now we find the same general plan, the development of a dramatic situation through surprise and disappointment to an unforeseen close; but since there is no big tragic theme to absorb the attention of the audience, the dramatist has to do other things. No longer do we find scenes like those between Haemon and Creon, Oedipus and Creon, in which one unbroken dramatic rhythm sweeps through the whole, from a level start to an exciting climax; the intrinsic importance of the dramatic material would not be big enough to support it. The events which compose the plot now have a different status; they have their dramatic value simply as events, not as the revelation of a tragic character or as the significant play of circumstances upon a tragic character. Accordingly the flow of events must be made as interesting and varied as possible; compare with the typical Sophoclean scene the long stichomythia between Ion and Creusa, which moves easily and naturally among half-a-dozen topics; or any scene in the *Helen*. Characteristic of the new style is the most amusing 'recognition scene' between Ion and Xuthus. Underlying all the wit and fun is the exciting possibility that Xuthus may after all turn out to be the father and not Apollo; there is the amusing contrast between Xuthus' happy confidence and Ion's puzzled reluctance; when all this has diverted us, Ion gives a sudden check to the plot, and to Xuthus' cheerfulness, by considering the situation in an analytical speech which is a new source of interest, and by deciding that on the whole he prefers to stay where he is. This typical stroke is repeated at v. 1340, when Ion thinks it better not to examine the tokens and not to search for his mother. The dramatist is, as it were, playing cat and mouse with his audience; he erects unforeseen obstacles in order to surmount them with éclat. In the same way, Theoclymenus comes near to wrecking the plan of escape in the *Helen*. Helen should stay on shore – lest grief for her dead husband should cause her to drown herself. The irony is pleasing, and we are set on the *qui vive* to see how Helen will overcome this unfortunate considerateness.

The *Iphigeneia* offers a good example of this new necessity of keeping the plot always on the move. Iphigeneia (578–96) suggests sparing Orestes and sacrificing Pylades, in order that the one who knows Argos so well may take her letter. Orestes objects; let her save Pylades, who has no cause to welcome death. She agrees, and the brother and sister discuss the manner of the sacrifice (617–43) – Pylades all this time remaining silent. Why? Is he screwing up his courage to the point of self-sacrifice? No; he is silent simply for the sake of the plot. He does not speak until v. 672 – and then he says the wrong thing; he insists not on dying instead of Orestes, but on dying with him. Is this because he is a romantic and foolish young man? If such he appears, it is an added point, but Euripides was not really concerned with Pylades' character – what indeed is Pylades? The whole manœuvre is intended simply to keep the situation moving. First the sister proposes, on pathetically flimsy grounds, to save the brother; then the dreadful substitution is made and allowed to pass unchallenged; then Pylades insists on dying, too, because if he does Iphigeneia cannot be rescued and the whole thing is ruined. The situation is screwed up tight, and our interest in the recognition-scene becomes the more intense.

Above all, now that there is no tragic climax, the dramatist must see to it that his ending does not fall flat. The *Iphigeneia* has its palpitating story of the contrary winds and the last-minute reprieve.[1] The *Helen* cannot be allowed to peter out in an easy escape followed

---

[1] This is very much like the reprieve at the end of *The Beggar's Opera*. (The obvious artificiality of it may be intended to suggest to us the more tragic ending, that 'Apollo' did in fact trick his client to his death.)

by the divine summary of things present and to come; therefore the messenger-speech itself is made exciting with its tale of sanguinary combat on the high seas, and then, in order to make the expected arrival of the *Deus* opportune, the wicked Theoclymenus must threaten to murder his sister. Now the god can step in to some effect – but no; Euripides still finds life in his plot, and gives us yet another thrill by producing a gallant slave who forbids the murder and cries 'Only across my dead body!' So, as in all these plays, the movement is kept up until the last possible moment – but the last moment, too, needs attention. The entirely artificial *Deus* is a happy way of bringing to a close plots which were artificial, too, in their inception,[1] but, unless the god is presented satirically, his winding-up speech may be a little perfunctory and dull. This danger Euripides meets with aetiology and topical allusions.

It is the *Alcestis* that has the most instructive ending. The simple restoration of Alcestis by Heracles, with speeches of bewildered gratitude from Admetus – Alcestis, too, saying something suitable to the occasion – would obviously be flat, and (because out of keeping) uncomfortable too. Shakespeare, in similar circumstances, would keep up the atmosphere of tragi-comedy by pretending that his restored heroine was a statue; Euripides is cleverer. Alcestis is veiled, and by a convenient excuse (1144 ff.) kept silent. This enables Euripides to present one of his few triangular scenes, one as cleverly used as any of Sophocles'. With a very piquant irony Heracles declares her to be the prize he has won in a wrestling-match, and his request that Admetus should look after her produces the delightful scene in which Admetus deplores temptation, protests, before the living Alcestis, his complete devotion to the dead Alcestis, rehabilitates his reputation with us, and lays the foundation for a future matrimonial happiness which otherwise must have seemed insecure. Now the happy disclosure of the truth can be made briefly, in the agreeable atmosphere of unreality. It is a brilliant scene which avoids all the dangers and brings the play to a triumphant close within the conventions.

[1] We may notice that had Euripides felt as apologetic about the *Deus* as do some of his critics, he might have ended the *Helen* with Theonoe, who is already on the premises, and knows things present and things to come quite as well as the Dioscuri (vv. 13 ff.). But it is much more interesting to see the deified brothers of our late heroine, and they also enable Euripides to contrive the little melodrama mentioned above.

The enacting of an exciting story makes for unity of plot, but the need for continuous piquancy of situation appreciably tempers the logic of that plot. The willing suspension of reason which we have to make in order to accept the initial situation is called upon again and again. For example, Pylades could have ruined the *Iphigeneia* by doing an obvious and natural thing, turning to the chorus at v. 669 and asking who the strange Greek woman was. In the *Helen* we are asked to assume that the fall of Troy was unknown in Egypt seven years after the event – this in spite of the presence of Theonoe the omniscient. In tragedy such weak links in the chain would be ruinous, for the strain on it is great; the succession of significant cause and effect must be close, and improbability in behaviour avoided. Now, since little depends on it except our own enjoyment, we are content to be bluffed if the bluff is worth while; and if the play is a comedy, we may even relish a *non sequitur* for its own sake. The entirely 'unjustified' introduction of Teucer is in keeping with the delicious comedy of the whole of the *Helen*; such invaders as the Boeotian or Meton in Aristophanes are not far removed from him in spirit.

The effect of the new theatrical reality can be traced a little further. Because the plays are not, as it were, about anything in particular, material can be used which would have been intolerable earlier. Because no serious theme is going to fill the *Ion* the play can start with an extended movement drawing most of its interest from sheer naturalism. Ion busy about his morning tasks – and dropping remarks like Φοῖβός μοι γενέτωρ πατήρ – is indeed both dramatic and naturalistic, for we both enjoy the scene for its own sake (saying with Aristotle τοῦτ᾽ ἐκεῖνο 'How very lifelike!'), and absorb the holy atmosphere of the temple, as at the beginning of the *Eumenides,* in order that the breaking of that calm may be the more effective. The chorus, however, wandering tourist-like about the precincts, is pure naturalism; we are very close now to Herondas and to Gorgo and Praxinoa in Theocritus. Tragedy may offer a touch of realism occasionally as a foil, but only the absence of a tragic theme can permit the complete diversion of our minds to naturalism for its own sake.

The point is even clearer in the messenger-speech. This has to announce that the plot against Ion has failed, that Creusa's guilt is patent, and that the Delphians are hot upon her trail to kill her for the attempted murder. The moment is one of extreme urgency, but this does not prevent the messenger from delivering a speech twice as long as those usual in Sophocles. What is stranger, the first third of this speech is devoted to the pitching and decorating of the marquee – a topic which surely could wait.

Obviously, if our minds were seriously engaged on an important issue this elaborate irrelevance would be unendurable; but they are not. Creusa's attempt on Ion's life has been treated in a perfectly conventional and non-moral spirit;[1] we are to be interested in the events simply as fact, and the more remarkable the facts, the greater our interest. Noble simplicity is in abeyance. In the *Septem* the messenger says 'The brothers have slain each other', and it is enough; if the messenger here had said 'Ion has escaped' it would be nothing at all. We must hear the manner of the escape, and it must be an interesting story, and if the poet chooses to elaborate it with a brilliant bit of descriptive introduction, so much the better. It is a new source of interest, and tragi-comedy is very hospitable.[2] Here we are even nearer to Alexandrianism, for example to the maker of that cup of ivy-wood and to Theocritus who describes it so vividly in his first idyll. Neither the carver nor the poet is possessed with any intrinsically important idea, so that both can devote themselves to showing the veins swelling in the old fisherman's neck. That Euripides knows perfectly well what he is doing here, and is not merely giving way to a brilliant garrulity, is shown by the fact that he keeps Creusa herself off the stage while the speech is going on.[3]

The opposite of naturalism is sheer theatricality, and this is admitted freely, particularly in the lighter plays. The delightful extreme is surely the appeal to Theonoe in the *Helen* (761 ff.). After the suicide-pact and the ensuing rhetoric from Menelaus comes in the omniscient priestess, to Helen's dismay, announcing that she is the arbiter between Hera and Aphrodite: shall she or shall she not reveal Menelaus' arrival to her brother? So ridiculous a situation

[1] See below, p. 326.

[2] Comparison with the messenger-speech in the *Hippolytus* is instructive. That brilliant description sounds a little frigid because it is, to some extent, mere decoration on a tragic theme.

[3] Similar examples of naturalism are to be found in the *I.T.*, 67–76 and 620–40. Both passages recall the *Philoctetes*; the reconnaissance of the temple is paralleled by the search for the cave, and both Iphigeneia and Philoctetes spend some time asking about old friends. There is no reason to suspect direct imitation: the effect is natural in each case.

cannot move in us any serious emotion, but we shall be ready to enjoy a neat piece of argumentation or any other intellectual pleasure that can be offered. Accordingly first Helen puts forward the appropriate arguments in an effective speech; then the chorus, perfectly appreciating the unreality of the occasion, says, 'Piteous words! Piteous art thou too! I long to hear what speech Menelaus will make in defence of his life.'

Menelaus is wonderful; the Rev. Mr Collins himself could have done no better. He cannot bring himself to weep – a disgrace to Troy – though they do say that it is quite proper to weep in misfortune; but such propriety, if it be propriety, he will not place before Courage. Theonoe may well think it right to save them; if not, he will be miserable and she wicked. But, he says, I can best do myself justice and touch your heart by addressing this tomb. Accordingly he invokes Proteus' aid, though 'I know that thou, being dead, canst never give me back Helen, but thy daughter here will never tolerate a blot on thy name.' Even this is surpassed by the terrific and convincing argument addressed to Hades: 'For her sake thou hast received many dead, slain by my sword; thou hast thy fee. Now either restore these to life again, or make Theonoe give me back my wife.' Finally to a shivering Theonoe the direful alternative to honour is proclaimed – two corpses slain by this sword lying side by side on this tomb.[1] 'There,' he says, 'action for me, not tears!'

The *Helen*, as is natural, is full of wit:

MEN. Gates whence I was driven away like a beggar.
HEL. What? Thou wert not begging, surely? Woe is *me*!
MEN. Such 'twas in fact, but 'twas not called so. (790–2.)

The wit approaches parody as the dramatist, no longer fiercely intent on the matter in hand, can look about him in a critical spirit. Thus Helen begins to outline her plot by saying that she will cut her hair in mourning-fashion:

MEN. And what help lies there? For there is a certain antiquity in the suggestion.

In the *Ion* fun and parody are used for a special purpose. Creusa's old servant, who arrives rather mysteriously from nowhere, is

---

[1] Τόδε, τοῦδε, clearly suggesting Menelaus' overacting.

funny first in the naturalistic way opened up by Clytemnestra's Watchman. He puffs his way up to the temple with αἰπεινά τοι μαντεῖα[1], and produces a stream of things like τοῦ ἀπόντος οὐ κρατῶ, τὸ τοῦ ποδὸς μὲν βραδὺ τὸ τοῦ δὲ νοῦ ταχύ[2] – excellent peasant-wit. But when he goes off on his poisoning errand, he is absurd in another way, for his apostrophe to his 'aged foot' is a deliberate parody of tragic diction; and it may legitimately raise doubts about v. 753:

Χο.	ἰὼ δαῖμον.
Πρ,	τὸ φροίμιον μὲν τῶν λόγων οὐκ εὐτυχές.[3]

Was Housman the first to write this kind of thing in fun? But calculation as well as ebullience lurks here, for all this fun surrounds the laying of the murderous plot by Creusa, and it is there partly to prevent us from taking the plot too seriously. There is none of it in the *Medea*, where also a murderous plot is laid; Euripides wants to see to it that we shall not make the mistake of turning Creusa into a Medea.

This whole scene is a good example of the new 'theatre'. Indignation and amusement, rage and despair, follow each other swiftly. Creusa's confession is put in the form of a monody not because that is the most natural form but because it is the most effective; in fact Euripides could scarcely afford sober simple eloquence, for that would at once raise Creusa from the theatrical to the tragic. Again, the laying of the plot is steeped in convention – to prevent us from considering it morally. There is the Old Man, the bad adviser, quite certain what has happened and what is going to happen. He puts forward the usual string of fantastic suggestions ('Burn down the temple!') which the clever Euripidean woman[4] disposes of before outlining her own plot. There is the assumption that to murder Ion is the most natural thing in the world: 'Come! do something womanly! Take to the sword, or to poison.' It is magnificent – but it is not anti-feminism. Finally, there is the absurd pedantry by which Creusa cannot mention her poisons without going back and back to

---

[1] 'Oracles are a bit steep!' (referring to their notorious obscurity).

[2] 'I can't do the impossible.' 'Slow in the legs but quick in the head.'

[3] CHOR. Ah! God!
   O.M.   The prelude of thy speech is not auspicious.

[4] These two characters already smack of New Comedy.

the 'battle of the earth-born'. The comedy must not obscure the pathos, but we must not mistake good 'theatre' for simple tragedy.

One more surface-effect should be mentioned, the new irony. The *Iphigeneia,* naturally not very rich in wit and fun, is full of this. At v. 149, just after we have seen Orestes in the flesh, Iphigeneia appears lamenting his death.[1] This ironical situation becomes the basis of further ironies; at v. 344, for example, when she hears that Greeks have come, Iphigeneia exclaims that before she was always full of pity when Greeks fell into her hands, but now, made cruel by the dream, she will have no mercy, whoever they are. The psychology of this does not seem very clear, but the theatrical effect is excellent. This is not tragic irony, though in this play it may make a similar effect, since Iphigeneia is in apparent danger of fulfilling the dream. Tragic irony assumes security where there is none, in order to emphasize the hero's blindness; now a state of affairs contrary to the truth is assumed merely to increase the piquancy of the situation. The real purpose of the dream is to make the eventual recognition more striking; not only does Iphigeneia not know that her brother is present, but she even has reason for thinking that he cannot be. In more strenuous days the gap between the real and the apparent truth was used for quickening our tragic apprehensions; now, at the most, it quickens our theatrical apprehensions. Very often (as at *I.T.,* 611, 627, 629) it amounts only to a double-entendre; in at least one passage in the *Electra* it becomes practically a stage-aside;[2] thus, being addressed only to our intellect it is really a kind of wit, akin to the ironies of comedy – which it soon becomes, in the *Helen.*

Tragi-comedy then may obey certain important canons derived from Middle Tragedy, but its style and its real logic are totally different. As it appeals to our sensations rather than to our apprehensions, it must make its plot continually exciting; in place of the steady development necessary to tragedy it must present sudden changes of mood and unexpected turns of plot. It can do this the more easily because there is much more room for sheer artificiality of contrivance, and because it can call upon a very wide range of

[1] The use made by Sophocles of Clytemnestra's dream affords an interesting contrast with this.

[2] Eur., *El.,* 224, where Orestes says to the frightened Electra, 'There is no one whom I have a better right to touch.' Since Orestes is not about to reveal himself – quite the contrary – the remark has no dramatic point but it does amuse the audience. The effect is repeated at v. 282.

M

effect – pathos, pure excitement, amusement in all its forms, simple naturalism, exciting even if irrelevant description. Besides plot there are two other elements of drama that we must briefly consider, the use of the Chorus, which we can more conveniently deal with in our next section, and characterization.

Characterization, like plot, becomes in Euripides' tragi-comedies something very different from what it was in his tragedies. We lose altogether the stridency which the tragic theme imposed on some characters and the inconsistency to which it condemned others, but for all that we do not return to Sophoclean standards of variety and conviction. It was, of course, impossible, for in plays which are essentially plays of incident, characterization cannot be very significant and becomes very largely a mere decoration. The *Alcestis*, inasmuch as one side of it is close to the comedy of manners, has its lifelike characters in Admetus and Pheres; and Alcestis, who might so easily have been a purely conventional figure in that unreal setting, derives individuality from her evident mistrust of her husband (cf. vv. 371 ff.); but in the *Iphigeneia* and *Helen* nothing depends on character except the contriving of an escape by a clever woman. The two savage kings must be conventionally pious and credulous, but Orestes and Pylades, Menelaus, Teucer and the minor characters can be, one might almost say, what they like (provided that they are interesting when they have a chance), while the fairy-godmother Theonoe can hardly be anything but a vague outline. But if they can be what they like they cannot be anything profound, for profound characterization implies a strict relation to significant action; they may, however, be interesting, and Euripides makes them interesting when he can.[1] Character-drawing has become an 'effect', like the others we have examined. Thoas' character goes a little beyond what his part demands; he is pleasantly and unexpectedly considerate – like the cannibal king in the parable, he, too, is a Balliol man. Menelaus' unfailing pomposity and complacency is a continual delight – but what are Orestes and Pylades? It would perhaps be possible to tabulate qualities for them, but they do not make an individual impression; the drama in which they move is too strong for playful or decorative character-drawing, and as it is not a drama of their own making (except for Iphigeneia's scheme)

---

[1] The qualification is added because Pylades and Orestes, for example, can have little chance to display character.

it does not vividly illuminate what they are. In the *Ion* we have, besides the hero, a pleasantly silly Xuthus, and a Creusa about whose characterization we must be careful, lest we turn her into a tragic, Medea-like person whom Euripides did not want. Ion himself is a brilliant sketch – as brilliant as Plato's Ion or his Euthyphro – and he has his *Aufklärung,* which is neatly done; but the contrast with the *Philoctetes* is interesting. Sophocles' play is serious drama with a brilliant plot as a subsidiary interest; Euripides' has a brilliant plot, and all the rest is subsidiary.

CHAPTER XII

New Tragedy:
Euripides' Melodramas

1. The 'Electra'

The *Electra* and the *Orestes* are of the same kind of drama as the tragi-comedies, though perhaps of a different species. That they are grim and not gay, and are based on character-drawing rather than on the excitements of an intricate plot, are important differences; but what is common to them is much more fundamental, and that is the new attitude towards the dramatic art. These two plays are melodramatic, not tragic; like the four plays we have just considered (and the two that we shall consider next) they aim first and foremost at being theatrically effective, and it is this that gives them their character and explains their form.

The first question that should suggest itself is what impelled Euripides to turn to this part of the Atreid legend – twice? On the moral aspect of the vengeance he had nothing new to say, and that little was not enough to make drama from. There was no point whatever in writing a play to show that vengeance by matricide was horrible, for who had ever, or could ever, say anything else? Certainly not Aeschylus; he makes it quite clear that though Apollo's command recognized a necessary principle, it was entirely unsuccessful as a solution of the problem, it was an outrage, and outraged the Erinyes. Not Sophocles, although he had made it an act of δίκη. As we have seen, this does not make it glorious; it is an awful deed brought about inevitably by a monstrous crime. To Euripides, Apollo was neither the defender of some principle in society nor the embodiment of a universal law; he was simply the god of Delphi, an immoral and reactionary institution. Therefore no longer does the power of the god permeate the whole action.

Apollo simply issues his order, as a tyrant might, and Euripides makes it as repulsive as he can. Then, in the second place, though the situation precipitated by Clytemnestra's act, properly treated, can be intensely dramatic, the actual problem of what to do with her is not dramatic at all. There is only one answer – public justice. Euripides gives that answer, but it was not a new one, for Aeschylus had given it too, and we cannot suppose that it was a desire to say so obvious a thing that led him to write these plays. Even in the *Choephori* and *Eumenides* the real drama is not the solution of a problem on which there is only one thing to say; the real drama is something very much wider of which this question and its answer become only symbols.

What is interesting in the comparison of the three dramatists is not their moral attitude to a very simple problem, but their dramatic attitude to the situation and to the actors in it. Aeschylus assumes that no system of public justice exists, because his real drama is the development of the moral order which results in its establishment. Sophocles assumes the same because his purpose is to present the act of vengeance as a particular instance of a universal law : crime begets its own recoil. He avoids any suggestion that the avengers could, or should, have used different and more civilized methods ; this would have transformed the play into something that he never intended – into a piece of social or juridical history. Euripides, in each of the two plays before us, uses a different method : in the *Orestes* Argos has its judicial assembly, and Tyndareus can make the obvious point (493 ff.) that Orestes should have appealed to the law ; but in the *Electra,* though the Dioscuri condemn Apollo and Orestes (1244, 1302), nothing whatever is said about the possibility of bringing Clytemnestra to judgement. The explanation of this difference is, naturally, purely dramatic. The point of the *Orestes* is the picture of three aristocratic degenerates who, completely lost to reason and devoid of any moral responsibility, do fly in the face of an ordered society ; therefore the existence of public justice is emphasized. In the *Electra* Euripides is doing something rather different. He is drawing a certain extreme type of character (reminiscent of Medea) and therefore wishes to place her in circumstances which push her to the extreme. The existence of public justice would have blurred the sharpness of the situation, as in the *Medea* it would have weakened and dissipated the drama to suggest that Medea could have sought legal redress for her wrongs. In each play the conception demands a terrifying character in an absolute situation.

But why does Euripides allow the Dioscuri to condemn the vengeance without stating the alternative? It seems hardly logical, and if Euripides had really been writing social drama this alternative would have been his triumphant conclusion; but he is writing melodrama. First, no alternative, in order to preserve the purity of the situation; then a hint, but no statement, of the alternative, to prevent us from taking the melodramatic Electra tragically – from thinking that she was a bedevilled creature who had to do something of this sort. For we may note another significant point. When the Dioscuri aetiologize about the trial on the Areopagus, they avoid saying 'And henceforth private vengeance shall be superseded by law'. That would have been natural, and it would have advertised Euripides' views if he had thought them worth advertising, but it would have implied that Electra and Orestes really had been in a tragic situation in which they could hardly have escaped murdering their mother. Therefore the trial is made to institute nothing more important than that henceforth equal votes shall bring acquittal.

It was not then a desire to say something new about the problem (as distinct from the situation) that attracted Euripides to this legend. Nor was it a simple desire to set Sophocles right. The vexed question of the priority between the two *Electras* need not detain us here. It has too often been attacked with arguments that work either way,[1] and on the assumption that the later play is full of implied criticisms of the earlier. Thus in Euripides' play, v. 94, 'I do not set foot within the walls', and v. 615, 'Thou couldst not, even if thou wouldst, enter the palace,' are a criticism of the improbable facility with which Orestes does this in Aeschylus and Sophocles. Was then Euripides so stupid a critic as not to know that a highly poetic drama can make assumptions impossible to a realistic one? In fact his play needs both of these remarks; the former emphasizes that this Orestes, unlike his predecessors, is hanging about the back-doors of Argos ready to run if recognized; the latter makes necessary the two

---

[1] The general tendency is to make the Sophoclean play the earlier. This I believe to be correct, though the belief has more faith than reason in it. One argument may be added to an already long list; would Sophocles have invited an unnecessary and unsatisfactory comparison by writing (v. 190) ὧδε μὲν ἀεικεῖ σὺν στολᾷ if Euripides' realistic play were already before the public? It is a small point but at least not an amphisbaena, like many of the comparisons adduced.

separate plots for entrapping Aegisthus and Clytemnestra. Therefore
the assumption that Euripides is indulging in pettifogging and
mistaken criticism is gratuitous.[1]

But even if we could determine the order of the two *Electras*, and
even if we were right in assuming that it was dissatisfaction with the
earlier work that prompted the later,[2] we should be no better off,
for it would remain that since neither is a still-born, academic play,
neither is in any way based on such a negative. Each embodies a very
positive attitude to a very dramatic situation. Let us first determine
what that was; then we may guess – if we must guess – what it was
that directed the later poet's thoughts to this extremely out-of-the-
way legend of Agamemnon and Clytemnestra.

The key lies in the different conception of Electra. The difference
is not merely that Euripides took Sophocles' heroine and with his
customary moroseness and hard realism turned her into a middle-
aged virago. Euripides may have taken a gloomy delight in blacken-
ing the characters of respectable heroes of legend; certainly had he
disliked doing this he could never have written the *Electra* and the
Orestes; but the important point to us is that the different conceptions belong to different types of drama and are therefore bound up
with all the other differences between the plays.[3]

Both plays are plays of character, but different kinds of plays.
Sophocles' Electra is a fully-drawn tragic heroine inasmuch as we
see how her many noble qualities have been hardened by the circumstances of her life. Yet she is no Aristotelian heroine; to look in
her for ἁμαρτία is to stultify Sophocles. Aristotle's Tragedy is one
in which the character, error and suffering of the central figure is the

---

[1] The skit on the *Choephori* is clearly in a different position. This may be mistaken,
but it is not pettifogging.

[2] Why should we not, for a change, begin to assume that Euripides and Sophocles,
being very great and sincere artists, though entirely different in temperament, were,
as artists, sympathetically interested in and appreciative of each other's works and
methods? There is no evidence for such a view, but neither, I think, is there real
evidence for the impression one is given that they were self-conscious, self-righteous
and censorious rivals. A good theme for an imaginary conversation: the two poets
in a group of Athenian notables, from Pericles downwards; the others try desperately
to start a philosophic or moral discussion between the poets, but the poets will talk
of nothing but dramatic technique – how to use the chorus, and whether a resolved is
more effective than an unresolved dochmiac.

[3] It is this that makes point-by-point comparison of the *Electras* so useless. We can
say that Sophocles is more natural here, Euripides more pathetic there, and the remarks
may be true; but until they are related to the different dramatic purposes that the
poets had they remain only the raw material of criticism.

meaning of the whole; in Sophocles' play the focus is not Electra, impressive though she is. The meaning is much wider, and when we have grasped it we see that every detail in the play is related to this, not to Electra's character. It is not that she must be ὅμοιος, 'representative of humanity', but that the action as a whole must be representative of human experience.

Neither is the other Electra Aristotelian, nor the play Aristotelian tragedy. This Electra is a woman in whom it is hardly possible to find a virtue; she is implacable, self-centred, fantastic in hatred,[1] callous to the verge of insanity. Why does Euripides invent this woman? What does she prove? What is the point of a dramatic hero who is all black? We must distinguish. In Xerxes and Agamemnon we had heroes whose characters, as presented, were nothing but error, yet they were tragic.[2] Electra is not one of these. Euripides does not limit himself to the catastrophic side of her nature and exclude the rest as irrelevant to her tragedy; he draws her in detail – and then omits the tragedy. She is not tragic in the Sophoclean way because she is not representative, 'like ourselves', and therefore cannot illuminate. She resembles Medea in not being representative, but no further; the whole meaning of Medea is that the ἁμαρτία which comprises practically the whole of her character is a universal one, so that Medea, though not Aristotelian, is symbolic of the human tragedy; but Electra, equally nothing but faults, is an entirely private and personal assemblage of faults with no universal significance. She is a Medea without the tragedy – but with all Medea's *Grand Guignol* effects; in other words, a heroine of melodrama.

Accordingly we find the whole play cast on melodramatic lines. The *Electra* and the *Orestes* are as pure melodrama as the *Iphigeneia*; they may contain incidental themes of wider interest, but their first purpose is to attract and sustain our interest by the sheer force of theatrical effect. The difference is that the *Iphigeneia* and the *Ion* do this through an exciting plot with characterization as an accessory, while the *Electra* and *Orestes* rely on exciting characterization with the interest of plot as an accessory. In discussing tragi-comedy we saw that plot had none of the ethical or spiritual significance that it

[1] Sophocles' Electra was wrong about Aegisthus, but this one is wild. Contrast the foolish monster she describes (326 ff.) with the courteous Aegisthus whom we meet later in the play.

[2] See above, pp. 103, 151.

has possessed in Middle Tragedy, no longer the illuminating inter-action of a typical character and typical circumstances, but only an exciting series of events; now we see that character, even in a 'play of character', loses that deeper significance and becomes only some-thing to move and hold our palpitating interest.

We must show that the melodramatic conception explains the general methods used in both plays; we may perhaps excuse our-selves from pursuing this into the details, since to point out how the frequent touches of realism, irony, piquancy in situation and satire are addressed to the audience rather than to the furtherance of a fundamental theme would be only to duplicate what was said in the last section.[1]

We may begin with the character of the heroine. Sophocles' Electra, because she is to be tragic, must remain in close touch with ordinary humanity, even though she is of necessity an unusual woman; we must be made to feel the tragedy that a loyal and affectionate woman should have been brought to hate her mother like this. Therefore her love for her father and brother is stressed everywhere, particularly at the end of the recognition-scene. But Euripides has no interest in modifying Electra's character by strong natural affections,[2] therefore, although for the sake of verisimilitude affection for Orestes is mentioned in the monody (130 ff.), when we come to business and to the actual recognition no transports of joy are allowed to come between us and the grim story that Euripides is working out for us. Desire for vengeance is, in this Electra, stronger than affection for a brother. This is the reason why the recognition-scene is finished off as brusquely as possible – though no doubt we must be prepared to hear that the real explanation was a desire to criticize Sophocles' undramatic prolixity at this point.

For this same reason, that the tragic Electra, however extreme, must remain broadly ὅμοιος, representative, Sophocles must palliate

---

[1] Typical points are: Realism – *Electra*, the invitation to the festival (167 ff.), Electra's nagging of her husband (404 ff.), and the general atmosphere of domesticity; in the *Orestes*, the keeping guard upon the stage (67 and 1246 ff.), the sick-bed scene, the escape of the Phrygian (1371 ff.). Irony – passim, especially in the symposium on the True Gentleman in the *Orestes*. Piquancy in situation – *Electra*, the recognition (552 ff.), the prolongation of suspense at 747 ff.; *Orestes*, Helen's secret return, her hair-offering (128 ff.), Orestes' sudden attack of madness and his delusion about Electra (255 ff.), Menelaus' failure to recognize Orestes (768 ff.), Diomedes addressing an Assembly (893). The sudden check to the plot common in tragi-comedy is hardly found here, as the plot-interest counts for much less.

[2] In the *Orestes* he has; see below, p. 347.

the horrors of the actual crime, or at least abstain from emphasizing its crudities, for we must not lose sympathy with Electra. It is not merely a matter of taste or literary judgement that Euripides emphasizes the crude details and Sophocles does not. It may be a matter of taste to write melodrama at all, but having chosen so to treat the subject, Euripides had to underline the hideousness of Electra and Orestes, and he does it with remarkable virtuosity. The plot to kill Aegisthus is based on a confidence in his courtesy; he is a very different person from the tyrant whom Sophocles presents. The plot sounds a little discreditable, but it is surpassed by Electra's heaven-inspired trap for her mother – again a trap based on confidence in her humanity. Orestes and Pylades kill Aegisthus with every circumstance of dishonour – he is their host, at a sacrifice, and the conspirators recognize the situation by refusing the lustral water that he offers; finally, after a delay (contrived for its theatrical value) Orestes hits him in the back, with a chopper. Sophocles' dramatic plan, if nothing else, excludes this kind of effect; his Aegisthus must be slain with that grim reticence, not described as lying on the ground with his back split, screaming and dying in convulsions.[1] Sophocles cannot pretend that the death of Clytemnestra is anything but a necessary horror, but he must not go further; he must show that his heroine rejoices at the deed, but he may not allow her to share in the physical act. Such extreme treatment would have ruined his tragedy by depriving it of any semblance of universality; Sophocles' reticence would have ruined Euripides' melodrama by robbing it of half its effectiveness. Far from making his chief actors as broadly human as the scene admits he must make them as striking as he can, true to the theatre rather than to life.

Between the murders comes the scene in which the melodramatic intention is most apparent and perhaps most surely achieved, the grisly passage with Aegisthus' head. Euripides makes it a practice to introduce these purely rhetorical speeches deliberately,[2] and the deliberateness is extremely effective here. There is no unreal pretence that Electra's emotions relieve themselves in a torrent of abuse. A certain stylization, the imitation of reticence, sets off the horror excellently; in particular, Electra, like her brother in the matter of the lustral water, has moral scruples whose light violation is an

[1] Eur., El., 842–3.

[2] See p. 328 on Helen, 943–5, and p. 344 on Electra, 297–300.

added indecency. In a speech conceived in this spirit we shall hardly expect the accents of simple tragedy, but shall look rather for point. Euripides, because he is using the situation only as a situation rich in dramatic thrills, is careful to satisfy our aroused interest by throwing new light on the old situation – not because the new light is something vital to his mind, but because the old light is useless to him. Accordingly we are given not Electra's joy at the death of one of her father's murderers, but a highly interesting analysis of Aegisthus' position as the husband of Clytemnestra.

The same sort of calculation underlies the treatment of Clytemnestra. The pomp of her arrival contrasts most effectively with Electra's poverty, and this is now an effect quite as important as any of the moral questions involved. In Sophocles' play Clytemnestra is the doomed criminal whose plea of justification must be, and is, demolished – because the force of Dike is the heart of the tragedy. Here, the debate is given a more personal tone because that is more immediately interesting. Clytemnestra uses a bold rhetorical argument for our pleasure, supposing the case that Menelaus, not Helen, had been stolen away; she brings in Cassandra, whom Sophocles had omitted because she was not the main issue; she explains (as if answering Electra from the other play) why she took Aegisthus: she had to. In reply Electra makes the point that Sophocles did not want – and a very interesting point – that as soon as Agamemnon was gone Clytemnestra showed herself a wanton, wishing only for his death. Euripides is not so anxious to raise the question of justice as to treat the situation in a naturalistic and interesting way.

But the finest stroke here is Clytemnestra's dissatisfaction with herself. Sophocles' murderess must have no regrets, that the revenge, from Electra's point of view, may be an unqualified act of justice. Therefore he makes her say:

$$\text{Ἐγὼ μὲν οὖν οὐκ εἰμὶ τοῖς πεπραγμένοις,}$$
$$\text{δύσθυμος.}[1]$$

But Euripides contrives a splendid effect when, with Aegisthus' head hidden in the cottage, he produces that gleam of a possible reconciliation now impossible. His Clytemnestra says:

[1] 'I then have no misgivings at what has passed' (vv. 549-50).

Συγγνώσομαί σοι· καὶ γὰρ οὐχ οὕτως ἄγαν
χαίρω τι, τέκνον, τοῖς δεδραμένοις ἐμοί.[1]

The dialogue continues:

EL. Why then do you whet your husband's wrath against us?
c. He is like that. Besides, you were always headstrong.
EL. Because of my grief. But my wrath will cease.
c. Then his anger too will cease.
EL. He is haughty; he dwells in my house.

But not, as Clytemnestra thinks, in the Palace.

It is splendid theatre, and it completes the utterly unqualified
picture of the heroine – except that we have still to learn that she
actually assists at her mother's murder.

And what of Orestes? It is evident that in determining his character Euripides had a wider choice than Sophocles. The tragic
nature of Sophocles' play dictated that Orestes should be neither
the dedicated servant of Apollo whom Aeschylus needed, nor a
complex character, overshadowing Electra, nor a conventional or
overdrawn figure, out of keeping with Electra. The fact that one of
his chief motives is the recovery of his rightful heritage prevents
him from standing in Electra's light, and materially helps to keep
him plausible and human. But Euripides was much less restricted;
his Orestes might with equal logic be an infatuated bigot, a cruel
avenger, a pathetic, misguided lad, a mere schemer – anything that
would allow him to perform the murders effectively. Euripides
chooses to make him irresolute, and it is interesting to see why.

That Orestes is no bold hero is at once made clear in the prologue;
he has come to spy out the land, ready to run if necessary. He has
made the offerings at Agamemnon's tomb by night, to escape the
notice of the authorities. This, to be sure, is mere prudence; still,
there was no reason for Euripides to mention the reason unless he
had wanted to reinforce the idea of Orestes' caution. But there is
more than this in the detail. M. Parmentier remarks, 'Euripide
affecte de faire prendre à son heros des précautions meilleures que
celles imaginées par ses devanciers'; but Euripides was much more
intent on his own play than on mistakenly criticising his predeces-

---

[1] 'I will pardon thee. For, my child, I am not so very glad at what I have done'
1105–6). Note the clever change from the impersonal 'what has passed' to the
personal 'what I have done'.

sors.[1] The point is that when Electra appears Orestes is not whisked away to perform his ritual duties as he is in Sophocles' play; these are already done, so that he can sit in hiding and listen to Electra's monody (109–111).[2] Therefore when he and Pylades jump out at v. 215 he knows who Electra is, and there is no reason why he should not in turn say who he is. But he pretends – for quite a long time. Then at v. 270, we suddenly see why:

$$\alpha\ddot{\iota}\delta' \ o\mathring{\upsilon}\nu \ \phi\acute{\iota}\lambda\alpha\iota \ \sigma o\iota \ \tau o\acute{\upsilon}\sigma\delta' \ \mathring{\alpha}\kappa o\acute{\upsilon}o\upsilon\sigma\iota\nu \ \lambda\acute{o}\gamma o\upsilon\varsigma ;^{3}$$

Of course: Orestes does not realize that these fifteen women are the Chorus, and therefore trustworthy. Electra reassures him, and Orestes' expected declaration – does not come. He still pretends, changing the subject. Electra makes her speech, the Peasant returns, they accept his hospitality, and still there is no disclosure. Can there be any reason but pure lack of resolution?

But if this is Orestes' reason, what is Euripides'? It is very interesting to see an Orestes so different from the hero of the *Choephori*, but there were other possibilities – for example, the criminal blunderer of the *Orestes* – which would have been no less interesting. There must have been something that made Euripides choose between equally possible alternatives, and that something was evidently the theatrical value of this Orestes in this situation. His nervous caution makes possible the obvious but effective ironies of this scene, Electra's tirades against the murderers,[4] the skit on

[1] If Euripides, not having found out that there are different kinds of drama and therefore of dramatic methods and conventions, were showing Sophocles and Athens how 'a Greek Play' should be made, we can be sure that he would have avoided the major improbability here which gives his critics such cynical pleasure, namely that the patient Pylades must already know all that this prologue contains. Melodrama, like Tragedy, has its conventions – and Euripides was neither a pedant nor a fool.

[2] This seems to me a strong argument for the priority of Sophocles' play. The 'overlap' is common to both, and it seems almost certain that the satirical use of it is the later. The recollection of tragedy is spice to satire, but the recollection of satire inconvenient to tragedy.

[3] 'Are these friends of thine that hearken to our words?'

[4] This speech is less 'naturally' introduced than the corresponding speech in Sophocles (354 ff.). But then, Sophocles is presenting a heroine in whose complete reality we must never cease to believe; an obviously 'made-up' speech would be a bad mistake. Euripides' Electra is much more a figure on the stage; she is there for effect, and this speech is here for effect. There is more room for artifice, and Euripides does, in fact, introduce the speech artificially; he even makes the chorus invite it, as at *Helen*, 945; a point which, whatever we think of it, at least shows that he was thinking theatrically and rhetorically, and was not anxious to pretend that this was tragedy.

Aeschylus, and the clever variant on recognition-scenes, whereby one of the parties, trying to avoid recognition, is unwillingly detected by a third. That is to say, characterization is close, vivid and consistent, but it is subordinated to stage-effect, as it was in the tragi-comedies.

Every dramatist must study stage-effect, but in the severer forms of drama this should be only a means to a further end; that this principle is no longer effective we can demonstrate further. We do not admit that Euripides was covertly criticizing Sophocles in the manipulation of his plot, but there is no question that he explicitly parodies Aeschylus in the scene between Electra and the Old Man. Whether this is a piece of impertinence or only an entertainment we need hardly discuss here;[1] from our point of view the significant thing is that it should have been possible for Euripides to turn aside from his theme to write such a passage at all;[2] the more significant since he does something not very dissimilar with the chorus.

For of the three odes in the play, two turn aside completely from the context in order to describe remote marvels, the Shield of Achilles and certain miraculous events in the history of Atreus and Thyestes.[3] The latter have indeed a mechanical kind of connexion with the plot, but the Shield has none at all – a fact which is emphasized by the rather awkward return to Clytemnestra at the end. Yet in Sophocles' *Electra* Euripides had (probably) an excellent model in the dramatic use of the chorus; and this play, unlike several of Euripides' tragedies, has an organic plot which might be supposed to invite and to benefit from a consistently dramatic chorus. There

---

[1] Euripides makes things so easy for himself – as for example by giving Orestes 'boots', which makes nonsense of the 'footprints' – that we cannot suppose him to have mistaken this for criticism. M. Parmentier, who writes temperately and sensibly about it, calls it 'une improvisation burlesque' (ed. Budé, p. 184). It is perhaps worth while to point out that the stupid Old Man proves to be right and the clever Electra wrong.

[2] This recalls the stray bit of dramatic criticism in the *Suppliant Women* (846–56). The play is a tragedy, but the report of the battle, which the dramatic criticism immediately precedes, contains very little of its essence. It is a necessary stage in the story, and Euripides, with disconcerting frankness, treats it as such. As there is nothing really tragic going on, but merely a dramatic narrative, he allows his attention to wander from the tragic theme to the criticism of dramatic narratives.

[3] The last, and very short, ode, sung during the killing, sticks closely enough to the drama; at such a moment even Euripides can refrain from writing a brilliant account of the chariot-race between Pelops and Oenomaus or the story of Tantalus. We may, however, notice what this ode does not do: it does not speak of justice, nor, on the other hand, does it question what Electra and Orestes are doing. It is objective: Clytemnestra killed Agamemnon; now she is being killed.

was material much nearer to hand than Thyestes: why did Euripides not use it? Why does he refrain from imitating Sophocles – and why is it that he made a better play by following his own judgement than he would have done by following Sophocles' example?

In both these odes, and in the parody, Euripides is evidently doing something to interest his audience, but presenting this directly and not through the drama; not as an interesting turn given to the plot or colour to the treatment, but as a separate decoration. This is worth a moment's consideration, especially as in all the non-tragic plays (except the *Alcestis* and the *Ion*) the chorus is given more or less decorative and 'undramatic' odes like these two in the *Electra*.

2. The Chorus in New Tragedy

There seem to be two separate points. The new drama deals with matters of purely private interest; even the subject of the *Electra,* which Aeschylus made so vast, is treated as only a personal matter. The chorus therefore can have no independent status in the play, as representing humanity or the City, but becomes either a useful Confidante or a nuisance. It is a small matter that the dramatist is put to the necessity of having to explain away the chorus when confidential affairs are being discussed on the stage; this is a convention that we can accept without demur.[1] More important is it that the old Parodos, the entrance-hymn, had to disappear. No longer could the chorus enter magnificently, as in the *Antigone* and the *Tyrannus,* with a song of communal importance; it now comes in pretending, on various excuses, that it is not a Chorus, but a group of individuals. In the *Iphigeneia* it enters singing a solemn hymn to Artemis, but alas! the religion is only a Wagnerian effect – not even that, for the purpose of their coming, we soon learn, is nothing but to hear of Iphigeneia's bad dream. This entrance no doubt was an impressive spectacle – that was what it was meant to be; but it is only the counterpart, suggested by the circumstances, of the realism of the Parodos in the *Ion*. It is now logical, and usually necessary, to bring on the Chorus realistically; the successor to the Parodos is the lyrical

[1] We may observe that the chorus never became a conventional lyrical appendage which could be simply ignored, one which the audience would never expect to be noticed from the stage. It remained an integral part of the play, and if it was in the way, the dramatist had to explain that it wasn't. (Cf. the chorus at Medea's murders, p. 191.)

conversation. As for the other odes, what was the richest source of material is now dried up. The chorus used commonly to illuminate the action from a different point of view – from a specifically dramatic one – as when the chorus of the *Tyrannus* defends Oedipus in its capacity of citizens of Thebes, or from the point of view of the 'ideal spectator' – but now, since the action raises no question of morality, religion, public policy, or even private philosophy, not even in the *Electra,* but only the question whether so-and-so will escape, and how, it becomes a little difficult for the Chorus to remain both dramatic and interesting. Certainly in the *Iphigeneia* (392 ff.) the chorus can participate in the curiosity that we also feel, and ask 'Who are the Greek strangers and how have they come?' but such speculations are in general an unpromising theme for lyric utterance, and Euripides does not use them often, nor without a good deal of adventitious ornament.

But even in Sophocles' *Electra* the dramatic action is treated as a private rather than a public matter – we saw that for this very reason the new style of Parodos is used – yet Sophocles can still manage to make his chorus not only relevant but actually one of the most eloquent of his dramatic instruments.[1] Was then Euripides not so clever, or did he care less for these things? We cannot escape so easily. Although Sophocles' theme was private and did not give the old scope to the chorus, the implications of the theme were more than personal, and these gave new opportunities. This is our second point. Events on the stage are in melodrama only events; there are no wider implications – or none that matter seriously. In the older drama the chorus, during a pause in the action, could dwell upon its significance, as when in Sophocles' *Electra* it likened the avengers to Erinyes or interpreted the dream as a sign that Dike was on the march. (It is interesting to note that there is no dream in Euripides' play.) Now, when the stage-action stops, what we most want is that it should begin again, for we are really interested in nothing else. It would have been idle for Euripides to imitate Sophocles and to write an ode which should carry over the spirit and personality of Electra from one scene to the next, or one which, going back to Agamemnon, should accentuate one of her motives or one of her tragic difficulties. This Electra stands out at once, complete, as a hard, vindictive woman; she is there only for our astonishment.

[1] Above, pp. 166 f., 175.

When Orestes goes off to encounter Aegisthus the chorus can in honesty neither speculate anxiously what the outcome will be – the pretence would be too hollow – nor talk of justice and vengeance. We know that Aegisthus will be killed; we await only the exciting details. The question whether the vengeance is just or not forms no part of the play; it was settled long before the play began. An Electra like this the chorus cannot praise without being revolting, nor blame without wasting our time. As for the plays of intrigue, it is even clearer that the gap between scene and scene is really empty space. Drama has become sensational, and when the actors leave off there is an intermission in the sensation. What can the chorus do to enhance the intrinsic excitement of the Iphigeneia or the comedy of the Helen? As far as it can, it keeps out of the way.

But it cannot keep out of the way for long (though Euripides writes eleven hundred lines of the Helen before introducing a stasimon), and, seeing that it can so well produce what the plays themselves are aiming at, namely theatrical effect, it is not desirable that it should. The chorus can very seldom contribute in the old way to the drama, but it can please or astonish us lyrically, as the messenger in the Ion did verbally. What the chorus sings about in these plays depends, naturally, on the dramatic context; if there is suitable material lying to hand they use it, if not they fill the gap with something else. In either case the ode does not profess to be anything but an effective diversion filling the gap which the actors have left. So in the Electra, Euripides prefers arresting narrative and vivid des-description, though of something quite remote, to an insincere imitation of tragedy; in the Helen (1301 ff.) he writes about Demeter – an intolerable irrelevance if our minds were to be seriously engaged on Demeter, but they are not; the ode is only a picturesque and brilliant piece of decoration.[1] Closer to the context are the three odes of the Iphigeneia and the remaining two of the Helen. Iphigeneia's servants ask who the strangers can be, they lament their own position, they tell how Apollo secured for himself the oracle at Delphi; but the curiosity and the pathos are little but an excuse for a graceful operatic movement, full of birds, festivals,

---

[1] Characteristic of the composition is the obvious imitative effect in the words, rhythm, and therefore probably music too in:

χαλκοῦ δ' αὐδὰν χθονίαν
τύπανά τ' ἔλαβε βυρσοτενῆ ... (1346-7).

mythological prettiness and pathetic verbal repetitions,[1] and the story of Apollo is quite Alexandrine in feeling. There is not a trace of reverence in the poem, nor of irreverence; it is simply a charming tale, told with due attention to the piquant details, and leading cleverly to the high light, the appearance of the precocious infant before Zeus, the request for the prerogatives of the golden shrine, and Zeus' indulgent smile. Again it is but a short step to Theocritus and his friendly Epyllia. The chorus of the *Helen* makes a very pretty song (1451 ff.) out of Helen's return; but the first stasimon is a little surprising. It begins conventionally enough by describing the inevitable bird, but in the second stanza it gets serious. The dramatic situation is that we are awaiting the King and the springing of Helen's plot. Of this the chorus can obviously take no lyrical notice, because there is nothing to say and nothing to do but wait; instead it occupies our minds and gives us a change from the prevalent flippancy of tone by singing seriously, consequently without verbal tricks, of war, chance and folly.

It is natural that the *Alcestis,* which, for all its burlesque, is very much closer to tragedy in manner than the later tragi-comedies and melodramas, should approach tragedy also in its use of the chorus. What is perhaps a little remarkable is that the *Ion* should have so much more dramatic a chorus than its fellows, though based no less than they on a private theme and an exciting plot. The first stasimon indeed relies on long invocations and commonplaces about having children, and can be called dramatic only because it is not obviously undramatic, but the second (676 ff.), foreshadowing Creusa's rage, and the third, praying for Ion's death and complaining of Apollo, attend strictly to the business of the play and do in fact contribute something to it. The reason for the difference between the *Ion* and the other tragi-comedies in this regard is not difficult to see. It is something that this chorus, as servants of Creusa and Athenian women, have a definite interest and a definite point of view of their own, but the important point is that the character of Creusa happens to count for much more in the action of this play than the characters of Iphigenia and Helen do in theirs. These heroines have simply to be ingenious at the right moment, and our chief interest is to see

---

[1] Some of these odes sound quite as empty and nearly as silly as some of Mozart's libretti; if we had Euripides' music, and Greek ears to hear it with, would it all perhaps sound as marvellous as Mozart's operas?

what will happen next; in the *Ion* also we want to know what will happen next, but that depends very much on what Creusa will think about it all. The play in fact is to some extent animated by that active personal will which was the unifying element in Middle Tragedy. The chorus, therefore, because it stands in close relation to Creusa and shares her sentiments, can contribute more to this play than it usually can in New Tragedy.

Thus we see that the chorus, like characterization, takes a new and a logical position in the new drama. Its odes are now never more than three, for speed and continuity in plot are the dramatist's chief object and whether their subject-matter is taken from the context or not their function is no longer to help, still less to illuminate the drama, but in an appropriate manner to fill the gaps in the action with lyrical ornament that will be acceptable for its own sake.

One point more may be mentioned. The dramatist may find it expedient to cut down the number of stasima, but music has charms, and he has no intention of foregoing more of them than he must, so that what the chorus loses the actors gain, now encroaching upon the chorus in its own field. In the quasi-parodi of the *Iphigeneia,* the *Helen* and the *Electra* the heroine is the *prima donna* and the chorus subordinate – this perhaps inevitably arising from the uncertain or sub-dramatic status of the chorus in these plays – while elsewhere we find an actor singing a solo aria when we might have expected a stasimon.

For example, the Messenger has informed Electra (*Or.* 957) that she and her brother are to die at once. For comparable moments in tragedy we may turn to the report of Orestes' death in Sophocles' *Electra* or to Tecmessa's discovery of Ajax' body. Electra, in Sophocles' play, says very little, and what she does say is provoked by her anger at Clytemnestra; then her grief begins to find its natural outlet in the exchange of brief ejaculations with the chorus. Tecmessa cries inarticulately, then masters herself sufficiently to tell the chorus what she has found, then laments to herself in a very natural way as she attends to the body. It is left to the chorus to express the emotion of the moment lyrically. Iocasta and Deianeira receive their death-warrants in silence, and Oedipus meets his discovery with a brief cry of despair; the Trachinian maidens can sing about Deianeira, and the Thebans can express something of the tragedy of Oedipus, but the actor is more convincing and eloquent if he remains silent. Imitating such eminently successful passages Euripides could have given to Electra wild cries of terror, and to the chorus an appropriate ode on the end of the royal house or some other suitable topic; but Euripides is not an imitator. Without a moment's hesitation his Electra sets to work and produces a long, elaborate aria which leaves the chorus nothing to say but 'Lo! here comes thy brother, with the faithful Pylades.'

This is perfectly correct, and the tragic imitation would be dull, even if not ridiculous. The whole drama, like the aria, is addressed to our nerves and sensations rather than to our minds; and at this stage of the play we are not going to accept Electra as a tragic heroine. Once more, it is the tragic poet who must be realistic in these matters. The melodramatist must attend to the conventions and demands of his own art, and use a moment like this operatically.

It is the same with Creusa's monody. We know how Sophocles would have made her tell her story; if we do not, we can see how dramatically Oedipus tells a tale that is filling him with terror.[1] Would the terror have been more obvious or dramatic if he had stopped his speech at v. 813 and gone off into lyrics? The difference obviously is that we do not want to see how Creusa's character and mind work under the strain; to us it is simply a sensational story. A speech of Sophoclean force and passion followed by a choral ode would have been insincere and far less to the purpose than Creusa's dramatic area.

But the *Orestes* contains a much more remarkable extension of stage-lyricism – a messenger-speech cast in the form of wild, incoherent arias; and this, far from being a sign of increasing laxity of form, is a fine and logical stroke in the making of a fine play.

3. The 'Orestes'

The *Orestes*, like the *Electra*, is a melodrama based on character-drawing and character imagined sensationally, not tragically; and its contrivance displays a control of dramatic rhythm more marked even than that of the *Electra*, for while the *Electra* proceeds steadily from hard unpleasantness to the limit of unnatural hatred, the *Orestes*, proceeding from folly to reckless criminality and from delusion to mania, advances from the usual dry prologue and com-

[1] *Tyrannus*, 771 ff.

mon Euripidean realism to nightmare; and in the engineering of this splendid spectacle the Phrygian's lyrics are an important structural feature, as we shall presently see.

Only in the most obvious sense is the play a continuation of the *Electra*; in conception and feeling it is very different. The earlier play has a grim concentration, the later a spectacular, almost frenzied, sweep of melodramatic action; but in spite of this we are nearer tragedy in the *Orestes*. The Electra and Orestes of this play are not the simple characters that they were in the *Electra*. The unaffected tenderness for each other that they display in the sick-bed scene stands in stark contrast with the utter folly shown by Orestes in all practical matters and the criminal recklessness that infects both. In itself such a contrast might be no more than a theatrical stroke, but it derives a tragic quality from one suggestion in the play, that these two are the last tainted offspring of a tainted house. It is natural, or at least conventional, that in the prologue Electra should proclaim her ancestry, but it is not inevitable that in doing this she should emphasize the crimes of which it has been guilty; and throughout the play Orestes and Electra, and Pylades too, are represented as degenerates, except for this streak of ordinary humanity; possessed, like the traditional Cleopatra, of a certain unhealthy brilliance, a menace to the society which has to endure them. We are to see how they send up the house of Tantalus in flames. The prologue prepares the way; the Chorus (vv. 345–7) continues the idea; Tyndareus declares that Electra, by her criminal suggestions to Orestes,

$$ὑφῆψε δῶμ' ἀνηφαίστῳ πυρί^1$$

Menelaus, in the last scene, cries

$$ἦ γὰρ πατρῷον δῶμα πορθήσεις τόδε;^2$$

and in obvious fulfilment of Tyndareus' accusation, Orestes calls out, in an access of frenzy,

$$ἀλλ' εἶ', ὕφαπτε δώματ', Ἠλέκτρα, τάδε.^3$$

Certainly the play is the spectacular portrayal of insane behaviour much more than the tragic working-out of this idea, yet the contrast

---

[1] She set her house on (metaphorical) fire. (V. 621.)
[2] What! Wilt thou destroy this, thy ancestral house? (V. 1595.)
[3] Come, Electra; set this house on fire! (V. 1618.)

between natural affection and inherited criminality does give a
tragic colour to the spectacle, though it may be a colour more like
that of romantic than of Aristotelian tragedy.

Euripides' firm control of dramatic rhythm is the making of the
play. Every scene is brilliantly constructed, but over and above the
individual strokes of dramatic surprise and pungency there is a
gradual crescendo in dramatic excitement keeping step with the
growing frenzy of Orestes and his accomplices. The stages are clearly
defined. The exposition is given in a dry prologue. The early
realistic scenes show first the hopeless position of Electra and
Orestes, and then the extreme folly of Orestes which makes it
worse. The arrival of the foolish Pylades quickens the tempo, and
with the announcement of the Assembly's verdict begins a wilder
passage in which criminal recklessness is added to folly and insane
vengeance to extreme danger. The third stage is one of fantastic
horror culminating in the wild scene in which Orestes is on the
point of murdering Hermione and setting fire to the palace; and the
finale, a brilliant return to the formality of the prologue, is the
tableau vivant in which Apollo, like a Shakespearian magician,
dissolves the mounting nightmare into familiar fact.

As for the details of the dramatic technique, we must restrict
ourselves to a few points. The difficulty of the chorus is met most
successfully. Not only does the general situation not readily accommodate a chorus, but as Orestes is asleep on the stage, its arrival is
actually a nuisance. Euripides boldly makes capital out of this by
allowing Electra to treat the chorus as a nuisance; it becomes fifteen
sympathetic but untimely visitors who are earnestly implored to
stop singing and to go home again – a new experience for this
ancient institution. We may notice, too, how cleverly Euripides
conveys the blindness of Electra and Orestes to realities, practical
and then moral. During the prologue Electra is anxiously scanning
all the roads for signs of Menelaus, their one hope; yet this same
Menelaus has had to smuggle Helen up from Nauplia by night, for
fear of the people. When Menelaus does arrive he clearly cuts no
very regal figure – though he contrasts effectively enough with the
ghastly Orestes – and Orestes' appeal to him is sentimentally argued
and obviously useless. At this point, most dramatically, Tyndareus
is announced. The unhappy father of Clytemnestra and Helen was
not a frequent visitor to the Athenian stage, and his arrival excites the

liveliest interest.[1] This is increased by the ecstasy of shame and dismay into which Orestes falls – natural feelings which, if only he could sustain them, might have earned him at least Tyndareus' pitying contempt; this would have been less injurious than the active hostility which he succeeds in provoking by his foolish speech. The speech is not sophistry but plain lunacy; the sophist pretends to answer his adversary's argument, but Orestes is so lost to all sense of reality that he does not see what the argument is.

Tyndareus departs, and now Menelaus, whose embarrassment has been doubled by the interruption, has to listen to Orestes' elaborately silly appeal; his reply to which, the only possible reply, is received with a volley of insults, and is later to be the excuse for the murder of his wife and daughter. The climax of this insane behaviour is the appearance of the death-like matricide and his exiled friend at the trial, and the speech which destroys his chance of escaping with a penalty lighter than death.

The mere folly of these young aristocrats is followed in the next scene by their natural facility in giving fair names to shameful deeds; and the dramatic skill which has led Orestes from his sick-bed to the climax in the Assembly repeats itself in the piling of crime on crime. They are as lost to moral as to practical realities. First the drama inherent in an enforced suicide is exhausted, and the self-deception of which Orestes is capable is crystallized in this outburst:

> 'Come! let us die nobly, accomplishing a deed worthy of Agamemnon. I will prove to the city my nobility by piercing myself to the heart with my sword; and thou must follow my courageous lead.'[2]

Then Pylades (who in the Argument attributed to Aristophanes of Byzantium is said to be the only character in the play who is 'not wicked') suggests that they may at least involve Menelaus in their ruin by murdering Helen. The scheme is taken up with a horrible enthusiasm, and Pylades, worthy companion to Orestes, translates it into moral terms as follows:

> If we unsheathed our swords against a better woman, the killing would be inglorious; but as it is, she will be making amends to all

[1] The juxtaposition of persons here recalls the scene in the *Troades* between Hecuba, Helen, and Menelaus.

[2] Vv. 1060–5.

Greece – those whose fathers she slew, those whose sons she destroyed, the brides whom she widowed of their husbands. A shout of joy will arise, fires they will light to the gods, vowing blessings to thee and to me, that we encompassed the death of an evil woman. Slaying her thou wilt not have the name Matricide, but casting this behind thee thou wilt mend thy fortune, acclaimed the Slayer of bloody Helen.

Pylades can yet continue:

Never, never must Menelaus prosper while thy father, and thou, and Electra are dead;

and he ends this fine oration by proclaiming that if they cannot slay Helen they will burn down the palace and themselves in it, thus either saving themselves like heroes, or like heroes dying.[1]

The only difficulty that this creates for Orestes is that of keeping within bounds his eulogy of Pylades' faithfulness; but when Electra adds the refinement that they should seize Hermione to be either a security for Menelaus' good behaviour or an easy victim to avenge his bad, his brotherly pride is stirred to the depths:

In beauty thou dost excel other women, but thy heart is a man's. How much more thou dost merit life than death! Such, Pylades, is the wife of whom, alas, Death will deprive thee – unless thou live to have her as thy wonderful bride.

It is fitting that the scene should end with an imitation of the triple invocation in the *Choephori,* which, shocking enough in the *Electra,*[2] sounds positively blasphemous here. As the two men proceed to the pointless murder of Helen, Pylades invokes 'ancestral Zeus and thee, Majesty of Justice'.

This Elizabethan excess of wickedness can hardly be carried through with a Periclean sobriety of dramatic method, especially as the miraculous escape of Helen is to take the action still further into the fantastic. For the contemplation of tragedy we need a certain repose of mind; quick and sensational action is the proper vehicle for this febrile melodrama. Accordingly we have at this point not a stasimon but an excited dialogue in lyrics while Electra and the two

[1] Vv. 1132–52.
[2] Vv. 671 ff.

halves of the chorus anxiously watch the approaches, then as Helen's shrieks are heard, Electra bursts into wild triumph; there is a sudden change to stealthy irony as Hermione arrives; she is seized by Orestes, Electra triumphs again, the chorus wonders what has happened within; and then comes a most unexpected diversion – a slave, terrified for his life, drops perilously from under the roof. He, though we hardly suspect it, is the *Exangelos,* the Messenger-from-within; but what messenger-speech could sustain the savage frenzy of the scene? He tells his frenetic story of treachery, slaughter and miracle in a series of wild lyrics, in which Euripides takes full advantage of the fact that the fellow is an excitable barbarian. As well as his terror will allow him he pours out his story. Then there is another swift change as Orestes comes out, sword in hand and now obviously a maniac, to play horribly with the slave, drive him back, and make all ready for the last frantic and bloodthirsty scene on the roof, Orestes still believing that Menelaus could 'persuade the city' if only he would.

The *Orestes* is an outstanding illustration of the freedom and strength of the Greek genius. Almost at one bound we have passed from a drama which is at least called statuesque to drama whose imaginative tumult rivals anything on the romantic stage; yet this is done with the minimum of interference with the traditional forms and with a firmness of control hardly surpassed by Sophocles himself.

4. The 'Phoenissae'

When Voltaire complained of the paucity of material in a Greek play he was not thinking of the *Phoenissae,* which contains enough to keep any modern dramatist going at full stretch for his five acts. Drama, as was suggested above, consumes material at this rate when the dramatic interest lies in the incidents themselves and not in what the actors think and feel and do in relation to them.

The *Phoenissae* is a remarkable play, and it illustrates, with the *I.A.,* yet another type of the late drama. It entirely excludes the comic, and makes no use of complication of plot; novelty in plot, so important in the *Ion* and presumably in Agathon's *Antheus,* is one element in the *Phoenissae,* but not the most important; characterization, whether complex as in the *Philoctetes* or melodramatic as in the

Electra, plays a very small part; and although both of these plays contain the material of tragedy, neither is, or was intended to be, tragedy. On the assumption that they were designed as tragedies it is impossible to explain either their material or their style and method, unless we abandon the hypothesis that Euripides was an artist and a good craftsman. We will abandon it if it fails, but until then it must obviously hold the field. We will set forth the structural and stylistic features in the *Phoenissae* that most attract notice, and we shall expect to find that one simple explanation covers all, and that we need not postulate shortcomings in the poet.

Some important facts are noted in the Argument. The play is πολυπρόσωπον, 'contains many characters'; there being in fact no less than eleven, without counting the chorus. The ancient critic has his misgivings about the Unity of Action; 'Antigone watching from the walls is no part of the action, Polyneices enters under safe-conduct to no purpose, and the scene of Oedipus being driven into exile, with its diffuse lyrics, is an idle addition (προσέρραπται διὰ κενῆς).' Of modern critics, some have exercised the Teichoskopia as an interpolation, others have drastically cut down the Exodos. From the Aristotelian point of view the criticisms implied are just, but what in fact is gained by these surgical operations? What is left is still nothing like a normal play, for it remains true that Polyneices' visit achieves nothing and is not even ethically or psychologically valuable; and what have the sacrifice of Menoeceus, Creon's attempt to save him, and the discussion on tactics, to do with the rest of the play or with each other?

Still dealing with structure, we may inquire why Euripides, having already so much material, arranged the catastrophe – if indeed the death of the brothers and Iocasta is the catastrophe – in such a way that it takes four messenger-speeches to cope with it? Why does Iocasta take Antigone to the battlefield? Why is the chorus elaborately made to consist of Phoenician women, not Thebans? Why has Oedipus been kept a prisoner in Thebes, and Iocasta been made to survive the disclosure of her tragedy?

As to style, why is the single-combat, far from being treated with Aeschylean reticence, described as if it were a gladiatorial fight? Is this an error of taste, brilliant drama, or both? Why does Euripides in almost every detail arrange the course of the battle differently from Aeschylus? Why is Antigone led to and from the roof with such ostentatious circumspection? Why does Teiresias go out of his way, twice, to inform us that being a prophet is not all jam?

As to characterization, why is Antigone represented first as simply a nice girl – curious, eager, naïve, but with no particular distinction – then as a devoted daughter and sister capable of driving Creon off the stage? What is the point? Is there any reason why in Eteocles melodramatic wickedness should be combined with puerility in military science? Or why Creon, who can teach Eteocles how to manage a campaign, cannot manage Antigone? Such combinations in a character are no doubt possible, but in a play possibility is not enough; we demand significance.

To ask all these questions is to see the answer at once. Euripides is not developing a tragic theme, or he would need neither this amount nor this variety of material; not even a non-tragic but dramatic theme, or the material would have more cohesion (as it has for example in the *Ion*). Out of the Theban legend he is creating what we may call a dramatic pageant, presenting scene after scene for the sake of their immediate and cumulative effect, but not for the sake of an inner drama; therefore he needs a lot of material, and need not be particular about its cohesion. He is bringing before us the whole lively history of the line of Cadmus, presenting on the stage the incidents attending its actual downfall, but bringing in, as opportunity offers, both earlier and later events. This explains the chorus, why it is composed of Phoenicians, and why it is both more active and more consistent than the chorus usually is nowadays. The picturesque origin of the house of Cadmus is dwelt on in the Parodos and in the first stasimon. Any chorus could have recounted these Phoenician legends, but it is infinitely more effective to have them recounted by a company of Phoenician maidens whose presence is a proof of the traditions they celebrate.[1] When it has discharged this task the chorus proceeds to such recent events as lie just out of the reach of the actors – the history of Oedipus (801–17) and the terror of the Sphinx. Oedipus is, of course, one of the actors himself, but he is being kept back to make the climax. If he covers this same ground himself – we must say 'if' as vv. 1595–1614 are spurious – the thrill of hearing the story from the lips of the chief actor in it will prevent us from feeling that it is an idle repetition. The Sphinx-ode

---

[1] The chorus has also the advantage of being more picturesque than a Theban chorus would have been. Cf. vv. 293 ff., 1301.

(1018 ff.) is especially noteworthy. It is written in the operatic style,[1] and like all the references to the incident (indeed, like the whole play itself) it is quite devoid of tragic colouring. We are not made to feel the tragic irony that Oedipus could be so brilliantly intelligent here yet so blind elsewhere. It is only a story of terrible danger, deliverance, and an astonishing sequel. The short stabbing phrases create an atmosphere of excitement and unrest, swiftly taking us through the startling series of events. The ode, in fact, is a chorus of the kind that a Covent Garden audience would insist on having repeated, accurately judging, in its unsophisticated way, its dramatic purpose and value.

The two scenes which separate Polyneices' exit from the messenger-speeches are interesting. There has to be an Eteocles-Creon scene in which Eteocles may provisionally hand over the sovereignty and so carry on the narrative smoothly, but no very intense dramatic interest develops inevitably from this. We may infer that it was to supply the deficiency that the passage on strategy was introduced. The end of the scene calls upon another source of interest that we meet more than once in the play, literary reminiscence; for the posting of the chieftains at the gates justifies itself dramatically (like the story of Polyneices' espousals, and like a great deal of Tennyson) as an echo from the great past. It is possible that there is a cheap sneer at Aeschylus in this passage when Eteocles says 'To give the name of each would be a great waste of time, when the enemy is before the gates' (751 f.). It is equally possible that there is nothing of the sort. Giving the names was not a waste of time in the *Septem,* and it would have been a waste of time in the *Phoenissae,* facts of which Euripides must have been aware; and Aeschylus had safeguarded himself against the criticisms of smart people by seeing to it that unfavourable omens should hold up the attack. Here we can be charitable without discredit, and suppose that Euripides is explaining to his audience why he omits a passage that they would certainly look for.

The Menoeceus scene is a bit unexpected, for it lies beside the

---

[1] For example:

> ἰάλεμοι δὲ ματέρων
> ἰάλεμοι δὲ παρθένων
> ἐστέναζον οἴκοις·
> ἰηιήιον βοάν
> ἰηιήιον μέλος κ.τ.λ. (1034–7).

main stream of the play, but if Euripides can justify it we shall not
object. This time there is no doubt why the scene is there. In the first
place it contains pathos of a dramatic kind, and an interesting and
characteristic novelty,[1] for Creon refuses to be a tragic character
and orders Menoeceus to run for his life. Euripides does, in fact,
make the best of both worlds – deadly sin in a would-be tragic poet,
but good business for the melodramatist – for he has his 'realistic'
Creon and can extract the heroics from Menoeceus. In the second
place, the scene has the advantage of showing us Teiresias once more.
After all, a Theban play without Teiresias would hardly do now.
But Teiresias is not the man he was. Gone are the days when his
supernatural machinery could crush a much stronger Creon than
this one is, or when he could successfully measure himself in strength
and majesty against Oedipus himself. Had not Eteocles tactfully
excused himself at the end of the previous scene we might have had
from Teiresias denunciation of a man hardly worthy of it; as it is,
only Creon is there, and the demand that he makes of Creon smacks
more of irrational magic than of the just anger of offended Heaven.
The demand, however, links us again with the legendary past, and
Teiresias does his best. To compensate for his loss of tragic dignity
he introduces a pathetic note which he had disdained in earlier plays.
His part, he feels, is in danger of being only a *succès d'estime,* so that
he plays on his blindness and weariness. To be the more interesting
he brings with him his 'lots', carried carefully by the daughter who
has succeeded to the boy-guide in the *Antigone.* He lets fall that he
has just had a distinguished success in Athens, and he gives us
glimpses of the man behind the prophet. It is very interesting to see
a great figure at closer quarters, and on the whole Teiresias carries
off a difficult situation with dignity, but there may have been those
who thought his coming a mistake.

When at the end of the Sphinx-ode the first of the two messengers bursts in we are for the moment made to feel that the late
Greek dramatist is as close to the neo-classic as the late Greek scientist
is to his sixteenth-century successor. If we are unwary, we shall
naturally assume that the messenger has come to announce Menoeceus' death – but no; it is the fortunes of Eteocles and Polyneices
that he has on his lips. Menoeceus receives a tribute as parenthetic

---

[1] Cf. the speech in which Iphigeneia, seeking to avoid the sacrifice, declares 'Ignoble
life is better than noble death' (*I.A.,* 1252).

as that accorded to Macaria in the *Heracleidae,* and he passes completely from our minds, until Creon opens the scene following with
a lament for his death; and then again Menoeceus is superseded by
Eteocles and Polyneices and is heard of no more. He is, in fact, very
like the hero of a by-plot, anticipating in his alternate appearances
'the happy loves of Theseus and Dirce'. In tragedy, where thought
is superior to incident, it was unnecessary and would have been
intolerable so to combine stories; now this is an agreeable source of
relief. Complication is succeeding to complexity.

Because incident is now superior to thought we are treated to
four messenger-speeches, and of these the first alone is the longest
we have yet heard. Not since the *Persae* has there been such a flood
of narrative. The reason why we have here five times as much
messenger as in the *Antigone* is plain enough. The usual function of
the messenger-speech was to make some decisive contribution to
the tragedy growing on the stage or in the orchestra; narrative-
detail was subject therefore to the chastening effect of the tragic
burden. But what tragedy is growing here, either on the stage or in
the orchestra? All that these speeches do is to follow and report
scenes of the pageant which escape the limits of the stage.[1]

The resemblance to the *Persae* is quite superficial. Aeschylus is
contriving a tragic theme, not reeling off a story; therefore he makes
the Queen direct things. She, naturally, so directs them that the
merely personal affairs – the safety of Xerxes, the names of the slain
– are cleared out of the way first; this being not only what probability suggests but also what the interests of the tragedy demand,
for in this way Aeschylus can develop, unhampered, his tragic
theme, the descent of Heaven's wrath upon the Persians. It is because
the speeches present a tragic action in the first place and a narrative
only in the second that they have such weight and poise. Incident is
subordinated to thought, and it is the thought that makes the form.
But Euripides is presenting narrative, and it is the events themselves
that must create the form, the presentation obediently following
them. He does not want weight and poise, but speed and vividness.

---

[1] This was one of the functions of the Teichoskopia. The brilliance and the extent
of the Argive host are used neither to emphasize the peril in which Thebes stands nor
to throw into relief the courage or wickedness of a hero. It is decoration, in the Epic
manner; that is why it can be set in a decorative frame – the careful emergence of
Antigone on to the roof and her careful descent are as much part of the total effect as
the Argive army itself.

Aeschylus, because he was using the dramatic form for a dramatic purpose, found that the arrangement which was tragically necessary was also natural; Euripides, because he is using the dramatic form (or at any rate the Greek dramatic form) for a purpose which is, strictly speaking, alien to it, namely narrative, finds that what is dramatically necessary is not natural. The actual situation demands that the Messenger should at once tell Iocasta the news which so urgently calls for her intervention, and that the story of the assault on the walls should be told afterwards to whoever cared to listen; the dramatic necessity, however, is that we should hear the whole thing from the beginning, and should realize gradually that there is to be no traditional meeting of the brothers at the seventh gate; and the dramatic necessity must prevail. Since we are, ourselves, all agog to hear the whole story in due order, and since our interest in Iocasta is sensational, not tragic and therefore paramount, the difficulty is not grave, and the pretence that the Messenger has a childish aversion from telling bad news is quite enough to lull our conscience. This is not a play in which we scrutinize motives and characters very closely. Indeed, the knowledge that the Messenger has something up his sleeve lends an extra thrill to his first story. Atossa directed the Persian, but Iocasta is led by the Theban.

Euripides' manipulation of the events invites comparison with Aeschylus' in the *Septem*. As he is using the same story as Aeschylus but omitting the thought, we must expect him to make good the loss in other ways, not only by covering more ground, but also in making that ground more superficially attractive. He must introduce novelty. To the tragic poet novelty of incident is a trifle; to the romantic or melodramatic playwright it is everything; so that either he invents an original plot, as Agathon did (and Euripides, virtually, in the *Ion* and the *Helen*), or, using a traditional plot, he gives it unexpected turns. Euripides completely refashions the story of the attack, partly for the sake of doing something new, but always in the interests of fuller and more exciting narrative.

The brothers do not meet at the seventh gate. As the *Phoenissae* has no moral basis worth mentioning, such an event could hardly be made significant of anything but chance – perhaps not a bad effect; but how much more melodrama there is in avoiding this classic dénouement and inventing a direct challenge and a single-combat. We have our assault on the walls notwithstanding, we have the dreadful thrill of seeing the brothers deliberately seeking each other out, we have the brilliant account of the fight (so studiously avoided by tragedy), the suicide of Iocasta, and a general battle to finish with. The vividness of the whole is increased by the serialist's device of breaking off at critical moments (1263, 1424). Euripides is not writing tragically, and the effect of immediacy given by this device actively prevents us from thinking tragically ourselves.

In the first speech Euripides retains the description of the Argive champions, but it is a purely physical description. Mottoes, boasts and taunts are left out; in this non-moral play they would have been so much lumber. In the interests of speed the Theban defenders are passed over; they were essential to Aeschylus, but would not have justified their presence here. Of Amphiaraus, so tragic a figure in the *Septem,* Euripides can make nothing; on the other hand Zeus' destruction of Capaneus becomes the sensational climax of the whole story, and when an enthusiastic interpolator added that Capaneus' limbs cart-wheeled in all directions, like Ixion's, his hair reaching Olympus and his blood the earth, he was but going too far along a road upon which Euripides himself had discreetly entered.

Iocasta's visit to the battlefield is a good stroke; even more picturesque is her summoning of Antigone – still fearful of the conventions. When she gets there Antigone does not do much, for all our attention in the fourth speech is concentrated upon the dying brother and Iocasta, but she had to be there in order to lead the procession home and so to be in position for the Exodos. In every conceivable way the old tragic material is rejuvenated – and 'rejuvenated' is the right word. Euripides will have no nonsense about tragic restraint, for he knows perfectly well that tragic restraint is for tragedy.

Some competent versifier, thinking more of the story than of the tragedy, added a scene to the *Septem*; but, nevertheless, the *Septem* ends where Aeschylus ended it, and the lean-to shed is a plain disfigurement.[1] Aeschylus' play is complete when his tragic thought is complete. But the death of Eteocles and Polyneices is not obviously the end of this pageant, and there is no train of thought here to reach its fulfilment. Without doing Euripides any injustice we can imagine him asking himself how and where he could best wind up

[1] As that very simple-minded metrician Hephaestion says of his 'hypercatalectic syllable', it is something added πρὸς τῷ τελείῳ.

his play. The succession of incidents goes on – there is for example
the burial of Polyneices. There cannot be a tragic full-close, for
there is no tragedy, but there can be a scene more impressive and
pathetic than any that has gone before. After the ten other characters,
after sacrifice, fratricide, suicide and battle, Oedipus himself is sent
in to bat. It was then for this that he has been kept in Thebes, hidden
in the palace. The old King can make a grand finale, telling his
astonishing story and then departing into hopeless exile. This must
be the end.

It involves one difficulty. If Antigone is to defy Creon and bury
Polyneices, she must suddenly grow into heroic stature. But the
audience has not been seriously interested in her and her character,
and Euripides can take the bold, and logical, course; he puts side by
side Antigone the nice girl and Antigone the heroine. In an ethical
drama this would be impossible; it is possible here because our
interest in her has been purely sensational and momentary. If she
helps to round off a grand story in a grand way, we shall not examine too ungratefully the means by which the dénouement is
brought about.[1]

It seems certain that the last scene, as we have it, is not what
Euripides wrote. It is most unlikely that he struggled into the confusion whereby Antigone both buries Polyneices and accompanies
Oedipus.[2] It is likely that it was an interpolator, not Euripides, who
provided Oedipus with his refuge at Colonus (a *contaminatio* with
the *Coloneus*), and that Euripides ended with Antigone remaining
in Thebes to bury Polyneices, and watching Oedipus as he groped
his sightless way into the unknown. This would be a spectacular
finish to a spectacular play, an interesting contrast with the end of
the *Coloneus*. Both are fine endings, but Sophocles' means more.

In the examination-paper with which we began we might have
asked this question: Explain why in the prologue these details are

[1] Some critics, naturally, have seen an interesting psychological development in
her character. This is impossible. Between the Teichoskopia and v. 1264 Antigone
has been in her dressing-room, neither seen nor mentioned; for us therefore she has
not existed – certainly not vividly enough to 'develop'. All that has happened to her
since v. 1265 is that she has been carried off (still fearful of the conventions) to a
battlefield and has witnessed the violent deaths of most of her family. If, then, development was intended it is quite unexplained and is therefore totally uninteresting. (See
below, p. 371, on Iphigeneia.)

[2] H. O. Meredith, in an attractive and ingenious paper (*C.R.*, LI, 97 ff.), has tried
to defend everything, but by using so many special assumptions that the result is
unconvincing. The view adopted here I have argued further in *C.R.*, 1939, pp. 104 ff.

mentioned; that Laius gave way to pleasure in the heat of wine, that Merope persuaded Polybus that the child was her own, that Oedipus gave Polybus Laius' chariot, that Oedipus named Antigone, Iocasta Ismene. None of these details comes to anything in the play; all might be omitted without loss – except, significantly, loss of brightness. The purely spectacular course that the play takes might be prophesied from the prologue. It is more than the conventional rehearsal of events which we have seen to be its usual and reasonable task in Euripides, for throughout it takes pains to be lively. We have distinguished three ways in which Greek drama has regarded past events: they have (as in the *Agamemnon*) been used as a living element in the present; they have been something affecting the present and therefore mentioned as required (as in the *Tyrannus*), and they have been only the causal prelude to the present, stowed away therefore in the conventional prologue. Now, in so far as the prelude is not conventional but bright and interesting, they are once more a real part of the play. Iocasta's intimate details, like Oedipus' narrative, are part of the pageant. They enable the dramatist to overstep the narrow limits of the stage in his search for the picturesque and dramatic; the chorus enable him to go still further back and to colour the present scene much more effectively. This is what it did in the *Agamemnon* – but now the colours are only pretty. The chorus in this play has a more assured position than it has enjoyed for some time, but its position so clearly depends on the accident of the dramatic setting that it must feel its end drawing near.

The *Phoenissae* then, because it is not tragic, but aims simply at creating a certain theatrical effect, falls into the same broad category as the tragi-comedies and the melodramas, but it differs from them in choosing for special development a different element of the complete dramatic form. Complication of plot, comedy and satire play no part in it, character-drawing hardly more; $\mu\tilde{\upsilon}\theta\sigma\varsigma$, in the form of extended narrative, and $\pi\acute{\alpha}\theta\sigma\varsigma$ predominate, with naturalism, operatics and a certain autumnal literary reminiscence to lend variety. A legend in which tragedy has found some of the noblest of its material is, for this new age, passed in review, with every attention paid to the possibilities of dramatic situation and narrative, but with no trace of tragic thought. Greek Tragedy in fact is ending where Wilamowitz said it began, in the presentation of Saga. Early tragedy (meaning, of course, the best of it) developed, as in a vertical plane, the tragic implications inherent in a situation that did not need to move at all. Now we are at the opposite pole; the situation must always be moving, and the inner drama, the vertical development, which had been everything, has ceased to exist.

Therefore we ought again to reconsider the meaning of Unity of Action. The criticisms made in the Argument to our play are true and irrelevant; if the scenes were as strictly related to each other here as they are in the *Ion*, we should have not a better play but a different sort of play. Aristotle's insistence on intellectual unity of plot must not be applied blindly to a play which is sensational and not intellectual.

Greek drama, Greek art in general, is conspicuously intellectual; what distinguishes the Greek dramatists from Shakespeare more perhaps than anything else is the point at which they begin to apply pure intellect to their work. In neither case is there the faintest doubt but that the drama originated where all living art must originate, in the intuitive, non-intellectual part of the mind; but with the Greeks it is impossible for criticism to penetrate to a point at which the poet's intellect is not already active; however far back we go, we find the pure tragic feeling already precipitated as a tragic thesis, already embodied in a plot; so that a Greek Tragedy without Words, if the thing were possible, would still be tragic; the 'meaning' is woven into the structure itself.

This suited Aristotle admirably. It was inevitable that he should insist on the intellectual virtues of Greek drama – not knowing that Shakespeare was going to exhibit some of the most marvellous of his pictures in makeshift buildings. But when we come to the *Phoenissae,* whose origin is not a tragic apprehension such as set the dramatist's intellect greedily at work, we must question the validity of Aristotle's intellectualism. His canons make for elegance of form, but elegance of form is a minor virtue; the Greek dramatists never made it their aim, but attained it, usually, as a by-product of the effort to present their idea as clearly as possible. In the *Phoenissae* the dramatic idea is to obtain a certain dramatic effect by presenting certain scenes from a certain legend; everything therefore which does in fact contribute to that effect is a logical part of the scheme, and a criticism which says that this scene or that is not 'logically' connected with the rest shows only that it has not realized what that scheme was. The self-sacrifice of Menoeceus has a connexion with the rest of the play which may be found but is not very close, yet since it gives depth to the story no objection can be taken to it. We are entitled to say that we think this a relatively poor form of drama, but we must not apply to it canons which have no validity. When the Athenians heard the fight between the brothers described with such relish, when they saw material which Aeschylus had charged with such tragic significance being used up for the sake of a romantic scene on the roof, some irreconcilable conservatives may have grumbled that Euripides was turning a church into a cinema. So he was, but it is very good cinema.

5. The 'Iphigeneia in Aulis'

The *I.A.* has its merits, but Greek Tragedy has its standards. Judged by these it is a thoroughly second-rate play; but it has considerable interest in literary history. It is important to realize that the play is relatively feeble not because Euripides missed his aim for once, being incompetent, tired or uninterested; he did what he set out to do, and did it with his accustomed sureness of touch. The play is second-rate because the whole idea was second-rate.

It might be interesting to speculate on the influences which led Euripides to write this West-end half-tragedy at a time when he had the elemental stuff of the *Bacchae* in him. Did he begin and nearly finish it in Athens, for and under the influence of an audience which no longer wanted tragedy pure and strong; then, going into the fresher air of Macedonia, drop this pretty but tired play unfinished in order to rise, like Samson, and shake the world with his *Bacchae*? In rescuing the *I.A.* from his father's literary remains Euripides the Younger did little to increase his father's fame, but he helped us to understand why the Alexandrian scholars thought nothing later in Greek Tragedy worth preserving.

Our affair, however, is not with speculation but with literary fact. What is the play about, and will its general conception explain its features without sending us for refuge to *ad hoc* assumptions of old age, political references, or ineptitude?

In order that the Expedition may proceed, Agamemnon has bidden his daughter to come to Aulis, nominally to be married to Achilles, really to be sacrificed. He is not a man of firm character (332), and in the romantic scene which follows the original plain prologue he is seen countermanding that order. The second letter is intercepted by Menelaus, a brutal ruffian who can see only that Agamemnon is breaking his word and letting a brother down. His scornful speech draws a picture of Agamemnon – one which passes unchallenged – as a mean careerist; Agamemnon in reply throws just as disillusioning a light upon Helen and upon the famous Oath of the Suitors. Suddenly Menelaus changes what we have to call his mind – but it is too late, for a messenger has announced the arrival of Iphigeneia and of her mother too. This is extremely awkward, but for a moment we may wonder how it justifies the tragic to-do that Agamemnon makes about it. The reason is that although apparently he could safely have refused to send for his daughter at all, now that she is here the army will insist on her being killed. Odysseus, a very wicked man indeed, who exercises a complete ascendancy over the Greeks, will stampede them, even to the sacking of Argos, and nothing can be done about it. Nor is this a private nightmare of Agamemnon's, for in the event the enraged army pursues Achilles – his own Myrmidons in the van – thirsting for Iphigeneia's blood and for the attack on Troy. Agamemnon has no choice but to go through with the miserable business, deceiving his wife and daughter as long as he can.

He does not deceive them for long. Achilles appears, demanding reasons for the delay in sailing; his men insist on going forward or going home.[1] But he meets Clytemnestra instead of Agamemnon, and the secret is soon out. He gallantly undertakes the defence of Iphigeneia, but this comes to nothing. Iphigeneia, who has at first tearfully protested, changes her mind as suddenly as Menelaus did, and goes willingly to the altar, where Artemis makes the miraculous substitution of a kid.

Now this is not a bad story, but it is not really tragic, and Euripides knows it. That is the reason why he does not trust to the story alone for his dramatic effect. There is tragedy in the story: Aeschylus showed us that when he made it part of the tragedy of Agamemnon who, sacrificing his daughter to his conception of duty and revenge, lays up retribution for himself. Agamemnon has his torments in this

---

[1] Why does Euripides so carefully avoid the strong contrary winds of Aeschylus? The Greeks are suffering from ἄπλοια (88), they lack favouring winds (352), and Achilles complains of waiting in the light breezes of the Euripus (813). The Myrmidons see no reason for waiting except the irresolution of the commanders.

play, but he has no tragic choice, and as the play proceeds the emphasis is laid not on what the guilty man will have to suffer but simply on the fate of the innocent Iphigeneia. Indeed we can hardly call Agamemnon a guilty sinner as he is here presented. The chorus in its only reference to the situation (1080–97) says something to this effect, but he is, in fact, drawn as a man who has levered himself into importance by unworthy means, a crafty, indecisive character, undeserving of our serious interest. His indecision at a critical moment lands him in a situation in which he has no choice but to commit an atrocious crime; but in order to apply the squeeze to him Euripides has to pretend that the Greek army is composed entirely of ogres. We see Agamemnon squirm; it may be a dramatic but it is not a tragic spectacle. Aristotle rightly said that the downfall of a bad man is φιλάνθρωπον but is not tragic;[1] here even τὸ φιλάνθρωπον is wanting, as the play moves right away from Agamemnon. Tragic illumination ought to be the justification of this cruel story, but we have only the story.[2]

There is no tragedy of Agamemnon, nor is there a tragedy of Iphigeneia. From her point of view the incident is nothing but a cruel blow of fate. As such it may, perhaps, be compared superficially with the blow that fell on Pelasgus, but the comparison is valueless. An incident is tragic or not tragic according to the treatment. We cannot, in fact, isolate an incident in literature from its treatment. What happened to Pelasgus is filled with significance; what happened to Iphigeneia remains what happened to Iphigeneia. We are no wiser; this combination of an unexplained demand from a goddess, an incompetent father and a frenzied army is a particular and not a universal, ἃ ἐγένετο but not οἷα ἂν γένοιτο.

These remarks would not surprise Euripides. He knew tha the was not, like Aeschylus, writing a tragedy of Agamemnon; that is the reason why he abandons him. He knew that the story, as he tells it, was melodramatic, with no illumination, no catharsis, to relieve

[1] Poetics, 1453a, 2 ff. Φιλάνθρωπον means, roughly, satisfactory to our sense of justice.

[2] Emerging once from a performance of a gloomy modern play which took itself to be tragedy, I met a stupid acquaintance who said to me 'I don't like these tragedies. What I always say is that there is enough tragedy in real life'. Now to be a critic no doubt one has to be clever, but a stupid man can tell one end of a stick from the other. My friend was not clever enough to see that the play was not a tragedy, but he had the sense to feel that it was a cruel story which meant nothing and was therefore an unnecessary infliction.

and justify its cruelty; that is the reason why Iphigeneia is not after all slain. Once more the happy ending replaces tragic catharsis.[1] Above all, this explains why the theme is subjected to such picturesque and diverse ornament. After reading the *Electra* and the *Orestes* we can imagine Euripides turning this incident into a morbid psychological study, and a very different play it would have been. After reading the *Hecuba* and the *Troades* we can imagine him turning it into social tragedy; that, too, would have made a very different play. The structure of this play is consistent with neither of these dramatic aims, but it is consistent with the dramatic aim that made the *Phoenissae*. Let us look at it a little more closely, beginning with the sacrifice.

Iphigeneia is first quite natural; recalling Creon in the *Phoenissae* she declares that it is better to live ingloriously than to die gloriously. Then she sings an elaborate and wild song against Paris, Helen, her father, the whole expedition. Finally, when it becomes clear that there is no defence and that Achilles is in serious danger, she readily offers herself for sacrifice; not as one still thinking the whole thing monstrous yet preferring to face the inevitable before it involves others, but as one who is going to die gloriously, save Greece and 'set it free', teach barbarians a lesson – all sorts of nonsense. Shakespeare at his most patriotic never wrote like this, and we are justified in calling it nonsense because even Menelaus has seen that Helen is not worth fetching back and that Iphigeneia has nothing to do with the affair.

Either Iphigeneia has changed her attitude fundamentally for reasons which are not divulged and for a dramatic purpose which remains obscure, or her characterization is, as Aristotle said, inconsistent. It is idle to defend the change of attitude by saying that it is possible; what indeed is not? Those who make this brave apology should look again at the *Poetics*: 'if a character is inconsistent ... let it be consistently inconsistent.' Inconsistency, to be permissible, must be significant of something, since a play, or any other work of art, exists not to record the possible but to create something of meaning. In the street we do not expect to see the meaning of everything; in a play we certainly do.

But why did Euripides do so extraordinary a thing? He was no novice, and if he were he would surely have avoided this error, and

[1] P. 315.

that, too, without much trouble. We have therefore to see if there is an explanation a little less improbable than that when he wrote the end of the scene he had forgotten the beginning. It may help if we recall Polyxena. Her sacrifice was a part of an undoubted tragedy, and it admitted of no miraculous substitution. She met death willingly, explaining that she had no reason to prefer life; the reason for this being that there was no need to add horror to tragedy. The tragedy would not have gained in significance had she had, like Antigone, every reason for clinging to life. Iphigeneia also goes willingly – because nothing else is dramatically decent. Why then does she first speak and sing so passionately on the other side? Because nothing else would have been interesting. That is to say, her character, like that of Antigone in the *Phoenissae,* is controlled entirely by what the situation of the moment requires; but since the two Antigones are separated by the length of the play while the two Iphigeneias could shake hands, the inconsistency is much more glaring here. Whether Euripides has justified his neglect of consistency here no one can say who has not seen the play acted, and acted properly; the real test is whether it comes off or not. To the reader it certainly appears that he has gone too far.

But if Iphigeneia's character is notoriously obscure, what of Menelaus'? When he first appears he is the simple melodramatic ruffian, outraged that Agamemnon has recanted; for entrapping and killing a daughter is, to him, a trifle compared with the crime of letting a brother down. But within a hundred verses he has veered round completely. Grasping Agamemnon's hand he is all repentance, magnanimity, clear-sightedness; he can even declare that Helen is better where she is – a point which Euripides has already suggested to him in several plays. He enjoys his repentance (502 f.) – but what has brought it about? The sight of Agamemnon's distress: really, until this very minute it had never occurred to him that killing a daughter might be unpleasant.

This, too, is no doubt possible, but it is a little thin. One would in fact easily suspect him of playing some deep game were it not that a moment later the reformed villain makes the constructive suggestion of murdering Calchas: dead men tell no tales. But, possible or not, where is the point? Euripides could easily have kept his Menelaus consistently brutal and yet dramatically interesting by not allowing Odysseus to have cognizance of the prophecy and making Menelaus tell him of it. The point is simply the sudden reversal of situation, Menelaus saying 'No, don't kill her', and Agamemnon 'Yes, I must'. We may look for deeper significance, but we shall not find it.

Because Euripides knows that his theme is not serious enough to sustain the play unaided, he does not rely on it. The play, like a modern biography, must at all costs be bright and interesting, but there is a brightness of truth, and there is a brightness that is preferred to truth. With a sort of satisfaction we have been learning lately that our heroes were not heroic; Athens at this time was experiencing similar delights. The wicked Menelaus of the *Andromache*, the cunning Odysseus of the *Philoctetes* were dramatically true, because their badness was a logical part of a serious dramatic plan; it is difficult to say as much for the meanness of Agamemnon here. Agamemnon is being 'debunked'. The picture of the King of Men 'on the make' is entirely consistent with the pictures of Iphigeneia unheroically natural and unreally heroic, and with this artificial reversal of situation of which at least the one half, Menelaus', can have no real significance.

In default of a real theme, Euripides taps every other source of interest. He plays for all he is worth on the sentimental appeal of the infant Orestes; he makes a very good and romantic scene out of Agamemnon's writing of the second letter.[1] But Clytemnestra and Achilles are more revealing. Clytemnestra gets out of her chariot with unrivalled impressiveness, and presently, when she is confronting Agamemnon with his wickedness, she speaks of her past relations with him and tells us something that Aeschylus never knew (1148 ff.). It is nothing to the point, but it is a vastly exciting piece of gossip. In this speech she does everything except what the situation, if it were a real one, would demand, namely that she should destroy Agamemnon in about ten verses. But then, the truth would have been a little too plain and unsophisticated; how much more elegant and interesting it is for us to see Clytemnestra getting into her stride and threatening Agamemnon with the *Agamemnon*.

The search for brightness magnifies Achilles' part beyond all recognition. His intervention alters nothing and affects nobody,

---

[1] It seems that Euripides the Younger still further brightened up his father's play by dropping the plain conventional prologue and starting off with the anapaestic passage between the King and the Slave. The scene in fact is extremely good, and sounds oddly Elizabethan.

except that its complete failure is used as an excuse for Iphigeneia's heroics. Achilles does nothing which, if this were tragedy, could not have been done through a reasonably competent Messenger – except one or two things which, if this were tragedy, would not have been done at all. Only Achilles in person could complete that intriguing scene of cross-purposes in which Clytemnestra, so very much the lady, greets Achilles, so very much the gentleman, as her imminent son-in-law. Only Achilles in person could provide us with that delicate character-sketch, so cleverly beginning with the word ὑψηλόφρων ('high-minded'), so full of ironical humour, so reminiscent of Plato's young men; or the sketch of the young aristocrat who has graduated in Chiron's cave and can therefore write himself a glowing testimonial – which includes parenthetically the fact that ten thousand girls are pining for his love. This has nothing to do with Iphigeneia, but it all helps to pass the time pleasantly and intelligently.[1]

The chorus, naturally, has to be very discreet. It may feel disposed to make the orchestra re-echo with gloomy prophetic thunders, but it has to be careful lest it blow the play to pieces. The long *parodos* is couched in the same style as the odes of the *Phoenissae* – non-moral, non-intellectual, a piece of pure description. The first stasimon philosophizes mildly about Love, with special reference to Paris; the second describes by anticipation scenes from the war; the third sings prettily about the marriage of Achilles' parents. Not until we reach the final stanza of this last stasimon is there any serious reference to the matter in hand.

We see then that neither in the chorus odes nor in the general lay-out of the play is there anything to persuade us that Euripides was thinking tragically about Agamemnon or Iphigeneia. The sacrifice is a dramatic and pathetic incident; but from the romantic night-scene with which we start to the miracle with which we end everything demonstrates that Euripides was less concerned with what he could put into the story than with what he could get out of it. In comparison with the *Phoenissae* the *I.A.* is weak, and the weakness seems to lie in this, that although the *Phoenissae* no less than the *I.A.* uses in a relatively superficial manner material which we might expect it to use tragically, the Theban pageant has a sweep

---

[1] Is it simply in order not to raise our tragic expectations that the winds are not allowed to howl against the waiting ships?

and a movement which lends itself to this objective treatment. The *I.A.* lacks this sweep, and it insistently raises but evades issues which we feel ought to be faced. It was very unconventional but clever of Agathon to invent a new plot for himself which he could treat as romantically as he chose without encountering at every turn the disconcerting ghost of Tragedy.

CHAPTER XIII

Two Last Plays

The *Bacchae* and the *Oedipus Coloneus* may seem an oddly assorted pair of plays, but they have an historical nexus which an historical study of Greek Tragedy may recognize with advantage: for both were produced posthumously. We may go further, for both plays are markedly different in form and in manner from their immediate predecessors. As if the thunder from Heaven that so impressively warns Oedipus of his approaching end had been audible in Macedonia as well as in Sophocles' native Colonus, Sophocles and Euripides alike seem to gather their forces for one last effort, each to embody, as in a testament, his final vision of the tragedy of man. Each develops a theme which is recognizably a continuation of earlier work, and the result is surprising; for Euripides writes a drama which, for all its wild movement and romantic colouring, is much more regular in form than most of his earlier tragedies, while Sophocles, the master of structure, approaches an almost Euripidean looseness of form.

1. The 'Bacchae'

The freshness and beauty of its poetry puts the *Bacchae* almost in a class of its own among the tragedies of Euripides; so does its dramatic style, which is our immediate concern.

This posthumous tragedy offers the remarkable spectacle of a dramatist returning to the methods and style – of his youth we cannot say, as he was nearly fifty when he wrote the *Medea,* but of a period of twenty or twenty-five years earlier. The *Bacchae* is the best constructed of all his tragedies. Many would claim this honour for the *Hippolytus,* perhaps rightly; yet the *Bacchae* has more unity, and it has a dramatic impetus not felt in every corner of the *Hippolytus.* With the tragedies that followed the *Hippolytus,* from the

Heracleidae to the *Troades,* the *Bacchae* has very little in common – a fact which of itself shows the absurdity of trying to treat dramatic style as something that develops and can be studied separately, independently of dramatic content. Nor can we attribute to any one external cause, whether old age or contemporary taste, both the relative looseness of the *Coloneus* and the unusual tautness of the *Bacchae.*

A very rapid survey of the *Bacchae* will establish the contrast that we are considering. The theme is begun, the impetus started, at the very beginning of the prologue. Already in the first ten verses we hear of a miracle, the still-burning fire that had consumed Semele – a miracle which ought to have been enough to silence the sophisms of Cadmus and to instil some doubts into the dogmatic mind of Pentheus. Another miracle follows: the god has caused the vine to grow over his mother's tomb. Next the prologue asserts the universality of the new religion (13–22), and continues by presenting the situation of the moment. Leaving Asia for Greece, Dionysus has come first to Thebes; his kinsmen, misled by Cadmus' sophisms, reject him, and, since his own city must be brought to accept him, he has driven the women out upon the mountains, mad; Pentheus, his particular opponent, must be made to recognize the new god-head.

Here, in fifty verses, not only is the scope of the play defined with perfect clarity, but also the dramatic rhythm is already started. Not often are these introductory monologues so incisive in style.

This incisiveness remains with the whole play. The first scene goes with an admirable vigour, and it has variety beyond what is usual in the tragedies. The old prophet, who sincerely accepts the new religion,[1] the old King, who accepts it, but not sincerely, and the young King, who rejects it utterly – these make a scene of a vividness which we can parallel from the tragi-comedies, but hardly from the tragedies. After the stasimon there is the terse Servant who brings in the disguised god with a warning story of fresh miracles; then a vigorous and natural stichomythia leads to the imprisonment of Dionysus by the infatuated Pentheus. There is his miraculous escape, the first Messenger's speech, so well placed – a final warning

[1] Perhaps, as Mr Grube thinks, only with the sincerity of the professional ecclesiastic. (My references to Mr Grube are to his interesting article on the play in *Trans. American Philolog. Assocn.,* LXVI, 37 ff.)

to Pentheus, which, however, serves only to provoke him to his last act of ὕβρις, the calling out of the army, as foreshadowed in the prologue. Now comes a very dramatic surprise. At v. 810 Dionysus, realizing that Pentheus is inaccessible to both persuasion and warning, changes his tactics; instead of overwhelming Pentheus and his Theban army as he had proposed (vv. 50–2), he decides to take a more terrible revenge on Pentheus alone, the revenge that we are soon to see.[1]

We need hardly continue. The whole plot moves with unwonted speed and directness, and is so well constructed and balanced that it is made to turn visibly at this one point. It is an organic unity, a complete contrast to the plots of all the surviving tragedies later than the *Hippolytus*. There is, indeed, one difficulty, the famous Palace-miracle,[2] but its solution is simple, and in any case it is a difficulty of a different order from the intrusive scenes and ill-made plots of the earlier plays.

To the schematic tragedies the *Medea* and *Hippolytus* also stood in sharp contrast, yet the *Bacchae* does not very closely resemble these either. The *Medea* has its formal inconveniences in the Aegeus-scene and the 'irrational' ending, while the *Hippolytus* falls dramatically (though not tragically) into two parts, and cannot make its chorus an integral part of its structure. No criticisms of this kind can be urged against the *Bacchae*; it has formal unity and it has a dramatic impulse which drives the action forward without deviation or slackening. The last scene is no exception. Critics who, in spite of the prologue, fix their attention exclusively on Pentheus have to make the familiar excuses. Tyrrell for example says[3] that a modern dramatist would have ended, with applause, at v. 1372. No doubt he would, but the reason why Euripides does not is not that he had no curtain, that he wanted to connect his story with the whole cycle of surrounding myths, that he wished at the end to raise the god above these mundane adventures. Such considerations have, sometimes, their place, but here the first point, which makes others unnecessary, is that Dionysus is not avenging himself on Pentheus only but on all those – Cadmus and his dupes – who have rejected him. The

[1] This point I owe to Mr Grube.

[2] Of this Norwood and Verrall had one explanation; a different one will be adopted below.

[3] Introduction to his edition of the play, p. 39.

theme is stated in the prologue and would be incomplete without the epilogue.[1]

It is perhaps in plot that the special position of the *Bacchae* among the tragedies is most evident, but in other respects it differs noticeably from at least the tragedies of the second group. For example, we cannot fail to be struck with the much more normal treatment of character. To assert that the characterization here is more convincing (in the ordinary dramatic sense) than that of the *Medea* and the *Hippolytus* might needlessly provoke dissent; certainly it is to those plays that we must turn for a parallel, and some would perhaps agree that in Medea, Jason and Hippolytus there is an exaggeration completely absent from Pentheus.[2] His honest narrowness makes him a round, not a flat character. Moreover, we see his defiance of the new religion growing; each successive event that ought to make him pause serves only to drive him to still more uncompromising opposition. Not since we saw Phaedra have we been so strongly reminded of Sophocles' methods. To make Pentheus even more Aristotelian Cadmus praises him (1308–12) for his filial respect and piety; he is a normally well-meaning man, but his complete lack of imagination ruins him.[3] We may notice, too, how the novelty of the Dionysiac religion is emphasized (e.g. 219, 467); this, as it is some excuse for Pentheus, plays its part in making him so much of a Middle Tragedy hero.

Situation as well as plot is handled more after the fashion of Middle Tragedy. We should look long in the Euripidean tragedy before we found another triangular scene as natural and significant as that between the two old men and Pentheus. The Helen-Hecuba-Menelaus scene is at least as successful – success is not in question – but it is rhetorical rather than natural; throughout the *Bacchae* there is real interplay between the characters. We have seen from the tragi-comedies that Euripides can manage these effects; we have seen why the earlier tragedies did not use them; now we are inquiring why the *Bacchae* does. Reminiscent, too, of Middle Tragedy is the unforced contrast between the Servant, who arrests Dionysus, and Pentheus. The Servant feels shame at his treatment of the

---

[1] As Wilamowitz impatiently asked, 'Kann man denn nicht lesen?'

[2] I do not wish to suggest that therefore the *Bacchae* is a better play. We are not awarding certificates but comparing methods.

[3] I cannot agree with Mr Grube's view of this passage, 'whitewashing of the villain'. It oversimplifies both Pentheus and the play to make him 'the villain'.

unresisting captive, fear too; Pentheus cannot feel either. It is a simple enough point, and would hardly deserve comment except that its naturalness is uncommon in the Euripidean tragedy. Characters like Medea's Paedagogus are natural, and effectively so, but their naturalistic touches do not illuminate the tragedy of the central figure in this intimate, Sophoclean way.

With this more normal treatment of character and situation there goes an actuality or imaginativeness in the treatment which has for some time been lacking. Not often does Euripides remind us of Aeschylus, but there is assuredly an Aeschylean flavour in the first of the scenes between Pentheus and Dionysus: Pentheus is so confident, so unconscious of his ὕβρις and the rationalistic infatuation that possesses him; he marches so blindly towards the doom that awaits him. His presumption is symbolized terribly in his actions. He cuts the lock (ἱερὸς ὁ πλόκαμος) from the unresisting god's brow; he wrests the thyrsus from his hand. It is the method of Clytemnestra's carpet over again.

Nor is it accidental that this same scene recalls Cassandra's 'To what house have I come?' The chorus prosaically answered 'To Atreus'. So here Dionysus says 'You know not . . . what you are doing nor who you are' (506), and Pentheus answers 'Pentheus, son of Agave and Echion'. Aeschylean, too, is the recklessness with which Pentheus orders the destruction of Teiresias' seat of augury. Sophocles' Oedipus may insult the prophet, or his Creon defy him:

> Him shall ye never bury in the tomb;
> No, not though Heaven's own eagles were to snatch
> And bear him in their talons to the throne.
> Not even so, for dread of that defilement
> Will I permit his burial.

It is shocking, but it is hyperbole:

> For well I know
> There is no mortal can defile the gods.[1]

Sophocles' characters remain in touch with the instinctive scruples of mankind;[2] this Pentheus is an Aeschylean infatuate, he is another Agamemnon burning the temples of Troy.

---

[1] *Antig.*, 1039 ff. Trans. Harrower.
[2] See above, p. 335 (the comparison between the two Electras).

But Euripides, at his most Aeschylean, does not cease to be Euripidean. Typical of his wry and rather disconcerting manner is the apparent comedy of the two old men dressed up for the dance. Since Euripides was not English, we must not hastily credit him with the doctrine that any joke is better than no joke; nevertheless the apparent comedy was avoidable. To Pentheus the two old men are a revolting sight, but it is part of the lesson which he must learn that the claims of Dionysus are absolute. The comedy is purposeful, and the clue has been given in the prologue. We have heard of the universality of the new religion, and that Dionysus has driven the women mad; it would be poor acting that allowed us to guffaw at Cadmus and Teiresias. Dionysus has nothing to do with Pentheus' respectability; the old men are to own his sway, as Pentheus himself will do, so much more terribly, in his last scene.[1]

Before we leave the topic of the general dramatic style of the *Bacchae* there is one further point to notice. It was suggested in an earlier chapter that some of the prominent features in Euripides' tragic style – the prevalence of rhetoric and dialectic, excursions into political, ethical or literary theory – were to be explained directly, though perhaps not wholly, by the general nature of those plays. If so, we should expect the *Bacchae,* a play much more akin in structure and feeling to Middle Tragedy, to be free from these things. In fact, it is. Reflections are made about 'wisdom', but they all arise directly out of the conflict of Pentheus with Dionysus; there is no discussion whatever of extraneous topics. Now at last the tragedy that Euripides is presenting on the stage fills his mind to the exclusion of everything else. There is nothing of the tragic idea left over.

Such is the real 'problem of the *Bacchae*', that suddenly Euripides returns to tragedy (Macedonia helps to explain this), and that he writes a tragedy in which plot, characterization, and general dramatic style are not only entirely different from anything that we have seen in his tragedy since the *Hippolytus,* but even more normal than the *Hippolytus* and *Medea* themselves. It is not difficult to see the explanation of this, but before we discuss it, we may conveniently deal with the one special difficulty of the plot, namely, the Palace-miracle.

The bleak rationalism of the last generation could not allow that

[1] 'The god has made no distinction, whether young or old are to dance to him. He will be honoured equally by all' (206–8).

in the *Bacchae* Euripides was doing anything but attacking, exposing and ridiculing the Dionysiac religion. Norwood and Verrall, sceptics more fortunate than Pentheus, seized on the Palace-miracle with delight; it was the refinement of wit that though in the middle of the play the palace should be shaken and burned to the ground, during the rest of it nobody should notice the fact and Pentheus himself should go in and out as if nothing had happened. There is a real difficulty here, not lessened by the silence of commentators.

But what does the Palace-miracle amount to? Mr Grube (to whom it occurred to read the text) points out that the chorus feels an earth-tremor, sees pillars and entablatures parting asunder, and predicts that the palace will fall to the ground – but does it? The chorus calls upon Dionysus to burn down the palace, and indeed a fire-miracle does take place (one that could be easily contrived on the stage), for the fire smouldering around Semele's tomb suddenly flares up. Dionysus escapes unquestionably, and that by wrecking or partly wrecking the building in which he was confined, namely the stables. There is no reason at all to suppose that these were visible to the audience.

But though a calm study of the text reduces the miracle to these dimensions a difficulty remains, namely, to explain why the difficulty arises. Why did Euripides so contrive matters that we have to look into the text so carefully before we can decide whether it is sense or raving nonsense?

We should remember that the back-scene was the usual palace-front and that the last thing the audience would look for would be an elaborate display by the stage-carpenter whereby pillars would be thrown to the ground and the orchestra filled with stage-rubble. The chorus could safely say that the palace-front was rocking and likely to fall; their excitement would be communicated to the audience through the dance and not by the contrivances of the stage-mechanician. Then this miracle, however great or small, is to be essentially an event in the minds of the actors and audience; its whole meaning is that Dionysus is a god with divine power. It is one of a series of miracles which is already begun in the prologue and continues up to the destruction of Pentheus; all serve the same purpose, though with increasing force. Euripides does not want this one to be given a significance different from that of the others; it may be more striking than the new flames at the tomb, but it is not different in kind. Therefore when it has made its effect Euripides passes on. Pentheus emerging frantic, completely under the god's control, might indeed have assisted us, who read these plays in our studies, by shouting 'What has brought my Palace (or Stables) to the ground?', but would this have assisted the audience, whose minds are now being filled with something else and whose eyes saw the pillars still standing intact at the back of the stage? Would it add to the poetic fact if every new arrival (who was not in fact picking his way among rubble) exclaimed 'Gods! What has happened to the Palace (or Stables)?' Each new arrival has new miracles to announce, fresh proofs of Dionysus' power; the palace-miracle, like the miracle of the fire, is superseded.

We may now turn to our chief question, why the *Bacchae* is so different in composition and style from most of the earlier tragedies. The answer lies, as so many answers do, in the nature of the theme. In this last tragedy we pick up a thread which we found in the first two, Euripides' feeling for the strength of certain natural and non-moral forces. Love and vengeance are the basis of the *Medea*; Aphrodite and Artemis in the *Hippolytus* are instinctive, non-moral forces, jealous of each other, beneficent to man only when each receives her due honour. The war brought a new tragic theme to the fore, and the tragedy of rational man preyed on by irrational but necessary passions is pushed into the background. The war continued and the spirit of Athens flagged. Athens, and Euripides with her, turned from high tragic issues to a lighter or a more intellectual drama. At last Euripides escaped from the agony and weariness of Athens, and in Macedonia, where spirits were fresher and the tragic implications of political life were out of sight, he returns to his sources.

The *Bacchae* does not present a conflict between rationalism and belief, for Pentheus is too pitiably weak to fight. It presents the overwhelming power of the god whom the narrow-minded Pentheus presumed to deny and the politically-minded Cadmus to patronize. Did Euripides approve or disapprove of Dionysus? The question is silly, as silly as to ask whether he approved or disapproved of Aphrodite. Dionysus, or what he typifies – for we need not tie Euripides to a literal belief in his mythology – exists, and that is enough.[1] We are not to suppose that Euripides believed in the

---

[1] In Euripidean criticism it is important to distinguish between gods. Euripides does not 'attack' Aphrodite or Dionysus, but he does 'attack' Apollo, who represents only Delphi, and such as Hermes, who represents nothing at all.

miracles, and we cannot suppose that he believed the primitive story he presents of the birth of Dionysus; we must, if we want poetry and drama, allow the poet his symbols. That done, we can see in this Dionysus the symbol of an ecstasy that is above, or beside, reason, one which the plodding rationalist or moralist rejects at his peril.

For Dionysus is more than the god of wine; in this play he is the god of ecstasy in religion (and the sender of panic), joy in nature, natural purity, happiness, beauty. He is not indeed the only source of these good things, but he is a very important one. It is interesting to note that the only other deities mentioned in the play, besides the Hesiodic, functional Zeus, are Aphrodite herself and Demeter the earth-goddess (274). Two deities, Teiresias says, are first among men, Demeter who gives food, Dionysus who gives wine, sleep, rest – a picture to which the chorus adds a great deal.

But we must mark that Dionysus, like Aphrodite, was non-moral and non-rational; not indifferent to morality, but it is not his province. This was more than Verrall could endure. The chorus (404 ff.) longs to be in Cyprus, in Paphos, haunts of Aphrodite; it longs, too, in the same stanza, for the holy slopes of Olympus, Pierian home of the Muses. That is to say, this chorus, unlike Hippolytus, Pentheus and other sectaries, can reconcile apparent contraries – but our modern rationalist will not let them do it; Cyprus and Paphos, painted in their blackest colours, are, by a fantasy of punctuation, made the object of the Bacchants' strongest reprobation.[1] But the conjunction of Paphos, the revels on Cithaeron, and the arduous slopes of Olympus is the very kernel of Euripides' thought.

This religion Pentheus cannot understand; to him it is a closed world. He is rooted in intellectualism and a narrow morality; characteristic of the man is his question 'What is the use (ὄνησις) of these rites?' (473) What, indeed, is the use of ecstasy? No answer is possible except what Dionysus says: 'They are worth knowing – but I may not tell thee.' Pentheus thinks that the revels are only an excuse for unchastity (225, 354, 686, 957–8), but the Messenger informs him (686–8) that he is wrong in fact, Teiresias and Dionysus that he is wrong in theory. Dionysus says (487) that daytime lends itself to evil no less than night, and Teiresias (314 ff.) that it is no concern of Dionysus' to make women chaste; that lies with them-

[1] C.R., viii, pp. 85–9; Tyrrell, Preface to 2nd edn. of the play.

selves. The chorus, indeed, shows us that Dionysus is not indifferent to morality, but this does not happen to be his province, and within his province his claims are absolute. As the chorus reconciles Paphos with Pieria, as we have to reconcile in ourselves Aphrodite and Artemis, so we must reconcile the claims of Dionysus with those of reason and morality. To deny either is to deny life itself. The confident dogmas of the 'wise' and the moral are not enough: οὐδὲν σοφιζόμεσθα τοῖσι δαίμοσιν.

Dionysus then is non-moral and especially non-rational. It is not his business to inculcate chastity and sobriety, nor will he obey the laws of our reason – resembling in this the deities in the *Hippolytus*. Aphrodite gains her ends ruthlessly, sacrificing Phaedra without a thought, and just as recklessly Artemis promises to avenge Hippolytus. Hippolytus' servant thinks vainly that the gods should be wiser than men; in the same way Agave protests that her punishment has been too heavy. It has been severe indeed, but these gods do not share our aspirations to mercy; natural forces are ruthless and insensitive. Dionysus therefore answers only 'Zeus my father consented to it long ago' (1349).

Now we can see why the *Bacchae* is so complete a contrast with plays like the *Troades*; it is because once more the tragic theme can be entirely projected into the action; there is real symbolism, not a diagram. No longer do we see collective or impersonal oppressors wronging collective victims whose characters can be of very little significance. The theme of the *Bacchae* is neither abstract nor passive; we have said good-bye to women crouching at altars. The theme is not public wrongdoing or folly, but a sharp opposition between one mind and another;[1] one that can not only be completely expressed in dramatic imagery, but also expressed in a single situation brought to a sharp focus and developed 'inevitably'. All the dramatic inconveniences of the earlier method have disappeared.

But we have suggested, too, that the composition of the *Bacchae* is superior even to that of the *Medea* and *Hippolytus*. For this also an explanation lies to hand. In the *Medea* the 'irrational' is the character of the heroine, and in order to give this full scope, to suggest that it

[1] Really between two minds (Cadmus' and Pentheus') and another. Each 'mind' can be projected into a life like character, and the dramatic genius of Euripides appears in the skilful way in which these two persons avoid obscuring each other. The sophistical, political attitude is given to Cadmus, and through him to his daughters, the moralism to Pentheus; and instead of making Dionysus (in a duplex plot) destroy these separately, he makes the one destroy the other.

symbolized a cosmic force, Euripides had to incur the censure of Aristotle, for Medea is subject to the limitations of being human. In the *Hippolytus* the 'irrational' is symbolized by the goddesses. These have to work behind the scenes, so that the drama exists on two planes at once. But in the *Bacchae,* thanks to the brilliant stroke whereby the god takes the form of a votary, the symbol of the 'irrational' is in the thick of the fight all the time, yet without the human limitations of Medea.

This stroke made possible another, the chorus of Bacchants. In the *Medea* and the *Hippolytus* the chorus is, at one time or another, of little dramatic use, if not even a positive inconvenience; certainly it is not in a position to keep before our minds, as this chorus does, the necessity and the power of that against which the victim is pitting himself: with this chorus Euripides returns to the great tradition. It is no ideal spectator but an actor; not in the obvious sense that it engages with the actors on the stage – though when it is involved with them, in Pentheus' threats which provoke it to call upon Dionysus, the result is highly dramatic – but that it presents always one of the spiritual forces at work in the play. It presents the mystery, the holiness, the joy of the Dionysiac religion, and (as Mr Grube acutely observes) it reflects the dramatic attitude of the god himself, for when he abandons all attempt to make Pentheus see the light and resolves to destroy him, the chorus sings of the thrill of triumph, the danger of being 'wiser than the laws', and prays that the 'Hounds of Frenzy' may destroy the blasphemer. These odes, most of them couched in the exciting Ionic rhythms, are full of that spirit of natural religion which Dionysus so terribly vindicates.

The Euripidean chorus often fails to remain continuously in touch with the action; this one succeeds. And not only that; no less than the chorus in the *Hecuba* and the *Troades* does it maintain the undertone of the tragic action, but it does this, not as they do by remaining aloof from the action; it is as much part of the action as any chorus in the whole of Greek Tragedy.[1]

For the first time therefore, certainly for the first time since the *Hippolytus,* we see Euripides dealing with a tragic theme

[1] It is the doubly dramatic position of this chorus that renders so idle the conventional attempts to extract from its utterances Euripides' own views. The Bacchants reprobate intellectualism and praise a natural, untaught virtue: if they did not they would not be Bacchants. We need not suppose that Euripides in his old age renounced the free use of the intellect, only that he saw that it has its limitations – and this we knew already, from the *Medea* and *Hippolytus.*

which lends itself to orthodox dramatic methods – once the transformation of Dionysus and the chorus of Bacchants had been
thought of. The result corroborates what we inferred in comparing
the tragedies with the tragi-comedies, that the structural and stylistic
shortcomings of the former cannot be put down to carelessness or
incapacity in the dramatist, but are the natural result of the nature
of his tragic inspiration. The war-tragedies presented passion rather
than action; therefore characterization was restricted, sometimes
downright inconsistent, and plot was disconnected and inert. The
Bacchae presents action and conflict again, therefore style changes
completely. The tragi-comedies assure us that Euripides could make
masterly plots when he had nothing more important to do; now for
the first time he is able to put this skill unreservedly at the service of
a tragic theme. The play as a whole is admirably planned. Of the
god's opponents, the women misled by Cadmus are sent off to
Cithaeron to serve the action as a sort of unseen chorus, leaving the
stage free for Pentheus, an opponent of a different kind – all being
at last united in the common woe of the epilogue. Equally admirable
are the details. The character-drawing is firm and natural, because
the theme allows it; and there are neither rhetorical or dialectical
diversions nor merely decorative lyrics. When we add the disconcerting comedy of the two 'comic' scenes and the sustained brilliance
of the messenger-speeches we can say that in the *Bacchae* we find all
the qualities of Euripides.

2. The 'Oedipus Coloneus'

This singularly impressive play is not easy to criticize. Its plot is
composed of two distinct themes, the reception and death of
Oedipus in Attica, and the attempts made by Creon and Polyneices
to claim him for some Theban interest. Even if we say of the Creon-
scenes that they are closely connected with the Attica-motif (which
is substantially true), we can hardly say it of the Polyneices–incident.
Looked at formally, the *Coloneus* is episodic, manifestly lacking the
unity and dramatic sweep of the *Tyrannus* and the *Electra*.[1] We can

---

[1] If dramatic style were as separable a part of drama and as obedient to the calendar
as is sometimes assumed, odd things might be said of the *Coloneus*. For example, that
since it resembles the earlier plays (*Ajax, Trachiniae, Antigone*) in its duplicity of
interest but shows an advance in technique (the Theban interest being cleverly
embodied in the Attic, A – B – A and not a mere A – B), it must have been composed
after these early plays but before the perfectly constructed *Tyrannus*.

see the same fact reflected in the choral odes. The Colonus ode,
however wonderful a poem, and the ode on old-age, however
poignant, do not link scene to scene as do the odes of the earlier
tragedies, while the second stasimon is a mere 'curtain' of the
Euripidean kind, relevant but not illuminating. It even begins with
the formula εἴθ᾽ εἴην.

This relative looseness of form we cannot ascribe to the inexperience of youth, for the play implies the *Tyrannus,* nor to the
weakness of age, for no play shows more strength; to say that
Sophocles was simply following the legend to its conclusion is to
offer the artist in him an affront which he has not yet been shown to
deserve, and to fall back on an abstraction, such as that Greek
Tragedy had by now relaxed the taut structure of an earlier time
would be neither true nor explanatory. The fact that the play feels
like a unity warns us that the real explanation lies deeper than this.

Before we inquire where it does lie, we may consider for a
moment this question of the dramatic style and Sophocles' old age.
The statement made in the second Argument that the *Coloneus* was
produced four years after Sophocles' death[1] is perhaps a mistake,
but there seems to be no good reason for doubting the tradition that
it was composed at the very end of the poet's long life. Signs of
extreme age have been seen in the excessive length of the concluding
lyrics and in the garrulity with which Polyneices gives the names of
his companions-in-arms (1313 ff.).[2] Only those can safely call the
lyrical ending tedious who have heard it sung in performance; to the
reader the lyrical ending of the *Antigone* approaches tedium; in the
theatre it is not a moment too long. Sophocles' judgement may for
once have erred; on the other hand, the death of Oedipus does leave
a big gap; this, and the scale of the whole play, may well be able
to carry the long lament. Nor is it necessary to see only garrulity in
Polyneices' list; an actor, we may suspect, would make much more
of it. Polyneices is nervously playing for Oedipus' support; that
terrible old man says not a word. Polyneices gives the names of his
companions – whom, we must remember, he is going to deceive
(1427–30). Is he trying to impress Oedipus? or to encourage himself?
or is he talking because Oedipus will not? Sophocles' stage-direc-

---

[1] 406 or 405 B.C. It is thought that this may have been a revival, not the first performance.

[2] So Masqueray, ed. Budé, pp. 152-3.

tions might have enlightened us, but we need not hastily assume that the passage is only a conventional fill-up.

On the other hand, the dramatic style and the poetry are finer than ever. No scene in Greek Tragedy is grander or more imaginative than the end of Oedipus. On that overwhelming apostrophe to Polyneices (1354) a scholiast cries out in just admiration. Hardly less impressive is the sudden prayer to the Eumenides in the prologue: 'Is the stranger gone?' 'Gone,' Antigone replies; 'you may say what you will at your ease. Only I am here.' We expect conversation; what we get is the sublime appeal.

$$\tilde{\Omega} \; \pi\acute{o}\tau\nu\iota\alpha\iota \; \delta\epsilon\iota\nu\tilde{\omega}\pi\epsilon\varsigma \; . \, , \, .$$

Such power is found everywhere. There is no longer scope for the frightening irony and tragic juxtapositions of the earlier plays; the dramatic power which invented these is directed to a new purpose, to suggest the almost supernatural stature of this Oedipus. The villagers are seen coming towards that sacred grove which they are afraid to look at; into that same grove Oedipus retires for safety. How simple the means, how great the effect! Or we may consider the strength of the contrast between the quiet prologue (into which the casual Stranger fits so exquisitely) and the succeeding passage with the chorus. The revulsion that they feel makes a splendid foundation for a play which is to end, so to speak, in the apotheosis of Oedipus.

Nor do the details show any sign of tiredness. There is the old vividness of minds in action:

THESEUS: Foolish man! Hot temper is no help to misfortune.
OEDIPUS: Censure me when you have heard. Till then, forbear.
THESEUS: Continue; I ought not to speak so hastily.

There is the old economy of dramatic effect, as when Creon announces 'Of thy two daughters the one I have seized already, the other I shall take now'. Very effective are the scenes between Oedipus and Creon. Creon, it has been observed,[1] is the Creon neither of the *Antigone* nor of the *Tyrannus,* but a smooth hypocrite. But why? One reason lies in Oedipus' first speech to him: he is made false in order that the prophetic knowledge which is now accorded to Oedipus may be the more triumphantly displayed.

[1] Jebb, *Introd.,* xxv; Masqueray, *Introd.,* p. 147.

After some twenty verses of fierce denunciation Oedipus tells him
the truth which he supposes to be his own secret, ending with the
prophetic curse launched against his own sons. He continues, in the
very accents of the blind prophet of the earlier play:

> ἆρ' οὐκ ἄμεινον ἢ σὺ τὰν Θήβαις φρονῶ;
> 'Do not I know better than you what passes in Thebes?'

It is magnificent; magnificent, too, is the later scene in which for the
last time Oedipus proclaims his innocence (939–1013). Again the
hypocritical Creon is the perfect foil. We can imagine how
effectively Euripides would have argued this theme; Sophocles is
still plastic, and fuses together Oedipus' passionate self-defence and
his indignant spurning of Creon.

Even more marked is the beauty and increased authority of the
verse. That is a noble speech in which Ajax proclaims the Greek,
and especially the Sophoclean doctrine of the instability of things:

> *All things doth long, innumerable time*
> *Bring forth from darkness and then hide from light . . .*
> *The snow-clad winter yields to fruitful summer,*
> *And night's dark orb makes room for shining day*
> *Whose horses blaze with light . . .*

But Oedipus' speech[1] is stronger, and less ornate:

> Ὦ φίλτατ' Αἰγέως παῖ, μόνοις οὐ γίγνεται
> θεοῖσι γῆρας οὐδὲ κατθανεῖν ποτε . . .

> *Dear son of Aegeus, to the gods alone*
> *Do age and death not come. All others things*
> *Doth Time, all-mastering Time confound. Earth's strength*
> *Decays, the body's strength decays; faith dies*
> *And faithlessness increases; never the same*
> *The spirit of friendship blows, nor man's to man*
> *Nor among cities . . .*

If the *Coloneus* was first produced posthumously, it must have been
with a shiver of emotion that the Athenians heard, later in this noble
speech, the dead poet's words:

> ἵν' οὑμὸς εὕδων καὶ κεκρυμμένος νέκυς
> ψυχρός . . .

[1] 607 ff.

And then my body, hidden in earth and sleeping,
And cold, shall sometime of their warm blood drink,
If Zeus be still Zeus, and Apollo true.

The comparison of two couplets illustrates the difference, both in power and in spirit, between the *Coloneus* and the *Tyrannus*. Oedipus taunted Teiresias with the verses

Ἀλλ᾽ ἔστι, πλὴν σοί· σοὶ δὲ τοῦτ᾽ οὐκ ἔστ᾽, ἐπεὶ
τυφλὸς τά τ᾽ ὦτα τόν τε νοῦν τά τ᾽ ὄμματ᾽ εἶ,

Twenty years later Oedipus can still speak like this; there is the same rush of monosyllables, the same harsh alliteration of σ and τ, the same string of elisions, and the same 'light ending' in his words to Creon:

Οὐκ ἔστι σοι ταῦτ᾽, ἀλλά σοι τάδ᾽ ἔστ᾽, ἐκει . . .

And the second verse? Weighty, smooth and awful, re-echoing like Cithaeron itself:

χώρας ἀλάστωρ οὑμὸς ἐνναίων ἀεί.[1]

There is no sign of relaxing grip here.

We have argued before that the special dramatic virtues of the middle plays of Sophocles were not sought independently, for their own sake, but were born of the effort to express a certain dramatic 'idea'. We have applied the same doctrine to Euripides; now we must apply it anew to Sophocles. The difference in form between the *Tyrannus* and the *Coloneus* is not a matter of age or circumstance, unless it was age or circumstance that made Sophocles in 430 or thereabouts dramatize a tragic action and in 406 a tragic passion. Age evidently had a real connexion with the play, but let us be clear about it. The form is relatively loose, not because the old man's hand is shaking, but because, his hand being still firm, his mind moves into a new region which demands, and finds, a new dramatic style.

The *Coloneus*, like other late works of genius, is more imaginative than the earlier works of that same genius. The late quartets of Beethoven – and if this particular parallel means nothing to the

[1] *O.T.*, 370-1, *O.C.*, 787-8. Translation, naturally, means little. 'There is (sc. power of Truth) except to thee. Thou hast it not, for | thou art blind in ears and mind and eyes.' 'That (sc. possession of Oedipus' body) is not for thee, but this is, there | on thy land my avenging curse dwelling in it for ever.'

reader he will be able to find his own illustration in Rembrandt or some other artist – are less definite in statement, more fluid in form, deeper and more remote in feeling, than the great works of his middle period. The difference between the *Coloneus* and the *Tyrannus* is similar; so, too, is that between the *Tyrannus* and the *Ajax* or *Antigone*. We have here a gradation which it is not ridiculous to compare with that in Beethoven; first a relative simplicity of outlook and positiveness in statement, then a period of greater complexity and depth (for the tragic philosophy of the *Tyrannus* and *Electra* is subtler and more penetrating than the comparatively simple, or at least clear-cut, moral contrasts of the earlier plays), and finally a purely poetic and almost apocalyptic vision which cannot be confined to the hard-won perfection of form of an earlier period. As Beethoven needed a much more fluid form for his last utterances than that which he had forged for the dramatic and intense utterances of his middle period, so Sophocles now transcends the bounds of his own Aristotelian perfection. This most poetic of plays convinces us of its unity, but as to where that unity lies, there is room for difference of opinion.

For since the play does not, in the old manner, display the inevitable march of a course of tragic action, such that the action or plot is itself the tragic idea, the meaning and therefore the unity of the play does not necessarily reside in that action. For example, Polyneices' request is not in itself a development of the plot as the statements of Teiresias were. Polyneices' coming is indeed part of the story, but that is not why it is here: the *Coloneus* is no *Phoenissae*. The real meaning must be looked for through the event, not in it; it lies, as we shall see, in the contribution it makes to the presentation of Oedipus.

There is, in fact, between the real unity of the play and the bones of the plot a slight but definite gap which distantly recalls Euripides' tragic technique. We must not exaggerate this, for Sophocles goes to no Euripidean extremes, but we must not overlook it, or we shall fail to explain the play. The real unity is impressionistic rather than factual. 'Pourquoi,' asks Masqueray in his excellent introduction to the play,[1] 'dans sa longue vie, Oedipe a-t-il été si malheureux? Etait-il coupable? C'est la question qui est annoncée, discutée, résolue dans la première partie de la tragédie, avant qu'Athènes

[1] P. 141.

donne asile au viellard. Et quand le jugement est prononcé, il reste acquis; on n'y revient plus.' 'Il est, en effet, fort remarquable qu'après le plaidoyer final d'Oedipe (960–1013) il ne soit plus dit dans la pièce un seul mot de cette culpabilité.' The play would be easier to understand if it had been built to this pattern – the self-defence of Oedipus, its acceptance by Athens, the protection actually afforded by Athens, and the passing of Oedipus; but at least in one respect it is not so neatly arranged, for Oedipus is definitely accepted by Athens, indeed offered asylum in his palace by the King, long before 'le plaidoyer final'. That the first part of the play disposes of Oedipus' guilt, even that it is mainly concerned therewith, is an illusion.

What, in fact, does happen during the play? There is a certain gradation. First the Stranger allows Oedipus provisionally to remain on sacred ground; then the chorus, which is so profoundly shocked first by the mere voice and aspect of Oedipus, then by his name and story, is with difficulty persuaded to allow him to remain, provisionally, in Colonus until the King shall decide. In this scene the motif of Oedipus' essential innocence is prominent. Now, if Sophocles' scheme were simply to dramatize the story, we should surely have an ode followed by the arrival of Theseus, then a grand vindication of Oedipus and his final acceptance by Theseus. There are no dramatic difficulties, and if the threat of Creon's interference were wanted to make Theseus' decision a more serious one, that could easily be introduced by Oedipus himself, or by a dramatic entry on the part of Ismene. We cannot suppose that a smooth progression like this could not have been engineered by Sophocles if he had wanted it. But instead of the expected Theseus we get Ismene with new oracles; and when Theseus does come the question of Oedipus' guilt or innocence is not raised at all, nor even is the benefit that Oedipus can confer on Athens made very prominent: Theseus is not one who needs bribing. The enlightened generosity of his first speech virtually assures Oedipus of protection before he has said a word, and in the question of Oedipus' innocence Theseus seems hardly to be interested.[1]

A plain presentation of the story was not Sophocles' idea – and

---

[1] Sophocles was no doubt as religious as everyone says he was, but his great characters noticeably act out of purely intellectual motives, except Antigone, who acts out of instinct. Theseus thinks like Odysseus in the *Ajax*; he is calm, unafraid, generous because he himself has experienced or may need generosity, and because ἔξοιδ' ἀνὴρ ὤν, 'I well know that I am a man, and have no greater share in tomorrow than you have' (*O.C.*, 567 f. Cf. *Ajax*, 1346 ff., and above, p. 298).

O

we need not be sorry for it. In the separate themes of the play – the local interest, the innocence of Oedipus, the working-out of the legend, the character of Oedipus – we shall find only variety, not unity; but if we stand back and look at the play from a distance, we see that there exists in the whole piece a certain governing movement or rhythm. We can see that Oedipus enters the play a disregarded outcast and leaves it – followed by the King of Attica – to keep a strange appointment with Heaven. This rhythm controls the play, and will explain it.

It is complex. We may notice, from our present point of vantage, that Oedipus enters as one who has learned resignation from suffering.[1] Perhaps he has; but gradually, through successive references to his sons, then through his resistance to Creon, finally in the tremendous scene with Polyneices, he passes from resignation to the full height of the wrath that is in him. We may notice that in the opening scene Oedipus is at everyone's mercy, a blind old man, dependent on the decency of a casual passer-by; at the end he towers above everybody.

This complex rhythm pervades everything in the play. There is no sudden revelation of a new Oedipus; Sophocles leads us step by step, almost insensibly, with the same skill that made the *Electra*. The important difference is that it is rhythm which cannot incorporate itself in one sweeping, heroic action, but must be created from the outside, out of separate actions or interests on which it draws as need arises. We may trace this rhythm in some of its aspects. Let us take our sense of Oedipus' power, not the power of his personality, which culminates in the scene with Polyneices, but that mysterious reflection of this, the power which is entrusted to him by the gods – or found in him by the gods, as there is no suggestion that a special gift or honour has been accorded him.

We must begin with the impression which the blind old man makes when first we see him. To the Stranger he is 'noble except in fortune' (76); the Chorus on the other hand, seeing him rise within the sacred grove, is terrified at the mere sight of him and the sound of his voice. Such is the figure whom we see, led in by his daughter. We hear that rest has been promised him at the grove which he has now reached, but of his strange power, that of benefiting Athens, we have only two bare hints (vv. 72 and 92–3).

[1] Vv 7–8.

The revulsion which the chorus feels towards Oedipus brings this rhythm, if we can yet call it begun, back to its starting-point. Oedipus has to fight to maintain his position, but it is maintained, and at v. 285 there is a slightly more explicit reference to his power. Then Ismene comes, with new oracles. We feel perhaps a little hazy about them all;[1] what exactly is the difference between these new ones and those that Oedipus had received before? As the earlier ones are not quoted we cannot possibly say. But why was the Ismene-scene wanted? Why cannot Oedipus have all the oracles at the beginning? Because our sense of his new power must be made to grow. As far as the action of the play is concerned Ismene's part could be considerably reduced; she might well, as we suggested above, enter after Theseus, and announce nothing but the coming of Creon. The rhythm of the play however needs the reinforcement that her fresh oracles give, and to emphasize the reinforcement Oedipus is twice made to refer to his present lowly position, both times before the oracles are declared.[2] Afterwards (455 ff.) Oedipus speaks with a new confidence, as one whom Athens may be glad to welcome and Thebes may vainly hope to capture.

The next stage is the Theseus-scene. What Oedipus can do for Athens is fully set forth; it is such as to outweigh even the chance of embroilment with Thebes. The stature to which Oedipus has now attained can be seen in the speech from which we have already quoted, Ὦ φίλτατ' Αἰγέως παῖ.[3] This is a very different Oedipus from the one who had to ask favours of the Stranger and of the old men of Colonus. Next, Creon and the violence which he is prepared to use emphasize Oedipus' importance even more; finally in the two scenes which concern Polyneices he is presented as the arbiter of destiny.

Here we have one aspect only of the dramatic rhythm of the play. We can in the same way follow the course of the growth of his wrath, from the resignation professed at the beginning to its climax just before the end. In vv. 339 f. Eteocles and Polyneices are the men who 'sit at home weaving', like Egyptians. During the tense dialogue in vv. 385–420 it becomes apparent to Oedipus that his

---

[1] As about other details on the outskirts of the play. (See below, p. 390.)

[2] Vv. 299 f. (to the Chorus) 'And do ye really think that Theseus will have care or thought for a blind man, and come to see him?' Vv. 385 f. (to Ismene) 'And didst thou come to hope that the gods would ever have regard for me and my deliverance?'

[3] Vv. 667 ff. 'Dear son of Aegeus.'

sons have betrayed him; this moves him to the terrible denunciation
in the speech 421 ff. Nothing, we may perhaps think, can be more
awful than this, except the actual meeting with Polyneices. But
Sophocles' hand has lost neither its cunning nor its daring.

There are two points to observe. This first denunciation is
couched in optatives, the wish-mood: 'May the gods not quench
their fated strife; may it become mine to decide the issue, for in that
case neither would he who now holds the crown keep it, nor
would the exile return home again.' When next the topic occurs it is
treated in more definite language: 'There remains to my own sons
an inheritance of my soil, enough – to die in' (789-90). Finally,
when the unhappy Polyneices stands before us, there are no longer
optatives and conditionals, but confident futures. The crescendo is
maintained; the gods have, it appears, given to Oedipus the decision
he hoped would be his. When? Where? We do not know; nothing
overt has happened. It is part of the general rhythm, a very imaginative way of increasing our sense of Oedipus' power.

This delicate piece of manipulation is the first point; the second
is very interesting. Sophocles seems to be very hazy about the
relative position of the two brothers and the Theban crown. It is
true that the Greek (and other) dramatists often leave out of focus
matters just outside the play, and that in such matters, which no
sensible audience would try to bring into focus, there may be
latent contradictions. But here, as the facts do come into the play,
the haze is noticeable, and Masqueray, penetrating it, points out
that there are four distinct situations assumed at successive moments
of the play: (1) that Eteocles and Polyneices have never enjoyed
royal authority at all (367 ff.), (2) that they might have prevented
Oedipus' exile (427 ff.), (3) that they jointly decreed this exile
(599 ff.), (4) that Polyneices was solely responsible for it (1354 ff.).
This, as Masqueray says, is too regular to be accidental – but what
is the explanation of it all? Sophocles had complete liberty, in spite
of what Aeschylus or Euripides may have done, to assume what
situation suited him best;[1] why has he assumed four? Because it
helps this dramatic movement. We thought that in this matter of
the sons there could be no climax after the denunciation of 420 ff.
We were wrong. Not only does the curse increase in definition and

[1] As he has done in making Polyneices the older. (See Jebb's note on v. 375.) For
other such deliberate confusions, see T. von Wilamowitz, *Dram. Technik.*, 20 ff.

certainty, but also, thanks to these delicate shifts, what was a curse launched impartially at two absent men becomes one launched with particular violence at the one who is present.[1]

We have now considered two aspects of the complex rhythm of the *Coloneus,* the way in which we are made to feel more and more the power of Oedipus, and the gradual revelation of his full personality. There remain two important points – the question of Oedipus' innocence, and the winning of his final rest. We may consider the latter first.

This theme is woven as one strand in the complex web of the play, largely by the use of the chorus. It is the chorus that insists that Oedipus shall leave the grove and comes near to driving him away forthwith. His peace is in jeopardy, but his demeanour, and the oracles that Ismene brings, alter the attitude of the chorus – how much, we can see by comparing vv. 139–236 with 510 ff.; in the latter passage the chorus can hear the worst without flinching. Oedipus, already accepted by the gods, is beginning to impose himself on men. The climax of this, the first part of the movement, is near when Theseus offers to the outcast the shelter of his palace. As to this Oedipus is quite clear; his real defence is spiritual, not temporal power, and he must remain at Colonus.

The climax is the ode. The point now reached, the culmination of a long development, is by the architectonic imagination of the

---

[1] This affects the word πρόσθε in v. 1375. Oedipus says to Polyneices 'I have let fly such curses at you before (πρόσθε) and I repeat them now'. Does 'before' refer to the two earlier passages in the play, or to an undisclosed occasion in Thebes? Most commentators prefer the former (though not the Scholiast, who had the advantage of knowing from the Thebais what that undisclosed earlier incident was); but why should Oedipus impede the torrent of his wrath by putting in a reference to vv. 420 and 789 – a reference unnecessary for us and unintelligible to Polyneices? The plain dramatic sense of the passage would be that Oedipus, as Polyneices well knows, uttered some kind of a curse before. This is inconsistent with the colourless reference to the brothers 'sitting at home weaving' – but so is the whole of this present speech. We are in the fourth situation; the sudden production of an earlier curse, of which we have heard nothing, is consistent with it and dramatically intensifies the present position.

Jebb objected to this view (*Introd.,* xxiv) that it makes of Polyneices a helpless victim of fate – a serious objection if true. But here Sophocles misses a theatrical opportunity in order to demonstrate that Polyneices is no victim of fate. Polyneices is not allowed, like Iocasta and several other characters, to stumble off the stage in an effective silence, though such an exit would be at least as dramatic as the farewell-scene that we have. Evidently Sophocles did this not for the sake of the pathetic farewell (he did not deal in such things), but in order to make it quite clear that Polyneices can nullify the curse by doing as Antigone suggests, by not being a fool and a traitor to his companions. As in the *Tyrannus,* curses and oracles do not compel; they only predict.

poet marked and emphasized with the first stasimon. The Colonus-ode, renowned for its beauty, famous as one of the few nature-poems in Greek, is no less notable for its dramatic qualities. It does not connect act with act, but it is no mere curtain. It marks an important point in the structure of the play, and it emphasizes a decision which is soon to be put to the test. To the blind man, who knows the inward peace and beauty of this appointed spot, the chorus describes its outward peace and beauty; on the sanctity of the grove it says nothing; Oedipus knows that already. It does, however, reinforce this sanctity with others in Colonus of which Oedipus knows nothing. 'The place,' said Oedipus, 'is here'; and the ode is here, outdoing in its supra-dramatic effect the dramatic 'timing' of the odes in the *Electra*.

As for the Creon-scenes, from our present point of view they do but reaffirm the position reached already; the wanderer is safely anchored at last. The second stasimon, which divides these scenes, does little more than fill a gap suitably. It describes, by anticipation, an event which the actors have neither time nor cause to describe. The third is very different. A mechanical dramatist might have placed here an ode that had particular reference to Polyneices; Sophocles does something else. Just before 'the god' summons Oedipus Sophocles places this harsh, frightful incident of Poly-neices, and across it, between the two scenes, he lets fall the even darker shadow of his bitterest ode. Like the earlier hyporchemata it prepares for the catastrophe, but by representing Oedipus' old age as a misery from which death will be welcome release.[1] The fine image of the storm-beaten cliff raises its head above the immediate surroundings. Even now a last storm is raging around its base, but the cliff, and the ode, too, look beyond that over the whole of Oedipus' past life, and, forward, to the end that is so near.

In this way the motif of Oedipus' release is finely kept moving until, with Polyneices' departure, the thunder from heaven is heard. Now all these separate threads are drawn together. He who was impotent and disregarded has come to wield, first tentatively and then with confidence, superhuman powers; he who was a

---

[1] It is surely not necessary to suppose that Sophocles was drawing upon his own experience of old age. What we know of his personality makes the description 'Impotent, lonely and friendless' a little surprising; what we know of his dramatic resources assures us that had a serene picture of old age been called for Sophocles could have written it.

homeless wanderer has been received, and defended, by the Athenian state, and is now summoned by the gods themselves; he who was resigned has been brought, gradually, to that last display of majestic wrath.

In a scene whose imaginative power only the end of the *Eumenides* can rival, the blind hero, like the blind prophet of an earlier play,[1] becomes guide to those who can see, and leads them with a sure step to the spot fixed for his end.

In this complex but always mounting rhythm one thing remains stationary, Oedipus' insistence that what he did was no sin. It remains stationary because it was no part of Sophocles' plan to develop it; it is an axiom, implicit in the assurance with which he first addressed the Eumenides. To the horrified chorus he develops his argument at length (285 ff.); later (510 ff.) this chorus is made to drag the most repulsive details from him in order that his innocence may be set in the strongest possible light. Yet, we must observe, there is neither discussion nor judgement. The chorus professes neither belief nor disbelief. Theseus comes, and before him no claim to purity is necessary; his large humanity can accept Oedipus as he is. When next the chorus speaks, in the Colonus-ode, there is no reference to this question; Oedipus is simply accepted.

Nevertheless we have one last passionate assertion before Creon – and how dramatically it is managed. Again, men and not arguments are at grips, for the speech is as much an onslaught on Creon as it is Oedipus' own apologia. In the mechanics of the play the apologia is nothing, for Theseus does not need it nor Creon merit it, and the substance has been given before. The argument is repeated because it has become part of Oedipus' very soul, and because it is the very core of Sophocles' philosophy, that virtue alone cannot assure happiness nor wickedness alone explain disaster. Oedipus has suffered ἀνθρώπινόν τι, one of those things which may happen to us whatever we are. His innocence is not a question that Sophocles cares to have discussed and judged; it is accepted instinctively by the fine intelligence of Theseus, and his acceptance of it is enough for the chorus.

Now we may try to answer the last and most fundamental question: what made Sophocles write, or at any rate complete, this play at the extreme verge of old age? We can well imagine that Oedipus,

---

[1] *Antig.*, 1014, ἐμοὶ γὰρ οὗτος ἡγεμὼν, ἄλλοις δ᾽ ἐγώ. 'He leads me, I lead others.'

Sophocles' most splendid symbol of humanity, must have been a close companion of his thoughts ever since he had finished his *Tyrannus*. Now, some twenty years later, no longer an oldish man but an extremely old man, he finds himself impelled to undertake the labour of composing the *Coloneus*. What has he to say now?

It is easy to see what the *Coloneus* is not. It is not, in the first place, a mere sequel, deriving its charm from its more mellow echoes of earlier work. Here there is no charm, no autumnal browns and gold. Nor is it a work of pious duty, the finishing of a great legend, for the play is as vital as the *Tyrannus* itself. It is not a study in the effects which years of suffering have had on Oedipus; in the *Philoctetes* Sophocles had used such a theme, but the *Coloneus* is no study of character. Nor is the play in this sense religious that it portrays resignation, wiser counsels, submission to the mysterious will of heaven. Oedipus is indeed too great a man to be querulous. He does say 'So the gods willed it, wroth perchance with my race from of old' (964), but it is no part of the dramatic idea that the sufferer, by learning to kiss the rod, wins peace – or why, when Oedipus has been established in Attica, when he might pass straight to his final peace, does Sophocles throw the dark shadow of the Polyneices-scene across the path? Oedipus does indeed end in peace, but it is a peace that is accorded him, not one that he wins for himself.

Further, 'On the part of the gods there is nothing that can properly be called tenderness for Oedipus.'[1] There is no friendly deity, like the Athena who cares for Odysseus in the *Ajax*. Apollo issues oracles – c'est son métier – but he is not in close relation with Oedipus as in the *Oresteia* he is with Orestes. The god who summons him is most impressively impersonal, like 'the god' who laid him low. Oedipus is remote from the gods. He is still the Oedipus of the earlier play – even more so : hot-tempered,[2] wrathful, with no trace of submissiveness. Nor are we told that the gods have repented for what they have done or forgiven him for what was no sin. What has happened is that adversity has not crushed Oedipus, and that strange new oracles gather round him.

In the *Coloneus* we have the same Oedipus, but now he can look back on his ruined life. He has nothing with which he can reproach

---

[1] Jebb, *Introd.*, xxiii.

[2] As Ismene (420), Creon (804, 852), and Antigone (1195) all point out.

himself; repentance is not in the picture at all: 'Pure before the law, unwitting I have come to this' (558). He thinks of some wrath of Heaven, but this is his explanation, not Sophocles'. To say that he could not have escaped is indeed neither true nor tragic; he could have escaped, but only if his towering intelligence had towered as high as the peculiarly malignant circumstances arrayed against him. It did not; if it had he would have been more than a man, he would have been a god. There was no sin, only the necessary frailty of being human.

Such was Oedipus, such he remains, and we may doubt if it was ever in Sophocles' mind to leave him crushed, hidden from sight in the Theban palace. Pessimist Sophocles may have been, with little faith in future bliss, with no confidence in present prosperity, but no Greek believed more firmly in the dignity of being a man, and it was because of this belief that he had to write the *Coloneus* before he died. Oedipus could not be left there. So, with even more sufferings and indignities heaped upon him, with his one fault, hastiness, defiantly unmodified, he is driven forth. To the gods he has made no concessions; just before his last summons he is at his most violent. But this play, though it presents the same Oedipus, reverses the movement of the *Tyrannus*, for Oedipus goes not from greatness to misery but from misery to greatness; and it reverses it in a higher plane, in the dark, not in the light. The kingly power that shines from him in the *Tyrannus* is still in him, but now, on the edge of death, it is transmuted into a superhuman power, and we see it growing. It is not a recompense given him by the gods; why should it be? Apollo in the *Tyrannus* was no enemy of Oedipus'; he merely saw what was coming and answered questions. So now, Apollo is no friend and champion of his; he sees the greatness that is in him and states facts. In taking Oedipus to themselves as a Hero the gods are but recognizing facts. By his stature as a man Oedipus imposes himself on the gods; it is not forgiveness, for there was no sin. The *Coloneus* is Sophocles' answer to the tragedy of life. He knows that he cannot justify God to man, but he can justify man to man.

We have said nothing about the imaginative use of topography in this play, how the sacred grove is gradually charged with as much significance as the Atreid Palace in the *Agamemnon*. At the end, the contrast between the familiarity of the spots which Sophocles so minutely describes and the remote majesty of Oedipus' passing must have given the scene a strange and thrilling colour which we can only faintly recapture.

This the *Coloneus* has now lost; in compensation it has gained something. A fate of which we have probably little reason to complain – none at all if the miserable *Rhesus* is a fair specimen of later tragedy – has decreed that for us Greek Tragedy shall end here; and where more suitably than at Colonus, with 'the towers that guard the city' in sight? No spot could be more appropriate; Tragedy comes home to die.

For Greek Drama is peculiarly the creation and glory of Athens. Athens and the Theatre of Dionysus are, in a very real sense, its Unity of Place. Not only were the plays performed in this theatre, not only was nearly every dramatic poet of eminence an Athenian, not only does the art as a whole bear indelibly the mark of Athenian intelligence and plastic imagination; beyond all this, Greek Drama is in a special degree the work of the Athenian people. All Attic drama, tragic and comic, was composed for one of the Festivals of Dionysus; this fact is capital. It was therefore religious in origin and for two or three generations remained religious in outlook; so was that tumultuous, hilarious and frequently obscene thing, Old Comedy – a contradiction which is disabling to the understanding until it is remembered how different are the Greek and the modern connotations of the word 'religion'. The difference is so wide that we may well avoid the word here and use the reality instead; for the essential point, the only one which a literary study of the subject can profit by, is that in practice the Festival was a solemn national celebration; not the celebration of an event, but of the City herself. It was serious and it was important, it had its origin in a religion and a ritual, but it did not compel the dramatist to be religious, still less Dionysiac; Aeschylus was a religious poet not because of the Festival but because of Aeschylus. To the dramatist the significance of the Festival was that it gave him as his audience nothing less than the Athenian people. That same people which, in a practical and political mood, met a few hundred yards away to discuss and determine high matters of state, met in the Theatre, in a more exalted mood, to watch plays; and the dramatists themselves appeared almost as their chosen laureates. Thus the dramatist, tragic or comic, was always writing for a big occasion, one which demanded and made natural big ideas and serious utterance, one which made impossible, in comedy as in tragedy, private themes and clever, coterie-literature. The modern world began in Alexandria; there for the first time in the history of Greek literature a homogeneous audience was lacking.[1]

To this public drama our nearest modern parallel is perhaps Church-music; in one sense the *Mass in B minor* is the modern *Oresteia*. But Attic tragedy was not restricted by creed or convention (the dramatist could take a political and contemporary subject if he chose), nor was it in any way an official art, an adjunct to politics. It was necessarily in close touch with its audience, as any living art must be, and its audience had come not as individuals looking for entertainment but as the City; an audience accustomed to handle the biggest issues in another place, not afraid of them therefore in the theatre. The Athenian drama necessarily reflects in its varied course the general aspect of contemporary thought and outlook; in Athens a dramatist who was not in touch with at least a substantial part of his audience would have been dumb, for there was no 'Little Theatre'. Nevertheless this art, as I hope we have seen, remained highly individual; remained, that is, an art. Greek myth provided the dramatist, as Pentelicus did the architect and sculptor, with as noble a quarry as a race of artists could hope for; the people, lively, sensitive, and educated in affairs, came to see plays, not merely to attend a ritual; and the occasion challenged the dramatist to clothe in this noble material his profoundest apprehensions about the life of man. Nothing less could live in this atmosphere.

The Festival conferred one other priceless advantage: it imposed external restrictions to which the poet had to conform; not cramping restrictions like those of a censorship, but liberating ones like the number of verses in a sonnet or of instruments in a string-quartet. His theatre was fixed; he could not choose between a big and a small one, nor could he elaborate beyond an elementary point the mechanical resources of the big one. He was restricted in the number of his actors,[2] and above all he had to make terms with the Chorus – which however was but the technical reflection of his major restriction, the audience. Thus he was protected from the easy subterfuges of more prodigal days, thrown more upon his own

[1] Hence the public and topical themes of Old Comedy, the public and universal themes of Old and Middle (and some New) Tragedy.

[2] This is not undisputed, but it still seems the better view.

intellect and artistic integrity, trained, like the Argive sculptors, on nothing softer than bronze. We have seen how the greatest of the Athenian dramatists responded. Within these restrictions they found a range of expression and a variety of form equal to their most exacting demands. There is no such thing as a typical Greek play; the form was something created anew, and differently, year by year, play by play, by dramatic poets of genius.

But dramatic poets of genius were not enough. Athens was necessary, and her spirit, and her spirit during this remarkable century, in which she gathered from the world around her what she wanted and could assimilate, until she became sufficient for herself and 'an education to Greece'. When Athenian Tragedy comes into our ken it ranges from Egypt to Argos, from Argos to the remote Caucasus, from the Caucasus to Egypt; if accidents can be inspired it is by an inspired accident that it passes from our ken in Attica itself, and with Oedipus; at Colonus the birthplace of Sophocles, not two miles from the Theatre of Dionysus. Here is the Unity of Place. Χῶρος δ' ὅδ' ἱερός.

Index

Actor:

—, single: 8

—, second: 25, 32, 42 f., 52, 53 f.

—, third, in Aeschylus: 57 f., 75; in Sophocles: 151–8

—, dramatic silence of: 58, 75, 110 and n., 306

Agamemnon: 64–78; 107–16 *passim*, 158, 159, 210 f., 281

Agathon: 2, 188, 351, 357, 369

αἴτια: 286, 332

Ajax: 120–5; 100, 152–4, 159, 160, 289 f.

Alcestis: 311–29 *passim*, 344

Allegory: 111

ἁμαρτία: 10, 102, 129, 191, 195, 197, 294

Andromache: 230–6; 257, 258 f., 263 f.

Anaximander: 135

Antigone: 125–31; 121, 122, 154 f., 171, 185

Aphrodite: 17, 18, 20, 68, 105, 128, 137, 204, 247, 383

Ares: 295

Aristophanes: 113, 190, 317, 318, 323

Aristotle's *Poetics*:

— and Aeschylus: 40, 97, 105; and Sophocles: 103; and Euripides: 190, 197 ff., 251, 263

(See also ἁμαρτία, *Catharsis, Character drawing, Logical construction, Natural Justice, the Revolting, Tragic Hero, the Universal.*

Artemis: 18, 20, 204, 205

—, at Aulis: 68, 105, 137, 314, 362 f., 366, 368

Athena: 137, 228 f.

Austen, Jane: 285 n., 325

Bacchae: 371–81; 201, 362

Bach: 97, 397

Beggar's Opera: 321 n.

Beethoven: 113, 384

Catharsis: 142, 235, 365

Chance: 146 f., 167, 183

Character drawing:

—, in Aeschylus: 14, 23 f., 26, 54, 85, 103, 374

—, in Sophocles: 119, 172 f., 176, 252, 374

—, in Euripides: 252, 373, 374

—, inconsistent: 255 f., 328, 359, 365 f.

Choephori: 78–87; 248, 339 f., 350

Chorus: 55, 160, 215 f., 219, 265

—, as actor, in Aeschylus: 24 ff., 49, 85, 87–95; in Sophocles: 159 ff., 305; in Euripides: 193 f., 380

—, as lyrical body: 107 f., 114 ff., 164–7, 221, 264, 341 ff., 392

—, characterization of, in Lyrical Tragedy: 27; in Aeschylus: 23, 25, 42, 49 n., 76, 114: in Sophocles: 23, 158–70; in Euripidean tragedy: 193 f., 215 f., 219, 221, 259–65; in New Tragedy: 340, 341–6, 348

Cinema: 362

Comparisons or contrasts:

—, Aeschylus and Sophocles: 23, 40, 44, 45, 53, 59, 79, 98 f., 103, 108

—, Aeschylus and Euripides: 212 f., 226, 265, 374

—, Sophocles and Euripides: style, 96, 198, 271, 272–5, 276, 277 f., 279; plot, 320, 330–46 *passim*, 384

(See also *Orestes-myth*.)

Conventions: 86

Dance:

—, in Aeschylus: 9, 22 n., 40, 41, 49 and n., 67, 114 ff.

—, in Sophocles: 164 f., 167

—, in Euripides: 376

(See also *Metre, Music*.)

Deus ex machina: 172, 200, 228, 285, 287, 309, 322

Dike:
—, in Aeschylus: 77, 79, 85, 86, 94, 95
—, in Sophocles: 133, 136, 139 f., 169, 176 f.
—, in Ionian philosophers: 135, 143
Diptych (Triptych): 121, 238, 241, 288
Dreams: 79, 133, 174, 327 n., 342

Electra (Sophocles): 131-7, 168-70, 172-7; 41, 59 n., 160, 162, 185, 330-46 passim
Electra (Euripides): 330-41; 208, 241, 346 f.
Enlightenment (XVIII century): 176, 188
Epic: 36, 41
Eros: 295
Eumenides: 87-95; 20, 97, 287

Fate: 48
Festival of Dionysus: 233, 396 ff.
Foreshadowing: 29 n., 73, 74, 204, 282 ff., 372

Gods, θεοί: 134, 313 f.
—, in Aeschylus: 19, 21, 39, 70
—, in Sophocles: 122, 295
—, in Euripides' tragedy: 201, 246, 247, 250 f., 377 f.; (in tragi-comedy) 317 f.
Gods and men: in Aeschylus: 70, 76, 85, 94; in Sophocles: 133, 136, 139 f., 169; in Euripides: 201, 250 f.

Hardy, Thomas: 276 n.
Hecuba: 216-23; 261 f., 316
Helen: 311-29 passim; 214
Heracleidae: 190 n., 253, 254 f., 275, 356
Heracles: 237-49; 264, 269
Herodotus: 130, 132, 138
Hesiod: 104
Hippolytus: 203-10; 268, 324 n., 375, 379
Historicism: 98
Homer: 57, 101, 104, 107
Housman, A. E.: 326

Imagery: 52, 69, 77, 82, 84, 87, 100, 112
'Increasing tension': 44, 57, 58 ff., 63, 74, 215

Ion: 311-29 passim; 256, 284, 344
Iphigeneia in Aulis: 362-9
Iphigeneia in Tauris: 311-29 passim; 188, 189, 341, 343 f.
Irony:
—, in Aeschylus: 51, 75
—, in Sophocles: 123, 133, 139, 163, 164
—, in Euripides: 254, 275 f., 327

James, Henry: 230 n.
Johnson: 101, 103
Juxtaposition: 113, 116, 124, 173

Logical construction (κατὰ τὸ εἰκὸς ἢ τὸ ἀναγκαῖον) 58 f., 105, 193, 195, 201 (See also 'Increasing tension'.)

'Meaning': v, vi, 126 n., 222, 314, 361
Medea: 190-202; 207, 260 f., 267, 331 f., 375, 379
Medieval drama: 101, 106
Messenger speeches: 193, 196 f., 207 f., 352, 355, 356
Metre: 1, 4, 5, 8, 13, 165 (See also Dance, Music.)
μιαρόν: see the Revolting
Milton: 60, 61, 88
Miracles: 39, 74, 128, 314
Modern prepossessions: 64, 97 f., 118, 121, 172
Mouthpiece of poet: 58, 160, 164
Music (of Euripides): 316, 344 n., 345 f., 354
Myth, manhandled by:
— Aeschylus: 16, 36, 65, 68, 87, 104-6
— Sophocles: 171 f., 296, 309
— Euripides: 239
— Shakespeare: 68, 104

Narrative element: 41, 106 f., 279, 356
Naturalism:
—, absence of: 27, 28, 30, 54, 103 f., 108 ff., 140 f.
—, presence of: 200, 319, 335 n.
Natural Justice (τὸ φιλάνθρωπον): 101, 102, 185, 364

Nature, rhythm of: 18, 123, 124, 146, 292, 384 (See also *Dike*, 135, 143; and *Pattern*.)

Oedipus Coloneus: 381–98; 150, 359, 370, 371
Oedipus Tyrannus: 138–44, 166–7, 177–86; 133, 155 f., 292, 294, 295
οἷα ἂν γένοιτο: see *the Universal*
Oresteia: 64–95; 15, 111
Orestes-myth in Aeschylus, Sophocles and Euripides, compared: 137, 159, 330–2

The Past: 159, 277, 360
Pattern: 145, 169, 170, 289 f.
Persae: 33–43; 108, 229, 356
Philoctetes: 298–310; 157 f., 171 f., 186, 200, 324 n.
Phoenissae (Euripides): 351–62
Phrynichus: 28, 33 f.
Pindar: 9, 19, 189
Plato: 62, 63, 329, 368
Plot-construction:
—, in Aeschylus: 104–8; in Sophocles: 118, 171 ff.; in Euripides' tragedy: 118, 198 f., 213–15, 216 f., 231 f., 257 f.; in his non-tragic plays: 311, 314, 320 ff., 351
Poetic style:
—, of Aeschylus: 26, 27, 123; of Sophocles: 154, 272, 384 f.; of Euripides: 271, 272
Politics:
—, references to contemporary events: 2, 7, 36, 95, 189, 224, 226 f., 230, 232
—, base necessities of: 221, 301 f.

Pope, Alexander: 102
Prometheus Vinctus: 55–63; 105, 111, 114
Prophecy, in Sophocles: 182, 183–5
Protagoras: 182

Reality, tragic and theatrical: 314, 320
Recognition scenes: 80 f., 320, 340
'Religious' drama: 313 (See also *Medieval drama*.)
The 'Revolting', τὸ μιαρόν: 10, 102, 190, 193, 254, 271, 285, 336
Rhesus: 396

Theocritus: 323, 344
Thucydides: 182, 185, 266
Timelessness of Art: 97, 101
Tragic dilemma: 10, 12, 29
Tragic Hero: 98, 102, 191, 195
Tragi-comedy: 312, 314, 334 f.
Trilogy: 106 f., 152, 211
Troades: 210–16; 261 f., 379

Unities:
—, of Place: 42, 110, 396
—, of Time: 60, 109
—, of Action: 99, 202, 227, 236, 361, 398
The Universal (οἷα ἂν γένοιτο): 36, 106

Voltaire: 351

Wagner: 341
Whitehead, A. N.: 143

Xenophon: 121

Zeus:
—, in Aeschylus: 12, 17, 70, 105
—, in Sophocles: 174, 289 ff., 297